Seen, Heard and Counted

T0344904

Development and Change Book Series

As a journal, *Development and Change* distinguishes itself by its multidisciplinary approach and its breadth of coverage, publishing articles on a wide spectrum of development issues. Accommodating a deeper analysis and a more concentrated focus, it also publishes regular special issues on selected themes. *Development and Change* and Wiley-Blackwell collaborate to produce these theme issues as a series of books, with the aim of bringing these pertinent resources to a wider audience.

Titles in the series include:

Seen, Heard and Counted: Rethinking Care in a Development Context
Edited by Shahra Razavi

Negotiating Statehood: Dynamics of Power and Domination in Africa
Edited by Tobias Hagmann and Didier Péclard

The Politics of Possession: Property, Authority, and Access to Natural Resources
Edited by Thomas Sikor and Christian Lund

Gender Myths and Feminist Fables: The Struggle for Interpretive Power in Gender and Development
Edited by Andrea Cornwall, Elizabeth Harrison and Ann Whitehead

Twilight Institutions: Public Authority and Local Politics in Africa
Edited by Christian Lund

China's Limits to Growth: Greening State and Society
Edited by Peter Ho and Eduard B. Vermeer

Catalysing Development? A Debate on Aid
Jan Pronk et al.

State Failure, Collapse and Reconstruction
Edited by Jennifer Milliken

Forests: Nature, People, Power
Edited by Martin Doornbos, Ashwani Saith and Ben White

Gendered Poverty and Well-being
Edited by Shahra Razavi

Globalization and Identity
Edited by Birgit Meyer and Peter Geschiere

Social Futures, Global Visions
Edited by Cynthia Hewitt de Alcantara

Seen, Heard and Counted
Rethinking Care in a Development Context

Edited by

Shahra Razavi

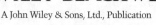

A John Wiley & Sons, Ltd., Publication

UNITED NATIONS
RESEARCH INSTITUTE
FOR SOCIAL DEVELOPMENT

The United Nations Research Institute for Social Development (UNRISD) was established in 1963 to create an independent, autonomous space within the United Nations system for policy-relevant research and dialogue on important social issues. The UNRISD mission is to generate knowledge and articulate policy alternatives on contemporary social development challenges and processes. Through its multidisciplinary research in collaboration with partners throughout the world, events and publications, the Institute works in support of policies and practices that reduce poverty and inequality, advance well-being and rights, and create more democratic and just societies.

This edition first published 2012
Originally published as Volume 42, Issue 4 of *Development and Change*
Chapters © 2012 by The Institute of Social Studies and UNRISD
Book Compilation © Blackwell Publishing Ltd.

Blackwell Publishing was acquired by John Wiley & Sons in February 2007. Blackwell's publishing program has been merged with Wiley's global Scientific, Technical, and Medical business to form Wiley-Blackwell.

Registered Office
John Wiley & Sons Ltd, The Atrium, Southern Gate, Chichester, West Sussex, PO19 8SQ, United Kingdom

Editorial Offices
350 Main Street, Malden, MA 02148-5020, USA
9600 Garsington Road, Oxford, OX4 2DQ, UK
The Atrium, Southern Gate, Chichester, West Sussex, PO19 8SQ, UK

For details of our global editorial offices, for customer services, and for information about how to apply for permission to reuse the copyright material in this book please see our website at www.wiley.com/wiley-blackwell.

The right of Shahra Razavi to be identified as the author of the editorial material in this work has been asserted in accordance with the UK Copyright, Designs and Patents Act 1988.

All rights reserved. No part of this publication may be reproduced, stored in a retrieval system, or transmitted, in any form or by any means, electronic, mechanical, photocopying, recording or otherwise, except as permitted by the UK Copyright, Designs and Patents Act 1988, without the prior permission of the publisher.

Wiley also publishes its books in a variety of electronic formats. Some content that appears in print may not be available in electronic books.

Designations used by companies to distinguish their products are often claimed as trademarks. All brand names and product names used in this book are trade names, service marks, trademarks or registered trademarks of their respective owners. The publisher is not associated with any product or vendor mentioned in this book. This publication is designed to provide accurate and authoritative information in regard to the subject matter covered. It is sold on the understanding that the publisher is not engaged in rendering professional services. If professional advice or other expert assistance is required, the services of a competent professional should be sought.

Library of Congress Cataloging-in-Publication Data

Seen, heard and counted : rethinking care in a development context / edited by Shahra Razavi.
    p. cm.
  Includes index.
  "Originally published as Volume 42, Issue 4 of Development and Change."
  ISBN 978-1-4443-6153-7 (pbk.)
  1. Work and family–Developing countries. 2. Child care–Developing countries. 3. Working mothers–Developing countries. 4. Caregivers–Developing countries. 5. Sexual division of labor–Developing countries. 6. Family policy–Developing countries. 7. Developing countries–Social policy. I. Razavi, Shahra.
  HD4904.25.S44 2012
  362.709172′4–dc23

2011047243

A catalogue record for this book is available from the British Library.

Set in 10.75/12pt Times by Aptara Inc., New Delhi, India

Printed in Malaysia by Ho Printing (M) Sdn Bhd

1   2012

Contents

Notes on Contributors   vii

1 Rethinking Care in a Development Context: An Introduction   1
  Shahra Razavi

2 The Good, the Bad and the Confusing: The Political Economy
  of Social Care Expansion in South Korea   31
  Ito Peng

3 South Africa: A Legacy of Family Disruption   51
  Debbie Budlender and Francie Lund

4 Harsh Choices: Chinese Women's Paid Work and Unpaid
  Care Responsibilities under Economic Reform   73
  Sarah Cook and Xiao-yuan Dong

5 A Widening Gap? The Political and Social Organization
  of Childcare in Argentina   93
  Eleonor Faur

6 Who Cares in Nicaragua? A Care Regime in an Exclusionary
  Social Policy Context   121
  Juliana Martínez Franzoni and Koen Voorend

7 A Perfect Storm? Welfare, Care, Gender and Generations
  in Uruguay   149
  Fernando Filgueira, Magdalena Gutiérrez and Jorge Papadópulos

8 Stratified Familialism: The Care Regime in India through the
  Lens of Childcare   175
  Rajni Palriwala and Neetha N.

9 Putting Two and Two Together? Early Childhood Education,
  Mothers' Employment and Care Service Expansion in Chile
  and Mexico   205
  Silke Staab and Roberto Gerhard

10 Going Global: The Transnationalization of Care   233
  Nicola Yeates

Index   255

Erratum

Notes on Contributors

Only the following contributors' works were included in this publication:

Debbie Budlender, Sarah Cook, Xiao-yuan Dong, Eleonor Faur, Fernando Filgueira, Juliana Martínez Franzoni, Roberto Gerhard, Magdalena Gutiérrez, Francie Lund, Neetha N., Rajni Palriwala, Jorge Papadópulos, Ito Peng, Shahra Razavi, Silke Staab, Koen Voorend, Nicola Yeates.

This error will be corrected in future printings of the book.

The publisher apologizes for any inconvenience caused.

Notes on Contributors

Debbie Budlender (debbie.budlender@gmail.com) is a specialist researcher with the Community Agency for Social Enquiry (C A S E), a South African non-governmental organization working in the area of social policy research. She has worked for C A S E since 1988.

Sarah Cook (Cook@unrisd.org) is the Director of the United Nations Research Institute for Social Development (UNRISD), Palais des Nations 1211, Geneva 10, Switzerland. She was previously a Fellow at the Institute of Development Studies at the University of Sussex. She has published extensively on China's social and economic development and on social protection in Asia. As Programme Officer for the Ford Foundation in Beijing (2000–2005) she supported the development of a gender and economics training programme and network in China.

Xiao-yuan Dong (x.dong@uwinnipeg.ca) is Professor of Economics at the University of Winnipeg, Manitoba, Canada, Adjunct Professor at the National School of Development, Peking University, and Co-director of the Chinese Women's Economic Research and Training Programme. She has published extensively on China's economic transition and development and gender/women issues. Her current research interest is time use and the care economy. She is an associate editor of *Feminist Economics* and has served on the board of the International Association for Feminist Economics since 2007.

Martin Doornbos is Emeritus Professor of Political Science at the Institute of Social Studies, PO Box 29776, 2502 LT The Hague, The Netherlands (e-mail: doornbos@iss.nl) and Visiting Professor of Development Studies at Mbarara University of Science and Technology, Uganda. He has done extensive research on state–society relations and the politics of resource allocation in Eastern Africa (mainly Uganda and the Horn) and in India, and is currently working on encounters between research and politics in the development arena. His most recent book is *Global Forces and State Restructuring: Dynamics of State Formation and Collapse* (Palgrave, 2006) and his forthcoming book (with Wim van Binsbergen) is entitled *Researching Power and Identity in African State Formation: Comparative Perspectives*.

Eleonor Faur (eleonorf@gmail.com) works with the United Nations Population Fund as Assistant Representative for Argentina, and teaches in the Doctoral Programme at UNGS-IDES. She has been involved in programme coordination on gender and human rights in international agencies, and has published several articles and books in Latin America. Her current research focuses on childcare, gender and social policy.

Fernando Filgueira studied Sociology at the Universidad de la República (Uruguay) and at Northwestern University (USA). He is currently Assistant Representative for the United Nations Population Fund in Uruguay. He can be contacted at e-mail: ffilgueirap@gmail.com.

Till Förster is director of the Centre for African Studies and professor of social anthropology (chair) at the University of Basel (email: till.foerster@unibas.ch). He has conducted long-term research on political transformations in Africa, in particular in Côte d'Ivoire and Cameroon, and is currently studying the interaction of local, state and rebel governance in northern Côte d'Ivoire. He is co-editor of *Non-State Actors as Standard Setters* (Cambridge University Press, 2009).

Juliana Martínez Franzoni is associate professor at the Institute of Social Research, University of Costa Rica (Apartado Postal 49–2060, Ciudad Universitaria 'Rodrigo Facio', University of Costa Rica, San José, Costa Rica; e-mail: juliana.martinez@ucr.ac.cr). Her research focuses on social policy formation and inequality in Latin America. Her most recent publications include 'Welfare Regimes in Latin America: Capturing Constellations of Markets, Families and Policies', *Latin American Politics and Society* (2008); *Latin American Capitalism: Economic and Social Policy in Transition*, a special issue of *Economy and Society* edited with Diego Sánchez-Ancochea and Maxine Molyneux (2009); and 'Are Coalitions Equally Crucial for Redistribution in Latin America? The Intervening Role of Welfare Regimes in Chile, Costa Rica and El Salvador', *Social Policy and Administration* (2009), with Koen Voorend.

Roberto Gerhard studied Political Science and International Relations at the Center for Research and Teaching in Economics (CIDE), Mexico, where he currently works as a Research Assistant for the Department of Public Administration. His main research interest is in child-oriented policies. He has published a book chapter on the provision of public childcare services in Mexico and is currently planning to develop an index to measure the quality of care, as well as a longitudinal study on the impact of different types of care on children in Mexico.

Magdalena Gutiérrez studied Sociology at the Universidad de la República (Uruguay) and Hispanic Studies at the University of Illinois at Chicago (USA). She is currently a technical advisor on information systems and labour policies for the Ministry of Labour of Uruguay.

Tobias Hagmann is a visiting scholar at the Department of Political Science, University of California, Berkeley and an associated researcher at the Department of Geography, University of Zürich (email: tobias. hagmann@geo.uzh.ch). He has researched resource conflicts, local and state politics in the Ethio-Somali borderlands and maintains a strong interest in the political sociology of the state, critical conflict research and development studies. He is the co-editor (with Kjetil Tronvoll) of *Contested Power: Traditional Authorities and Multi-party Elections in Ethiopia* (forthcoming).

Asnake Kefale is assistant professor at the Department of Political Science and International Relations, Addis Ababa University (email: asnakekefale@gmail.com). He has done extensive research and published on issues of federalism, conflict, governance and civil society in Ethiopia.

Francie Lund (lundf@ukzn.ac.za) is the director of the Social Protection Programme of WIEGO (Women in Informal Employment: Globalizing and Organizing), and is a Senior Research Associate at the School of Development Studies, University of KwaZulu-Natal, Durban.

Lalli Metsola is a researcher at the Institute of Development Studies, University of Helsinki, Finland (email: metsola@mappi.helsinki.fi). For his PhD, he has researched and published on state formation, citizenship and political subjectivity in Namibia through the case of ex-combatant 'reintegration'. Recently, he has also done research on policing, violence and the rule of law in Namibia.

Neetha N. is a Senior Fellow at the Centre for Women's Development Studies. She has worked as Associate Fellow and Coordinator, Centre for Gender and Labour at the V.V. Giri National Labour Institute, NOIDA. Her current research interests are women's employment, care work and migration. She can be contacted at CWDS, 25 Bhai Vir Singh Marg, Delhi-110 001, India; e-mail: neetha@cwds.ac.in; neethapillai @gmail.com

Rajni Palriwala is currently Professor of Sociology at the University of Delhi. Her research falls within the broad area of gender relations, covering kinship and marriage, dowry, women and work, care, women's movements and feminist politics, and methodology. Her publications include Care, culture and citizenship: Revisiting the politics of welfare in the Netherlands (with C. Risseeuw and K. Ganesh, Het Spinhuis, 2005). She can be contacted at the Department of Sociology, Delhi School of Economics, University of Delhi, Delhi-110007, India; e-mail: rajnip@gmail.com

Didier Péclard is senior researcher at the Swiss Peace Foundation (swisspeace) in Bern and lecturer in political science at the University of Basel (email: didier.peclard@swisspeace.ch). He has worked and published extensively on Christian missions and nationalism as well as on the politics of peace and transition in Angola. As a fellow of the Swiss National Centre of Competence in Research (NCCR) North–South, his current main research focus is on the dynamics of statehood in societies after violent conflicts.

Jorge Papadópulos studied Sociology at CIESU (Uruguay) and Political Science at Pittsburgh University (USA). He was a Director at the Social Security Bank in Uruguay (BPS) and is senior researcher at the Centre for Studies and Information in Uruguay (CIESU).

Ito Peng is a Professor at the Department of Sociology and the School of Public Policy and Governance, University of Toronto, Canada (e-mail: itopeng@chass.utoronto.ca). She teaches and researches in areas of political sociology, comparative welfare states, gender and social policy and specializes in the political economy of East Asia. Her current research includes an UNRISD-sponsored research project on the political and social economy of care; a joint research project with the Global Centre of Excellence at University of Kyoto on changing public and intimate spheres in Asia, in which she looks at social and economic policy changes and care and labour migration in Asia; and a Canadian Social Science and Humanities Research Council funded research project on social investment policies in Canada, Australia, Japan and Korea.

Shahra Razavi is Senior Researcher at the United Nations Research Institute for Social Development (UNRISD), Palais des Nations, 1211 Geneva 10, Switzerland; e-mail razavi@unrisd.org. She specializes in the gender dimensions of social development, with a particular focus on livelihoods and social policy. Her recent publications include *The Gendered Impacts of Liberalization: Towards 'Embedded Liberalism'?* (Routledge, 2009), *Workers in the Care Economy*, edited with Silke Staab (*International Labour Review*, 2010), and *The Unhappy Marriage of Religion and Politics: Problems and Pitfalls for Gender Equality*, edited with Anne Jenichen (*Third World Quarterly*, 2010).

Timothy Raeymaekers is lecturer of Political Geography at the University of Zürich (timothy.raeymaekers@geo.uzh.ch). He has done extensive research on cross-border trade and local politics in eastern Democratic Republic of Congo. Amongst others, he is currently working on a book manuscript about cross-border trade in the borderland of Congo-Uganda based on his PhD thesis.

Marleen Renders is a post-doctoral research associate at the Human Rights Centre, Ghent University (email: marleen.renders@ugent.be). She currently works in Kenya's Coastal Province, investigating women's human rights in contexts of legal pluralism involving customary and Islamic law. She conducted her PhD fieldwork in Somaliland in 2002/2003 and was a research fellow at the Academy for Peace and Development, a local dialogue

NGO carrying out participatory action research, in Hargeisa. Her work on Somaliland is shortly to be published by Brill (Leiden).

Inge Ruigrok is a consultant for the European Commission and an associate researcher at the Centro de Estudos Africanos (CEA/ISCTE) in Lisbon (email: ingeruigrok@gmail.com). She holds a PhD in Political Anthropology and an MSc degree in International Relations. Her doctorate research was on governance, culture and political change in post-war Angola, with a special focus on the redefinition and negotiation of central-local relations. She previously worked as a journalist in Europe and Southern Africa.

Anita Schroven is a researcher at Max Planck Institute for Social Anthropology, Halle/Saale, and the Center for Interdisciplinary Studies, University of Bielefeld Germany (email: schroven@eth.mpg.de). She has conducted extensive research on state, governance, decentralization and oral tradition in Guinea as well as on gender and post-war societies in Sierra Leone and Liberia. She is author of the book *Women after War* (LIT Verlag, 2006).

Silke Staab is currently pursuing an MPhil/PhD at the Politics Department, University of Sheffield (Department of Politics, University of Sheffield, Northumberland Road, S10 2TU, UK; e-mail: s.staab@sheffield.ac.uk). Her research project examines patterns of continuity and change in Latin American social policy from a gender perspective, seeking to assess how far recent social policy reforms represent a shift away from the tenets of 'high-tide' neoliberalism, as well as the implications of this shift for gendered rights and responsibilities. Over the past six years, she has worked for different UN agencies and NGOs on issues related to gender, care, social policy and migration.

Jason Sumich is a research fellow for the SARChI Chair on Social Change, University of Fort Hare, 4 Hill Street, East London, 5201, South Africa (email: j.m.sumich@googlemail.com). His main areas of interest concern nationalism, urban ethnography, the middle class, social class formation and social stratification in Mozambique. He is currently researching nationalism, Islam and Indian Ocean trade networks in Mozambique and India.

Ulf Terlinden is a research associate at the Institute for Development and Peace (INEF) at the University of Duisburg-Essen (email: contact@ ulfterlinden. de). He has been a resident political analyst in Somaliland since mid-2005 and his main research interest revolves around governance and post-conflict peacebuilding in the Horn of Africa. He has worked as research fellow and capacity builder with the Academy for Peace and Development, a local dialogue NGO carrying out participatory action research, in Hargeisa.

Koen Voorend is lecturer at the School of Communication of the Faculty of Social Sciences and researcher at the Institute for Social Research, University of Costa Rica (Apartado Postal 49–2060, Ciudad Universitaria 'Rodrigo Facio', University of Costa Rica, San José, Costa Rica; e-mail: koen.voorend@ucr.ac.cr). His current research is on gender equality in Latin American welfare regimes, migration and the formation of universal social policy in the periphery. Some of his recent publications include 'Are Coalitions Equally Crucial for Redistribution in Latin America? The Intervening Role of Welfare Regimes in Chile, Costa Rica and El Salvador', *Social Policy and Administration* (2009), and 'Sistemas de patriarcado y regímenes de bienestar. ¿Una cosa lleva a la otra?', Fundación Carolina-CeALCI (2009), both with Juliana Martínez Franzoni. He recently entered the doctoral programme of the Institute of Social Studies in The Hague.

Nicola Yeates is Professor of Social Policy at the Department of Social Policy and Criminology, The Open University, Walton Hall, Milton Keynes, MK6 7AA, UK. She has published widely on issues of gender, migration, care and social policy across diverse country settings and from a transnational perspective. For a list of her recent research publications, see http://oro.open.ac.uk/

1

Rethinking Care in a Development Context: An Introduction

Shahra Razavi

INTRODUCTION

The restructuring of production systems on a global scale and the recurrent financial and economic crises to which liberalized economies are prone, have received considerable attention, both scholarly and policy-oriented, in recent decades. While it may not have made it to the front page of *The Wall Street Journal*, a great deal has also been said about the social disruptions associated with the ascendancy of the neoliberal agenda — reminiscent of Polanyi's (1957) analysis of the 'disembedding' of markets from social priorities in eighteenth and nineteenth century Europe (Beneria, 1999; Standing, 1999). One long-standing critique originating in response to the stabilization and adjustment measures of the 1980s came from feminists who pointed to women's intensifying unpaid work as 'shock absorbers' of last resort (Elson, 2002). While bankers and governments have periodically worried about how to respond to the crises of finance, including the most recent episode that erupted in Wall Street, others have voiced concern about the long-term repercussions for social reproduction (Bezanson and Luxton, 2006).[1] It is indeed tempting in this context to think about a generalized crisis of social reproduction, or a 'crisis of care',[2] as some have framed it (Beneria, 2008).

I would like to thank Chantal Stevens and Ji-Won Seo for excellent research assistance during the preparation of this volume. I am also grateful to Debbie Budlender, Sarah Cook, Silke Staab, Nicola Yeates and two anonymous referees of the journal for their useful comments on previous drafts of this paper. This volume draws on research commissioned by UNRISD under the project, 'The Political and Social Economy of Care'. The project was funded by the United Nations Development Programme (UNDP) Japan/WID Fund, the International Development Research Centre (Canada), and the Swiss Agency for Development and Cooperation (SDC).

1. Social reproduction has been defined in a variety of ways. We understand the concept to include the social processes and human relations associated with the production and maintenance of people and communities on a daily and generational basis, upon which all production and exchange rest (Bakker, 2003: 67); it involves 'the provision of food, clothing, shelter, basic safety and health care, along with the development and transmission of knowledge, social values and cultural practices and the construction of individual and collective identities' (Bezanson and Luxton, 2006: 3; see also Elson, 1998).
2. Care is defined as the activities and relations involved in meeting the physical and emotional needs of dependent adults and children, and the normative, economic and social frameworks within which these are distributed and carried out (Daly and Lewis, 2000). It is thus one important component of social reproduction.

Seen, Heard and Counted, First Edition. Edited by Shahra Razavi.
Chapters © 2012 The Institute of Social Studies. Book compilation © 2012 Blackwell Publishing Ltd.

However, as the contributions to this volume show, even if the care crisis is global, it is far from homogeneous. Moreover, care arrangements in developing countries have not received the same level of scrutiny as those in advanced industrialization countries — a lacuna that the present collection of papers seeks to address. Hence, our assessment of care systems and public policy responses is largely focused on these under-studied contexts in Africa, Asia and Latin America.

Women's entry into the paid workforce — a near global trend[3] — may have reduced the time hitherto available for the provision of unpaid care. But this shift has taken place alongside many other changes, some of which may have intensified care burdens, while others may have had a more favourable impact on the capacity of households to meet such needs. A clear illustration of the former is the pressure brought to bear on family care providers by the HIV/AIDS pandemic, especially in Southern Africa where prevalence rates are high and health systems under enormous strain (Budlender and Lund, this volume).

Care systems are also under stress where families are reconstituted, whether through internal or cross-border migration. In China, due to the residential registration system (*hukou*) and land use rights, migration remains temporary and results in a large 'left-behind' population. Cook and Dong (this volume) cite estimates suggesting that close to one-third of rural children are 'left behind', either living with only one parent (mostly mothers), or with grandparents or other relatives. This resonates with the growing literature on 'transnational families', also covered in the contribution by Yeates (this volume), which draws attention to care deficits experienced by children in migrant-sending peripheral countries like the Philippines while their mothers seek paid work elsewhere in the world (Ehrenreich and Hochschild, 2003; Parrenas, 2005). There are clearly hidden costs of migration that are not easy to capture, not only those involved with the dislocation of families but also psychological ones (Beneria, 2008). Yet it is also important not to assume that 'abnormal' family arrangements necessarily result in a care deficit.[4]

The rising prevalence of households with young children maintained by women who have to manage both income earning and care giving, whether in Uruguay (Filgueira, Gutiérrez and Papadopulos, this volume) or in South

---

3. That is, if developments in the previously planned economies of East and Central Europe, Central Asia and China are excluded.

4. As Parrenas's (2005) research in the Philippines shows, ideologies of gender and the naturalization of motherhood frame both the practices and the discourses of loss and deprivation in these households: children constantly complain about the deprivation they experience in terms of lack of maternal love, and the inadequacy of the love they receive from fathers and grandmothers — even where fathers are very present in their lives and other kin (grandmothers, aunts) provide support and care. Migrant mothers, likewise, often justify their work overseas as a household strategy to meet family goals (e.g. putting children through school or lifting the family's circumstances), even though in reality family and personal goals are often interwoven in the migration project (see also Asis et al., 2004).

Africa (Budlender and Lund, this volume), presents yet another scenario where the demand on women's time is enormous. It is also among this cluster of largely lower-income households that access to care services, whether public or market-provided, remains limited. It is important again not to assume that children in these households are necessarily more deprived, for example in nutritional terms, than children in families where both parents are present (Moore, 1994). There is nevertheless a tendency over time towards what Chant (2010) has called 'the feminization of responsibility and/or obligation', whereby women with young children are having to assume an increasing share of the responsibility for meeting household needs with little or no support from the fathers of their children.

However, the past two decades have also seen rapid fertility decline in many parts of the developing world (which may mean fewer children and less time devoted to childcare),[5] the increasing availability (though at rates that are far from adequate) of amenities such as clean water, electricity and time-saving domestic technology, and increasing rates of enrolment of children in primary and — to a lesser extent — pre-primary education and care services. Taken together, these developments may well have reduced the drudgery of domestic work among some social groups, and shifted at least a small part of care to institutions other than the family. It is not clear therefore that the overall need for the provision of unpaid care has increased over time in all places, although in some contexts and for some groups it clearly has.

While the present moment may not necessarily be marked by a generalized care crisis, as we have suggested so far, there is nevertheless something new about the current juncture. Care has emerged, or is emerging, as a legitimate subject of public debate and policy development on the agendas both of those making claims — be it through social movement activism or NGO advocacy — and of many governments, not only in the advanced industrialized countries, but also in developing countries.[6] The contributions in this volume present a first picture of differences and commonalities in these trends across a series of developing countries, and the ways in which care dynamics across developing and developed countries are interlinked.

How is this change — the eruption of care onto the public/policy agenda — to be explained? Many would argue that the period of state roll-back and retrenchment which marked the 1980s was superseded in the late 1990s by a reorientation in mainstream thinking, with the shift to the 'post-Washington Consensus'. This entailed a tacit recognition, at least by the international financial institutions, that effective governance was not simply

---

5. Demographic variables alone do not determine care needs and burdens. Rather, they are filtered through social, cultural and economic factors which, in turn, shape what is considered to be 'sufficient' or 'good' care. For example, time allocated to adult–child interaction tends to increase as ideas of what constitutes 'good care' change. Another implication of fewer children may be that they cannot look after each other.
6. Perhaps indicative of 'the moment', the United Nations Commission on the Status of Women that meets annually in New York, selected as its theme for 2009 the issue of care, with particular reference to HIV and AIDS.

about shrinking the state.[7] There was also a willingness to recognize the need for social expenditure — now recast as 'social investment'[8] (Jenson, 2010; Jenson and Saint Martin, 2006) — if the liberalization agenda was to stay on course. In the context of a more enabling ideational environment, regional and global development agencies called for social policies that could restore the social fabric 'through activating greater participation, more "community level" networks and ties of social solidarity' (Molyneux, 2002: 173), and agencies such as ECLAC, OECD, UNICEF and the World Bank advocated in favour of both cash transfer programmes and early childhood education and care services (Bedford, 2007; Mahon, 2010).[9]

As is evident from the contributions in this volume, these global policy pronouncements have been taken up enthusiastically in several Latin American countries where governments have developed social policies to address the needs of children, women and the family through care-related policy innovations. These have included conditional cash transfer schemes, different modalities for expanding the availability of early education and care services, and the introduction of child-rearing credits in pension schemes. One suspects that beyond the ideational shifts associated with the social investment approach, which have had particular traction in this region (Jenson, 2010), there has also been some contagion or 'spill-over' effect across countries (in the form of 'best practices' and the like). Emblematic of a new wave of social policy and based on the pioneer schemes in Brazil (*Bolsa Familia*) and Mexico (*Oportunidades*), cash transfer programmes, largely targeted to mothers, have been piloted and/or institutionalized in at least fifteen countries in Latin America. We return to some of the gender implications of these schemes below.

Less remarked on, but no less significant, is the extent of experimentation in childcare policy and programme development — historically a priority area in national women's movements advocacy. Given the declining efficacy of stratified social security systems in Latin America, there has been little effort to implement or expand the scope of earlier legislation that had made childcare a right for formally employed mothers (Mahon, 2011). Instead, states in the region have taken significant steps to expand both formal and

---

7. The neoliberal reform agenda has been criticized by some of its own architects for its failure to unpack the different dimensions of 'stateness' and distinguish between state scope and state strength (e.g. Fukuyama, 2004).

8. Jenson (2010) suggests that it is the polysemic character of 'social investment' that facilitated its diffusion, i.e. that it was open to multiple interpretations. As she argues, 'the ideas that spread most are ones that can draw together numerous positions and sustain a moderate to high level of ambiguity' (ibid.: 71).

9. It is legitimate to ask if the world is not entering a new 'roll-back' phase given the austerity measures being taken in many developed countries. The gender implications of the budget cuts in the UK have been amply analysed by the UK Women's Budget Group (2010). The global repercussions of these measures, both ideological and economic, are yet to become clear.

non-formal or 'community-based' forms of care and pre-school education. This is covered in some detail by several contributions to the present volume, most notably the comparative paper on Chile and Mexico (Staab and Gerhard), and the single country analyses of Argentina (Faur) and Nicaragua (Martinez Franzoni and Voorend).

Social policies responding to care needs have also been at the centre of public debate and policy experimentation in South Korea and South Africa, energized and facilitated by processes of democratization. In South Korea a combination of both 'progressive and pragmatic' motivations, namely a stated concern for gender equality and worries about the very low fertility rates coupled with economic slowdown, has catalysed a relatively sizeable state response over a short period of time (Peng, this volume). The extent of state social provisioning in South Africa since the end of apartheid has also been remarkable for a developing country (Budlender and Lund, this volume). State response seems to have been elicited, in part at least, by the tragic scale of the AIDS pandemic, combined with the historical legacy of family disruption and high levels of structural unemployment. Great anticipation that the post-apartheid state would address the injustices of the past, especially in a context where macroeconomic policy has remained fairly orthodox and incapable of tackling unemployment, has been another critical trigger.

Yet care needs have not uniformly 'broken out of the domestic' (Fraser, 1987: 116) and onto the public agenda. The meek policy responses in the highly diverse contexts of Nicaragua, China and India are an important reminder of the multiple forces and structural impediments that stand in the way of making care a legitimate public policy concern. China and, to a much lesser extent, Nicaragua share a history (albeit short in the case of Nicaragua) of socializing care needs through their state-socialist projects. The rejection of that model by pro-market forces — whether of the heterodox (in the case of China) or neoliberal kind — has led to the 'reprivatization' (Haney, 2003) of care. Indeed, comparative work on the family in post-socialist Eastern Europe shows how 'the familial' was deployed to assist states' reform of, and often retreat from, social life (Haney and Pollard 2003).[10] In India, meanwhile, strong notions of familialism undergirding state discourse and policy have placed serious limits on the state's willingness to entertain the idea that care giving could be made, even if only partially, a public responsibility (Palriwala and Neetha, this volume).

Most of the contributions to this volume provide country-based analyses of the social economy of care and relevant policy developments. As such,

---

10. It is important to note that while in Hungary, according to Haney (2003), 'familialism' was deployed to rationalize welfare retrenchment, in the Czech Republic 'familialism' was appropriated to justify welfare expansion. The argument in the Czech Republic was that precisely because the family served as a site of refuge and social anchor under state socialism, it should be supported with public funds in the post-socialist era.

they are grounded in methodological nationalism — a feature they share with social policy analyses following the welfare regime approach. This is not to suggest that they are necessarily blind to global forces, whether in the form of care personnel (nurses, domestic workers) who migrate in and out of the country, or the role of global ideational factors in framing national policy options, or indeed the far less subtle role of donors in dictating 'policy conditionalities' on macroeconomic lending or in shaping social programmes. But their focus is on national-level processes: the institutional dynamics of care provision, its gendered/class/racial character, its intersection with policy processes, and its interactions with broader trends of social differentiation and polarization.

Taking a different methodological approach — one that privileges the 'border-crossing webs of socio-economic relationships' — the contribution by Yeates examines the diverse contours of care transnationalization in the contemporary era. By putting care in a global context, she examines the connections between internal policy processes and what happens in other countries, between internal and transnational migration, and the impact of developed country policies (e.g. international recruitment strategies) on developing countries. In doing so she takes the reader beyond the well-trodden theme of care worker migration. What her contribution illustrates is not only a facet of economic and social restructuring that tends to be neglected by mainstream literatures — the 'invisible' or 'other economy' as Donath (2000) calls it — but also the ways in which social relations and practices of welfare and care are being 'stretched' over long distances across national borders. We include this contribution in the hope of furthering the dialogue between these methodologically divergent perspectives.

The rest of this introductory paper is structured as follows. The first section provides a general background to the special issue, explaining its country selection and working hypotheses. It then turns to the family as the institution that stands central in defining and mediating the actual tasks of caring and its gendered character. However, as the subsequent section shows, we need to avoid the 'ghettoising of care' (Daly, 2009) in the family. The notion of a 'care mix' (Daly and Lewis, 2000) or 'care diamond' (Razavi, 2007) has been used to draw attention to the diversity of strategies, institutions and practices for providing care.[11] Moreover, what goes on inside families is not hermetically sealed from developments in the broader context. Processes of economic and social change, as well as policy developments, play a key role in how care needs are defined, who is seen

---

11. The 'care diamond' metaphor, which draws attention to the four ideal-typical institutional sites mediating care — families, markets, states, not-for-profit sector — was used as an *organizing* device in the UNRISD research project from which this collection originated, since the project included research on unpaid care provided by household and family members, market-based and state-based care provision, as well as the role of the not-for-profit sector in the countries where it was most pertinent. The care diamond was not meant to provide an analytical scaffolding or serve as a conceptual framework.

as needing care, and how their needs are to be met. The concluding section reflects on the politics of care, and what the analysis of care in developing countries can say about care in developed countries.

ABOUT THIS VOLUME

It is often assumed that care policies are a relatively late development in a country's welfare architecture. Daly and Lewis (2000), for example, argue that care policies provide a fruitful point of entry for analysing welfare state change, and Daly (2011) argues that policy relating to family life is one of the most active domains of social policy reform in Europe. Morel (2007) likewise sees care policies as part and parcel of the current restructuring of the welfare state, a restructuring that involves both a recasting of the overall relationships between family, market and state, and a transformation of gender relations and norms.

Where does this leave developing countries (clearly a heterogeneous group)? Is there an evolutionary pattern in the development of social policies, whereby care policies appear at a relatively advanced stage of welfare state development? If this were the case, then developing countries with nascent social policies would have to wait some time for care to become an active domain of policy experimentation. However, evidence from other policy domains suggests that countries can leap-frog and that there can be institutional learning (Mkandawire, 2001). Looking at the relationship between late industrialization and welfare development, Pierson (1998) for example notes that after 1923 there was a tendency for 'late starters' to develop welfare state institutions earlier in their own individual development and under more comprehensive terms of coverage than the pioneer countries. He also notes that in general 'the larger and more entrenched a welfare state becomes, the more difficult it is to change. . . . The move toward an active social policy is easier where there are fewer with an immediate interest in the maintenance of passivity' (Pierson, 2004: 15).

Encouraging as this may be, there are a number of factors that are likely to prove important, if not decisive, in shaping a country's capacity to respond effectively to care needs. Although not a determining factor in itself, the availability of resources at the national level will always affect the state's provision of services, infrastructure and transfers/subsidies that can facilitate care giving. However, the translation of resources into the pre-conditions for care will be mediated by specific historical and conjunctural factors, including both political and ideational ones. On the political front, while the presence of gender equality lobbies within both the state and society may help turn care issues into a public policy concern, it is not likely to be sufficient for eliciting policy response. Gender-equality issues that include a redistributive dimension, such as the provision of public care services, invoke questions of socio-economic inequality as well as gender inequality, and may therefore be shaped by patterns of class politics, such as the power of left parties or trade unions (Htun and Weldon, 2010; Huber and Stephens, 2001). However, state response to care needs can also take a more top-down form, driven by political elites and technocrats, and underpinned by more instrumentalist or 'productivist' motivations, such as building 'human capital', generating service sector employment, and ensuring 'family cohesion'. It may also be driven by more mundane concerns such as appearing more 'modern' or enhancing state legitimacy in the eyes of both domestic and international constituencies. What we see emerging from the contributions to this volume are not linear processes of policy development, but a more messy picture punctuated by both horizontal movements indicative of institutional learning/borrowing as well as policy reversals and institutional disarray.

Apart from the prerequisite of having a time use survey, countries in the UNRISD project were purposefully selected from three different regions to include from each region one country with a relatively more developed system of social welfare (e.g. Korea, Argentina, South Africa), and one that was considered to be a welfare laggard (e.g. India, Nicaragua, Tanzania).[12] The aim was to have maximum variation in terms of social policy development so as to have some policy development in the area of care, and to capture some variation in policy responses to care. While the project intended to include policy developments with respect to different groups of care recipients (young children, those with severe illnesses/disabilities, the frail elderly), at the country level researchers focused on areas of care around which more significant policy developments were taking place. Childcare, as is evident from the contributions to this volume, turned out to be a significant area of policy experimentation across all the countries included in the project, while care for people living with HIV/AIDS became a research focus in the case studies on South Africa (this volume) and Tanzania (see Meena, 2010).

Elderly care is a neglected area in the countries included here (with the exception of South Korea and China). Policy debates on population ageing often focus on financial issues, such as pensions. Meanwhile, the need for practical support in carrying out daily activities and the demand for long-term physical care are often neglected. In many middle-income countries these are now urgent issues requiring policy attention (but perhaps less so in those countries where populations are skewed to young ages). The contribution on Uruguay in particular draws attention to the urgent need to develop a system of elderly care, almost from scratch, in a context where the 75+ age group, which is more prone to disability, is increasing rapidly. China has also seen interesting demographic shifts: while the ratio of the population aged 0–14 to the working population fell sharply from 1990 to 2006 (from 41.5 to 27.4

---

12. The UNRISD project, 'The Political and Social Economy of Care', commissioned original research in seven countries: Argentina, Nicaragua, India, Korea, Japan, Tanzania and South Africa. This was complemented by desk studies on Chile, Mexico, Uruguay and Switzerland. Most of the papers included in this volume were part of the UNRISD project, the two exceptions being the contributions on China and on transnationalism.

per cent), the ratio of the 75+ age group to the working age population rose (from 2.5 to 4.7 per cent). The burden of elderly care is particularly acute in this context in the aftermath of the 'one-child policy' (though not implemented in rural areas).

Despite the diverse trajectories, periodization and authorship of economic reform packages, all countries in our cluster have seen the promotion and consolidation of a market-led development path, albeit with notable variations in the specific templates followed. These reforms have been marked by rising levels of income inequality almost everywhere, and poverty levels that have remained persistent in some contexts. The contributions to this volume are particularly interested in how social policy provision for care has emerged, evolved and is changing in line with altered political and economic conditions. The tension between patterns of economic development that are largely exclusionary and polarizing, and processes of social and family change that raise new risks and demands forms the backdrop. Many of the tensions are being addressed (though not resolved) in the messy realm of social policy formulation and implementation where policy elites (sometimes in conjunction with external actors) interpret, appease, deflect or subvert the articulated 'needs'. 'Needs' are always interpreted through the existing forms of political power distribution so that those who are the most marginal are the least likely to have their 'needs' recognized (Fraser, 1987). Unequal care in turn reinforces inequality (Tronto, 2006). Masquerading under different banners — poverty reduction, social protection or community participation — a broad range of social programmes has been put in place to address the needs of the most disadvantaged, yet without abandoning the neoliberal basics centred on economic liberalization and a nimble state that facilitates the integration of people into the market.

FAMILIES AND THE PROVISION OF UNPAID CARE

Families are clearly central to the welfare regimes of many developing countries, as they are elsewhere. In fact one of the early criticisms directed at Esping-Andersen's (1990) *Three Worlds of Welfare Capitalism* was his neglect of the family and of women's unpaid work as important contributors to societal welfare (Lewis, 1992). Nearly a decade after the publication of his classic study, Esping-Andersen (1999: 11) explained this oversight in terms of 'the blindness of virtually all comparative political economy to the world of families. It is, and always has been, inordinately macro-oriented' (and gender blind!). In his more recent work he argues emphatically that the revolution in demographic and family behaviour, spearheaded by women's embrace of personal independence and lifelong careers, has triggered the proliferation of new and less stable household and family arrangements, which in turn demand a new welfare state (Esping-Andersen, 2009). A similar position has been adopted by several other welfare state analysts who distinguish between 'old' and 'new' social risks and argue for the adaptation of welfare states to the latter (Bonoli, 2006).[13] This resonates with the approach taken by Filgueira et al. in their analysis of welfare, care and gender in Uruguay in this volume, which underlines that the failure to adapt to the new social conditions is even more devastating in middle-income countries such as Uruguay which are marked by very high levels of inequality.

Household and family arrangements are heterogeneous and unstable in the contexts we are concerned with, as well as being unable to meet welfare needs without support from other sectors of the economy. However, the forces underpinning change have been far more insidious, associated more with persistent economic crises and lop-sided development models, and less with women's embrace of personal independence and lifelong careers, as Esping-Andersen puts it (for Europe). Work on welfare regimes in Latin America has underlined the point, overlooked in much welfare regime analysis and theorizing by feminists and non-feminists alike, that the heterosexual nuclear family form may not be the norm everywhere, and has attempted to integrate more complex family forms into such analysis (Martinez-Franzoni, 2008). In countries such as Nicaragua, India and South Africa a significant proportion of households are complex and extended, and a substantial number of children continue to grow up with adults other than their parents, who possibly share childcare and other care work among themselves. Even in South Korea, where the economy has undergone massive structural transformation, high levels of co-residency amongst the elderly and their adult children allow multi-generational family members to share housing, pool resources and exchange child and elderly care services. In many of these contexts, families and extended kin networks remain important cultural and survival resources. Feminist social policy analysts by no means argue for a notion of individuals as atomized and autonomous beings. Yet even the limited forms of 'de-familialization' that have been proposed (for example, women's capacity to uphold a socially acceptable standard of living independently of the family) are difficult to apply in contexts where family and kinship networks remain important to people's livelihoods and security, and where non-familial provision of social security is weak (Hassim and Razavi, 2006).

This kind of social embeddedness is not only a primary source of identity, but also structures women's entitlements by offering them some access to resources such as land, housing and childcare even if only as a consequence of their conjugal or maternal status. In the midst of economic crisis, when jobs disappear and the little state provision that there is becomes eroded, these networks take on an even more critical role. In the context of recurring crises in Latin America during the 1980s and 1990s, the proportion of extended households increased in some countries as a response to the economic

---

13. The 'new' risks invariably include tensions between work and family life (due to women's entry into the labour market), single parenthood, having a frail relative, possessing low or obsolete skills, and insufficient social security coverage (due to labour market changes away from full-time lifelong employment) (Bonoli, 2006).

privations that lower-income sectors experienced and as a means of pooling resources and meeting needs such as shelter (Jelin and Diaz-Munoz, 2003). Similarly, household strategies, such as the tendency for women to take on paid work, the out-migration of younger and able-bodied members, or pooling and sharing of resources across extended kin networks can change, sometimes very rapidly, in response to the broader context within which these networks are embedded (Cerrutti, 2000; Gonzalez de la Rocha, 1988). This underlines the critical point that the family is not an isolated institution (Jelin and Diaz-Munoz, 2003). Nor is it autonomous. Domestic units, whatever their composition and form, are rooted in social networks which provide support and solidarity, sometimes across national borders, as well as being connected to the wider political economy through the flow of goods and services (Moore, 1994). However, while households and families play a crucial role in social protection and reproduction, the extended nature of economic crises in many developing countries, as well as structural changes associated with migration and HIV/AIDS, may have exhausted kinship solidarity networks (Therborn, 2004: 180).

Another feature exemplified by several countries in our cluster, most notably South Africa, Uruguay and Nicaragua, is the relatively high incidence of households with children that are maintained primarily by women (mostly mothers and grandmothers) without male support. As the evidence from Uruguay shows, it is among the lower-income strata that the presence of such households is particularly high (around 21 per cent) — more than double the rate found for higher income groups. A similar pattern can be seen in Argentina, and also in South Africa if race is used as a proxy for social class. There may be certain advantages for women of forming such households, in terms of greater decision-making power, freedom from violence, or more control over assets (Chant, 2008). It is nevertheless a constrained choice which leaves mothers in the difficult position of having to both earn a living and care for their dependants, in a context where income-earning opportunities are limited and family networks already strained.

A stark illustration of how broader political and economic processes shape and disrupt families comes from the South African contribution. Here the legacy of colonial domination and apartheid/racial capitalism has left a deep mark on family structures and gender relations, with important implications for the organization of care. The migrant labour system, which was most formalized in the country's mining industry,[14] effectively removed men from their families for most of the year while they worked in mines and lived in single-sex compounds. Women and children were for the most part restricted to an increasingly impoverished hinterland of subsistence agriculture. As is well known, the migration routes from these mines and

---

14. There is a tradition of both functionalist (anthropologist) and Marxist analytical work on the migrant labour system in Southern Africa; in a review of this work, O'Laughlin (1998) reiterates the importance of seeing the labour migrant system in Southern Africa as a regional labour system.

colonial construction projects also became paths for the spread of venereal disease and more recently AIDS (Caldwell et al., 1992).

These patterns, Budlender and Lund suggest, are still visible fifteen years after the end of apartheid: the majority of children are still living apart from their biological fathers. In 2005, only 35 per cent of children (0–17 years) were resident with both their biological parents while 39 per cent were living with their mother but not their father. South Africans continue to have lower rates of marriage and higher rates of extra-marital childbearing than most other countries. Women in South Africa are likely to end up responsible for providing for their children both financially and in terms of care.

Budlender and Lund are reluctant to claim any causal relations between the patterns of residence and marriage, on the one hand, and the persistently high rates of male unemployment, on the other. For Botswana, however, O'Laughlin (1998: 24) has argued that the reason many women and men do not marry and establish common households 'is because they cannot and not because they do not wish to do so'. In the context of long-term structural unemployment — which afflicts the southern African region — many poor men do not form households at all and effectively 'disappear'. Both rural poverty and the high incidence of households maintained by women, O'Laughlin suggests, derive from the dominant model of accumulation in the region that continues to be exclusionary and polarizing.

Beyond the political economy, 'the family' also embodies strong ideological and normative dimensions or a social imaginary that defines the rights and responsibilities of its members, and identifies who should provide care, as well as the legitimate recipients, and the best location for such provision. Across the wide range of countries included in this cluster, regardless of cultural and religious traditions, political configurations and socio-economic variations, the actual tasks of caring are defined as family responsibilities, and within families, as quintessentially female/maternal duties. In China, the care of the elderly by the family is even endorsed by several pieces of legislation and the Constitution, and it is a criminal offence for an adult child to refuse to support an aged family member (Cook and Dong, this volume). Women, however, tend to experience stronger pressures to care than men do in most societies, as the experience of caring is very often the medium through which they are 'accepted into and feel they belong to the social world' (Graham, 1983 cited in Giullari and Lewis, 2005: 11).

The inequalities in the provision of unpaid care work — unpaid housework, care of persons and 'volunteer' work — are captured in the time use survey data referred to in many of the contributions to this volume.[15] It should

---

15. Much of the literature on the developed world has tended to focus on the relational aspects of care, i.e. the face-to-face activities that strengthen the physical health and safety and the physical, cognitive, or emotional skills of the care recipient. This emphasis on nurturing, face-to-face interactions has sidelined domestic work that provides the basis on which personal care giving can be carried out. In developing countries where time-saving domestic

not come as a surprise that, in all countries, women's hours of paid work are less than men's, while men contribute less time to unpaid care work. Among six of the countries in our core cluster (India, South Korea, South Africa, Tanzania, Nicaragua and Argentina) the mean time spent by women on unpaid care work was more than twice the mean time spent by men (Budlender, 2008a). When paid and unpaid work were combined, women in all six countries allocated more time to work than men — meaning less time for leisure, education, political participation and self-care. In general, therefore, it is fair to say that 'time poverty' is more prevalent among women than men. But this statement relates to averages calculated across the population. In fact, the distribution patterns for men and women are very different, with low variability among men (that is, men seem to do a consistently low amount of unpaid care work) and high variability among women (some women do significantly more unpaid care work than others). As a consequence, there is a notable level of in-group inequality among women. Age, gender, marital status, income/class, race/caste and the presence of young children in the household are some of the factors that influence variation in the time people spend on unpaid care work. Being male tends to result in doing less unpaid care work across all countries. As far as the age of the care giver is concerned, the common pattern is an initial increase, with age, in the amount of unpaid care work done, followed by a decrease. Household income, meanwhile, tends to have an inverse relation with women's time inputs into unpaid care work. In other words, in low-income households women allocate more time to such tasks than in high-income households, possibly a reflection of the fewer possibilities of purchasing care services, the absence of infrastructure and larger household size. Having a young child in the household has a major impact on the amount of unpaid care work assumed by women and men.[16]

Yet despite the construction of care work as deeply familial and maternal, care is not and has never been confined to the family and family-mediated relations. Many of the intimate tasks associated with care slip out of the unpaid domain of family and 'go public' (Anttonen, 2005). This happens in a variety of ways, for example when households resort to market-mediated relations to access care assistance provided by domestic workers or child minders, or through public sector or not-for-profit sector service provision. In some instances the 'publicness' of care is straightforward, for example when families resort to a public old age home or crèche for the care of an elderly parent or a young child; here both the location of care and the

---

technology and basic social infrastructure are not readily available, domestic tasks can absorb a huge amount of time, leaving little time for the more 'interactive' part of care. Even in the developed countries, domestic work continues to absorb a significant share of women's time among low-income households who are not able to hire help or purchase market substitutes. The contributions to this volume have therefore tended to include non-relational aspects in their analysis of care.

16. Detailed analyses of the time use data for the UNRISD project countries can be found in the edited volume by Debbie Budlender (2010), *Time Use Studies and Unpaid Care Work*.

relations mediating it, as well as the source of funding, partially shift away from the family. In other instances, families can make their own financial arrangement for hiring care that is provided in the home or in another location (for example a private crèche). The relations can become even more complex and fuzzy where states show a propensity to give financial support to families to provide childcare at home, either by the parent or through the employment of a home-based childcare worker. In this case, as in the case of child-oriented cash transfer schemes already referred to, while the state assumes some financial responsibility for childcare, 'the bottom line is that the family [mother] is still seen as the appropriate provider of care to young children, although not as the sole provider' (Daly, 2011: 15).[17]

Notions of familialism[18] and maternalism[19] resonate across the countries covered in this issue, regardless of how families arrange their actual tasks of caring. These normative assumptions are often carried over into the policy domain where almost by default it is women/mothers who are seen as the ones who have to bear responsibility for the care of other family members. In periods of rapid change, as in the case of China with the declining influence of socialist ideology that accorded at least formal equality to women and men, traditional patriarchal values can see a revival: the growing references to China's Confucian cultural heritage in policy circles, Cook and Dong suggest, not only frees the government from assuming fiscal responsibility for welfare provision, but is also likely to reinforce traditional gender norms and/or simply leave care needs unaddressed.

Even when it is not mothers or other family members who provide care — when care is shifted out of the family — the workforce tends to be predominantly female and workers often face significant wage disadvantages *vis-à-vis* workers with comparable skill levels in non-care related occupations (Budig and Misra, 2010; England et al., 2002).[20] Caring seems to be widely devalued, no matter where it takes place and who performs it, the low pay often justified by constructing such work as 'low-skilled' and/or as work which carries its own rewards.

---

17. Daly's paper deals with European policies only; however, the point being made can be extended to the cash transfer schemes in developing countries as well.

18. Familialism can be understood as an ideology that promotes family as a way of life and a force for social integration. A familialist welfare system, more specifically, is one that relies heavily on the family for the provision of welfare and care.

19. Maternalism has been defined by Koven and Michel (1993: 4) as a variety of ideologies that 'exalted women's capacities to mother and applied to society as a whole the values they attached to that role: care, nurturance and morality'. Unlike the papers on India and Argentina in this volume that use the term maternalist to describe state policy, Koven and Michel's analysis was grounded in women's social movements and *their* engagement with welfare policies. However, they also drew attention to 'the protean character of maternalism, the ease with which it could be harnessed to forge improbable coalitions' and the 'subtle shift from a vision of motherhood in the service of women to one serving the needs of paternalists' (ibid.: 5).

20. An analysis of workers in the care economy of UNRISD project countries appears in a Special Issue of *International Labour Review* (Razavi and Staab, 2010).

Running counter to predictions that paid domestic service would disappear with economic development, rising income inequality seems to have acted as a major driving force behind its growth. It is therefore not surprising that paid domestic labour remains an important source of employment for poor women in some of the most unequal parts of the world, such as Latin America and South Africa. Similarly, in both India and China, the recent period of economic growth has witnessed an increase in the number of women employed in domestic service, with the rise of an urban 'servant-employing' middle class as the pull factor, and shrinking employment opportunities in rural areas as the push factor.[21] In the context of growing inequalities, the movement of domestic labour across borders has also increased, not only from South to North, but also within Southern regions (e.g. from Peru to Argentina, from the Philippines to Singapore). Hovering at the most informal end of the labour market spectrum, most of these workers are excluded from regulations on minimum wage, maximum working hours, or mandatory employer contributions.

CARE AS PUBLIC POLICY

As analysts of care have often remarked, one of the complexities of care is that it cuts across conventional policy boundaries — 'in fact, there is no policy for care as such in most national policy settings' (Daly, 2009). Yet this very complexity also points to the marginal status of care in the currently dominant paradigm of growth. 'Can we imagine another centrally important human activity, e.g., national defence, or transportation infrastructure, that would be spread so thinly and unevenly across the four corners of the care diamond?' (Tronto, 2009).

Good care requires a variety of resources. Time is a key input into care provision. However, the question of time cannot be considered without the material/income dimension. It is one thing to be time-poor and income-rich (middle-class professionals), another thing to be time-poor and income-poor (women wage labourers in rural India), and yet another to be time-rich and income-poor by being forced into idleness because of very high rates of structural unemployment. Hence the concern about time needs to be much more firmly connected to income and poverty (Elson, 2005). In the welfare regimes literature, care-related interventions have been broadly categorized into three areas, dealing with time (e.g. paid care leaves), financial resources (e.g. cash transfers) and services (e.g. pre-schools, homes for the elderly) (Daly, 2001). While the broad trend across Europe favours multidimensional responses to care, it also reveals that overall spending on family policy varies

---

21. As Yeates's paper (this volume) shows, in Britain too, household spending on paid domestic labour quadrupled between 1986 and 1996, and the number of people employed as domestic workers increased by 17 per cent during the late 1990s when average employment growth was 3 per cent.

(indicating different degrees of state commitment to care) as do policy emphases. One of the key policy lessons emerging from this evidence is that time, money and services are complementary policy inputs, rather than being substitutes. This is an important point to bear in mind, especially in view of the enthusiasm with which donors have been advocating for child/family-oriented cash transfer schemes in developing countries — albeit aimed at enhancing children's capabilities and/or reducing poverty, rather than facilitating care *per se* or reducing gender inequality — without sufficient reflection on the critical role of care services.[22]

A Decent Income for Care

One way in which care giving can be supported is by providing allowances, financed through public funds, so that the primary care giver can temporarily withdraw from full-time paid work. This is equivalent to what Fraser (1997) has termed the 'care-giver parity model'. One problem with this scenario, as she points out, is that even if the system of allowances-plus-wages provides the equivalent of a basic minimum breadwinner wage, it is likely to create a 'mommy track' in employment — a market in flexible, non-continuous full- and/or part-time jobs (Fraser, 1997: 57). Recent policy discussions in Europe on welfare restructuring have placed the accent on the need for labour market 'activation', especially of women with young children, including lone mothers, who have tended to have lower rates of labour force participation and some degree of financial assistance on the basis of their maternal status. It is in this context that Orloff has written about 'farewell to maternalism' (2005). Others have looked into what the new 'adult worker model' can mean for gender equality, both in the home and in the market (Daly, 2011; Giullari and Lewis, 2005).[23]

Governments do not seem to be bidding 'farewell to maternalism' in some of the countries covered in this special issue. In the case of several Latin American countries which have been experimenting with different types of cash transfer schemes aimed at children and the family in recent years, feminist analysis suggests a revival of maternalism (Molyneux, 2006). One issue that is considered problematic is the requirement that mothers contribute a set amount of hours of community work, such as for cleaning schools and health centres, in addition to the commitments they have to make to taking their children for regular health checks and attending workshops on health

22. This is similar to a broader concern which has been raised about conditional cash transfers, namely that while cash stipends may enhance poor people's access to services (by enabling parents to purchase school uniforms and books, for example), they do little to strengthen the supply and quality of public health and education services, which are often in a dire state after years of neglect and under-funding.
23. Concerns have been raised about the quality of jobs that women are getting, particularly in view of the European policy emphasis on the need for more 'flexible' employment regimes that are necessary for global competitiveness (Giullari and Lewis, 2005).

and hygiene (ibid.), intensifying women's unpaid workloads. Attention has also been drawn to the ways in which women in such programmes seem to be 'primarily positioned as a means to secure programme objectives; they are a *conduit of policy*, in the sense that resources channelled through them are expected to translate into greater improvements in the well-being of children and the family as a whole' (ibid.: 439). Endorsing these concerns, Faur's analysis of Argentine social policies (this volume) suggests that the appeal to mothers' responsibility and commitment to their children and families as a prerequisite for obtaining the minimum resources needed for subsistence from the State, reflects a traditional maternalistic perspective 're-packaged into a modern criterion for eligibility to social assistance'.

Such a critical stance is not shared by other contributors. South Africa has been another pioneer in the public provisioning of social assistance grants for children, old people, and a number of other social groups. Indeed the proportion of households that receives at least one of these grants is significant. Similar to other cash transfer programmes, women predominate among the beneficiaries: 98 per cent of those who receive the Child Support Grant (CSG) and 73 per cent of those who receive the pension for elderly people are women. The other important characteristic of the South African grants is that they are unconditional (though means-tested), going against the orthodoxy that insists on behavioural conditionalities.[24] Hence, the concern that conditional cash transfers increase women's unpaid care burdens, as the contributions on Argentina and Nicaragua in this volume suggest, is not pertinent here.[25] Budlender and Lund (this volume) argue that these grants 'crowd-in' care, especially for children, by substituting for employment-based income in a context where many adults and prime carers are unemployed or discouraged from even looking for work. They also cite evidence that suggests that receipt of an old age pension grant may enable grandmothers to care for their grandchildren while the younger women migrate to seek paid work.

There are, apart from the problematic conditionalities, multiple impediments that stand in the way of making these transfers a rights-based entitlement: their weak legal basis in many countries; the fact that some of these programmes rely on external funding of unknown duration; the means-testing that very often lacks transparency to beneficiaries; abusive behaviour by officials within the system; and the absence of automatic redress

---

24. However, there have been attempts to introduce conditionalities in South Africa since 2010; see Lund (2011) for clarification and an argument on why linking the CSG to school attendance is 'a step in the wrong direction'.
25. Although there is evidence to show that conditional cash transfers increase children's school enrolment and attendance rates and improve their health, there is little if any research that proves that it is the conditionalities that cause this 'rather than simply the injection of additional cash into the household' (Budlender, 2008b: 8–9). If the positive impacts are not the result of the conditionalities, there is little reason for the state to face the challenges and administrative costs associated with implementing them and for beneficiaries to face the difficulties that conditions will create for them (ibid.).

mechanisms.[26] Most important perhaps, what needs to be borne in mind is that social assistance payments ideally should be one component of a much more comprehensive system of social security. They can nevertheless be a useful component for many as a reliable (albeit small) source of regular income. In other words, the baby (transfer) should not be thrown out with the bathwater (conditionality).

Being set at a relatively low level, social assistance payments can usually defray only a small percentage of the cost of raising children (or caring for other dependants). Hence, for better or for worse, the income to support care giving will at least have to be partially provisioned through paid work. In developing countries, however, labour markets tend to be extensively informal, with far-reaching implications for people's lack of access to social and economic security. Countries like India and Nicaragua, whether we label them 'exclusionary' (Filgueira, 2007) or 'informal' (Martinez Franzoni, 2008) welfare regimes, are characterized by extensively informal labour markets where social protection measures such as pensions and maternity/parental leave are largely directed to the small strata who are in formal (very often public) employment.

Although there is an inverse relationship between the informalization of labour and economic growth (confirming the counter-cyclical nature of informal work), informal employment has been growing not only in contexts of low economic growth but also where rates of growth have been modest or good, suggesting a more complex relationship between the two (Heintz and Pollin, 2003). In China, Cook and Dong suggest that despite high rates of growth, rising levels of unemployment in the late 1990s led to stronger arguments for having less secure 'flexible' forms of employment as re-employment measures, especially in sectors where women dominate. In the case of India the entire net employment increase between the high-growth years 1999/2000 and 2004/5 has been that of informal workers (Srivastava, 2008). While Indian women's economic activity rates are low in comparative terms (the lowest in our cluster of countries), those who enter the workforce often do so as a 'distress strategy'. Hence, it is very often poverty that pushes women into the paid workforce, and often into marginal forms of employment offering very low levels of income. For vast sections of the workforce earnings are so low that even the existence of multiple earners in the household is not sufficient to pull the household above the poverty line (UNRISD, 2010). This is despite the exceptionally long hours spent on such work.[27] Similarly, the contribution on China documents the 'harsh

---

26. These issues have been elaborated at some length in the report of the Independent Expert on the Question of Human Rights and Extreme Poverty, Magdalena Sepúlveda Carmona (UNGA, 2009).
27. According to the time use survey data, Indian men and women have the longest working hours and the shortest time allocated to 'non-productive work' (i.e. sleeping, leisure, studying) compared to other countries in our cluster (Budlender, 2008a).

choices' that rural women in low-income villages have to make between caring for their young children and earning a livelihood in a context where grandmothers and older children are the only care substitutes available to them. The extensive informality of labour markets in such contexts also makes a mockery of the care-related social protection measures that may be on the statute books, such as entitlements to maternity[28] or parental leave — minimal measures for reconciling paid work and unpaid care responsibilities (historically targeted to women, but now increasingly embracing men too).

While labour markets are more formalized in Argentina, Uruguay, South Africa and South Korea, and the coverage of social protection programmes more extensive, a number of relevant issues nevertheless stand out. In both Argentina and Uruguay, even during the 'golden age', women's primary role in care and reproduction was firmly maintained, and their access to social protection was very often mediated through marriage. Argentina, as the contribution by Faur makes clear, exemplifies significant discontinuity marked by recurrent crises and abrupt changes in its welfare regime. Over a period of important structural reforms (1975–2000), the country has gone from being a regional pioneer in social policy that offered social security coverage, albeit of different quality, to its economically active population and basic education and health services to nearly all citizens, to what may be called a dualist regime. Close to half the workforce is today informally employed and increasingly dependent on the social assistance programmes that have moved to centre stage. This is also the period when falling earnings, especially of male breadwinners due to unemployment or underemployment, have propelled women into the paid workforce.

The fact that today close to half of all economically active women work informally means that they have no entitlement to paid maternity leave or to workplace-based care services, which are differentially available even to those who work formally (depending on the sector, province and the strength of trade unions). In fact the policy direction in Argentina, as in Uruguay and Mexico (Staab and Gerhard, this volume), seems to be moving away from the implementation or expansion of earlier legislation on employment-based rights to childcare for women. Instead, the state has taken significant steps to expand both formal and non-formal pre-school education and care services.

However, there are also elements of continuity and path-dependency. Despite its significantly downsized formal workforce, Argentina stands out regionally for the resurgence of its historically strong labour movement in recent years. This has helped large portions of the formal workforce to recover their wage levels (and some non-wage benefits like family allowances) in the midst of relatively robust growth rates (Etchemendy and Collier, 2007). While the reasons for this resurgence are complex, one contributing factor has been the coming to power of a government which has been favourable

---

28. The origins of maternity leave were not in facilitating care, but rather in protecting the welfare and health of mother and child.

to unions and to union activity. However, in some ways similar to the situation in South Africa, unionism and some form of corporatism in both countries has not been able to overcome the deep segmentation that separates the insiders (mostly formal sector workers) from the outsiders (the informal workforce) amongst whose ranks women predominate. The few social provisions that low-income families and women draw on to reconcile their informal paid work with their care responsibilities are accessed not through employment, but through poorly funded social services and social assistance programmes of diverse kinds.

South Korea stands apart from both Argentina and South Africa given the extent to which employment-related social protection mechanisms are being used by the state to help families (read women) to reconcile their paid work with their family responsibilities, by legislating, regulating and financing maternity and parental leaves (in addition to legislating and financing childcare services and elderly care). However, as the contribution by Peng shows, the 'caring' side of the state is taking shape almost in parallel with, and perhaps as a sweetener to, the bitter and more contentious post-1997 labour market reforms that have facilitated the extremely rapid growth of non-standard employment. [29] In 2005, non-standard employment accounted for 24.1 per cent of men's and 40.3 per cent of women's employment (Grubb et al., 2007). These labour market trends beg the question as to how effectively the newly mandated maternity and parental leave provisions will be applied across sectors, especially in the smaller enterprises where women tend to be clustered.

Infrastructure and Basic Social Services

Besides income from work (or, in its absence, social transfers), there are at least two other critical pre-conditions for care giving: public provisioning of appropriate infrastructure and technology (water and sanitation, decent housing) to reduce the burden of unpaid domestic work; and enabling social services (health, primary education) to complement unpaid care giving. Both the welfare regime literature and its feminist critiques assume a fairly capable state that will collect taxes and finance basic amenities like electricity, roads and safe water, and at the very least provide basic health and education services. These preconditions cannot be taken for granted in a developing country context.

---

29. 1997 marked the Asian financial and economic crisis which brought in the IMF with a bailout plan 'that became an occasion for overhauling the labour market regime in South Korea, to make it more "flexible"' (Woo, 2007: 18). Woo argues that the South Korean government in fact used the IMF as a political cover to push through the labour market reforms that the corporate sector had long been demanding but which the government had failed to impose due to trade union militancy.

The issue of poverty and resource constraints — not only of the majority of the population, but also of the state — is an important theme in Martinez Franzoni and Voorend's analysis of care in Nicaragua (this volume). Both women and men engage in the labour force at relatively high rates. The problem rather is that the kinds of work people undertake give very low levels of income. This also means that the state's capacity to generate revenue through personal taxation is constrained. The marginal role of the state becomes clear when the figures for public social expenditure are placed alongside those for cross-border remittances and overseas development assistance.

Public health and education services in many countries have been commoditized over the past decades and their quality eroded because public investment in them, though rising in recent years in some countries, has not kept up with growing needs and expectations. In India and Nicaragua, however, even the reach of basic public health and education services remains inadequate, especially in remote rural areas and among socially disadvantaged groups.

Palriwala and Neetha argue that even the supposedly universal components in the Indian welfare regime — health and education — have always been unevenly and minimally available or not accessed by those who have had the means to resort to private facilities. Matters have been made worse since the 1990s with the substantial increase in private healthcare provision (Baru, 2003), as part of the government strategy to develop medical corporations catering to both wealthy domestic and foreign customers (see Yeates's discussion of medical tourism in this volume). The lack of affordable medical treatment means that the care of the ill falls on family members, usually women and girls, or the sick are left to recover on their own as best they can. In education, primary school enrolment has expanded significantly, although the quality is very uneven and standards very low, especially in rural areas and among poorer religious and caste groups. High drop-out rates in schools also mean that neither the education nor the care of children (at least during school hours) can be shifted out of the household and made a public responsibility. Much the same could be said about public welfare services in Nicaragua. In both countries regional disparities in the availability of public services have been made worse through policies of decentralization, to the extent that wealthier districts have more easily been able to raise local revenue to supplement national transfers than poorer ones.

Care Services and the Public–Private–'Community' Mix

The previous two sections dealt with some of what we called the preconditions for care giving. This section turns to care services for children, which have been a source of expansion in many institutionalized welfare states, and which have also emerged on the policy agenda in some of the countries included in our cluster. This may be in part at least a reflection of the diffusion of the 'social investment perspective' which has a particular interest in children, their 'human capital' and capabilities, which are seen as long-term 'investments' that will reap rewards in the future. As such the social investment perspective is fully in tune with the notion of 'equality of opportunity' that has become part of the common sense in current thinking about equality, displacing the earlier concern with equality of outcome (Phillips, 2006). But care service expansion could also be responding to other pressures and needs, for example facilitating women's labour market activation or creating employment opportunities for them — other tenets of the social investment approach (Jenson and Saint Martin, 2006).

The feminist social policy literature has tended to rate the provision of publicly financed and/or delivered services for care-related needs rather positively.[30] While it acknowledges that this strategy carries heavy financial implications for the public budget, it has several important advantages from a gender perspective (Huber and Stephens, 2000). It tends to legitimize care work, provide relatively well-protected jobs for women (at least compared to the market or charitable sectors), give unpaid carers greater choice in seeking employment, and improve access and quality for recipients of care (especially those on low incomes). However, the direct provision of public care services is not the norm even in Europe (apart from the Nordic countries), where there has been a shift to more hybrid forms of service provision.

In the middle- and upper-middle income countries in our cluster (Argentina, Chile, Mexico, Uruguay, South Africa and South Korea) governments have been actively experimenting with a range of care-related measures, including early childhood education and care (ECEC) services. The challenge faced by most of these countries (perhaps with the exception of South Korea) is not only to expand coverage, but to do so in a way that reduces class and regional inequalities, rather than reproducing and reinforcing them. This becomes a formidable challenge when a mix of public–private–community is used, and where different types of programme are developed for different social groups. This seems to be the model favoured by the World Bank which eschews the kind of universal ECEC services recommended by organizations such as the OECD; inspired by US 'Head Start' and related programmes, the World Bank favours ECEC programmes that target the very poor through less formal types of service provision (Mahon, 2011).

In countries where the education system is segmented, there is the risk of reproducing those inequalities in the ECEC services. However, 'path dependency' does not mean that there is no room for policy change, as illustrated by the Chilean case analysed by Staab and Gerhard (this volume).

---

30. The disability movement has tended to lean towards cash benefits (as opposed to service provisioning). Cash benefits, it has been argued, allow care recipients greater choice in accessing the type of services they need and hence more 'independent living' (see Williams, 2010 and references cited therein).

The fact that coverage of children under the age of four was extremely low before the reforms arguably increased the government's room for manoeuvre in shaping the institutional setting in which services would be provided. Their analysis suggests that the government of Michelle Bachelet (2006–2010) may well have used this leeway to strengthen the role of public institutions — in contrast to the larger educational system where powerful private-sector interests have been a major obstacle to equity-oriented reforms.

In all these countries, while higher-income groups usually have a range of options, such as private childcare or hiring domestic/care workers, the ability of lower-income households to purchase care is limited. Pluralism of service provisioning can slip into fragmentation as gaps are filled by providers offering services of varying quality and catering to different segments of the population, as Faur shows for Argentina. In Argentina class and regional differences in access to pre-school education for five-year-olds have been reduced substantially by making enrolment mandatory for this age group and by bolstering public provision. However, for the younger age groups where public provision is limited and the market plays a dominant role, enrolment rates of children from lower-income households remain only a fraction of their higher-income counterparts. Since low-income families cannot access the fee-based private childcare facilities, they face long waiting lists for public crèches, or have to resort to the less professionalized 'community' services (Childhood Development Centres) being promoted by the Ministry of Social Development.

A somewhat similar situation prevails in Mexico (Staab and Gerhard, this volume), where from the early 2000s the Ministry of Public Education made public pre-school education mandatory for all three- to five-year-olds, while the Ministry of Social Development (Sedesol) has, since 2007, put in place a large day-care programme (Federal Day-care Programme for Working Mothers) targeted to a younger cohort of children (one- to four-years) from low-income households. The latter programme, like its Argentine counterpart, also relies on less professionalized staff. Interestingly, and in some contrast to the maternalist thrust of the Mexican cash transfer programme, the Federal Day-care Programme's main aim has been to expand employment opportunities for women (rather than enhancing child welfare or school-readiness); it aims to do this by giving mothers access to affordable 'community-based' childcare options, and by creating employment opportunities for women as 'self-employed' carers offering their services under the programme. As Staab and Gerhard rightly argue, while care work is often devalued even when it is institutionalized and professionalized, the 'community' strategies being pursued in Mexico and many other countries raise serious questions about both the working conditions and pay of women carers, as well as the quality of care that is being offered to children from low-income households.

South Korea's overall performance in terms of number of children enrolled in pre-school is comparable to the Latin American countries. Here the state has sought to partially finance, regulate, but not necessarily deliver care services. Indeed, only around 6 per cent of the childcare centres are truly public; the rest are subsidized, private for-profit and non-profit centres (mimicking the role of the private sector in the delivery of healthcare). Government subsidies on a sliding scale based on parents' income are paid directly to the institution where the child is enrolled. Hence, the same institution may be frequented by children from low- and high-income groups, as the participation of those with lower incomes is subsidized by the state. An effective and equitable mix of public and private provision thus demands a fairly capable state that can regulate market and not-for-profit providers *and* subsidize the access of lower-income households. Yet a 'public–private' mix is often advocated in contexts where such capacity, both administrative and fiscal, is weak.

In the lower income countries, such as India and Nicaragua, care services tend to be rudimentary and inadequate. However, some of the infrastructure for providing these services may be already in place. Examples include the crèche-nutrition units (*anganwadis*) in India, or the childcare centres in Nicaragua. Yet public financing of these schemes is extremely low, and their reliance on very low-paid and 'voluntary' work is not supported by adequate training and resources.

The temptation by states, especially when fiscally constrained, to rely on 'voluntarism' is a theme that reverberates across several contributions to this volume, in particular Martinez Franzoni and Voorend's analysis of 'voluntarism' as an important pillar of Nicaraguan social programmes. As their study amply shows, 'voluntarism' is also deeply gendered. Although the costs of social programmes can be reduced, it is highly questionable whether this 'volunteer' support is appropriate in a context where families, especially women, already face multiple demands on their time. It is also not clear what 'voluntarism' means in a context of extensive poverty or high structural unemployment, where many 'volunteers' may have joined the programme in the hope of acquiring skills that will channel them into paid employment. The latter concern has been raised widely in response to the Home Based Care programmes relying on 'volunteer' work that have mushroomed across African countries because formal health systems are not able to cope with the burden of HIV/AIDS-related care (Akintola, 2004; Meena, 2010).

THE POLITICS OF CARE

The contributions to this volume challenge the view that only advanced industrialized countries are able to develop care-related policies and programmes, while developing countries are indelibly stuck on a 'familialist' track. While severe resource constraints at the national level tend to reinforce reliance on the unpaid work of women, whether as mothers or 'community' workers (as we saw in Nicaragua), the relationship between income and policy development is not linear or univocal.

Classical European-style care policies in the form of employment-related measures such as paid and unpaid leave, severance pay and flexi-time, may be non-existent or rudimentary in many developing countries, but they are also out-of-sync with the 'real' labour markets in these countries which leave a large proportion of the workforce outside formal systems of labour regulation. However, other care-related policy areas are receiving attention. Several developing country states have been active around early childhood development programmes, and some have even outpaced developed countries in terms of actual coverage of children. In a developing country context, policies apart from leave and care services — such as infrastructure development, basic social service provisioning and social protection programmes — have particular salience in facilitating care giving. Many developing country governments are experimenting with different ways of responding to care needs in their societies. The variations across countries in how social and care policies are taking shape hold some useful policy lessons. One is the danger of relying on 'voluntarism' — a useful message at a time when the role of the 'community' is being reified in some developed countries to fill the gap in the context of welfare state retrenchment. The other message is the risk, in particular for women, of labour market 'flexibility' and the danger of de-linking social policy from employment issues and macroeconomic policy more broadly. On this last point it is important to underline that social policy more broadly, and care provisioning more specifically, effectively help (re)produce labour and replenish the labour pool; and conversely, to create a welfare system that is more than a thin safety net of last resort requires state revenues that can be generated and sustained by fully employing the human resources of a country in high-productivity activities. As Heintz and Lund (2011) remind us, drawing on Esping-Andersen's 1990 influential book, *The Three Worlds of Welfare Capitalism*:

> a de-commodifying welfare state must maintain something close to full employment. There is no way of de-linking employment policy from the broader welfare regime. This includes macroeconomic policies which have a direct impact on the level of employment. Given the impact of the recent financial crisis, it also requires policy which disciplines capital in ways that support broader social objectives — in today's economies, this means regulating financial capital in particular. (Heintz and Lund, 2011: 22)

Another emerging message clearly relates to the intersecting inequalities of gender/class/race/location and the risk of market-driven care arrangements reinforcing those inequalities. A final note of caution underlined by developments in China is the risk of policy reversals and patriarchal resurgence. The latter only goes to underline how tenuous and contested the gains in gender equality often are.

In particular historical junctures women's movements have been able to rally around care issues, build political and institutional alliances, and call on the state to fund good quality services for the care of young children or the elderly. Sweden may be a case in point. It may also be a rather exceptional case. Care concerns have often been thrust upon the state by virtue of exigency, for example in the context of rapid population ageing and fertility decline (as in South Korea) or in the midst of health epidemics such as HIV/AIDS, both of which have intensified care needs and provided an opening for putting the issue on the policy agenda. In other instances, interest in children's well-being on the part of both policy elites and children's rights advocates seems to have driven the policy process, especially at a time when attention to child poverty has been heightened. This seems to have been the case in Chile, Uruguay, South Africa and Argentina, for example. However, as the following contributions make clear, policy responses in all these countries have been facilitated by specific historical and political conjunctures: the coming to power of left-leaning governments, sometimes with feminists in critical positions (as the contributions on Chile and Uruguay show), the momentum created by democratic openings (as in South Africa). Alternatively, it may reflect the search by politicians for a 'winnable' strategy, as Peng's analysis of the Roh Moo-hyun administration suggests for South Korea. Here the government responded positively to the demands of feminists and welfarists for care-related policies, because childcare was an effective reform package with which the Roh government could address several key policy issues simultaneously: high unemployment, low economic growth, low fertility and gender equality.

The key question is how to sustain the pressure and ensure that the measures that are put in place meet the needs of all those who require care, and the rights/needs of all those who provide care. The fact that care giving is so easily naturalized — even by women themselves — as 'something that women do', and hence not an issue that could be rendered the subject of public contestation and policy-making, often acts as a barrier to its politicization. A key challenge that confronts countries examined in this volume is the inequalities in the quality of care that different social groups receive — inequalities which closely mirror the configurations of social class and racial/ethnic status. These imbalances fly in the face of all the rhetoric about 'equality of opportunity'. In a world where elites can satisfy their care needs by hiring others (domestic workers, nannies, and so on) and by accessing fee-paying crèches and homes for the elderly, while others rely on under-funded public services and over-stretched kinship and family networks while they struggle to meet their family's subsistence needs, it is not easy to construct alliances around common human needs for care. The conundrum has been eloquently captured by Joan Tronto:

> as long as care is privatised and individualized it is possible to praise oneself for one's caring and decry the ways in which others care. Such praise and blame will likely follow lines of race, class . . . [and] will likely make it more difficult to see inequalities as a result of lack of choice and to see them more as the result of deliberate bad actions, decisions, and ways of life of others. (Tronto, 2006: 11)

Providing meagre allowances (for families, children or the elderly) or 'community services' to support care, financed through the public budget, then become subject to all kinds of paternalistic conditionalities in order to police the behaviour of the welfare recipients or 'dependants' (Fraser and Gordon, 1994; Standing, 2011). The inequality in care then creates a vicious circle, and people are unlikely to recognize the structural underpinnings (unequal power, economic and social inequality and patterns of discrimination) of care imbalances. Thus, they are unlikely to see that the care imbalance requires social responsibility and a collective response. Turning the vicious circle into a virtuous one where the costs of care can be socialized and its benefits maximized becomes a formidable challenge, but one that must be faced if we are serious about creating really equal societies.

REFERENCES

Akintola, O. (2004) 'A Gendered Analysis of the Burden of Care on Family and Volunteer Caregivers in Uganda and South Africa'. Working Paper, Health Economics and HIV/AIDS Research Division. Durban: University of KwaZulu-Natal.

Anttonen, A. (2005) 'Empowering Social Policy: The Role of the Social Care Services in Modern Welfare States', in Olli Kangas and Joakim Palme (eds) *Social Policy and Economic Development in the Nordic Countries*, pp. 88–117. Basingstoke and New York: Palgrave Macmillan for UNRISD.

Asis, M.M.B., S. Huang and B.S.A. Yeoh (2004) 'When the Light of the Home is Abroad: Unskilled Female Migration and the Filipino Family', *Singapore Journal of Tropical Geography* 25(2): 198–215.

Bakker, I. (2003) 'Neoliberal Governance and the Reprivatization of Social Reproduction: Social Provisioning and Shifting Gender Orders', in Isabella Bakker and Stephen Gill (eds) *Power, Production and Social Reproduction*, pp. 66–82. Basingstoke and New York: Palgrave Macmillan.

Baru, R. (2003) 'Privatization of Health Services: A South Asian Perspective', *Economic and Political Weekly* 38(42): 4433–7.

Bedford, K. (2007) 'The Imperative of Male Inclusion', *International Feminist Journal of Politics* 9(3): 289–311.

Beneria, L. (1999) 'Globalization, Gender and the Davos Man', *Feminist Economics* 5(3): 61–83.

Beneria, L. (2008) 'The Crisis of Care, International Migration and Public Policy', *Feminist Economics* 14(3): 1–21.

Bezanson, Kate and Meg Luxton (2006) 'Social Reproduction and Feminist Political Economy', in Kate Bezanson and Meg Luxton (eds) *Social Reproduction: Feminist Political Economy Challenges Neoliberalism*, pp. 3–10. Montreal: McGill-Queen's University Press.

Bonoli, G. (2006) 'New Social Risks and the Politics of Post-Industrial Social Policies', in K. Armingeon and G. Bonoli (eds) *The Politics of Post-Industrial Welfare States: Adapting Post-War Social Policies to New Social Risks*, pp. 3–26. Oxford and New York: Routledge.

Budig, M.J. and J. Misra (2010) 'How Care-Work Employment Shapes Earnings in Cross-National Perspective', *International Labour Review* 149(4): 441–60.

Budlender, D. (2008a) 'The Statistical Evidence on Care and Non-Care Work in Six Countries', GD Programme Paper No. 4. Geneva: UNRISD.

Budlender, D. (2008b) 'Feasibility and Appropriateness of Attaching Behavioural Conditions to a Social Support Grant for Children Aged 15–17 Years'. Report prepared for Department of Social Development (Government of South Africa), Final Version.

Budlender, D. (ed.) (2010) *Time Use Studies and Unpaid Care Work*. New York and Oxford: Routledge/UNRISD.

Caldwell, J.C., P. Caldwell and I.O. Orubuloye (1992) 'The Family and Sexual Networking in Sub-Saharan Africa: Historical Regional Differences and Present-Day Implications', *Population Studies* 46(3): 385–410.

Cerrutti, M. (2000) 'Economic Reform, Structural Adjustment and Female Labor Force Participation in Buenos Aires, Argentina', *World Development* 28(5): 879–91.

Chant, S. (2008) 'The "Feminisation of Poverty" and "Feminisation" of Anti-Poverty Programmes: Room for Revision?', *Journal of Development Studies* 44(2): 165–97.

Chant, S. (2010) 'Towards a (Re)conceptualisation of the "Feminisation of Poverty": Reflections on Gender-Differentiated Poverty from The Gambia, Philippines and Costa Rica', in S. Chant (ed.) *The International Handbook of Gender and Poverty: Concepts, Research, Policy*, pp. 111–16. Northampton: Edward Elgar Publishing Limited.

Daly, M. (2001) 'Care Policies in Western Europe', in M. Daly (ed.) *Care Work: The Quest for Security*, pp. 33–55. Geneva: International Labour Organization.

Daly, M. (2009) 'Care as a Challenge for Public Policy in Europe'. Unpublished paper. Geneva: UNRISD.

Daly, M. (2011) 'What Adult Worker Model? A Critical Look at Recent Social Policy Reform in Europe from a Gender and Family Perspective', *Social Politics* 18(1): 1–23.

Daly, M. and J. Lewis (2000) 'The Concept of Social Care and the Analysis of Contemporary Welfare States', *British Journal of Sociology* 51(2): 281–98.

Donath, S. (2000) 'The Other Economy: A Suggestion for a Distinctively Feminist Economics', *Feminist Economics* 6(1): 115–23.

Ehrenreich, B. and A.R. Hochschild (eds) (2003) *Global Woman: Nannies, Maids and Sex Workers in the New Global Economy*. London: Granta Books.

Elson, D. (1998) 'The Economic, the Political and the Domestic: Businesses, States, and Households in the Organization of Production', *New Political Economy* 3(2): 189–208.

Elson, D. (2002) 'Gender Justice, Human Rights, and Neo-liberal Economic Policies', in Maxine Molyneux and Shahra Razavi (eds) *Gender Justice, Development and Rights*, pp. 78–114. Oxford: Oxford University Press.

Elson, D. (2005) 'Unpaid Work, the Millennium Development Goals, and Capital Accumulation'. Paper presented at the conference on Unpaid Work and the Economy: Gender, Poverty and the Millennium Development Goals, United Nations Development Programme and Levy Economics Institute of Bard College, Annandale-on-Hudson, New York (1–3 October).

England, P., M.J. Budig and N. Folbre (2002) 'Wages of Virtue: The Relative Pay of Care Work', *Social Problems* 49(4): 455–73.

Esping-Andersen, G. (1990) *The Three Worlds of Welfare Capitalism*. Princeton, NJ: Princeton University Press.

Esping-Andersen, G. (1999) *Social Foundations of Post Industrial Economies*. Oxford: Oxford University Press.

Esping-Andersen, G. (2009) *The Incomplete Revolution: Adapting to Women's New Roles*. Cambridge: Polity Press.

Etchemendy, S. and R.B. Collier (2007) 'Down but Not Out: Union Resurgence and Segmented Neocorporatism in Argentina (2003–2007)', *Politics & Society* 35(3): 363–401.

Filgueira, F. (2007) 'The Latin American Social States: Critical Junctures and Critical Choices', in Yusuf Bangura (eds) *Democracy and Social Policy*, pp. 136–63. Basingstoke: Palgrave.

Fraser, N. (1987) 'Women, Welfare, and the Politics of Needs Interpretation', *Hypatia* 2(1): 103–21.

Fraser, N. (1997) 'After the Family Wage: A Postindustrial Thought Experiment', in Nancy Fraser *Justice Interruptus: Critical Reflections on the 'Postsocialist' Condition*, pp. 41–66. London and New York: Routledge.

Fraser, N. and L. Gordon (1994) 'A Genealogy of Dependency: Tracing a Keyword of the US Welfare State', *Signs* 19(2): 309–36.

Fukuyama, F. (2004) 'The Imperative of State-Building', *Journal of Democracy* 15(2): 17–31.

Giullari, S. and J. Lewis (2005) 'The Adult Worker Model Family, Gender Equality and Care: The Search for New Policy Principles, and the Possibilities and Problems of a Capabilities Approach'. SPD Programme Paper No. 19. Geneva: UNRISD.

Gonzalez de la Rocha, M. (1988) 'Economic Crisis, Domestic Reorganisation and Women's Work in Guadalajara, Mexico', *Bulletin of Latin American Research* 7(2): 207–23.

Graham, H. (1983) 'Caring: A Labour of Love', in J. Finch and D. Groves (eds) *A Labour of Love: Women, Work and Caring*, pp. 13–31. London: Routledge and Keegan Paul.

Grubb, D., J.K. Lee and P. Tergeist (2007) 'Addressing Labour Market Duality in Korea'. OECD Social, Employment, and Migration Working Papers No. 61. Paris: OECD.

Haney, L. (2003) 'Welfare Reform with a Familial Face'. in L. Haney and L. Pollard (eds) *Families of a New World: Gender, Politics, and State Development in a Global Context*, pp. 159–78. New York: Routledge.

Haney, L. and L. Pollard (2003) 'In a Family Way: Theorizing State and Familial Relations', in L. Haney and L. Pollard (eds) *Families of a New World: Gender, Politics, and State Development in a Global Context*, pp. 1–14. New York: Routledge.

Hassim, S. and S. Razavi (2006) 'Gender and Social Policy in a Global Context: Uncovering the Gendered Structure of "the Social"', in S. Razavi and S. Hassim (eds) *Gender and Social Policy in a Global Context: Uncovering the Gendered Structure of "the Social"*, pp. 109–29. Basingstoke: Palgrave/UNRISD.

Heintz, J. and F. Lund (2011) 'Welfare Regimes and Social Policy: A Review of the Role of Labor and Employment'. Unpublished paper. Geneva: UNRISD.

Heintz, J. and R. Pollin (2003) 'Informalisation, Economic Growth and the Challenge of Creating Viable Labor Standards in Developing Countries'. PERI Working Paper Series No. 60. Amherst, MA: University of Massachusetts, Political Economy Research Institute.

Htun, M. and J.L. Weldon (2010) 'When Do Governments Promote Women's Rights? A Framework for the Comparative Analysis of Sex Equality', *Perspectives on Politics* 8(1): 207–16.

Huber, E. and J.D. Stephens (2000) 'Partisan Governance, Women's Employment, and the Social Democratic Service State', *American Sociological Review* 65(3): 323–42.

Huber, E. and J.D. Stephens (2001) *Development and Crisis of the Welfare State: Parties and Policies in Global Markets*. Chicago, IL: University of Chicago Press.

Jelin, E. and A.R. Diaz-Munoz (2003) 'Major Trends Affecting Families: South America in Perspective'. Report prepared for United Nations Department of Economic and Social Affairs, Division for Social Policy and Development, Programme on the Family, New York.

Jenson, J. (2010) 'Diffusing Ideas for After Neoliberalism: The Social Investment Perspective in Europe and Latin America', *Global Social Policy* 10(1): 59–84.

Jenson, J. and D. Saint-Martin (2006) 'Building Blocks for a New Social Architecture: The LEGO Paradigm of an Active Society', *Policy and Politics* 34(3): 429–51.

Koven, S. and S. Michel (1993) *Mothers of a New World, Maternalist Politics and the Origins of Welfare States*. New York and London: Routledge.

Lewis, J. (1992) 'Gender and the Development of Welfare Regimes', *Journal of European Social Policy* 2(3): 159–73.

Lund, F. (2011) 'A Step in the Wrong Direction: Linking the South Africa Child Support Grant to School Attendance', *The Journal of Poverty and Social Justice* 19(1): 5–14.

Mahon, R. (2010) 'After Neoliberalism? The OECD, the World Bank and the Child', *Global Social Policy* 10(2): 172–92.

Mahon, R. (2011) 'Work–Family Tensions and Childcare: Reflections on Latin American Experiences', *Sociologica* 1, Symposium/Gender and Welfare State. A Feminist Debate.

Martinez Franzoni, J. (2008) 'Welfare Regimes in Latin America: Capturing Constellations of Markets, Policies and Families', *Latin American Politics and Society* 50(2): 67–100.

Meena, R. (2010) 'Nurses and Home-Based Caregivers in the United Republic of Tanzania: A Dis-continuum of Care', *International Labour Review* 149(4): 529–42.

Mkandawire, T. (2001) 'Social Policy in a Development Context'. SPD Programme Paper No. 7. Geneva: UNRISD.

Molyneux, M. (2002) 'Gender and the Silences of Social Capital: Lessons from Latin America', *Development and Change* 33(2): 167–88.

Molyneux, M. (2006) 'Mothers at the Service of the New Poverty Agenda: *Progresa/Oportunidades*, Mexico's Conditional Transfer Programme', *Social Policy and Administration* 40(4): 425–49.

Moore, H. (1994) 'Is There a Crisis in the Family?'. Occasional Paper No. 3. Geneva: UNRISD.

Morel, N. (2007) 'From Subsidiarity to "Free Choice": Child- and Elder-Care Policy Reforms in France, Belgium, Germany and the Netherlands', *Social Policy and Administration* 41(6): 618–37.

O'Laughlin, B. (1998) 'Missing Men? The Debate over Rural Poverty and Women-headed Households in Southern Africa', *The Journal of Peasant Studies* 25(2): 1–48.

Orloff, A.S. (2005) 'Farewell to Maternalism? State Policies and Mothers' Employment'. Working Paper WP-05–10. Evanston, IL: Institute for Policy Research, Northwestern University.

Parrenas, R.S. (2005) *Children of Global Migration: Transnational Families and Gender Woes*. Stanford, CA: Stanford University Press.

Phillips, A. (2006) '"Really Equal": Opportunities and Autonomy', *The Journal of Political Philosophy* 14(1): 18–32.

Pierson, C. (1998) *Beyond the Welfare State?* Cambridge: Polity Press.

Pierson, C. (2004) 'Late Industrializers and the Development of the Welfare State'. SPD Programme Paper No. 16. Geneva: UNRISD.

Polanyi, K. (1957) *The Great Transformation*. Boston, MA: Beacon Press.

Razavi, S. (2007) 'The Political and Social Economy of Care: Conceptual Issues, Research Questions and Policy Options'. GD Programme Paper No. 3. Geneva: UNRISD.

Razavi, S. and S. Staab (eds) (2010) 'Workers in the Care Economy', *International Labour Review* 149(4), Special Issue.

Srivastava, R. (2008) 'Towards Universal Social Protection in India in a Rights-Based Paradigm', *Indian Journal of Human Development* 2(1): 111–32.

Standing, G. (1999) *Global Labour Flexibility: Seeking Distributive Justice*. Basingstoke: Macmillan Press.

Standing, G. (2011) 'Behavioural Conditionality: Why the Nudges Must be Stopped – An Opinion Piece', *The Journal of Poverty and Social Justice* 19(1): 27–38.

Therborn, G. (2004) *Between Sex and Power: Family in the World, 1900–2000*. London and New York: Routledge.

Tronto, J. (1993) *Moral Boundaries: A Political Argument for an Ethic of Care*. New York: Routledge.

Tronto, J. (2006) 'Vicious Circles of Unequal Care', in M. Hamington and D.C. Miller (eds) *Socializing Care*, pp. 3–25. Lanham, MD: Rowman & Littlefield Publishers, Inc.

Tronto, J. (2009) 'Democratic Care Politics in an Age of Limits'. Unpublished paper. Geneva: UNRISD.

UK Women's Budget Group (2010) 'A Gender Impact Assessment of the Coalition Government Budget'. Women's Budget Group, London.

United Nations General Assembly (UNGA) (2009) 'Promotion and Protection of All Human Rights, Civil, Political, Economic, Social and Cultural Rights, Including the Right to Development'. Report of the Independent Expert on the question of human rights and extreme poverty, Magdalena Sepúlveda Carmona. Human Rights Council, Eleventh session, Agenda item 3, A/HRC/11/9, 27 March. www2.ohchr.org/english/bodies/hrcouncil/docs/11session/A.HRC.11.9_en.pdf, accessed on 5 August 2010.

United Nations Research Institute for Social Development (UNRISD) (2010) *Combating Poverty and Inequality*. Geneva: UNRISD.

Williams, F. (2010) 'Claiming and Framing in the Making of Care Policies. The Recognition and Redistribution of Care'. GD Programme Paper No. 13. Geneva: UNRISD.

Woo, M.J. (2007) *After the Miracle: Neoliberalism and Institutional Reform in East Asia*. Basingstoke: Palgrave Macmillan.

2

The Good, the Bad and the Confusing: The Political Economy of Social Care Expansion in South Korea

Ito Peng

INTRODUCTION

The South Korean welfare regime is a quintessential case of a familialistic male breadwinner welfare regime: it not only 'assigns a maximum of welfare obligations to households' (Esping-Andersen, 1999: 45), the structure of its social welfare system and labour market is also based on a male breadwinner model characterized by a strict gender division of labour (Lewis, 1992). Historically, the Korean state devolved individual welfare and care responsibilities to households (affecting women in particular) by providing almost no alternatives to family-based care. Unlike social democratic welfare states which provide public care services to children, the elderly and the disabled, and unlike liberal welfare states in which market-based care services are available to middle- and higher-income households, both public and private sources of care in Korea were very limited until the 1990s.

This tight interlock between familialism, the male breadwinner household model and women's unpaid care role is, however, becoming disjointed. While maintaining a familialistic male breadwinner orientation, the Korean social policy regime has been remodelling itself since the 1990s, from what may be considered an *extensive familialism* premised on women's uncommodified care work, to a *modified familialism* through the partial commodification of women's care work.[1] In short, the state's preference for assigning maximum welfare obligations to households is being modified by attempts to lessen women's care responsibilities through social care expansion. The process of shifting some of women's child and elderly care burdens out of the family has resulted in the commodification of some of women's hitherto uncommodified care work at home.

In this article, I use the case of recent family–work harmonization policy reform to illustrate how Korea's social policy regime has been reconfiguring,

I would like to thank my Korean colleagues, particularly Professor Hyekyung Lee, Dr Seung-Ah Hong, Dr Joo-Hyun Park, and colleagues at KIHASA and KWDI for their time and support in this research. I would also like to thank my UNRISD colleagues, especially Shahra Razavi and Silke Staab, for their support in reading and commenting on the earlier versions of this article. Finally, I am grateful to Seonggee Um for her research assistance and the reviewers for their very helpful feedback. This research was supported by grants from UNRISD (Political and Social Economy of Care Project) and the Social Science and Humanities Research Council of Canada.

1. See Leitner (2003) for a discussion of different forms of familialism.

Seen, Heard and Counted, First Edition. Edited by Shahra Razavi.
Chapters © 2012 The Institute of Social Studies. Book compilation © 2012 Blackwell Publishing Ltd.

and what this means for women and gender equality.[2] I call this a case of 'The Good, the Bad and the Confusing' because, from a gender perspective, the seemingly 'good' or positive story of social policy development has to be understood in the light of the rather 'bad', or adverse, labour market policy developments. The result is a confusing mix of policies that simultaneously supports and impedes gender equality. The first section sets the context by describing the Korean social policy regime in relation to care and how it has changed over the last few decades. The following section then presents competing policy developments. Here, I present the family–work harmonization policy and the labour market and employment reforms to illustrate how the two sets of competing policies have proceeded in parallel since the 1990s. The case of recent childcare reforms is then used to show how the politics of instrumentalism and compromise may have contributed to this confusing policy mix. Finally, the last section explores the implications of these policy reforms for women and gender equality.

CONTEXT: THE CHANGING SOCIAL POLICY REGIME IN KOREA

In Korea, the state relies extensively on the family to provide individual welfare and personal care.[3] As a result, direct public support for the family is minimal and social assistance is strictly means tested. There were, however, fairly high levels of employment protection and stratified social insurance systems that favoured and protected (predominantly male) full-time workers and their families until employment reforms were introduced in the 1990s. Prior to the 1990s, the rigid labour market and high economic growth contributed to near full (male) employment. The job security for male breadwinners resulting from this system afforded (middle class) married women the chance to opt out of the labour market to devote themselves to family care, and thus provided the main basis of family welfare. The recent family–work harmonization reforms have set in motion the modification of a previously familialistic and patriarchal welfare orientation by expanding the state's role in family support. The percentage of total general government expenditure that is allocated to the family is, however, still modest. It increased from 0.16 per cent in 1990 to 1.9 per cent in 2006. This is not

---

2. I define the family–work harmonization policy as a set of policies that aims to support working parents with dependent children. It includes maternity and parental leaves, flexible work hours, childcare support, family allowances and other supportive policies for workers with family responsibilities. There has been an expansion of elderly care as well, which is not addressed here.

3. This is comparable to other familialistic welfare regimes such as those of Japan and Southern Mediterranean countries, where the state's reliance on the family has led to a lack of family support programmes and personal social services.

Table 1. Composition of All Households with Older People (65+), 1990–2000

| Household composition | 1990 | 2000 | Age groups in 2000 | | |
			65–69	70–79	80±
			Percentages		
One generation	16.9	28.7	35.5	27.5	12.8
Two generations	23.4	23.9	27.3	19.9	26.5
Three generations	49.6	30.8	23.2	33.3	45.1
Single person	8.9	16.2	13.7	18.9	15.0
Total	100.0	100.0	100.0	100.0	100.0

Source: National Statistical Office (2004), quoted in Choi (2006).

Table 2. Changes in the Relation between Family and Old-age Support

| Year | Live with children (%) | | Children provide material support (%) | |
	Yes	No	Yes	No
1994	n/a	n/a	62.1	37.6
1998	54.5	44.9	58.2	41.6
2002	42.7	56.7	53.3	46.3

Source: National Statistical Office (2004), quoted in Choi (2006).

an insignificant rise, but the total amount remains considerably less than its common comparators, Japan, Sweden and the UK, which allocated 2.8 per cent, 6.4 per cent and 7.2 per cent respectively in 2005 (OECD, 2011).[4]

The family therefore continues to play an important role in welfare provision in Korea. For example, though declining, the high level of co-residency among the elderly and their adult children allows multi-generational family members to share housing, pool resources and exchange child and elderly care services (see Table 1). Similarly, a little over half of those who are sixty and older claim that they receive financial support from their children (Table 2). In 2001, 20.1 per cent of all the elderly, and 45.8 per cent of the elderly living on their own, cited financial support from their children as their main income source (Kwon, Kim and Jung, 2009).

Korean families also continue to spend a significant amount of money on education and health, despite the sizeable and increasing levels of public spending in these areas. Public expenditure on education as a percentage of GDP rose from 4.6 to 6.2 per cent between 1990 and 2004; however, private expenditure on education as a percentage of total household consumption

4. See OECD (2009a) for the definition of social spending on the family.

(in urban areas) also rose from 8.1 to 11.5 per cent during the same period (Ministry of Education, Science and Technology, 2004). The huge increase in the public share of total health spending (from 36.3 per cent in 1995 to 54.9 per cent in 2007) is also offset by a high level of household spending.[5] Because of the high co-payment rate, even with the increased public health spending, the private share of health spending (including both insurance contributions and out-of-pocket payments) in Korea is among the highest in the OECD, at 36 per cent (OECD, 2009c). In sum, despite the increase in public expenditure on social welfare and family support, facilitating the shift to a modified form of familialism, the family continues to play a major role in protecting individuals from social risks.

In addition, despite the expansion of its welfare state, Korea still has to contend with its legacy as a developing country. Health and pension insurances were universalized in 1989 and 1999, respectively. The Employment Insurance reform of 1998 extended coverage to almost all waged workers, including most non-regular workers. In 2000, non-regular employees, the self-employed and unpaid family workers were included in the Workers' Compensation Insurance. At the same time, the National Basic Livelihood Security Programme (NBLS) — the public social assistance programme — made low income the sole criterion for receiving public assistance. These developments show that the main purpose of social insurance in Korea has indeed shifted from its original aim of serving as a limited system of protection for core workers in key industries to being a tool for social risk pooling and income redistribution (Peng and Wong, 2008).

Yet, Korea's total social spending is still noticeably lower than that of other industrialized nations. We can arguably attribute this to its developmental status; despite the doubling of total social spending from 3 per cent of GDP in 1990 to 6 per cent in 2000, it will take time for the country to reach the OECD average. Similarly, even with the expansion of social insurance programmes, labour market status still makes a difference in individual entitlements to social security. Although this is also true of other welfare regimes, the issue of labour market status is more pronounced in Korea because of the large number of workers in non-standard employment.[6] For example, the Employment Insurance coverage is still limited to waged workers (i.e. formal sector employees). Given that over 30 per cent of all workers in the labour force are in the non-standard sector, the lack of Employment Insurance coverage makes them economically vulnerable. In 2003, only about 50 per cent of all workers (57.1 per cent of all male workers and 40 per cent of all female workers) were covered by Employment Insurance (Kim, Moon and Kang,

---

5. During this time, total health spending in Korea rose from 4.1 per cent to 6.8 per cent of GDP (OECD, 2009a).
6. I use 'non-standard employment' to refer to the self-employed, own account holders and unpaid family workers. This differs from 'non-regular employment', which refers to part-time salaried and wage employment.

2004).[7] Thus, while formal social insurance programmes are in place, the large non-standard employment sector creates barriers to workers accessing these social insurances.

RE-ARTICULATION OF LABOUR MARKET AND SOCIAL POLICIES

Since the 1980s, Korean society has been undergoing a number of social, economic and political transformations which are placing pressures on the government. The first is a combination of structural and normative transformations, including defamilialization, individualization, fertility decline and demographic ageing, and increased expectations of gender equality. For example, the average household size declined from 4.5 in 1980 to 3.12 in 2000, due to the decline in the total fertility rate (from 2.8 in 1980 to 1.2 in 2002) and the decline in the number of multi-generational households, as well as the increasing prevalence of single-person households. The proportion of people sixty years and older living with their adult children dropped from 80 per cent to 39 per cent between 1981 and 2006. The proportion of women over the age of twenty-five with college and higher education rose from 5.2 per cent in 1985 to 25.4 per cent in 2005, and the mean age at first marriage increased from 27.8 to 31.4 years for males, and 24.8 to 28.3 years for females between 1990 and 2008 (KWDI, 2008). The last two factors have directly contributed to the decline in the total fertility rate. Public opinion surveys also show that the majority of Koreans believe women should continue to work after marriage and/or childbirth (KNSO, 2002; Na and Moon, 2004), and that younger Korean men prefer to marry women who are employed rather than housewives.[8] Norms about marriage and gender relations have changed as evidenced by the rise in the crude divorce rate[9] (from 0.6 in 1980 to 2.9 in 2004) (OECD/Korea Policy Centre, 2009), and the increased employment rate among married women (from 41.0 per cent in 1985 to 49.9 per cent in 2007) (KWDI, 2008). These changes have not only contributed to a decline in the fertility rate and exacerbated the pace of demographic ageing — which made problems associated with elderly care and a rising dependency ratio a policy imperative — but they have also increased public expectations regarding gender equality.

---

7. These features make the Korean welfare regime somewhat akin to Latin American welfare regimes which are strongly characterized by informality (Barrientos, 2004). Unlike Latin American welfare regimes (e.g. Mexico), where informally employed workers are often excluded from health and pension insurance, Korean health and pension insurance is universal, and the Korean government has made efforts to broaden other social insurance schemes to include non-standard workers.
8. 'Survey of Young People, 2007', interview with Seung-Ah Hong, Ministry of Gender Equality and Family, 14 December 2007.
9. Crude divorce rate refers to the number of divorces per 1,000 persons.

Second, Korea has also experienced two critical political and economic transformations since the 1980s: political democratization beginning in 1987, and the Asian economic crisis of 1997. The process of democratization ended more than twenty-five years of authoritarian rule. Labour gained the right to form independent unions and to strike. The number of trade unions multiplied (from 2,742 in 1987 to 7,883 in 1989) and the number of labour disputes jumped (from 276 in 1986 to 3,749 in 1987) (Lee and Lee, 2004). The combination of labour activism, rigid labour laws and positive economic growth led to rapid wage escalation. Korea's political democratization also hastened its integration into the global economy; in the context of growing economic competition, Korea's rigid employment system and higher wages rendered the economy increasingly uncompetitive, particularly in relation to other newly industrialized Asian economies. Employers responded to these changes by demanding that government deregulate and flexibilize the labour market. By the beginning of the 1990s, employers and some pro-liberalization advocates within the government began to call for wage control and employment flexibility.

The Asian economic crisis of 1997 put the country into the receivership of the IMF. It also ended Korea's three decades of continuous high economic growth. The pressure to deregulate the labour market intensified as the IMF economic bailout package stipulated an overhaul of the labour market. The economic crisis also led to a political regime change. In 1997, Korean voters rejected the conservative government headed by President Kim Young-sam (1993–1998) in favour of the populist Kim Dae-Jung (1998–2003). In response to IMF conditionalities, the Kim Dae-Jung government forged a tripartite state–business–labour agreement that allowed employment deregulation in exchange for welfare state expansion. Employment legislation had, until then, restricted employers from hiring non-regular workers and laying off employees. In effect, Korean labour law provided what Woo (2007) refers to as '*de facto* lifetime employment' for male workers in standard full-time employment. The 1998 Labour Standard Act amendment almost did away with this system by allowing 'urgent managerial need' as a legitimate reason for employers to discharge workers, and by legalizing temporary dispatch work through temporary employment agencies.

The combination of layoffs and forced retirements, the replacement of regular with non-regular employees and a low rate of economic growth led to a sharp rise in income inequality and poverty. The rate of registered male unemployment rose from 2.8 per cent in 1997 to 7.6 per cent in 1998, while the average monthly income of urban wage earners' households dropped by about 7 per cent. To ameliorate the impact of labour market restructuring, the government expanded social insurance, social welfare and employment support programmes. Public expenditure on unemployment benefits rose from 10.46 billion Won in 1996 to 1,030.3 billion Won in 2003. Expenditure on active labour market programmes such as job creation, skills training and job search also increased from 118.8 billion Won in 1996 to 3,346.8 billion in 1999 (OECD, 2009a). However, these were small consolations for overall employment insecurity.

Women were much more adversely affected by these labour market reforms than men. The proportion of women in regular employment (as a percentage of all economically active women) declined from 25.5 to 19.1 per cent between 1995 and 2000, while those in non-regular employment rose from 34.0 to 42.4 per cent, suggesting that many women were laid off and/or withdrew from full-time employment and opted for temporary and daily work (KWDI, 2008). Many women also dropped out of the labour force after 1997 because they were frustrated by employers' discriminatory behaviour (Lee and Cho, 2005). The new post-crisis era was thus marked by labour market deregulation, increased job insecurity, a decline in real wages and rising income inequality. The notion of the male breadwinner household had not only become untenable for most households, but a second wage earner was now essential to maintaining a middle-class lifestyle.

By the time Roh Moo-hyung took power in 2003, issues of unemployment, low economic growth, income inequality and population ageing were dominating public and policy debates. Although the Roh government was elected with the mandate to make politics more accountable to the grassroots, the public also expected it to solve all the emergent issues at once. The government responded to this with a number of family–work harmonization policies, including childcare reforms. The reforms were based on the idea that increased public investment in human and social capital would create positive returns between economic growth and social welfare. The government sought to counterbalance its push for increased labour market flexibility with an expanded social security and social welfare system. And it did this by effectively reframing social welfare expansion (particularly in child and elderly care) as the new 'growth engine' for future economic development (Lee, 2007).[10]

EVIDENCE: RECENT REFORMS

The Good: The Caring State

Since 2003, the Korean government has assumed (and promised to continue assuming) more welfare responsibilities by legislating, financing and providing welfare, particularly child and elderly care, through the public, market and community sectors. For example, Early Childhood Education and Care (ECEC) policies have been revised, resulting not only in the expansion of

---

10. See also interview with Lee Sook Jin, KIHASA, 18 December 2007.

ECEC and a commitment to equalize ECEC opportunities for all children, but also in more integrated pre-school education and pre-school care.[11]

Since the introduction of the Early Childhood Education Promotion Act in 1982, the number of kindergartens has increased, from 2,958 in 1981 to 8,294 in 2007. Similarly, since the Child Care Act of 1991, the total number of childcare centres also increased, from 1,919 in 1990 to 29,823 in 2007,[12] with the number of children enrolled in childcare centres rising from 48,000 to 1,062,415 (KICCE, 2008a).[13]

The new education reform plan proposes the establishment of a new public pre-school system for three- to five-year-olds that will integrate ECE and early childcare. Pointing out that ECE is 'the best educational investment' a country could make, the Presidential Commission on Educational Reform framed the integration of ECE and ECC as a way to reduce families' financial burdens and raise women's social and economic participation (Presidential Commission on Education Reform, 1997, cited in Na and Moon, 2003). The plan also emphasizes its role in creating a 'level playing field' by giving priority to children from disadvantaged and low-income families to access ECEC programmes, ensuring at least one year of free pre-school education for all five-year-olds. Indeed, the enrolment rate of pre-school children in formal care or early education services for nought- to two-year-olds rose from 19.6 per cent in 2004 to 37.7 per cent in 2006, while the figure for three- to five-year-olds increased from 59.5 per cent to 79.8 per cent during the same period (OECD, 2004, 2009b).

The 2004 Early Childhood Education Act and the 2005 Child Care Act reforms have led to increased national and local government commitment to expand and develop ECEC programmes, and to monitor their quality; this includes increasing government funding for childcare-related programmes and stronger certification requirements for ECE teachers, childcare staff and

---

11. Early childhood education (ECE) in Korea mainly consists of kindergartens and *hakwons* (private educational institutions specializing in English, music, arts, sports, etc.) and caters for three- to five-year-olds, while early childcare (ECC) provides institutional and home-based childcare to nought- to five-year-olds. The main objective of ECE is pre-school education, while for the ECC it is care, although since the 1990s, the two objectives have begun to merge as many ECE and ECC institutions are providing both education and care. A current policy issue in Korea is the institutionalization of these two separate and often private systems into a public education system.

12. The formalization of the national childcare legislation has prompted the registration of private childcare centres in the national registry. Some of this huge increase in the number of childcare centres may therefore be due to better registration of private childcare arrangements which were already in place but not hitherto registered with the government.

13. In Korea, the majority of publicly funded childcare is provided by 'private' (for- and not-for-profit) childcare centres. Currently, only 5.6 per cent of all childcare centres are truly public, that is governmental institutions which employ childcare workers who are considered to be public servants. Most private childcare centres in Korea are not-for-profit, meaning they are run by NGOs and other registered non-profit organizations. All publicly funded childcare institutions are regulated by the government.

facilities. The national government's ECE budget jumped from 356 billion Won to 886 billion Won between 2002 and 2006, while that of childcare increased almost five-fold, from 435 billion to 2,038 billion. Several tax benefit programmes were also introduced to help families with pre-school children, including: 1) an annual income tax deduction of up to 1 million Won per child for families with children under six years old; 2) a deduction of 2.5 million Won from annual taxable income for families with two or more children under twenty years of age; 3) an annual income tax deduction of up to 2 million Won on education fees for families with children of three to five years old attending kindergarten and childcare facilities; 4) an annual income tax deduction on medical expenses for children of amounts exceeding 3 per cent of income; and 5) a tax exemption of up to 100,000 Won per month for childbirth and childcare allowances paid by employers (KICCE, 2008b).

The proportion of newborn to five-year-old children enrolled in childcare centres receiving childcare allowance increased from 43.4 per cent in 2005 to 50.7 per cent in 2006 (KICCE, 2007). The government promises to extend the childcare allowance to 80 per cent of all families with children under the age of five by 2010 (Korea.net, 2006b). An additional 2.6 billion Won was allocated in 2007 for parents with children under one year to provide low-cost babysitting and night-time babysitting services (Chosun Daily, 2007).

The 2001 Maternity Protection Act extended paid maternity leave from sixty to ninety days (at 100 per cent wage replacement) and increased financial support for parents taking one year parental leave.[14] The 2005 maternity leave legislation reform bolstered state support for maternity leave by shifting the financial burden of wage replacement from the employer to the state and social insurance. A flat-rate wage replacement of 300,000 Won per month (approximately US$ 250, which in 2003 represented about 10 per cent of average urban household income) was added to the remaining nine months of parental leave in 2004. This rate was subsequently raised to 400,000 Won (US$ 400) in 2006 and 500,000 Won (US$ 500) in 2007. Finally, in 2006, parental leave was extended from one to three years on a flexible basis for public servants (Korea.net, 2006a), and a three-day paternity leave, 'no overtime on the sixth of every month' campaign,[15] and 'daddy quota' schemes were also introduced (Choi, 2008).

Attempts were also made to recast the male breadwinner model into a dual earner model. The comprehensive women's workforce development plan for 2006–10, introduced in 2006, for example, attempts to activate women's employment and to support their human capital development through legislative reforms, such as the Equal Employment Act and policies to support women-owned enterprises. Affirmative Action for women in the labour market was

---

14. Although fathers are encouraged to take parental leave, Korea has yet to introduce a formal 'daddy leave' policy. Parental leave is, however, transferable between the two parents.
15. 'Six' sounds very similar in Korean to 'raising (children)' or 'taking care of (children)'.

also introduced in 2006, and currently applies to workplaces employing 500 or more on a full-time basis (Choi, 2008). Self-Reliance Support Programmes have been instituted within the NBLS Programme, particularly targeting single mothers to engage in paid work.

In sum, the good news is that the Korean government has made a significant commitment to financing and regulating social welfare and care of families with dependent children. As illustrated by family–work harmonization reforms, the government has not only taken steps to lighten women's care burden by increasing support for ECE and childcare services, but it has also expanded parental leaves and employment support schemes to facilitate mothers' employment outside the home.

The Bad: Increasing Labour Market Insecurity

While family–work harmonization reforms are reinforcing support for women to enter the labour market, employment legislation reforms have made the labour market much more insecure for everybody. Although Korea's rigid employment system has been the main cause of its labour market dualism, the system did provide some measure of employment security and a 'family wage' for male breadwinners.[16] The relaxation of employment protection has, instead of breaking down this dualism, further intensified the dual labour market structure by shrinking the core employment and displacing a large number of workers to the periphery.

Increased economic insecurity intensified the pressure on women to enter paid work, while at the same time the expansion of non-standard forms of employment, particularly in the service sector, pulled married women into the labour market. The number of employed women in their forties and fifties increased from 3.423 million to 4.117 million between 2001 and 2006 (Korea Labour Institute, 2006). Women's increased employment was, however, complicated by pervasive labour market discrimination against them. The gender gap in median earnings of full-time workers in Korea is about 40 per cent (OECD, 2009b); over 60 per cent of working women are in non-standard employment and about three-quarters of female

---

16. By labour market dualism I mean a structural bifurcation of the labour market into 'core' and 'periphery', with the core consisting of regular, full-time employment, often accompanied by union representation, family wages and generous company welfare, and the periphery consisting of non-regular and informal employment, characterized by the lack of union representation, lower wages, precarious working conditions, limited social insurance coverage and limited access to company welfare benefits. In addition to the core/periphery and regular/non-regular employment divides, significant differences in wage and employment conditions exist between large and small and medium enterprises. In Korea, the peripheral labour market tends to be made up of small and medium size companies and non-standard forms of employment where the majority of women workers are found. For further discussion on labour market dualization in South Korea, see Peng (forthcoming).

non-standard employees are married. Rather than breaking down the rigidity of the dual labour market structure, labour market deregulation has rather 'levelled down' labour market standards by replacing standard full-time jobs with non-standard employment (into which women have been drawn in large numbers).

The bad news is therefore that post-economic crisis labour market reforms have significantly increased economic insecurity. In the Korean labour market context, it is evident that what seems to have motivated the state to support women's employment and to shore up the family may not simply have been its renewed commitment to gender equality; rather, state policy was also reacting to the adverse economic and labour market transformations that were taking place at the time.

The Confused: Childcare Services Expansion

Its equivocal motivations notwithstanding, it is nevertheless curious that the Korean government committed itself to such an extensive expansion of childcare services and supports. Given the variety of policy tools available, why did it choose to focus on childcare? True, childcare is a reasonable target of social welfare expansion, but so are higher education and skills training for youths and unemployed workers. In fact, logic would dictate that attending to skills development and retraining of the current unemployed and under-employed and new labour market entrants should be a high priority. In other words, pre-school childcare was not the only sector the government could focus on. The main reason for this choice is the Roh government's instrumentalist approach to social policy. Childcare was an effective reform package with which the Roh government could address several key policy issues simultaneously — high unemployment, low economic growth, low fertility and gender equality. It also embodied the principle of social and economic development through 'social investment' (Dobrowlosky and Lister, 2008; Jenson, 2004). A close look at childcare reform policy making from 2004 to 2006 reveals that the Roh government tried to solve multiple policy agendas through a single reform package. And it is precisely this political instrumentalism that has created the confusing policy mix alluded to in the title of this article.

The timing for the Roh government could not have been worse. After a few years of what appeared to be a post-crisis recovery (1999 to 2002), economic growth plummeted to 3.1 per cent in 2003, the lowest since 1998. Public expectation that President Roh would solve the economic problem was, however, dashed by the government's inability to turn the economy around in its first year in office. The President's ability to manage the economy was unavoidably questioned, as the media attacked his lack of economic understanding and political diplomacy. Public support for the President fell. In an attempt to come up with effective policies, Roh Moo-hyun created several

Presidential Committees in 2004, including the Committee on Social Inclusion to mediate an inter-ministerial dialogue and develop a national agenda to reduce poverty and discrimination, and the Committee on Ageing Society and Population Policy to develop policies to deal with fertility decline and population ageing. Both committees focused on childcare policy reform.

Childcare was an attractive social policy agenda because it addressed a number of important policy concerns shared by the inter-ministerial group members. More to the point, policy makers understood that if carried out well, childcare policy reform could satisfy the public demand for both economic growth and social welfare. For those in the social welfare sector, childcare expansion addressed the huge demand for accessible and affordable childcare services and support for a growing number of working mothers. For those in the educational sector, it was an opportunity to push for more ECEC resources and a possible base from which to attempt ECE law reform, which the Ministry of Education and Human Resource Development has been proposing, without much success, since 1997. For those concerned with economic growth, childcare expansion promised potential economic stimulation and employment creation. And finally, for women's issues advocates, childcare was an important measure to facilitate women's economic and social participation, and thus ultimately, gender equality. Many policy makers in the Ministry of Health and Welfare (MOHW) also believed that childcare expansion and family–work harmonization policies would help counter fertility decline and thus moderate rapid population ageing.

Getting inter-sectoral support for childcare expansion was therefore not very difficult. Different political partners had different reasons to support childcare at that point. Many economists and policy bureaucrats in ministries such as Ministry of Planning and Budget (MPB), Ministry of Labour and the Korean Development Institute (KDI) had been arguing that Kim Dae-Jung's productive welfare policy was 'inconsistent' and 'old-fashioned' (Cho, 2005: 84), and that the new government should adopt more 'market-friendly welfare policies'. They pointed to the OECD recommendations of further governance and financial reforms, along with support for new labour market entrants, such as women, youths and workers with dependent children, as evidence of an international policy trend in support of a market-oriented social policy. In addition to the human capital enhancement potential, this group of experts also saw childcare reform as an opportunity to cultivate a new social service market and create jobs. Those more concerned about income inequality and social exclusion, on the other hand, saw childcare expansion as a way not only to provide needed services, but also to equalize opportunities and (through the creation of a social market) nurture more active civil society engagement in social service delivery (Lee, 2007). In all cases, childcare was one social investment strategy everyone could support. As the report of the Ministry of Labour noted, childcare expansion promised to contribute to the virtuous economic cycle of providing needed services, creating jobs and stimulating the economy:

> Creating social service jobs has boosted our economy's growth potential as it has helped the economically inactive population, including housewives and the aged, to be integrated into the economically active population. In particular, the provision of social services, such as childcare, housekeeping and patient care, has liberated women from domestic work, which in turn, has increased employment levels. The project of creating social service jobs has not only created jobs for vulnerable groups of workers ... (but) has also played the role of providing social services which are in short supply, thereby largely contributing to providing social services for low-income lower middle classes who need such services but have little purchasing power. The project has great significance in that it has opened up new horizons by creating jobs in the social service sector, which is often called the third sector, beyond the private and public sectors and needs to expand its share of employment, through cooperation between NGOs and the government. (Ministry of Labour, 2008)

While all the members in the inter-ministerial group were able to agree on the expansion of childcare, opinions on how to achieve this differed widely. The Ministry of Gender Equality and Family (MOGEF) supported a proposal for universal public childcare provision advanced by the Korean Women's Development Institute (KWDI), the policy research think-tank affiliated to the MOGEF.[17] The KWDI's research had found significant public dissatisfaction with the existing childcare system. Most mothers they surveyed felt that the government subsidy they received for childcare was too low and that there were not enough public childcare centres. The KWDI's care paradigm was also informed by social democratic exemplars like Sweden and Denmark. Many of their researchers had studied the Scandinavian welfare model and were inspired by it. Their preference, therefore, was to socialize care through public childcare service provisioning. They argued that it would be more cost-effective for the government to provide public childcare rather than subsidize for-profit and non-profit private providers given the low transaction cost — the infrastructure for such services already existed.[18]

Although the MOGEF was supportive of universal public childcare, its most logical policy ally, the MOHW, was divided. Within the inter-ministerial group, a huge difference also existed between the 'economic ministries' — the Ministry of Planning and Budget (MPB) and the Ministry of Labour — and the 'social ministries' (the MOGEF and the MOHW). The MPB proposed the total deregulation of childcare, preferring the state to use subsidies and tax benefits to incentivize and stimulate market demand and increase market competition. They argued that individual needs

---

17. Interview with Seung-Ah Hong, Fellow, Family Policy Research Centre, Korean Women's Development Institute, 14 December 2007.
18. Interview with Seung-Ah Hong, 14 December 2007. Hong was also involved in the KWDI research on childcare as a researcher during childcare policy reform in 2005 and 2006.

for childcare services could be met most efficiently by the market. While not entirely convinced of the merit of public provision of childcare services, the MOHW was also not comfortable with the MPB's idea of total deregulation, worried that the quality of care might be sacrificed. The Ministry of Labour, meanwhile, saw the burgeoning childcare market as an excellent opportunity to advance its interests in job creation and employment facilitation for women.

Parallel debates also took place outside the government. Most NGOs and researchers supported the idea of publicly provided childcare services. However, nearly 95 per cent of the childcare providers belonged to the private sector; thus, the Private Childcare Providers' Association (PCPA) formed the largest opposition to the idea of universal public childcare. Pointing to the lack of efficiency and flexibility in the public childcare system, they fiercely opposed the KWDI and MOGEF position. The PCPA formed a powerful political voice outside of the government and it played a very similar role to that of private providers in the health care arena, such as hospitals and physicians. The Korean Childcare Teachers' Association (KCTA), the majority of whose members worked in private sector childcare centres, was also divided on the issue. The universal public childcare policy presented both opportunities and constraints for them. Making childcare centres public meant the formalization of their employment status as public service workers, which came with employment security, union representation, higher wages and better working conditions; but it was also likely to be accompanied by stricter certification requirements. In the end, the KCTA avoided potential risks by accepting the position of private provision of childcare.

The inter-ministerial debate over childcare policy reform lasted nearly two years. During this time, the committee's policy proposal was given to the Vice Ministers of all the relevant ministries, discussed within each ministry, and debated within the committee before an agreement was reached and presented to the President. The President then called an all-ministers meeting, inviting academics and policy experts, along with stakeholders in civil society, to finalize the plan. The timing was critical as the government faced growing public discontent due to the lack of economic improvements and growing income disparity. The pressure on the government to come up with an effective solution to multiple problems increased.

Childcare policy had received much political and policy attention at this point due to the fact that the total fertility rate in Korea had dropped to a historic low of 1.08 in 2005 and public anxiety about the future of the Korean nation was growing.[19] The government now faced a few additional social and political problems — not just a slowing economy and high unemployment, but also income inequality, alleged government corruption and the lowest-ever fertility rate. As concerns over job creation and fiscal constraint grew,

---

19. Interview with Joo-Hyun Park, Secretary General, and Chairman of Operating Committee, Presidential Committee on Ageing Society and Population Policy, 17 December 2007.

the proposal for universal public childcare, which many associated with more government spending, became less sellable. At the same time, the MOHW also began to lose some of its earlier vested interests in childcare when the family and childcare portfolio was moved to the MOGEF in 2005. Furthermore, the MOHW had, by this time, switched its attention to pension reform and the Elderly Care Insurance proposal, fiscally much larger issues than childcare. The MOHW thus did not oppose the MPB position to stay on the existing policy course, increasing childcare subsidies rather than pushing for universal public childcare. Without the active support of the MOHW, MOGEF had little choice but to concede to the dominant position of staying with that course. The reform concession was a significant fiscal commitment to childcare through subsidies to parents and to businesses to establish workplace childcare facilities, while leaving intact the structure of private sector dominated provision. It was not a victory for the MOGEF, but neither was it a total defeat.

Childcare policy reform in Korea therefore entailed an expansion and elaboration of the existing path. It expanded through the financial broadening of subsidies to parents, and multiple-sector concerted efforts to develop the childcare market. The process was far from harmonious. It involved nearly two years of ongoing political debate within and outside the government as multiple actors struggled to push forward diverse policy agendas. There was a moment when a real breakthrough from the traditional private sector dominated childcare to public childcare seemed possible but, in the end, instrumentalist politics prevailed as the government sought the policy solution that would appease all parties.

CONCLUSION

Increasing public support for the family and social care is an important departure in Korea's social policy regime, but it should not be interpreted as simply an expression of the state's intention to relieve women of family care obligations. A more careful analysis suggests a combination of both progressive and pragmatic political-economic motivations. Recent social care reforms have responded to feminist and pro-welfare demands for more welfare expansion and gender equality, as well as to pro-economy demands for a flexible labour market and active labour market strategy. Using the social investment framework, the government managed to achieve social welfare expansion, job creation, mobilization of women's human capital and labour power, and steady labour market deregulation.[20] Policy reforms have therefore been both family supportive and employment targeted. Many feminists who supported the Roh Moo-hyun government saw the expansion of social care as part of a larger and more complex set of policies necessary

---

20. Since 2003, 100,000 new jobs have been created in the care sector (MHWFA, 2009).

to achieve gender equality. Their demands for gender equality and social welfare expansion were met by family–work harmonization policies, such as expanded maternity and parental leave and childcare and elderly care, and increased support for families, particularly single-parent families. But these progressive changes were also offset by extensive labour market deregulation that pushed a large proportion of women and men workers into non-standard employment. Commodifying unpaid family care work such as childcare was therefore an important social and economic policy measure; it freed women to enter the labour market (i.e. to commodify their labour) and it created new economic growth engines.

The story of Korea's recent social policy reforms is thus as follows. First, the good news: family–work harmonization reforms are real and significant, and they have the potential to support women's employment and thus promote gender equality. Now for the bad news: at the same time, labour market deregulation has led to a levelling down of labour standards, thus significantly increasing employment insecurity for working adults. Because women are over-represented in non-standard, non-regular and service sector employment, these reforms will have a particularly adverse effect on them. In short, this is more likely to impede than to facilitate the attainment of gender equality. Third, the confusing mix of gender equality promoting and impeding policy reforms is problematic because it completely sidesteps an important political issue: a clear and coherent articulation of the government's vision and principles *vis-à-vis* social welfare, family and women. Yet, in hindsight, it also makes perfect sense given the socio-economic and political context of Korea in the early 2000s. The government was saddled with multiple policy problems and it needed an effective strategy in which different actors could invest their political capital. Social investment through family–work harmonization, particularly childcare, was something all parties could agree on. In a competitive democratic condition, welfare state politics is rarely straightforward: politics of compromise almost always result in a confusing mix of progressive and regressive policies.

The Korean case also raises two important issues. First, it underscores the importance of social policy in determining and defining the nature of women's work. Without the work–family harmonization and childcare reforms, the bulk of childcare would be likely to remain in uncommodified forms within the household. Social policy reforms thus provided institutional and legal bases to defamilialize women's care work and to facilitate the commodification of female labour in the market. However, these institutional and legal mechanisms for the externalization of care were clearly informed by the imperatives of labour market deregulation, the erosion of the male breadwinner household model and new expectations regarding women's work outside the home. It is important therefore not to read the commodification of women's unpaid care work as a sign of expanded choices for women or the reduction of women's overall work burdens. Rather, it implies a new social norm about women's responsibility to work and a shift in the location and financial accounting (however imperfect) of women's work.

Second, the Korean case also illustrates new policy innovation in response to multiple social and economic imperatives. The increased government commitment to social welfare through social investment is neither a return to the Keynesian welfare state model, nor is it exactly a tool of neoliberalism. Rather, it is an adaptation to the post-industrial situations marked by changes in demography, family and gender relations, and increased global economic competition. It is an acknowledgement of the fact that the economy cannot be left to the market alone, and that the state has an important role to play in preparing individuals and families to adjust to new employment conditions and to respond to new social risks. The new model of social risk prevention marks a shift from the traditional male breadwinner household to a dual-earner model. For feminists, the key question is whether the commodification of women's labour will lead to greater gender equality. One crucial test of this would be to see whether it could lead to women's reduced reliance on marriage/kin/family for economic security and enhanced power. This would require the creation of sufficient decently paid and protected employment. So far, the evidence suggests that the commodification of women's labour in Korea has been happening in the absence of improvements in employment conditions. In other words, so far, family–work harmonization reforms in Korea may have been good politics, but they have not been such a great deal for women.

REFERENCES

Barrientos, A. (2004) 'Latin America: Towards a Liberal-informal Welfare Regime', in I. Gough (ed.) *Insecurity and Welfare Regimes in Asia, Africa, and Latin America: Social Policy in Development Contexts*, pp. 121–67. Cambridge: Cambridge University Press.

Cho, W.H. (2005) 'Productive Welfare: Welfare of Korea', in L-J. Cho, H. Moon, Y.H. Kim and S-H. Lee (eds) *A New Paradigm for Social Welfare in the New Millennium*, pp. 55–98. Seoul: Korea Development Institute.

Choi, E. (2008) 'New Social Risks in Korea: Balancing Work and Family, Income Polarization'. Paper presented at the Trilateral Social Policy Research Project Health Care, Work–Family Responsibilities and Income Redistribution in Diversified and Ageing Societies, Tokyo (16–17 February).

Choi, Y. (2006) 'Transformations in Economic Security During Old Age in Korea: The Implications for Public-pension Reform', *Aging & Society* 26: 549–65.

Chosun Daily (2007) 'Family Ministry to Offer Low-Cost Nanny Care'. *Chosun Daily* 5 April.

Dobrowolsky, A. and R. Lister (2008) 'Social Investment: The Discourse and the Dimension of Change', in M. Powell (ed.) *Modernizing Welfare State: The Blair Legacy*, pp. 125–42. Bristol: The Policy Press.

Esping-Andersen, G. (1999) *Social Foundation of Post-industrial Economies*. Oxford: Oxford University Press.

Jenson, J. (2004) 'Changing the Paradigm: Family Responsibility or Investing in Children', *Canadian Journal of Sociology* 29(2): 169–92.

Kim, J., Y. Moon, V. Kim and M. Kang (2004) 'Ten Years of Employment Insurance and Female Workers'. Seoul: Korea Women's Development Institute.

Korea Institute of Child Care and Education (KICCE) (2007) 'Percentage of Children Supported for Child Care Fees'. http://www.kicce.re.kr/english/resources/m01.asp (accessed 14 April 2008).

Korea Institute of Child Care and Education (KICCE) (2008a) 'Annual Numbers of Childcare Centres (1990–2007)' and 'Annual Number of Children Enrolled in Childcare Centres (1990–2007)'. http://www.kicce.re.kr/english/resources/m01.asp (accessed 23 September 2009).

Korea Institute of Child Care and Education (KICCE) (2008b) 'Child-Rearing Support Policies in Korea 2007'. http://www.kicce.re.kr/english/data/ChildRearing%20Support%20Policies%20in%20Korea%202007.PDF (accessed 16 June 2008).

Korea Labour Institute (2006) 'Labour Statistics'. http://www.kli.re.kr/ (accessed 14 April 2008).

Korea National Statistics Office (KNSO) (2002) 'Report on Social Statistics Survey'. Seoul: NSO.

Korea.net (2006a) 'Childcare Leave to Extend to 3 Years'. http://www.korea.net/News/News/NewsView.asp?serial_no=20061004019 (accessed 14 April 2008).

Korea.net (2006b) 'Childcare Allowance to be Introduced in 2010 to Boost Birth Rate'. http://www.korea.net/news/news/newsprint.asp?serialno=20060607023 (accessed 16 June 2008).

Korean Women's Development Institute (KWDI) (2008) 'Statistical Handbook 2008: Women in Korea'. Seoul: KWDI.

Kwon, S., S. Kim and Y. Jung (2009) 'Introduction of Long-term Care Insurance in South Korea'. Paper presented at the Association of Public Policy Analysis and Management, International Conference, Singapore (7–9 January).

Lee, H. (2007) 'Keynote Speech: Future Direction of Social Services in Korea'. Paper presented at International Symposium: Social Service Provision System: The Issues of Public–Private Partnership in Korea, Seoul (11–12 December).

Lee, K.W. and K. Cho (2005) 'Female Labour Force Participation during Economic Crisis in Argentina and the Republic of Korea', *International Labour Review* 144(4): 423–50.

Lee, W. and J. Lee (2004) *Industrial Relations: Recent Changes and New Challenges*. Seoul: Korean Labour Institute.

Leitner, S. (2003) 'Varieties of Familialism', *European Societies* 5(4): 353–75.

Lewis, J. (1992) 'Gender and the Development of Welfare Regimes', *Journal of European Social Policy* 2(3): 159–73.

Ministry of Education, Science and Technology (2004) 'The 2004 Statistical Yearbook of Education'. Seoul: MOEST. (Also available at: http://english.mest.go.kr/main.jsp?idx=040101).

Ministry of Labour (2008) 'News Update: Social Services Expansion'. http://english.molab.go.kr/english/Employment/print.jsp (accessed 17 June 2008).

Na, J. and M. Moon (2003) 'Integrating Policies and Systems for Early Childhood Education and Care: The Case of the Republic of Korea'. UNESCO Early Childhood and Family Policy Series. Paris: UNESCO.

Na, J. and M. Moon (2004) 'Country Note: Early Childhood Education and Care Policies in the Republic of Korea'. OECD. http://www.oecd.org/dataoecd/42/43/33689774.pdf (accessed 14 June 2008).

OECD (2004) 'Early Child Education and Care 2004 – Country Profiles: Korea'. http://www.oecd.org/dataoecd/15/61/3723628.pdf (accessed 10 September 2009).

OECD (2009a) 'OECD Social Expenditure Database'. http://stats.oecd.org/index.aspx (accessed 7 July 2009).

OECD (2009b) 'OECD Family Database'. http://www.oecd.org/document/4/0,3343,en_2649_34819_37836996_1_1_1_1,00.html (accessed 10 January 2009).

OECD (2009c) 'OECD Health Data 2009'. Paris: OECD.

OECD/Korea Policy Centre (2009) 'Society at a Glance — Key Findings: Korea'. www.oecd.org/els/social/indicators/asia (accessed 10 September 2009).

OECD (2011) 'OECD Social Expenditure Aggregate Data'. http://stats.oecd.org/index.aspx? datasetcode=SOCX_AGG (accessed 5 August 2011).

Peng, I. (forthcoming) 'Labor Market Dualization: Case of Japan and South Korea', in P. Emmenegger, S. Housermann, B. Palier and M. Seeleib-Kaiser (eds) *The Age of Dualization: Structures, Policies, Politics*. New York: Oxford University Press.

Peng, I. and J. Wong (2008) 'Institutions and Institutional Purpose: Continuity and Change in East Asian Social Policy', *Politics and Society* 36(1): 61–88.

Statistics Korea (2007) 'Divorce Statistics in 2006'. http://kostat.go.kr/eboard_faq/BoardAction. do?method=view&board_id=106&seq=157&num=157&parent_num=0&page=11&sdate= &edate=&search_mode=&keyword=&position=&catgrp=eng2009&catid1=g01&catid2= g01b&catid3=g01bi&catid4= (accessed 20 September 2009).

Woo, M.J. (2007) (ed.) *After the Miracle: Neoliberalism and Institutional Reform in East Asia*. Basingstoke and New York: Palgrave.

3

South Africa: A Legacy of Family Disruption

Debbie Budlender and Francie Lund

INTRODUCTION

All social policy analysis, and social policies themselves, explicitly or implicitly contain a model of family life. Such a model expresses the care roles of men and of women, and the role of paid and unpaid work in earning income and providing for the material security and well-being of family members. Esping-Andersen's ground-breaking work (1990, 1999) on welfare regimes presented a framework for comparative analysis of social provision in advanced industrialized states. Criticized initially for its gender blindness, it nevertheless catalysed a new approach to social policy analysis and a new body of scholarship which has attempted to pin down axes along which welfare provision in different countries converge and diverge.

Perhaps inevitably, Esping-Andersen's initial focus on selected OECD countries has been expanded to the analysis of other parts of the world, including Latin America, Asia and to a lesser extent Africa (Gough et al., 2004). This raises interesting questions about the extent to which policy analysis which is grounded in post-industrial countries can travel successfully to very different arenas. In particular, it raises questions about the extent to which family and household structure, labour markets and concepts of 'employment', and assumptions about social provision, are implicit in the Esping-Andersen framework and in subsequent variations thereof. It also raises questions about how far it can then be useful as a framing template in analysing other regions.

Armando Barrientos (2004) tackled Latin America as a region, characterizing it as moving towards a liberal-informal regime. Juliana Martinez-Franzoni (2008) took this further in her attempt to incorporate complex and extended family and kinship networks which she rightly argued may be the norm in some developing country contexts. Welfare regime analysis of the Asian region has been undertaken by, *inter alia*, Gough et al. (2004), Ha Joon Chang (2004) and Ito Peng (this volume, which references her earlier work in this area).

The African continent has received less scholarly attention. Authors such as Gough et al. (2004) and Bevan (2004) have characterized Africa as having 'in/security regimes'. Bevan points to features such as weak or failed states, small economies, local despotism, the absence of social benefits through work (due to the small size of the formal employment sector) and little social

Seen, Heard and Counted, First Edition. Edited by Shahra Razavi.
Chapters © 2012 The Institute of Social Studies. Book compilation © 2012 Blackwell Publishing Ltd.

spending. South Africa is invariably treated as an outlier in the sub-Saharan region, where it stands apart for its sheer economic size. It has a relatively strong state, a large formal and small informal sector, and significant public social spending constituting a welfare regime within which the state plays a central part. In this contribution, we draw together unusual characteristics of the legacy created by the apartheid system, namely the state-orchestrated destruction of family life, high rates of unemployment and a high prevalence of HIV/AIDS. These lead to questions regarding who can be counted on to provide care, as well as who is assumed, in state policies, to fulfil the role of care giver. The disruption of family life has resulted in a situation in which many women have to fulfil the role of both breadwinner and care giver in challenging circumstances of high unemployment and very limited economic opportunities. This crisis of care raises a number of questions: who is actually providing the care and to what extent can or will social provision and employment-related social policies mitigate the care and provisioning crises in order to provide adequate support and security to women and children?

To pursue these questions, this article uses the lens of care for (and by) children. A foretaste of the starkness of the figures: in South Africa, only about 35 per cent of children live with both their mother and father, while at least an equal number live only with their mother. The majority of women have children, but a large number of them do so outside of marriage and with different fathers for successive children. Almost one fifth of children have lost at least one parent. Only about one third of the 12.7 million households conform to the 'nuclear norm' of children and parents, with about one fifth having three generations or more present in one household. Many grandmothers care for their grandchildren, often in the absence of the children's parents. When family life is so disrupted and complex, is it necessary to use different approaches to the issue of care than those developed in advanced industrialized countries?

The paper first presents survey data on marital patterns and living arrangements, and their implications for care. It shows the origins of the disruption of family life in the migrant labour system, a legacy which persists fifteen years after the formal end of apartheid. Using data from the 2000 Time Use Survey (TUS; see Statistics South Africa, 2000), it shows the significant differences in the amount of time men and women spend on care activities. It shows the large numbers of children living away from their parents, in particular from their fathers, and reveals that where relationships have formally broken down, relatively few fathers comply with the legal obligation to provide financial support for their children. The paper also presents data on the catastrophic HIV/AIDS epidemic which changes fundamentally who needs and who provides care. It then considers the extent to which labour market participation can act as a source of material well-being for men, women and their children. Women are increasingly working in paid employment (though with low earnings), as well as having to provide more care. We suggest that, unlike in other countries where young girls may be withdrawn from school to provide care, in South Africa it is likely that unemployed adult women, and older women pensioners, are filling in as care givers.

Since the democratic transition in 1994, the South African government has held fast to social spending on an array of programmes in the fields of health, education and welfare. We select those which may, intentionally or unintentionally, assist with care directly, or provide support to women carers in this role. An intervention such as the Expanded Public Works Programme (EPWP) in the field of early childhood education has the dual objective of providing more childcare for more children, at this time of HIV/AIDS, as well as providing vocational skills leading to employment. The grants for elderly people are known to have redistributive effects in that they assist older women in their care responsibilities for younger people and enable younger women with children to seek employment. The post-apartheid government has, however, been unable to address the unemployment problem, and it has moved away from its initial commitment to universal free services in health and education. The inequality-creating effects of these trends are somewhat mitigated by the pensions and grants to which select vulnerable groups are entitled. It is also unclear whether the programmes have a transformative effect on the continuing patterns of family disruption or the burden of responsibility borne by women in an unequal environment. Indeed, they might well help to maintain the unequal burdens.

LIVING ARRANGEMENTS, MARITAL PATTERNS AND THEIR IMPLICATIONS FOR CARE

It is often assumed that it is 'normal' for parents to provide for children financially and otherwise. As we have noted, however, the nuclear family is not the norm in South Africa. Many households do not consist of two parents plus children, and a substantial number of children do not live with their biological parents. Furthermore, where children are living with their parent/s, fathers tend to play a much smaller role than might be expected.

Drawing on data from the General Household Survey of 2005 and ignoring gender for the moment, Table 1 groups households with various combinations of 'generations' with age groups where 'children' are those up to 18, 'middle' those between 18 and 49, and 'older' being 50 years and above. The table shows that only just over a third (34.5 per cent) of all South African households conform to the 'nuclear norm' of children and a middle generation. About a quarter (25.7 per cent) have the middle generation only, including couples who have not yet had children, people or couples whose children have grown up and moved on, people who have not had children, student households, and so on. About one fifth, or 20.5 per cent, include three generations — children, middle and older people (and some households may include more than three generations).

Table 1. South African Household Composition, 2005

Household composition (generations)	Number of households	Per cent
Children only	67,590	0.5
Children and middle	4,386,951	34.5
Children and older	390,512	3.1
Children, middle and older	2,611,256	20.5
Middle only	3,270,368	25.7
Older only	1,120,835	8.8
Middle and older	865,339	6.8
Unspecified	13,418	0.1
Total	**12,726,270**	**100**

Source: own calculations based on General Household Survey 2005 data set (Statistics South Africa).

Adding gender to the equation reveals further deviation from a nuclear norm of mother, father and children. The gender patterns can, at least in part, be explained by the country's political past and, in particular, migrant labour and apartheid. Apartheid's vision was, in crude terms, to reserve the cities for the white population, with the African (as defined by apartheid legislation) population, in particular, living in separate 'homelands'. However, the apartheid economy could not have survived without the poorly-paid labour of (mainly male) African workers who were allowed to live in the cities, towns and on commercial farms on a migrant basis in order to work for white-owned interests. They were for the most part required to do so alone, leaving wives, children and other family members behind in the homeland areas.

In its most formalized system, which operated in the large mining industry which underpinned the economy for much of the twentieth century, men were given eleven-month contracts during which time they were housed in single-sex compounds. They were thus able to be with their families for a maximum of four weeks a year — less if one deducts travel time. Inevitably, the system resulted in high rates of extra-marital sex. It also provided very little opportunity for men to get to know and engage with their children. The pass laws, which restricted the movement of Africans, were formally abolished in 1986. However, the patterns that had been established during the preceding decades did not disappear with these laws. Instead, as seen below, South Africans continued to have lower rates of marriage and higher rates of extra-marital childbearing than found in most other countries. Further, men continued to engage very little with their children.

In all countries for which data are available, men are found, on average, to be significantly less involved in childcare activities than women. The situation in South Africa is extreme. Analysis of the Time Use Survey of 2000 (Statistics South Africa, 2000) reveals that men aged 15–64 years spend an average of three minutes a day on care of persons while women

Table 2. Living Arrangements of Children Aged 0–17 years,
2002–2008 (per cent)

	2002	2003	2004	2005	2006	2007	2008
With both parents	37.8	36.6	35.7	35.2	35.1	34.3	35
With mother only	38.1	37.9	39.5	39.4	38.7	39.8	40
With father only	2.9	2.9	2.7	2.9	3.0	2.8	3
With neither parent	21.1	22.5	22.1	22.5	23.3	23.0	23

Source: http://www.childrencount.ci.org.za/indicator.php?id=1&indicator=2 (accessed 22 October 2010).

in the same age category spend an average of thirty-nine minutes per day caring for children in their own households. The estimate for women might at first glance seem low, but there are similarly low estimates for direct person care (most of which is childcare) in other developing countries (see, for example, Budlender, 2008: 16). The relatively low figure is explained by the fact that only about a third of women of this age spend time on childcare on an average day. The average time thus includes large numbers of women who do not fulfil any direct care duties. South Africa's estimate for men, however, is unusually low when compared to other developing countries.

The 'average' situation in South Africa can be at least partly explained by the fact that the majority of children are still — fifteen years after the end of apartheid and two decades after the abolition of the pass laws — living apart from their biological fathers. In 2008, only 35 per cent of children (0–17 years) were resident with both their biological parents,[1] while 40 per cent were living with their mother but not their father. More than four-fifths (81 per cent) of the 23 per cent of children living with neither parent had at least one parent who was still alive. Thus the fractured family set-ups cannot easily be explained by orphanhood due to AIDS-related deaths. Table 2 reveals that the proportion of children living with both parents declined further over the period 2002–08. Grandmothers account for the largest single grouping of those caring for children not living with their parents, thus again placing the burden of care firmly with women.

Residence patterns of fathers and children cannot, however, fully explain the extremely small amount of childcare done by the average man. Indeed, the TUS 2000 found that men living in households which contained their own biological children under the age of 18 recorded fewer minutes per day (six minutes) spent on childcare than the average of nine minutes per day recorded by women living in households that contained no children at all (Budlender et al., 2001: 68).

This lack of fathers' contribution to care activities runs parallel with little financial support. Many countries have legislation in place to ensure

1. www.childrencount.ci.org.za (accessed on 22 October 2010).

that parents provide financially for their children in the event of family disruption or dissolution. The South African Maintenance Act states that a non-resident biological parent must provide for his or her child, whether or not either parent of the child was married at the time of conception or birth of the child, or at some other point. However, the Act brings little relief to the many women who bring up their children without the father's assistance. Many men simply deny paternity or 'disappear', while those who are deceased obviously cannot provide. Even if the father is identified and acknowledges paternity, the Act places an obligation only on those non-resident parents the courts consider able to afford the payment. With high levels of unemployment and many people earning low and uncertain incomes, there are many who are judged non-liable. Finally, the Maintenance Act is poorly enforced even when the man is identified and able to pay, and even where a court order has been issued.

Turning now to marital patterns, these could affect care responsibilities in different ways. Firstly, it is generally assumed that marital patterns will affect fertility, although in South Africa the relationship between the two is much weaker than in many other countries, due to high rates of extra-marital childbearing. Fertility will, in turn, affect the number of children who need care. Secondly, marital patterns will in part determine the extent to which carers can depend on others for assistance with financial provision as well as care. Thirdly, marriage in itself usually creates obligations in respect of care between the partners. Finally, marriage and sexual relationships are important factors in the spread of HIV and AIDS, which in turn generates care burdens.

Household surveys over the period 1996–99 suggest that only between 30 and 35 per cent of women aged 15–49 years were married, while a further 4–6 per cent were co-habiting with partners. Well over half — 58 to 60 per cent — of women in their prime reproductive (and caring) years (15–49 years) had never been married. Yet, according to Moultrie and Dorrington (2004: 9), in 1998 more than 30 per cent of never-married African women aged 45–49 years had more than three children.

Examination of census statistics reveals that the marriage rate among Africans has been declining since at least the 1960s (Mhongo and Budlender, n.d.). Furthermore, in the period 1960 to 2001, the date of the most recent census, there was a larger increase in the reported number of never-married women than among men. This pattern persists if the analysis is restricted to those aged 50 years and above. Thus in 1960, 2.9 per cent of African women aged 50 years and above were reported as never married, while in 1996 the percentage stood at 19 per cent and in 2001 at 17 per cent. This pattern suggests that the decline is not simply the result of a higher age at first marriage. Instead, greater numbers of women, in particular, are remaining unmarried throughout their lives.

It is clear from the above that large numbers of children are being brought up away from their mothers, and in households where they are being taken care of by other (largely female) relatives. The question arises as to the degree of choice exerted by mothers over this. In exploring the association between the feminization of poverty and the increase in female-headed households, Sylvia Chant suggests that in the Latin American context women are choosing separation from partners/fathers of their children, having seen the advantages of being on their own, such as control over their income, and freedom from coercion and violence (Chant, 2008: 175). O'Laughlin (1998) on the other hand, writing about Botswana, suggests that women's choices to set up autonomous households with the father of their children are greatly constrained. These debates are relevant from a policy perspective insofar as they suggest that interventions oriented towards children, women and poverty should target female-headed households. But how relevant are they to South Africa?

In South Africa as elsewhere, 'household head' as a concept has both theoretical and empirical flaws (Budlender, 2003). The most common understandings are that the household head is the main income earner and the person who is the primary decision maker. Yet these two characteristics may not be attached to the same person, and different household members may have different views on who is the main decision maker, or who is the head of the household in terms of some other definition. The 2001 Labour Force Survey (Statistics South Africa, 2001) left it to the respondent to decide what the meaning of household head was. In 11 per cent of households the main income earner was not named as head. In the 2002 General Household Survey (Statistics South Africa, 2002), two out of five (41.5 per cent) female-headed households contained at least one male aged 18 years or more, and 20 per cent of all female heads of household reported that they were married.

In South Africa, many of the women who bear the main responsibility for both financial and other care of the children will not be the head of the household. This applies, in particular, to those who are the mother of the children rather than to those who are the grandmothers. Some will be living in households where their father is the head, some will have their mother or mother-in-law as the head, and others will have brothers, sisters or people in a range of other relationships as head. And while many women with young children live apart from the fathers of the children, it does not follow that they are bringing them up on their own. A policy that focused on female-headed households would thus be of little benefit for the majority of women with whom we are concerned.

HIV AND AIDS AND ITS CARE IMPLICATIONS

According to the AIDS and Demographic Model of the Actuarial Society of South Africa (ASSA), 11.4 per cent or 5.5 million people in South Africa were infected or living with HIV/AIDS in 2007. In 2005, African people were at least six times more likely to be infected than other population

Table 3. *HIV/AIDS Prevalence Rates among Women and Men in South Africa*
2000 and 2007 (per cent)

	Total population	Women 15–49	Men 15–49	Women 20–64	Men 20–64
2000	7.9	15.2	12.2		
2007	11.4	21.6	15.4	20.8	17.9

Source: ASSA Demographic and HIV/AIDS Model available at www.assa.org.za.

groups (Government of South Africa, 2007: 30) and this pattern will have
continued.

   Table 3 shows changes in the prevalence rates for men and for women
between 2000 and 2007, making a distinction between the primary reproductive years (15–49) and primary economically productive years (20–64).
The primary reproductive years are ones in which women are most likely to
be rearing, in addition to bearing, children. The rate has changed relatively
rapidly during the rampant epidemic. As is common in heterosexually-driven
AIDS epidemics, such as that of South Africa, women are more likely than
men to be infected, for both biological and social reasons. Women are also
more likely than men to be infected at an early age, reflecting in part the fact
that women tend to partner with men older than themselves.

   Using data from thirty-three sub-Saharan African countries, Bongaarts
(2007) shows that the prevalence of HIV tends to increase in countries where
a high average age of first marriage is combined with long periods of pre-
marital sex, including with different partners. This finding helps to explain
the high rate of infection in South Africa and neighbouring countries, all of
which experienced high levels of male migrant labour during the twentieth
century. Bakilana (2005) compares data from South Africa, Tanzania and
Zimbabwe. She finds that while South Africans tend to have their first sexual
experience somewhat later than Tanzanians, the average age of marriage is
much later than in the two other countries. This, she argues, increases the
likelihood of multiple partners and the risk of HIV infection. What she
does not say, but which follows from the above, is that it also increases
the likelihood of having children outside of marriage, and perhaps multiple
children with different fathers (see the earlier and related hypothesis by
Moultrie and Timaeus, 2002: 52).

   High HIV/AIDS rates in the prime reproductive and productive years cast
doubt on a social model which envisages that men in this age group will
provide financially for their families while the women provide the care. HIV
infection need not necessarily mean that a person is unable to provide for
their and their family's material and care needs. During the first years of
infection, in particular, people are generally able to continue to function
'normally'. However, this is generally not the case once people reach the
stage where they are actually ill with AIDS. Instead of providing for others,
those who are AIDS-sick will need to be provided for by others. This is

the case unless, perhaps, they have access to anti-retroviral therapy (ART), which increasing numbers of people now receive: in 2007, over 370,000 of the estimated 890,000 people in South Africa who needed it were receiving ART, 78 per cent of them through the public health services.

The use of ART is likely to have a number of care-related impacts. There will be fewer orphans and sick babies and adults who need care. Also many on treatment will need intermittent or continuous but lighter care. Some adults and children who would otherwise have died will continue to be available to participate in caring. There will be decreased household expenditure on equipment for caring, but there may be additional expenditure on ART itself for those procuring it privately, and on monthly transport for those procuring it 'free' from government. There will likely be a strong positive impact on the morale of health carers, as the people they care for get healthier, and have hope for the future. This is likely to be important as well in the motivation of the many household and community members who provide home-based care for others while being HIV-positive themselves.

The post-1994 government failed to develop a coherent policy on HIV/AIDS. A number of civil society actors — non-profit organizations (NPOs), religious organizations, human rights lawyers and leading academic researchers, among others — confronted the government, and much of their advocacy work has focused on securing more effective treatment for people with HIV/AIDS. Little, if any, attention has been given to the needs of carers, and the focus on treatment through ART may have displaced some of the policy attention that might otherwise have been given to the care needed by the seriously ill. There is also growing agreement that the ART policy itself, in Africa as a whole but especially in South Africa, offers too little to too few people, too late into the development of the illness. This has implications not only for those who are ill but also for home-based carers and for those working within the health system, and on other resources within the health system (Ford, Mills and Calmy, 2009).

PARTICIPATION IN THE LABOUR MARKET AS A SOURCE OF SECURITY

The above description of marital patterns, living arrangements and the pervasiveness of HIV/AIDS suggests that women are likely to end up responsible for caring for their children both financially and otherwise. How important is the labour market as a source of income security, and hence of securing the money necessary for childcare? In this section we look at shifts in the structure of the economy, and at gendered trends in labour force participation, migration and unemployment.

In the South African economy as a whole, a marked shift has taken place away from the primary sector (mining and agriculture) towards the tertiary sector, with 79 per cent of women's (and 56 per cent of men's) employment being in the tertiary sector in 2006 (Labour Force Survey, September 2006, own calculations). The shift from mining is especially important given the key role this sector played in the country's economic development. The reliance on mining had an impact beyond the economic sphere. The migrant labour system and accompanying laws controlling movement between rural and urban areas (often referred to as the 'influx control laws') played a major role in ensuring the profitability of mining. At the same time, it gave rise to many of today's demographic and social patterns, through the fracturing of households over generations. We have seen that the fractured household pattern persists despite the relative decline of the mining industry.

Van der Westhuizen et al. (2007) examine the increasing feminization of the South African labour market, with women's share of the labour force growing from 41.8 per cent in 1995 to 48.8 per cent in 2005. This feminization has entailed an increase in female unemployment rates, alongside the increase in the number employed. In addition, a large number of the new jobs accessed by women have been low paid, unskilled ones. Van der Westhuizen et al. (2007) offer several reasons for the greater increase in female labour force participation (compared to men) over the last decade. These include a decline in the income of men to which women might have access, the HIV/AIDS epidemic (presumably as women are under increased pressure to earn when other sources of money are no longer available as a result of illness or death), an increase in the number of female-headed households (which often equates to households without adult men), the abolition of apartheid restrictions on movement and employment and the impact of the Employment Equity Act (which stipulates equal opportunities for women and for men).

While female labour force participation has increased, the returns to women's work continue to be lower than those of men. In 2001, employed women within each of the four population groups tended to record lower hourly earnings than men, with the average hourly earnings of women expressed as a percentage of men's hourly earnings ranging from 91 per cent among coloured women and men to 71 per cent among white women and men (Budlender, 2002: 47). Nevertheless, the earnings gap between women and men in different population groups was greater than that between women and men within a particular population group. At the extreme, the average earnings per hour of African women stood at R8.40 compared to R39.92 for white South African men.

Of those fortunate enough to find employment, more than one-third are in the informal sector, with 8 per cent working as domestic workers (almost all of whom are women). Excluding domestic workers, 34 per cent of employed women were in the informal sector, but only 25 per cent of employed men. African people were more likely than those from other population groups to be working in the informal sector. As in other countries, the informal sector tends to yield lower incomes than formal sector jobs.

Within-country migration for employment continues to be common in South Africa, but the characteristics of those who migrate have changed in important ways. In particular, the number of female migrants has increased relative to that of men. Thus already in 1999, women accounted for about a third of people who were absent from the home for at least four nights a week for purposes of work or work-seeking (Budlender, 2002: 54–5, drawing on the General Household Survey, October 1999). The great majority (83 per cent) of these migrants were from rural areas. Among both men and women, 60 per cent or more were in the age group 20–39. This age group encompasses the primary childbearing and -rearing years, raising questions as to how the care burden is then dealt with. While men's tendency to migrate has been offered as a reason for their limited involvement in childcare, an increase in women's migration does not seem to have affected the extent of *their* engagement in childcare. Instead, it has probably increased the extent to which older women engage in childcare. Large household surveys in two quite different rural areas found a significant association between the receipt of a pension by an elderly woman, and the departure of a younger mother in order to seek work (Ardington et al., 2007; Posel et al., 2006). We return to this theme later.

Turning to unemployment, current unemployment rates are high for both women and men, but higher for the former. Thus, in September 2006 the female unemployment rate was 30.7 per cent, compared to 21.2 per cent for men. The unemployment rate for African women was 36.4 per cent (Statistics South Africa, 2007: iv, xviii), compared to 25.3 per cent for African men. There have been lively debates about both the measurement of unemployment and the factors driving and sustaining it. There is general agreement about the detrimental role played by the creation of the homelands, in which millions of people were trapped or forced to move to areas disconnected from markets, and in which there was very limited paid employment aside from the civil service. Since the democratic transition, the government and unions have held summits about economic growth and employment, leading to statements which are high on rhetoric but do not translate into realistic programmes. Employment creation at a time of slow economic growth is not easy. There is general agreement, also among government officials, that the mechanisms employed to catalyse and support small enterprises were poorly designed and targeted. The spatially segregated settlement patterns of apartheid still situate poorer people far from markets. While opportunities have been created for new elites, it is difficult to create jobs for people whose low level of skills does not match labour market requirements. The public works programmes may provide a bridge into the market for a few, but they are essentially poverty alleviation programmes, and cannot create sustained employment for many. Finally, the apartheid era over-regulation and size of the formal economy may itself have 'crowded out' space for smaller enterprises to develop (for example, through the penetration into deep rural areas of formal supermarkets).

In sum, South African women are increasingly engaging in paid work, but many who would wish to do so — and, indeed, need to do so to cater for their own and their family's needs — are unable to find work. An unintended outcome of the combination of high rates of unemployment with large, complex households within a context where HIV/AIDS is rife is that some unemployed women can pick up the burden of care for children — inside or outside their own households — that would otherwise fall to men or to the state.

POLICY AND PROGRAMME INTERVENTIONS

We have discussed the impacts of the political and economic history of South Africa on family life and employment, as well as the double burden of breadwinning and care giving that befalls women. We have shown how, among middle generation women, the HIV/AIDS epidemic has resulted in an increase in the need to be cared for, in addition to being providers of care. We now turn to the question of whether and how state provision of social and employment programmes alleviate or intensify the double burden women bear. We focus particularly on programmes that intentionally (the early childhood development component of the public works programme, and the grant for young children) or unintentionally (pensions that go to older people and especially women) have impacts on the care of children, and women's participation in the labour market. How states provide or support care can alleviate care burdens and enable better quality of childcare which may be reconcilable with higher rates of women working. Conversely, failure to provide or support affordable care may trap women (and their children) in poverty.

With the first democratic elections in 1994, it was expected that the new government would pursue redistributive social policies in accordance with the Freedom Charter of the 1950s which expresses the right to social services, especially free health and education, for all. The ANC government rapidly withdrew from commitments made in the Reconstruction and Development Programme (RDP) through adopting a conservative macroeconomic policy, Growth, Employment and Redistribution (GEAR), in 1996. GEAR had many neoliberal features, but the government also increased the size of the civil service, included land reform (though the land reform process has been very slow), and increased allocations to social provision (as a percentage of GDP). State expenditure trends on education, health and welfare services (the latter covering personal social services and state social assistance) between 1997/98 and 2007/08 show a clear increase in the absolute amounts allocated for social spending over this period, with a relative decline of the proportion spent on education and health respectively, but a rise in the welfare proportion (a category that includes social assistance grants). The proportion of GDP spent on these three items combined remained constant, at 13.1% in both 1997/98 and 2007/08 (Budlender and Lund, 2007). Nevertheless GEAR has signally failed to make a dent in unemployment or address income poverty, though there is evidence of a significant increase in non-income welfare through the provision of basic services, as pointed out by Bhorat et al. (2007).

There has been some progress. Almost all children now attend school: enrolment rates for primary school and upwards are over 95 per cent for children aged 7–17 years (Monson et al., 2006: 72). The quality of education is, however, poor. In the public health sphere, there is now free primary healthcare for all, with free specialized services for children under six years old and pregnant mothers. There has been a significant expansion of facilities to rural areas; a district health system, meant to further the idea of integrated local-level services, has been introduced, with primary facilities for preventive and elementary curative care as first port of call. Abortion has been legalized, giving women more control over unwanted pregnancies, and generic drugs have been introduced, giving more people access to affordable medicines. However, there are parts of the country where health services are collapsing, staff refuse to comply with the demand for abortions, and preventive services are overwhelmed by the need for clinical care for those with HIV/AIDS. Also, a small proportion of the population benefits from high-quality health services provided by the private sector and through private insurance, while the majority are poorly served by inadequate public services. And while many services could be seen to be biased towards women in the sense of reaching more women than men, the bias does not adequately address the unequal burdens borne by women and men. Universal access to good quality healthcare can significantly reduce the unpaid care burden assumed by women in households, especially in the context of a pandemic such as HIV/AIDS. When access is hampered or difficult, and the service of dubious quality, then the burden shifts back to unpaid care in households.

Starting in the late 1980s, organizations in the welfare sector started advocating a shift towards 'developmental social welfare', or 'social development'. This was a change from curative care to a more preventive, developmental and community-based approach. The vision is worthy, and the government now provides financial support to a more inclusive range of NPOs, with easier regulatory processes. The rhetoric of 'community', however, obscures the fact that funds are cut back on the very services (such as institutional care for the elderly and for those with psychiatric problems) which provided much-needed support to those who cannot function independently, and which relieved the burden on the (largely female) household members who must otherwise provide or buy in care.

Early Childhood Development

We focus now on two programme areas which impact on childcare and potentially on women's employment: the early childhood development (ECD) arena, and pensions and grants for elderly people and for children.

ECD programmes in South Africa focus, at least in policy papers, on children up to the age of nine. In the 1980s there was an active lobby among NPOs for ECD policy and provision. The policy choices put forward were posed as 'width versus depth', with the choice between either an adequate level of care for many children, cared for by a large cadre of women with little formal training, or on proper preparation of children for school readiness, provided by women at a much higher level of skills, with the implication that fewer children would be reached at least in the short term. Government resources have tended to focus on the latter approach with substantial expansion of what is known as Grade R, a single pre-primary school year which government hopes to have universally implemented within the next few years. Much of this provision takes place in public primary schools.

The annual General Household Survey has also captured a steady increase in the percentage of children between two and six years old 'attending educational institutions', from 22 per cent in 2002 to 32 per cent in 2007 (own calculations). However, this still leaves the majority of younger children requiring full-time care from elsewhere. Even those attending facilities will require care for most of the day as provision for young children is often only half-day. Many children in better-off households will be cared for by paid domestic workers, of whom there are about one million in South Africa (the vast majority of whom are African women).

The government subsidizes some NPOs to implement ECD services (somewhat similar to what Peng shows for South Korea in this issue). The small size of the subsidies means that the care givers of the children would generally have to pay fees to supplement the funds. The public sector support to the NPOs has for a long time been supplemented by unsubsidized, formal fee-paying pre-school care, attended mostly by middle class children. There are also innumerable informal facilities in poorer people's private homes and backyards in urban townships and informal settlements. Fees are charged, but often paid erratically. In order to obtain a subsidy, ECD centres need to register both as an NPO and as an ECD provider. They must meet health and other standards, requirements which prevent many facilities in poorer communities from becoming registered, and thus from obtaining the subsidy.

The South African government has included ECD support as a component of its public works programmes, aiming to improve access to childcare facilities and childcare, provide employment opportunities for women (and some men) in the programmes, and promote the professional development of (mainly) women working in childcare. These goals explicitly relate to care work, and the programme is an interesting example of a government promoting interaction between public and private provision. For this the state relies on the extensive network of existing NPOs, some of which receive some government subsidy, and in which it is estimated that only about 10 per cent of care givers are qualified. Within the public works programme, the state subsidizes learnerships (a form of apprenticeship) for staff of NPO ECD organizations. The programme currently concentrates on site-based provision (i.e., specialized community-based facilities). Its potential importance is in developing better care and school preparation for children, combined with employment creation for women, all being run through NPOs, with government support.

Statistics about the scope, coverage and impact of the ECD public works are unreliable, and implementation has been much slower than planned (Budlender and Parenzee, 2007). There are few existing ECD organizations in the rural areas where the needs are the greatest, both in terms of the absence of facilities and of the lack of employment for women (Berg, 2007). In some of the EPWP projects only training is given, with no work being available after the training. The stipends paid in the social programmes of the EPWP are appallingly low. Rates as little as R9 per day can be found and even the higher rates are lower than stipends paid in the more traditional public works programmes where men more typically work (Budlender, 2009). Thus the state, which is usually seen as a 'good employer' with high standards of both employment security and income, allows in this arms-length programme, through the NPO sector, the endorsement of lower-than-poverty earnings, especially for women carrying out care work.

Pensions and Grants and the Implications for Care

Non-contributory and unconditional cash transfers played a vital role in the alleviation of poverty for a number of years before the collapse of the apartheid system. They also enable care for and by elderly people, people with disabilities, and those who care for children. The system was introduced for whites early in the twentieth century and then gradually extended to include the whole population. Anticipating the democratic transition, towards the end of the 1980s the racially discriminatory aspects of the system were gradually removed (with the exception of the grant for women and children), culminating in parity in 1993.

The role of grants in the reduction of inequality between white and black people, and in the redistribution of wealth from the rich to the poor, is clear. Using household income and expenditure data for 2005/06, the official statistical body claims that: 'The Gini coefficient based on disposable income (from work and social grants) for the whole country was 0.72. . . . If social grants and taxes were excluded, the Gini coefficient for the whole country would be 0.80 rather than 0.72, i.e. the reduction of inequality through redistributive policies reduces the Gini coefficient by 8 percentage points' (Statistics South Africa, 2008: 3).

The best known of the grants, and the one whose impact has been most closely studied, is the pension for elderly people. It is means tested on income. Historically, eligible women received it at 60 and men at 65, but the eligible age for men has been lowered to 60. Its receipt has thus far been biased towards women, who have received it at a younger age, tend to live longer and are more likely to pass the means test. It is well-targeted for rural areas, is presently valued at R1,010 per month in late 2009 and goes to well over 85 per cent of elderly South Africans (the vast majority of whom are poor Africans).

The direct beneficial impacts of this pension have been well-measured — impacts both on the elderly themselves and on those in their households with whom it is typically shared. When the pension started being a significant force in African households, in the mid-1980s, early studies focused on the positive impacts for pensioners themselves — their health, self-esteem and role in the household. Attention soon turned to the impacts on pensioners' households. In all studies, and measuring a number of different variables, with large sample sizes, it makes a pronounced difference whether the pension money comes in through the male or female pensioner. As expected, that which goes to women is 'spent better' than that which goes to men. Case and Deaton (1998) found this in regard to pension spending on household goods. Case and Menendez (2007) found that money accruing to women pensioners increases the likelihood of girl children staying longer in school more than it does for boy children (though it makes a positive difference to boy children as well). In a study conducted in 2001, Case highlights the positive impact of all pension income on pensioners themselves, and on the health status in general in the household. Results are significantly better for the health status of children when the pension recipient is an older woman. And pension households have more younger children in them than non-pension households. It is very difficult, given available data, to establish whether pensions 'cause' changes in household structure — it would be extremely unlikely, however, that they do not do so.

There has been a tendency in some studies to try and prove that public spending on pensions 'crowds out' private savings (Jensen, 2003). A counter-argument is that, on the contrary, pensions 'crowd in' care by pensioners of other household members (Lund, 2002). Other quantitative analysis has tried to show that pensions coming in to households are associated with prime age adult men voluntarily leaving employment to come and live off the older pensioner who now has an income (Bertrand et al., 2003). However, these findings have been countered: Ardington et al. (2007) found that pensions in fact increased employment among prime-age household members; Posel et al. (2006) showed an association between receipt of the pension by the older woman and a younger mother in the household going away to seek work, and leaving her child with her mother, aunt or mother-in-law. Finally, study after study points to the support pension money provides to older women who care for grandchildren when the mother has died of AIDS. Pension pay-days in rural areas have become vibrant informal market days on which locally produced and retailed goods from urban areas are traded.

The major change to this system of social assistance since the democratic transition was the introduction in 1998 of the child support grant (CSG), which is now one of three types of grants aimed at children and their carers. It is targeted at children in very poor households, and paid to the child's primary care giver (not necessarily the biological parent). The grant is means-tested on income. Eligibility was initially for children up to their seventh birthday; since then this has been extended up to their fifteenth birthday, with a further phased extension to eighteen years of age starting in 2010. Introduced at an amount of R100 per child per month, it had risen to R230 per month by the end of 2008, when it reached 8 million children. The vast majority of applicants are women, the majority of whom are the biological mothers, the rest being largely grandmothers or other older relatives, though increasing numbers of fathers have recently applied (see Lund 2006 for specifically gendered questions around the take-up of various grants). By 2008, over 80 per cent of eligible children were getting the grant. There are still substantial administrative and bureaucratic hurdles, and isolated pockets of the country where the grant seems not to penetrate at all. Children who are not in the care of a person aged 16 years and above cannot access it, and two vulnerable groups of children who are thereby excluded are children in child-headed households, and children who live on the streets (Budlender and Woolard, 2006).

Evaluations show that the grant is acting as a small but useful supplement to the household budget. With regard to impacts, grant recipients stay in school for longer (Case and Ardington, 2004); one study in KwaZulu-Natal finds that it has beneficial effects on children's nutritional status (measured in height-for-age) (Agüero et al., 2009). Both of these outcomes should contribute to longer-term improvements in the life chances of children. The amount of the grant is so very small that one would not expect an impact on work-seeking or employment patterns of either men or women.

All of the social assistance grants are unconditional. This is unlike most of the Latin American programmes and runs counter to the World Bank's policy stance that they should be conditional — in other words, that women's receipt of the money should be contingent upon their having to perform certain tasks which may themselves incur investments of women's time and energy, such as to ensure that all family members go to a clinic. Thus in South Africa there is no concern, such as that expressed by Molyneux about the PROGRESA programme in Mexico (Molyneux, 2006), that formal features and requirements of the programme increase women's care responsibilities even further. There is, however, clear evidence of sexist and abusive behaviour by officials within the system towards the elderly, and towards young female applicants for the CSG (Goldblatt, 2005).

CONCLUSION

We have argued that the years of colonialism followed by apartheid left South African society with a legacy of disrupted family life which has, and will continue to have, long-term consequences on care givers' responsibilities and ability to care for children. The gendered patterns of care remain, in which men take little responsibility for financial or other forms of support, while women try and reconcile the need to be both carers and income earners. Government has invested significantly in social provision. A number of good social policies were developed, some were implemented and others reneged on or distorted in the process of implementation.

Government has continued to shape care arrangements among beneficiaries through extending and to some extent making more accessible education, health and welfare services. However, the parallel systems in health and in education, of poor public services for the poor and expensive private services for the better off (McIntyre and Thiede, 2007), continue to entrench patterns of inequality. Chisholm (2005) describes the historical continuity with the racialized apartheid past that is still found in education, and this is similarly the case in health. Some of this inequality is mitigated through the systems of pensions and grants, a large portion of which go to women and children. However, at least some of that grant money for the poor is spent on buying poor people's access to health and education services, in the form of transport, money for medicines and for expensive school fees and uniforms.

The public works project in the ECD field attempts to develop an employment market for women in this field, as well as address the need for extension of facilities for childcare. However, in poorer rural areas, where the need for child facilities and for employment for women is greatest, there is simply no 'market' — there is a demand for services, but there are insufficient jobs in the ECD field and care givers (such as mothers) do not have the money to pay for the service. The exceptionally low stipends for women participating in the public works programmes are rationalized through hopes of future work availability; at present, however, women derive almost no short-term material benefits from their participation.

This extent of state involvement in social provision is remarkable when compared to developing countries in general, and in African countries in particular. Some of the forms of provision may seem to accept too readily that mothers, wives and daughters are 'natural' care providers. However, the historical legacy of disrupted family life and distorted markets has meant that women, and especially older women, shoulder a large part of the care work for children. This is now exacerbated by the HIV/AIDS pandemic, in which mothers in their reproductive and productive years are dying in large numbers, further increasing the burden of care by the elderly. It is likely that the high unemployment rate among women is enabling unemployed women to shoulder some of the care responsibilities of women in paid work.

South Africa's history has led to these patterns of profound disruption and inequality. Nevertheless, some of the characteristics of fractured family life, high HIV/AIDS rates, and severe unemployment and under-employment, are shared with other countries — countries that do not, however, have the same resources to allocate to social spending. An exploration of the South African situation demonstrates well how commonly made assumptions in social policy — about 'typical' family forms, about parental responsibility for children, about the role that is likely to be played by the labour market in supplementing state provision — simply cannot be taken for granted. This problem for policy analysis cannot be solved by 'tweaking' welfare regime analysis with caveats. It may be that a reconceptualization of the approach to the analysis of care is needed.

REFERENCES

Agüero, J., M. Carter and I. Woolard (2009) 'The Impact of Unconditional Cash Transfers on Nutrition: The South African Child Support Grant' (unpublished manuscript). www.aae.wisc.edu/carter/papers/acw2009.pdf (accessed 26 August 2009).

Ardington, C., A. Case and V. Hosegood (2007) 'Labour Supply Responses to Large Social Transfers: Longitudinal Evidence from South Africa', *American Economic Journal: Applied Economics* 1(1): 22–48.

Bakilana, A. (2005) 'Age at Sexual Debut in South Africa', *African Journal of AIDS Research* 4(1):1–5.

Barrientos, A. (2004) 'Latin America: Towards a Liberal-informal Welfare Regime', in I. Gough and G. Wood et al. *Insecurity and Welfare Regimes in Asia, Africa and Latin America*, pp. 121–68. Cambridge: Cambridge University Press.

Berg, L. (2007) 'Reconciling Employment Creation and Childcare Services through Early Childhood Development Provision: A Comparison of Selected Models of Provision'. Master's thesis submitted to the School of Development Studies, University of KwaZulu-Natal, South Africa.

Bertrand, M., S. Mullainathan and D. Miller (2003) 'Public Policy and Extended Families: Evidence from Pensions in South Africa', *The World Bank Economic Review* 17(1): 27–50.

Bevan, P. (2004) 'The Dynamics of Africa's In/security Regimes', in I. Gough and G. Wood et al. *Insecurity and Welfare Regimes in Asia, Africa and Latin America*, pp. 202–52. Cambridge: Cambridge University Press.

Bhorat, H., C. Van der Westhuisen and S. Goga (2007) 'Welfare Shifts in the Post-apartheid South Africa: Comprehensive Measurement of Changes'. Development Policy Research Unit Working Paper 07/128. Cape Town: University of Cape Town.

Bongaarts, J. (2007) 'Late Marriage and the HIV Epidemic in Sub-Saharan Africa', *Population Studies* 61(1): 73–83.

Budlender, D. (2002) 'Women and Men in South Africa: Five Years On'. Pretoria: Statistics South Africa.

Budlender, D. (2003) 'The Debate about Household Headship', *Social Dynamics* 29(2): 48–72.

Budlender, D. (2008) 'The Statistical Evidence on Care and Non-Care Work across Six Countries'. Gender and Development Programme Paper Number 4. Geneva: United Nations Research Institute for Social Development.

Budlender, D. (2009) 'Towards Minimum Wages and Employment Conditions for the Expanded Public Works Programme Phase II'. Report prepared for Shisaka Development Management Services by Community Agency for Social Enquiry.

Budlender, D. and F. Lund (2007) 'Setting the Scene: Factors Framing the Political Economy of Care work in South Africa'. Research Report for the UNRISD Political Economy of Care Project. Geneva: UNRISD.

Budlender, D. and P. Parenzee (2007) 'South Africa's Expanded Public Works Programme: Exploratory Research of the Social Sector'. Cape Town: ON PAR Development and Community Agency for Social Enquiry.

Budlender, D. and I. Woolard (2006) 'The Impact of the South African Child Support and Old Age Grants on Children's Schooling and Work'. Report for International Programme on the Elimination of Child Labour. Geneva: ILO.

Budlender, D. with N. Chobokoane and Y. Mpetsheni (2001) 'A Survey of Time Use: How South African Women and Men Spend their Time'. Pretoria: Statistics South Africa.

Case, A. (2001) 'Does Money Protect Health Status? Evidence from South African Pensions'. NBER Working Paper 8595. Cambridge, MA: National Bureau of Economic Research.

Case, A. and C. Ardington (2004) 'The Impact of Parental Death on School Enrolment and Achievement: Longitudinal Evidence from South Africa'. CSSR Working Paper 97. Cape Town: University of Cape Town.

Case, A. and A. Deaton (1998) 'Large Cash Transfers to the Elderly in South Africa', *The Economic Journal* 108: 1330–61.

Case, A. and A. Menendez (2007) 'Does Money Empower the Elderly? Evidence from the Agincourt Demographic Surveillance Area', *Scandinavian Journal of Public Health* 35(3): 157–64.

Chang, H.-J. (2004) 'The Role of Social Policy in Economic Development: Some Theoretical Reflections and Lessons from East Asia', in T. Mkandawire (ed.) *Social Policy in a Development Context*, pp. 216–46. Basingstoke and New York: Palgrave Macmillan.

Chant, S. (2008) 'The "Feminisation of Poverty" and "Feminisation" of Anti-Poverty Programmes: Room for Revision?', *Journal of Development Studies* 44(2): 165–97.

Chisholm, L. (2005) 'The State of South Africa's Schools', in J. Daniel, R. Southall and J. Lutchman (eds) *State of the Nation: South Africa 2004–2005*, pp. 210–26. Cape Town: HSRC Press.

Esping-Andersen, G. (1990) *The Three Worlds of Welfare Capitalism*. Cambridge: Polity Press.

Esping-Andersen, G. (1999) *Social Foundations of Post-industrial Economies*. New York: Oxford University Press.

Ford, N., E. Mills and A. Calmy (2009) 'Rationing Anti-retroviral therapy in Africa: Treating too Few, too Late', *Global Health* 360(18): 1808–10.

Goldblatt, B. (2005) 'Gender and Social Assistance in the First Decade of Democracy: A Case Study of South Africa's Child Support Grant', *Politikon* 32(2): 239–57.

Gough, I. and G. Wood with A. Barrientos, P. Bevan, P. Davis and G. Room (2004) *Insecurity and Welfare Regimes in Asia, Africa and Latin America*. Cambridge: Cambridge University Press.

Government of South Africa (2007) 'HIV and AIDS Strategic Plan for South Africa, 2007–2011'. Draft 9, March. Pretoria: Government of South Africa.

Jensen, R. (2003) 'Do Private Transfers "Displace" the Benefits of Public Transfers? Evidence from South Africa', *Journal of Public Economics* 88: 89–112.

Lund, F. (2002) '"Crowding in" Care, Security and Micro-enterprise Formation: Revisiting the Role of the State in Poverty Reduction, and in Development', *Journal of International Development* 14(6): 681–94.

Lund, F. (2006) 'Gender and Social Security in South Africa', in V. Padayachee (ed.) *The Development Decade? Economic and Social Change in South Africa 1994–2004*, pp. 160–79. Cape Town: Human Sciences Research Council. www.hsrcpress.ac.za

Martinez-Franzoni, J. (2008) 'Welfare Regimes in Latin America: Capturing Constellations of Markets, Policies and Families', *Latin American Politics and Society* 50(2): 67–100.

McIntyre, D. and M. Thiede (2007) 'Health Care Financing and Expenditure', in S. Harrison, R. Bhana and A. Ntuli (eds) *South African Health Review 2007*, pp. 35–46. Durban: Health Systems Trust.

Mhongo, C. and D. Budlender (n.d.) 'Declining Rates of Marriage in South Africa: What do the Numbers and Analysts say?'. Unpublished manuscript.

Molyneux, M. (2006) 'Mothers at the Service of New Poverty Agenda: The PROGRESA/ Oportunidades Programme in Mexico', in S. Razavi and S. Hassim (eds) *Gender and Social Policy in a Global Context*, pp. 43–67. Basingstoke and New York: Palgrave Macmillan.

Monson, J., K. Hall, C. Smith and M. Shung-King (2006) *South African Child Gauge 2006*. Cape Town: Children's Institute, University of Cape Town.

Moultrie, T.A. and R. Dorrington (2004) 'Estimation of Fertility from the 2001 South Africa Census Data'. CARe monograph no. 12. Cape Town: Centre for Actuarial Research, University of Cape Town.

Moultrie, T.A. and I. Timaeus (2002) 'Trends in South African Fertility between 1970 and 1998: An Analysis of the 1996 Census and the 1998 Demographic and Health Survey'. Technical Report prepared for Burden of Disease Research Unit. Cape Town: Medical Research Council.

Moultrie, T.A. and I. Timaeus (2003) 'The South African Fertility Decline: Evidence from Two Censuses and a Demographic and Health Survey', *Population Studies* 57(3): 265–83.

O'Laughlin, B. (1998) 'Missing Men? The Debate over Rural Poverty and Women-headed Households in Southern Africa', *Journal of Peasant Studies* 25(2): 1–48.

Posel, D., J. Fairburn and F. Lund (2006) 'A Reconsideration of the Effects of the Social Pension on Labour Supply in South Africa', *Economic Modelling* 23: 836–53.

Statistics South Africa (2007) 'Labour Force Survey September 2006'. Statistical release P0210. Pretoria: Statistics South Africa.

Statistics South Africa (2008) 'Income and Expenditure of Households 2005/2006'. Statistical Release P0100. Pretoria: Statistics South Africa.

Van der Westhuizen, C., G. Sumayya, and M. Oosthuizen (2007) 'Women in the South African Labour Market 1995–2005'. Working Paper 06/118. Cape Town: Development Policy Research Unit, University of Cape Town.

Data sets used in author's calculations

Statistics South Africa (2000) Time Use Survey data set. Pretoria: Statistics South Africa.

Statistics South Africa (2001) Labour Force Survey February 2001 data set. Pretoria: Statistics South Africa.

Statistics South Africa (2002) General Household Survey data set. Pretoria: Statistics South Africa.

Statistics South Africa (2006) Labour Force Survey September 2006 data set. Pretoria: Statistics South Africa.

Statistics South Africa (2007) General Household Survey data set. Pretoria: Statistics South Africa.

4

Harsh Choices: Chinese Women's Paid Work and Unpaid Care Responsibilities under Economic Reform

Sarah Cook and Xiao-yuan Dong

INTRODUCTION

China's remarkable economic transformation over the past three decades is well documented. An unprecedented pace of structural change has moved the country from a poor, agrarian and centrally planned economy, largely closed to foreign investment and international trade, to one that has dramatically reduced poverty, raised incomes and is now remarkably open and globally integrated. China has become the world's second largest economy, the 'workshop of the world', a major consumer of primary commodities and intermediate products from across the globe, and increasingly a major trading partner and source of investment for low-income countries.

Associated with this dramatic rise in economic power are profound economic, social and demographic transformations. The mechanisms for allocating goods and labour in both market and non-market spheres have fundamentally changed; the role of the state and the work unit (*danwei)* as a provider of social goods and services has been eroded; responsibility for social reproduction and 'care' — a domain principally of the state in the urban sector under the planned economy — has returned to the household. These processes have considerable — but largely under-researched — implications for the work and status of women in both the home and the marketplace.

The question of how women have fared relative to men in the transition process has received considerable attention. The reform era started with high levels of female labour force participation and relative (to many other countries) gender equality in the workplace. But this occurred within a state system of labour allocation which created huge inefficiencies and redundancy. A large body of economics literature on the reform era has thus focused on the spread of market allocation mechanisms, the extent to which a more competitive labour market has emerged and, to a more limited

This paper is based on a series of research papers prepared for a project funded by the Heinrich Böll Foundation entitled 'Care for Children and Elders and its Impact on Chinese Women during the Economic Transition'. The outcomes of the project have been published as part of an edited volume in Chinese by the authors of the present paper (Dong and Cook, 2010). This paper presents these findings in English for the first time. We would like to thank the Beijing Office of the Heinrich Böll Foundation for its financial support and Shahra Razavi for her valuable comments.

Seen, Heard and Counted, First Edition. Edited by Shahra Razavi.
Chapters © 2012 The Institute of Social Studies. Book compilation © 2012 Blackwell Publishing Ltd.

degree, the gender consequences of these changes in areas such as labour force participation, enterprise employment and wage rates.[1]

This article attempts to broaden the scope of our understanding of the impacts of economic reform on women by focusing on a critical but ne-glected area — the issue of social reproduction and unpaid care work. The analysis seeks to address the following questions: what are the implications of the reform process for non-market activities, such as care for children and elders, activities which traditionally are the domain of women? How does a care-giving responsibility affect women's labour market outcomes? And what are the implications of work–family conflicts for the well-being of women and their families? Before addressing these important issues, we provide an overview of the economic reform and its impact on women's paid work.

ECONOMIC REFORM AND WOMEN'S WORK

During the Maoist era (1949–76), the status of women in China improved considerably. Much of the progress was attributable to a labour system modelled in accordance with the theory of Marx and Engels that social pro-duction is an integrated process of the production of material products and the reproduction of human beings under socialism (Engels, 1972; Grapard, 1997). Inspired by the Marxist doctrine that women's emancipation is con-tingent on their participation in socialized labour, women's full participation in the labour force played a key role in the leadership's attempt to alleviate discrimination against women (Croll, 1983). In the cities, most working-age women and men were employed on a full-time basis in state-owned enterprises (SOEs). The status of state employees entitled women as well as men to secure lifetime employment and a wide range of social services and benefits, from maternity leave, childcare, healthcare and subsidized housing to retirement pensions. Job security, public health care, death ben-efits and pension entitlements provided by the employer gave working men and women a sense of economic security for old age. However, the provi-sion of care for children, the elderly and the sick remained, for the most part, women's responsibility.

While Chinese women bore the double burden of paid work and unpaid domestic labour, the socialist labour regime minimized the market 'penalties' that women had to endure due to their role as care givers in a market economy. Because workers were employed for life and wage structures were centrally determined and not closely linked to job performance, women did not have to relinquish employment opportunities for care-giving responsibilities, nor did

---

1. See Berik et al. (2007) for a literature review on gender and economic transition in China.

they suffer substantial wage losses due to reduced work hours or lower labour productivity as a result of their care-giving role. Social services provided by the employer, such as childcare, healthcare and access to retirees' service centres, also helped alleviate the emotional and physical strains resulting from competing care-giving demands on women's time (Liu, Zhang and Li, 2008). Thus, despite women's role as primary care givers for children and elders, during Mao's era China's female labour force participation rate was among the highest in the world, and the gender wage gap was remarkably small by international standards (Jacobsen, 1998; Kidd and Meng, 2001).

Economic Reforms in the Urban Sector

In 1978 China embarked on a transition from a planned to a market economy. This transition has fundamentally changed the landscape of the urban labour market, with far-reaching implications for gender equality in paid and unpaid work. The decentralization and privatization of the SOE sector have brought an end to the era of lifetime employment and egalitarian labour compensation for urban workers, eroding the institutional mechanisms that internalized the costs of reproduction and protected women's reproductive role under central planning. Under pressure for profits, enterprises are increasingly reluctant to accommodate employees' care-giving needs; as a consequence, caring for family members places the care giver at risk of losing earnings or being dismissed from the job altogether. Moreover, the dismantling of the employer-based socialist welfare system in China has led to a substantial decline in state and employer support for care provision in the form of subsidized childcare and paid maternity leave, shifting care responsibilities predominantly to the family.[2] Furthermore, SOE and social welfare reforms have also significantly reduced pension benefits and made healthcare more costly, thereby increasing the needs of the elderly for financial and physical assistance (Zhan and Montgomery, 2003). Under the post-reform social security system, individual entitlements to social security, such as unemployment support, healthcare insurance and pensions, are all directly linked to the individuals' labour market outcomes.[3] The employment-based social security system exacerbates the adverse financial consequences of care giving for those who have to forego earnings

---

2. See He and Jiang (2008), Liu, Zhang, and Li (2008), and Du and Dong (2009) for references on the impact of welfare reforms on childcare, elderly care and healthcare in China.

3. For instance, the essence of pension reform is to replace retirement benefits provided by state enterprises with benefits linked to the amount that an individual worker contributes to a retirement account while employed. The idea is to build up individually funded accounts along with social pools that can provide a minimum pension benefit. Payments to both social pools and individual accounts are to be made by employees in the form of wage deductions, as well as by employers (Fan et al., 1998).

or employment to look after their children, elderly parents and disabled family members.

The declining influence of socialist ideology also led to a re-emergence of traditional patriarchal values and increasing pressures on women to return to the home. A widely held view in China is that women's labour force participation in China is too high to be justified by market forces. Hence their withdrawal from the labour force, permanently or periodically, would be a solution to rising unemployment in the cities (Yee, 2001). This sexist attitude is clearly revealed by China's gender-differentiated retirement policy[4] and the government's support for creating flexible forms of employment for women (Liu, Zhang and Li, 2008). Indeed, in policy circles, rising urban unemployment in the late 1990s has led to arguments in favour of less secure, 'flexible' forms of employment as re-employment measures, especially in sectors where women predominate (Cook, 2010).

State withdrawal from social reproduction and social protection has increased the difficulty urban Chinese women experience in participating in the labour market. Studies document that women were more likely to be laid off than men and experience greater difficulty finding re-employment in the private sector (Appleton et al., 2002), partly because women are deemed inflexible and unreliable due to their family responsibilities. Consequently, the unemployment rates for women, especially married women, were higher than that of men and women's spells of unemployment were longer (Du and Dong, 2009; Giles et al., 2006). Women have also withdrawn from the labour force at much higher rates since the 1990s (Dong et al., 2006; Maurer-Fazio et al., 2007).[5] The decline of women's employment was concentrated among those who were married to husbands with low earnings, and the fall in married women's employment rates was a major driving force for rising income inequality among urban Chinese households (Ding et al., 2009). Studies also found that women were more likely than men to experience downward occupational mobility, moving into jobs with less pay and lower skill requirements following the public-sector restructuring (Song and Dong, 2009). A growing number of urban workers, predominately women, have been pushed into the informal sector where jobs are typically temporary or part-time, insecure and low paid (Cook and Wang, 2010; Yuan and Cook, 2010). Consequently, the gender wage gap widened markedly in

---

4. In accordance with this policy, the retirement age is sixty for men and fifty-five for women for white-collar employees, and fifty-five for men and fifty for women for blue-collar workers. During the downsizing of the public sector, mandatory early retirements were widely applied to employees who were within five years of the legal retirement age (Fan et al., 1998).

5. Based on nationally representative labour force surveys and urban household surveys, Dong et al. (2006) estimated that urban Chinese women's inactivity rate went up from 35.4 per cent in 1997 to 45.9 per cent in 2002, and their unemployment rate increased from 9 per cent in 2000 to 12.7 per cent in 2003.

the post-reform period (Dong and Zhang, 2009; Gustafsson and Li, 2000; Maurer-Fazio et al., 1999; Zhang et al., 2008).

Economic Reforms and Developmental Transformations in the Rural Sector

Prior to the reform, Chinese rural households lived in a collective farm system with three levels of administration — team, brigade and commune. The provision of childcare programmes was primarily the responsibility of communes and brigades. While the pre-reform childcare system permitted a broad-based distribution of services among urban families, publicly subsidized childcare in the rural sector was available only in the more prosperous communes and brigades.

China's rural economy has also undergone radical change since the onset of economic reforms in 1978. The household responsibility system, which replaced the commune system, was followed by the expansion of off-farm rural industrial employment in Township and Village Enterprises (TVEs) in the mid-1980s. These enterprises were rapidly privatized in the mid- to late-1990s. At the same time, rural–urban migration became a major feature of the Chinese economy as tens of millions of peasants moved around the country in search of work (Davin, 1998; Tan et al., 2006). The rural transformations have brought about rapid income growth and massive poverty reduction in rural areas (Chen and Ravallion, 2004).

Although rural women have benefited from rising rural incomes and the growth of non-agricultural employment in the post-reform era, they have not had the same opportunities to participate in new income-generating activities as men. Studies show that women in rural areas are less likely to be involved in local off-farm work than men (Chang et al., forthcoming; Knight and Song, 2003; Xia and Simmons, 2004). In the cities, female migrants are found largely in labour flows to export factories in south China, whilst in the service sector, they work as domestic help, in hotels and restaurants. The pattern of female migration raises a number of issues including the difficulty of accessing services, such as healthcare, education for their children, decent housing and childcare in destination areas. There are also concerns about labour conditions, such as long working hours, particularly in factories, non-payment of wages and poor working conditions which affect workers' health (Pun, 2007).

While a large body of work has emerged examining the impacts of economic reforms on women's labour market outcomes, most of the studies focus on the paid economy and pay little attention to changes in the reproductive economy and the tensions between women's dual role of care giver and income earner. As a result, the unpaid care sector is an understudied area and its implications both for women's participation in the paid workforce and well-being (whether of women, children, the sick or elderly) remain inadequately understood. We seek to address some of this knowledge gap by examining the institutional, economic and demographic changes that have reshaped the care economy in post-reform China, and exploring the impacts of the changing care economy on women's role as income earners and care givers.

THE CARE ECONOMY UNDER STRAIN

As pointed out in the previous section, the overriding concern of the Chinese government in the post-reform period has been to find the most efficient way of restructuring the productive economy, assuming that social reproduction will adjust itself accordingly. As a result, social protections for women's reproductive role have been severely eroded; the support of the government and the employer for care provision has been substantially cut back; and the contribution of women's unpaid care work has been completely ignored in the design of the emerging social security system. These policy changes have exacerbated the labour market penalty on women for their care-giving role, contributing to the deterioration of women's position in the labour market, as the studies cited in the previous section demonstrate. In this section, we take a close look at the institutional, economic and demographic changes that affect childcare and elderly care and intensify the pressure on women to play the dual role as care givers and income earners in China's transitional economy.

With respect to institutional changes, nowhere have the changes adversely affected women with young children more than in the area of childcare provision. During the Maoist era, as in the socialist countries of Central and East Europe and the Soviet Union, China established a public childcare system which provided care to children from the earliest months of their lives until they entered primary school (Liu, Zhang and Li, 2008), although publicly subsidized childcare was more accessible to families in the urban sector than in the rural sector. The economic reform has brought about two major changes in China's childcare policy. First, the post-reform policy discourse stressed the role of formal childcare for promoting early childhood education while downplaying its role for supporting working women. This decoupling of the dual functions of childcare programmes was a key feature of the 1989 Regulations for Kindergartens, according to Zhu and Wang (2005). In accordance with the new regulations, publicly subsidized childcare programmes should no longer cover children aged nought to two years for whom provision of education is considered unimportant. As a result, publicly funded nurseries for children aged nought to two years became almost non-existent (Liu, Zhang and Li, 2008).

The second and the most sweeping change has been the substantial cutback in the childcare support provided by the government and employers. With the pace of reforms accelerating and pressure for profits mounting, the vast majority of Chinese enterprises in the urban sector ceased to offer subsidized childcare services to employees. According to the Chinese enterprise social responsibility survey undertaken in 2006, enterprises that still ran kindergartens accounted for less than 20 per cent of SOEs and only 5.7 per cent of all enterprises in the sample (Du and Dong, 2010). Due to the cutback in government funding for social services, many publicly subsidized care facilities were either shut down or transformed into service-for-fee commercial programmes. In the rural sector, the privatization of township and village enterprises in the late 1990s weakened the capabilities of local governments to finance public childcare programmes. As a result, the number of kindergartens and kindergarten enrolments in rural areas fell from 10,700 and 1.6 million in 1995 to 5,000 and 0.9 million in 2003, respectively (Ministry of Education, 2007).

Recognizing the changing patterns of childcare provision, in its 2001 Guidelines for Kindergarten Education the Chinese government formally endorsed a pluralistic approach to childcare, with 'state-run kindergartens as the backbone and exemplar' and 'social forces [an ideologically convenient term for market forces] as the primary providers'. Between 1997 and 2006, the number of publicly funded kindergartens in China fell from 157,842 to 55,069, while private kindergartens grew rapidly with their share rising from 13.5 per cent to 57.8 per cent. For China as a whole, the number of kindergartens decreased by 28.5 per cent between 1997 and 2006 (Ministry of Education, 2007). The childcare reforms have raised concerns about availability, affordability and quality of childcare programmes in China (Corter et al., 2006; He and Jiang, 2008; Liu et al., 2008).

As with childcare, the institutions of elderly care have also faced new challenges during the economic transition. Like many countries in the world, the provision of care for the elderly is primarily the responsibility of families in China. The Marriage Law of 1950 and the Constitution of 1954 stipulate that care for the elderly is the responsibility of Chinese citizens and that it is a criminal offence for an adult child to refuse to perform her or his proper duty to support an aged family member (Palmer, 1995). China's institution of familial care was traditionally sustained by the Confucian ethic of filial piety and was built on the social structure of a patriarchal, patrilocal and patrilineal family system (Liu, 1998). Women were expected to live with their husbands' families after marriage and to take care of their parents-in-law on a daily basis. Increases in women's economic independence since the founding of the People's Republic of China have markedly weakened patrilocal and patrilineal care norms (Cooney and Di, 1999; Davis, 1993).

In post-economic reform China, family members continue to be the primary care givers to the elderly. Consistent with the approach to childcare, the post-reform elderly care policy discourse emphasizes family responsibility and the role of markets for care provision. The Elderly Rights and Security Law which was enacted in 1996 reiterates that care for frail elderly parents is a non-evadable responsibility of adult children, despite employers' increasing reluctance to accommodate employees' care-giving needs in the workplace. There is growing reference to China's Confucian cultural heritage in policy circles, emphasizing the reliance on the family for welfare services (White, 1998). Although promoting the Confucian ethic of filial piety may offer a way to free the government from assuming fiscal responsibility for elderly care provision, it is likely to reinforce the traditional familial gender norms, and/or simply leave some care needs unaddressed.

China's continuing demographic transition to an increasingly aged society has further increased care burdens on families. According to official statistics, the proportion of the Chinese population aged sixty-five years and above rose from 4.9 per cent in 1982 to 8.3 per cent in 2008 (NBS, 2009: 90). Analysts project that China's age dependency ratio will surpass that of industrialized countries in 2020 and become the highest of any population in the world by the middle of the twenty-first century (Poston and Duan, 2000). Due to the effect of the one-child policy on family demographics, growing numbers of married couples will have sole responsibility for four parents and one child, with the main burden of care again likely to fall on women (Chen and Standing, 2007).

The structural change of the Chinese economy from an agrarian to an industrial base has also created new tensions for the care economy. The rapid growth of industrial production and high rates of urbanization separate the workplace from the home, increasing women's needs for non-parental childcare services. However, without access to publicly subsidized childcare programmes, the vast majority of women in rural areas and migrant women in cities have to rely on informal care substitutes or fee-for-service day-care programmes to enable their participation in the labour market.

Rural–urban migration also creates dislocation for migrant families. Due to institutional arrangements related to the residential registration system (*hukou*) and land-use rights, as well as various other economic and cultural factors, migration remains temporary, resulting in a large left-behind population consisting of children, non-elderly married women and the elderly (Fan, 2009). Indicative of the size of the left-behind population, almost 59 million children under the age of eighteen years — 28 per cent of rural children — are left behind, living with only one parent (mostly mothers), grandparents or other relatives (All China Women's Federation, 2008). A growing number of rural elderly people live in 'empty nests' in which elderly females take care of their spouses, while having no one to take care of them after the spouse passes away (Liu, Zhang and Li, 2008).

Economic growth, together with privatization and commercialization of care services and population ageing, have led to a rapid expansion of markets for domestic and care services. Analysts estimate that about 15 to 20 million Chinese workers earn a living by cleaning, cooking and taking care of children, the elderly and the sick for middle- and high-income families (Hu, 2010). Laid-off urban female workers and female migrants account for the majority of paid domestic workers. In China, as in many other countries, the domestic service market is poorly regulated: the work is low status, low pay and not covered by the existing social security system, while domestic workers also face societal discrimination (Hu, 2010; Wang, Si and Chen, 2010). The development of domestic and care service markets has transferred part of the domestic and care burdens from middle- and upper middle-class women to women struggling at the margin of the labour market, thereby perpetuating socio-economic inequality.

THE TENSION IN WOMEN'S DUAL ROLE AS CARE GIVER AND INCOME EARNER

The changes in the care economy associated with policy reforms and de-mographic transition have heightened the tensions between women's dual role as care giver and income earner. In the remaining part of this contri-bution, we draw on findings from new empirical analyses to examine the implications of the growing work–family conflicts women face for the well-being of women and their families. We focus on three aspects: first, the way that access to childcare services shapes women's labour force participation; second, caring for elderly parents and parents-in-law and married women's labour supply; and third, 'care deficits' and the well-being of children and elderly people in rural areas.

Access to Childcare and Women's Labour Force Participation

It is widely recognized that the lack of affordable, decent childcare ser-vices represents a major obstacle to the participation of women with young children in paid work. Market provision of childcare is generally deemed inadequate because out-of-pocket payments are regressive and often create cost barriers for low-income families. Du and Dong (2010) examine the im-pact of the childcare reform on women's childcare choices and labour force participation in urban China using data from the China Health and Nutrition Survey (CHNS) for the period 1991 to 2004.[6] They point out that China's pluralistic approach to childcare provision in conjunction with the legacy of employer-based welfare entitlements has created a two-tier system. In this system, subsidized high-quality childcare services mainly reach the already well-off parents — employees of non-profit public organizations and large SOEs which are still able to provide childcare services — while other parents

---

6. The CHNS was carried out for the years 1989, 1991, 1993, 1997, 2000, 2004 and 2006. Each survey covers about 3,800 households and 14,000 individuals in both urban and rural areas from nine provinces: Heilongjiang, Liaoning, Shandong, Henan, Jiangsu, Hubei, Hunan, Guizhou and Guangxi. The survey provides rich socio-economic information on individuals, households and communities in the sample.

have to rely on the fee-based services of private or commercialized public kindergartens to meet their needs.

Applying multinomial logit regression techniques to a sample of women with children aged six years or younger, Du and Dong explore the implications of China's childcare reform for women and children from different socio-economic groups. The authors find striking disparities in women's labour force participation and children's access to formal childcare among different socio-economic groups. Women with less education or lower levels of family income are more likely to withdraw from the labour market and are less likely to use centre-based childcare. For working women, those married to husbands with higher levels of educational attainment are more likely to enrol their children in centre-based childcare. Comparing a family where both parents have primary education to one where both parents are university graduates, the labour force participation rate of the mother is about 11 percentage points higher for the latter than for the former and the probability of using childcare services by the two groups is 34 percentage points apart. The analysis also confirms that public childcare services are less accessible than commercial care services to women with lower levels of education, indicating that public childcare programmes in urban China are failing to play a redistributive role.[7] In addition, the SOE-sector restructuring appears to have hit mothers with children aged nought to two years the hardest, as evidenced by their declining labour force participation. These findings suggest that gender-blind, market-oriented childcare reforms are reinforcing socio-economic inequalities, including gender inequality as well as inequality in the quality of childcare and early education.

Rural migrant families are among the most vulnerable socio-economic groups in post-reform urban China. They have limited access to publicly subsidized social services, including childcare, primary or secondary education for their children, and therefore rely on families and for-profit provision to meet these needs. Yuan (2010) explores how married migrant women cope with the tension between paid work and childcare using data from the 2007 Beijing Migrant Family Survey. The analysis shows that in response to the growing demand of migrant families, private childcare services have grown rapidly in the migrant communities in Beijing. In line with the fact that migrant workers are concentrated in low-paying jobs, the childcare accessible to migrant families is typically characterized by charging low fees and providing low quality services. Most of the childcare facilities are non-registered because they do not satisfy the regulations on safety, sanitation, teacher qualification, student–teacher ratios, and so on. The presence

---

7. Public childcare programmes are more accessible to women with higher educational attainments because women with more education have a better chance of working in public organizations and large SOEs which continue to provide subsidized childcare services to their employees in the post-reform period.

of low-fee childcare appears to be important for migrant women's labour force participation. In interviews, many migrant women indicated that they have to stay at home, or choose self-employment or work irregular hours in order to look after pre-school children. Some working women expressed the view that if they could afford it, they would prefer to stay at home and take care of their children themselves because the childcare services accessible to migrant families are of poor quality. This viewpoint is evident in regression results: the probability that a mother does not participate in paid work and chooses to look after her children increases with the income level of the husband. This finding is thus indicative of the harsh choices women from low-income migrant families have to make, between earning an income and their children's well-being, in the absence of affordable, quality childcare programmes.

The tensions between work and childcare provision are felt not just by migrant women in the cities but also by women in low-income rural villages, where services that can substitute for family provision are generally unavailable and economic pressure to work is enormous. Wang and Dong (2010) investigate the impact of childcare on women's occupational choices in low-income villages using survey data covering 592 households from four state-designated 'poverty' counties in 2001. The authors find that in these low-income villages, grandmothers and older children are the only care substitutes available to women and the lack of access to affordable, decent childcare is a main obstacle to women's participation in off-farm employment. The authors estimate the effect of having young children on the likelihood of women and men participating in off-farm self-employment or wage employment versus farm work. The regression estimates show that, controlling for human capital and demographic characteristics, having an additional child under the age of six increases women's participation rate in agricultural production by 1.94 percentage points and reduces their participation in off-farm self-employment by 1.22 percentage points and in wage employment by 0.7 percentage points. With respect to work hours, having a child younger than six decreases a woman's participation in wage labour by about half an hour a day (-0.586 hour), amounting to more than a third of the difference in mean wage hours between men and women in the sample. These findings thus provide strong evidence that care for young children constitutes a barrier to women's access to more lucrative off-farm employment and wage work.

Care for Parents and Married Women's Labour Supply

The ageing of China's population has increased the burden of elderly care for Chinese families. According to official statistics, the proportion of the Chinese population aged seventy-five and above and eighty-five and above rose from 1.65 and 0.21 per cent respectively in 1990 to 3.39 and 0.53 per cent in 2008.[8] If we assume that those eighty-five years and older are likely to require care and assistance in their day-to-day living, then the care implications of these numbers are clear. Looking at the relative care burdens of children and the elderly, we can see an interesting shift. While the ratio of the population aged nought to fourteen years to the working age population (fifteen to sixty-four years) fell sharply from 41.5 per cent in 1990 to 27.4 per cent in 2006, the ratio of the population aged seventy-five years or older to the working age population rose from 2.5 per cent to 4.7 per cent.

While research is still limited, some evidence exists for the impact on care givers. In a case study of 110 urban care givers for elderly parents in 1999, Zhan (2002, 2006) examines the impact of elderly care on the psychological well-being of care givers. The study shows that higher care burdens were reported by care givers with higher levels of disability, fewer siblings or lower household incomes. Care givers who were unemployed and had poor self-rated health reported higher levels of depression.

Liu, Dong and Zheng (2010) study the impact of caring for parents on married women's labour supply in urban China using data from the CHNS for the period 1993–2006. The study focuses on women aged between thirty-five and fifty-one years old, as adult children aged thirty-five or older are more likely to provide care to an elderly relative than those in the younger age group. To take into account the influence of patrilineal familial norms, the authors explore the differences between caring for parents and caring for parents-in-law. They argue that as a reflection of patrilineal norms, married Chinese women are expected to care for parents-in-law to gain their husbands' approval and support. Furthermore, the pressure to participate in paid work is likely to be greater for women who care for their own parents than those caring for their parents-in-law. This is because husbands would arguably be more supportive of wives foregoing employment or reducing paid work hours if they cared for their parents-in-law than if they cared for their own parents. Thus, the authors contend that, all else being equal, caring for parents has a less negative effect on the care giver's labour supply than does caring for parents-in-law.

The authors first explore the determinants for the care patterns classified as (a) not providing elderly care, (b) caring for own parents, and (c) caring for parents-in-law. The regression results indicate that women confront competing care demands, not only between their own parents and their parents-in-law but also between older parents and their young children. Patrilineal norms still play a role in prioritizing care-provision

---

8. The figures are from the 1990/2000 Population Census of the People's Republic of China for 1990–2000; China Population Statistics Yearbook for 2001 to 2005; and China Population and Employment Statistics Yearbook for 2006–08 (National Bureau of Statistics, 2001, 2006, 2009).

responsibilities by adult children in that having a living mother-in-law reduces the probability of providing care for one's own parents, whilst it
increases the probability of caring for parents-in-law. In addition, having
a young child reduces the probability of a woman taking care of elderly
parents and parents-in-law.

The authors next examine the impact that caring for parents has on
women's employment status and labour supply. The regression results reveal
marked differences between caring for parents and caring for parents-in-law:
caring for parents does not affect the care giver's employment status and
work hours, whereas caring for parents-in-law has a significant, sizeable
negative effect on the care giver's probability of working and hours of work.
This finding supports once again the contention that traditional patrilineal
norms still play a role in shaping the intra-household allocation of care
responsibilities in urban China. The result suggests that, intertwined with
gender and familial norms, the effects of unpaid care are multifaceted. For
those who provide care for parents-in-law, unpaid care work means the
loss of income and employment-based entitlements to social welfare and
security and thus leads to greater economic dependency and vulnerability.
By contrast, for those who look after their own parents, unpaid care work
implies longer work hours and less time available for rest, personal development and socializing. Regardless of what form it may take, women are
paying the price for the rising elderly care burdens under the existing familial
care system.

'Care Deficits' and the Well-being of Children and the Elderly in Rural Areas

Massive rural–urban migration has left behind tens of millions of children,
non-elderly married women and elderly people. The gendered, generational
patterns of internal migration tend to modify the household division of
labour along gender and generational lines, with adverse implications for
girls, their mothers and grandmothers. Using data from the CHNS for the
period 1997–2006, Chang and Dong (2010) examine how labour migration affects the time-use patterns of left-behind wives, school-age children
and elderly people. The study focuses on the amount of time that married
women aged between sixteen and fifty years, elderly people aged fifty years
or older, and children aged between seven and fourteen years spend on two
types of activity: farm work and domestic work (including care provision).
The authors find that because agricultural labour and land markets and social services are underdeveloped, labour migration has increased the work
burdens of left-behind rural populations. Specifically, in the event a family member migrates, an increase occurs in married women's time spent
on farm work, children's time on domestic work, elderly men's time on
farm work, and elderly women's time on both farm and domestic activities.
Migration has striking gender differentiated impacts with the increase in

work time being greater for elderly women and girls than for elderly men and boys. The presence of pre-school children also has a significant impact on time-use patterns, increasing the time spent on farm and domestic work for married women and the time spent on domestic work for school-age children and elderly men and women. The changing time-use patterns highlight the adverse effect of domestic responsibility on women's occupational choice and time autonomy and raise concerns about the quality of care provided for left-behind pre-schoolers, children's time available for school work and childhood development, and elderly people's time available for leisure and rest.

The rural economic transformation over the past three decades has also dramatically altered the patterns of labour force participation for rural women, exacerbating the tensions between the demands of work and childcare for working mothers. These tensions are commonly framed as involving a trade-off between the negative effect of reductions in the quantity as well as the quality of time spent on childcare and the positive effect of additional income (Glick and Sahn, 1998). The potential negative effects of maternal labour supply can be mitigated by making high quality maternal childcare substitutes widely accessible to rural households. Using data from the CHNS for the period 1991–2006, Liu and Dong (2010) estimate the effects of maternal labour supply and maternal childcare substitutes on the health status of pre-school children in rural areas using three anthropometric indicators: height-for-age Z score, weight-for-age Z score and age-adjusted body mass index (BMI). The results confirm the presence of a potential trade-off: increased time spent on paid work worsens children's health status, while the increased income accruing to the household partly through women's labour earnings[9] improves children's health status. The overall impact will thus depend on which effect dominates.[10] The results also indicate that maternal childcare substitutes in rural areas are of poor quality as increased non-parental childcare hours have a negative effect on child health status. Why would rural mothers engage in paid work given its negative consequence for children's health? In interviews by one of the authors, women claimed that they must work to earn enough money to offer their children a better education and to support the women themselves when they are old. The findings of this study once again shed light on the harsh choices women from

---

9. To reduce the required number of instrumental variables, the earnings of a wife and a husband are aggregated into one variable. As a result, the authors were unable to assess the increased earnings resultant from a mother's labour supply and the net effect of maternal labour supply on children's health.

10. In a separate study, Liu (2009) estimates the net effect of maternal labour supply on children's weight-for-age Z score using the CHNS data. She finds that the negative labour hour effect of maternal labour supply dominates its positive income effect and therefore maternal labour supply overall has a small but statistically significant negative effect on children's health.

disadvantaged socio-economic groups have to make between paid work and unpaid care work, and between meeting short-term economic needs and long-term investment in future capacity and human capital.

CONCLUDING REMARKS

Since the reforms began in 1978, China's economic growth has been impressive and women as well as men have gained much from the new opportunities. However, studies on the process of economic transition indicate that women have been adversely affected in terms of their ability to participate equally in the new market-oriented economy. This article adds to the growing body of literature on gender and economic transition by looking at the social and economic trends that intensify the burden of care provision, and the pressures this places on women, in particular in their dual roles as care givers and income earners.

The article shows that the state's retreat from the sphere of reproduction during economic transition has exacerbated the weight of domestic responsibilities which women have to balance alongside their participation in the labour force, limiting their occupational choices and time autonomy. Women from disadvantaged socio-economic groups are most affected. Privatization and commercialization of childcare services not only limit the occupational choices of women from disadvantaged socio-economic groups but also deny their children access to quality childcare. Population ageing, in conjunction with the growing emphasis on Confucian values and family responsibility in policy circles, has exacerbated the dilemma for middle-aged, married women who attempt to fulfil multiple responsibilities as income earners as well as care givers for family members at different stages of the life cycle. Social dislocation associated with labour migration has increased work burdens of the left-behind middle-aged, married women, school-age children and elderly people. The emergence of off-farm wage employment and the lack of affordable, decent out-of-home childcare substitutes, force rural women with pre-school children into making harsh choices, intensifying the conflict between the employment of mothers and their children's well-being.

These choices may compromise the care and education of children as well as the care of the elderly. They also constrain women's labour force participation and options, and thus ultimately their own incomes and well-being. It is increasingly clear that women have been disproportionately pushed out of formal employment opportunities, are more likely to drop out of the labour market than men, and are concentrated in low paid, irregular forms of informal employment. While analysis on the side of labour demand suggests explanations arising both from human capital and discrimination, the studies reported here point to the need for analysis of the supply-side constraints — particularly the need to balance care responsibilities — that undermine women's capacity to undertake wage employment. The longer-term outcome is that these women have limited access to social protections or pensions, thus perpetuating the care responsibilities of the next generation. Ultimately, a gendered approach to both social and labour market policies, with investments in support for social reproduction services, will be needed to break this cycle.

REFERENCES

All-China Women's Federation (2008) 'Zhongguo Nongcun Liushou Ertong Qingkuang Yanjiu Baogao'['A Study Report of the Situation of the Left-behind Children in Rural China']. Beijing: All-China Women's Federation.

Appleton, Simon, John Knight, Lina Song and Qingjie Xia (2002) 'Labor Retrenchment in China: Determinants and Consequences', *China Economic Review* 13(2/3): 57–252.

Berik, Gunseli, Xiao-Yuan Dong and Gale Summerfield (2007) 'China's Transformations and Feminist Economics', *Feminist Economics* 13(3/4): 1–32.

Chang, Hongqin and Xiao-Yuan Dong (2010) 'Labor Migration and Time Use of the Left-Behind Married Women, Elderly and Children in Rural China', in Xiao-yuan Dong and Sarah Cook (eds) *Gender Equality and China's Economic Transformation: Informal Employment and Care Provision*, pp. 267–83. Beijing: Economic Science Press.

Chang, Hongqin, Fiona MacPhail and Xiao-Yuan Dong (forthcoming) 'The Feminization of Labor and the Gender Work–Time Gap in Rural China', *Feminist Economics*.

Chen, Lanyan and Hilary Standing (2007) 'Gender Equality in Transitional China's Health Policy Reforms', *Feminist Economics* 13(3/4): 189–212.

Chen, Shaohua and Martin Ravallion (2004) 'How Have the World's Poorest Fared Since the Early 1980s?', *World Bank Research Observer* 19(2): 141–70.

Cook, Sarah (2010) 'Informality and Gender Inequality: The Challenge of China's Labor Market Restructuring', in Xiao-yuan Dong and Sarah Cook (eds) *Gender Equality and China's Economic Transformation: Informal Employment and Care Provision*, pp. 27–47. Beijing: Economic Science Press.

Cook, Sarah and Meiyan Wang (2010) 'Feminization of Informal Employment? The Impacts of Urban Labor Market Restructuring on Women's Work and Welfare', in Xiao-yuan Dong and Sarah Cook (eds) *Gender Equality and China's Economic Transformation: Informal Employment and Care Provision*, pp. 48–68. Beijing: Economic Science Press.

Cooney, Rosemary S. and Juxin Di (1999) 'Primary Family Caregivers of Impaired Elderly in Shanghai, China', *Research on Aging* 21(6): 739–61.

Corter, Carl, Zeenat Janmohammed, Jing Zhang and Jane Bertrand (2006) 'Strong Foundations: Early Childhood Care and Education'. Paper commissioned for the EFA Global Monitoring Report 2007.

Croll, Elisabeth (1983) *Chinese Women Since Mao*. London: Zed Books.

Davin, Delia (1998) 'Gender and Migration in China', in Flemming Christiansen and Junzuo Zhang (eds) *Village Inc.: Chinese Rural Society in the 1990s*, pp. 230–40. Honolulu, HI: University of Hawaii Press.

Davis, Deborah S. (1993) 'Financial Security of Urban Retirees', *Journal of Cross-Cultural Gerontology* 8(3): 1979–96.

Ding Sai, Xiao-Yuan Dong and Shi Li (2009) 'Employment and Earnings of Married Women and Family Income Inequality during China's Economic Transition', *Feminist Economics* 15(3): 163–90.

Dong, Xiao-yuan and Sarah Cook (2010) (eds) *Xingbie pingdeng yu Zhongguo Jingji Zhuanxing: Feizhenggui Jiuye yu Jiating Zhaoliao* [*Gender Equality and China's Economic Transformation: Informal Employment and Care Provision*]. Beijing: Economic Science Press.

Dong, Xiao-Yuan and Liqin Zhang (2009) 'Economic Transition and Gender Differentials in Wages and Productivity: Evidence from Chinese Manufacturing Enterprises', *Journal of Development Economics* 88(1): 144–56.

Dong, Xiao-yuan, Jianchun Yang, Fenglian Du and Sai Ding (2006) 'Women's Employment and Public-Sector Restructuring: The Case of Urban China', in Grace Lee and Malcolm Warner (eds) *Unemployment in China: Economy, Human Resources & Labor Markets*, pp. 87–107. London and New York: Routledge Contemporary China Series.

Du, Fenglian and Xiao-yuan Dong (2009) 'Why Do Women Have Longer Unemployment Durations than Men in Post-Restructuring Urban China?', *Cambridge Journal of Economics* 33(2): 233–52.

Du, Fenglian and Xiao-yuan Dong (2010) 'Women's Labor Force Participation and Childcare Choices in Urban China during the Economic Transition', in Xiao-yuan Dong and Sarah Cook (eds) *Gender Equality and China's Economic Transformation: Informal Employment and Care Provision*, pp. 173–91. Beijing: Economic Science Press.

Engels, Frederick (1884/1972) *The Origin of the Family, Private Property and the State*. New York: International Publishers.

Fan, C. Cindy (2009) 'Flexible Work, Flexible Household: Labor Migration and Rural Families in China', *Research in the Sociology of Work* 19: 377–408.

Fan, Gang, Maria Rosa Lunati and David O'Connor (1998) 'Labor Market Aspects of State Enterprise Reform in China'. Technical Paper 141. Paris: OECD Development Center.

Giles, John, Albert Park and Fang Cai (2006) 'Re-employment of Dislocated Workers in Urban China: The Roles of Information and Incentives', *Journal of Comparative Economics* 34(3): 582–607.

Glick, Peter and David E. Sahn (1998) 'Maternal Labor Supply and Child Nutrition in West Africa', *Oxford Bulletin of Economics and Statistics* 60(3): 325–55.

Grapard, Ulla (1997) 'Theoretical Issues of Gender in the Transition from Socialist Regimes', *Journal of Economic Issues* 31(3): 665–86.

Gustafsson, Björn and Shi Li (2000) 'Economic Transformation and the Gender Earnings Gap in Urban China', *Journal of Population Economics* 13(2): 305–29.

He, Jianhua and Yongping Jiang (2008) 'An Analysis of China's Childcare Policy and Current Situation from the Perspective of Supporting Women and Balancing Family and Work', *Xueqian Jiaoyu Yanjiu* [*Studies in Pre-school Education*] 8: 3–7.

Hu, Xinying (2010) 'Paid Domestic Labor as Precarious Work in China'. PhD dissertation. Simon Fraser University, Burnaby, BC, Canada.

Jacobsen, Joyce P. (1998) *The Economics of Gender* (2nd edn). Malden, MA: Blackwell.

Kidd, Michael M. and Xin Meng (2001) 'The Chinese State Enterprise Sector: Labour Market Reform and the Impact on Male–Female Wage Structure', *Asian Economic Journal* 15(4): 405–25.

Knight, John and Lina Song (2003) 'Chinese Peasant Choices: Migration, Rural Industry or Farming', *Oxford Development Studies* 31(2): 123–47.

Liu, Bohong, Yongying Zhang and Yani Li (2008) 'Reconciling Work and Family: Issues and Policies in China'. ILO, Asia. Available at: http://www.ilo.org/asia/library/pub4.htm.

Liu, Jing (2009) 'Non-Agricultural Employment, Maternal Care and Children's Health: Evidence from Rural China', *Jingji Yanjiu* [*Economic Studies*] 9: 136–49.

Liu, Jing and Xiao-yuan Dong (2010) 'The Impacts of Maternal Labor Supply and Non-parental Care on Children's Health in Rural China', in Xiao-yuan Dong and Sarah Cook (eds) *Gender and China's Economic Transformation: Informal Employment and Care Provision*, pp. 242–66. Beijing: Economic Science Press.

Liu, Lan, Xiao-Yuan Dong and Xiaoying Zheng (2010) 'Parental Care and Married Women's Labor Supply: Evidence from Urban China', *Feminist Economics* 16(3): 169–92.

Liu, William T. (1998) *Elder Care Policies in China: The Social Value Foundation is in the Family*. Singapore: World Scientific/Singapore University Press.

Maurer-Fazio, Margaret, James Hughes and Dandan Zhang (2007) 'Gender, Ethnicity, and Labor Force Participation in Post-reform Urban China', *Feminist Economics* 13(3/4): 189–212.

Maurer-Fazio, Margaret, Thomas G. Rawski and Wei Zhang (1999) 'Inequality in the Rewards for Holding up Half the Sky: Gender-Wage Gaps in China's Urban Labor Market, 1988–1994', *China Journal* 41: 55–88.

Ministry of Education (2007) *Educational Statistical Yearbook of China*. Beijing: China Statistics Press.

National Bureau of Statistics (2001) *The 1990/2000 Population Census of the People's Republic of China*. Beijing: China Statistics Press.

National Bureau of Statistics (2006) *China Population Statistics Yearbook 2001–2005*. Beijing: China Statistics Press.

National Bureau of Statistics (2009) *China Population & Employment Statistics Yearbook 2006–2008*. Beijing: China Statistics Press.

Palmer, Michael (1995) 'The Re-emergence of Family Law in Post-Mao China: Marriage, Divorce and Reproduction', *China Quarterly* 141: 110–34.

Poston Jr., L. Dudley and Chengrong Charles Duan (2000) 'The Current and Projected Distribution of the Elderly and Eldercare in the People's Republic of China', *Journal of Family Issues* 21(6): 714–32.

Pun, Ngai (2007) 'Gendering the Dormitory Labor System: Production, Reproduction, and Migrant Labor in South China', *Feminist Economics* 13(3/4): 233–53.

Song, Yueping and Xiao-yuan Dong (2009) 'Gender and Occupational Mobility in Urban China during the Economic Transition'. Chinese Women Economists (CWE) Working paper series. Beijing: National School of Development, Peking University.

Tan, Lin, Zhenzhen Zheng and Yueping Song (2006) 'Trade Liberalization, Women's Migration and Reproductive Health in China', in Caren Grown, Elissa Braunstein and Anju Malhotra (eds) *Trading Women's Health and Rights? Trade Liberalization and Reproductive Health in Developing Countries*, pp. 121–42. London: Zed Press.

Wang, Heng and Xiao-yuan Dong (2010) 'Childcare Provision and Women's Participation in Off-Farm Employment: Evidence from China's Low-Income Rural Areas', in Xiao-yuan Dong and Sarah Cook (eds) *Gender Equality and China's Economic Transformation: Informal Employment and Care Provision*, pp. 228–41. Beijing: Economic Science Press.

Wang, Jufen, Min Si, Yuexin Chen (2010) 'Domestic Workers' Access to Social Security in Shanghai: A Case Study', in Xiao-yuan Dong and Sarah Cook (eds) *Gender Equality and China's Economic Transformation: Informal Employment and Care Provision*, pp. 113–28. Beijing: Economic Science Press.

White, Gordon (1998) 'Social Security Reforms in China: Towards an East Asian Model?', in Roger Goodman, Gordon White and Huck-ju Kwon (eds) *The East Asian Welfare Model: Welfare Orientalism and the State*, pp. 175–97. London and New York: Routledge.

Xia, Qingjie and Colin Simmons (2004) 'The Determinants of Labour-time Allocation between Farm and Off-farm Work in Rural China: The Case of Liaoning Province', *Journal of Chinese Economic and Business Studies* 2(2): 169–84.

Yee, Janet (2001) 'Women's Changing Roles in the Chinese Economy', *Journal of Economics* 27(2): 55–67.

Yuan, Huina (2010) 'Migrant Family's Choices of Mother's Employment and Childcare: Empirical Evidence from Beijing', in Xiao-yuan Dong and Sarah Cook (eds) *Gender Equality and China's Economic Transformation: Informal Employment and Care Provision*, pp. 192–205. Beijing: Economic Science Press.

Yuan, Ni and Sarah Cook (2010) 'Gender Patterns of Informal Employment in Urban China', in Xiao-yuan Dong and Sarah Cook (eds) *Gender Equality and China's Economic Transformation: Informal and Care Provision*, pp. 48–68. Beijing: Economic Science Press.

Zhan Heying, Jenny (2002) 'Chinese Caregiving Burden and the Future Burden of Elder Care in Life-course Perspective', *International Journal of Aging and Human Development* 54(4): 267–90.

Zhan Heying, Jenny (2006) 'Joy and Sorrow: Explaining Chinese Caregivers' Reward and Stress', *Journal of Aging Studies* 20: 27–38.

Zhan Heying, Jenny and Rhonda J.V. Montgomery (2003) 'Gender and Elder Care in China: The Influence of Filial Piety and Structural Constraints', *Gender & Society* 17(2): 209–29.

Zhang, Junsen, Jun Han, Pak-wai Liu and Yaohui Zhao (2008) 'Trends in the Gender Earnings Differential in Urban China, 1988–2004', *Industrial and Labor Relations Review* 61(2): 224–43.

Zhu, Jiaxiong and Christine Wang (2005) 'Contemporary Early Childhood Education and Research in China', in Bernard Spodek and Olivia Saracho (eds) *International Perspective on Research in Early Childhood Education*, pp. 55–78. Greenwich, CT: Information Age Publishing.

5

A Widening Gap? The Political and Social Organization of Childcare in Argentina

Eleonor Faur

INTRODUCTION

The feminist response to the welfare regime literature (Esping-Andersen, 1990) has enhanced the prominence and relevance of the issue of care for research and policy agendas, especially in advanced industrialized countries with institutionalized welfare regimes, but also in Latin America. Major arguments have been that different welfare regimes can actually consolidate different care regimes (Sainsbury, 1996); that welfare regimes can express weaker or stronger proximity to a male breadwinner family model (Lewis and Ostner, 1991); and, ultimately, that they are based on certain gender and family ideologies which are rarely gender-neutral (O'Connor, 1993; Orloff, 1993).

It is now widely recognized that the design and implementation of social policy within a national context has a significant impact on how care strategies and activities are organized at both macro and micro level (Daly, 2001; Daly and Lewis, 2000), as well as on the extent to which childcare is 'defamilialized' (Lister, 1994). From a gender equality perspective, these are key aspects. Stated simply, where social policies assign much of the burden of childcare to families, this load is usually assumed by mothers, and women's participation in the labour market tends to be hampered (by being either excluded from the workforce or confined to part-time and casual work). Access to care services, in contrast, facilitates both the defamilialization of childcare as well as the commodification of female labour.

Although both public and private institutions intervene in the provision of care, the State plays a particularly significant role, since it simultaneously offers services and regulates contributions from other 'welfare pillars', to use a term coined by Esping-Andersen (1990). Furthermore, in countries where high levels of inequality prevail, the state may act as the great leveller of opportunities through universal provision of public goods and services.

I am very grateful to those who gave me valuable feedback and comments on previous drafts of this article. In particular, I thank Shahra Razavi, Valeria Esquivel and Silke Staab for their suggestions. I am also grateful to Chantal Stevens for her comments and careful editing of the paper. Finally, I would like to thank the anonymous reviewers for their very inspiring comments on a previous version of the paper. The views expressed herein are those of the author and do not necessarily reflect the views of UNFPA or the United Nations.

Seen, Heard and Counted, First Edition. Edited by Shahra Razavi.
Chapters © 2012 The Institute of Social Studies. Book compilation © 2012 Blackwell Publishing Ltd.

This article examines the way in which state social policies are shaping care arrangements for children under five in Argentina. Over the past three decades, Argentina has undergone profound, and at times abrupt, changes in its political, economic and social configurations. The weakening of the welfare model that began with the military coup of 1976 and deepened in the 1990s resulted in increased levels of poverty and social inequality, turning economic privation into a widespread phenomenon. These changes have modified both women's economic roles and the capacity of households to care for their youngest, placing new demands on public institutions. While familial childcare is still the most prevalent strategy for households, it coexists with other caring institutions which are assuming an increasingly important role in the supply of care: states, markets and communities. Yet, given the deep transformation of the Argentine social structure and family dynamics, how do social policies address emerging care needs? How do they actually tackle the issue of inequality in the shaping of the political and social organization of care? Can we identify what Sainsbury (1996) calls a 'care regime' (a model — whether it be liberal, conservative-corporatist or social-democratic — that predictably delimits and defines family obligations and State involvement with respect to care responsibilities), or what Razavi (2007) refers to as a 'care diamond'? Or do we find ourselves before a different type of structure — one in which there is not one singular configuration of care arrangements but rather one where different models coexist?

First, it should be noted that Argentina lacks a truly unified 'care policy'. Different types of facilities act, by default, as complementary components in the constitution of the political and social organization of care, which is both multifaceted and complex. So far, the right to childcare has been weakly protected by Argentine legislation. Care is only understood within a framework of rights in labour legislation pertaining to women, and in the educational system. This means that two different subjects overlap as right-holders in connection to childcare: women workers in their role as mothers, and boys and girls who require early education services or crèches. Therefore, on the one hand, there are employment-related parental leave and care services, historically designed to contribute to work and family 'reconciliation', which posit women as the main subject responsible for familial care. On the other hand, pre-school schemes and kindergartens are meant to enhance children's opportunities through the education sector, but families also resort to them to get their children cared for. Indeed, given the weakness of other conciliatory mechanisms, education services for children of all ages continue to be one of the main resorts parents have in order to reconcile their remunerated work obligations with their care responsibilities (Faur, 2009).

Additionally, childcare services related to the 'social development' sector are being installed. These facilities do not respond to a framework of rights, but rather form part of the country's 'compensatory' measures. They are based on a different logic from kindergartens (which fall within the education sector), as they focus on poor children, and for the most part sidestep any pedagogical considerations. Last but not least, means-tested programmes are increasing, especially in the guise of poverty-reduction cash transfer schemes which, by delivering transfers mainly to women and making them responsible for the fulfilment of the attached conditions — usually related to their family's care needs — tend to put 'mothers at the service of the state' (Molyneux, 2007).

By analysing this constellation of social policies, this article sheds light on the different logics that underpin and animate childcare provision. That is, far from offering equal rights to citizens through a system with a strong universalist cast, these institutional arrangements reflect the ethos of the current welfare 'model' in Argentina — a fragmented set of social policies based on different assumptions for different social groups, which in turn filter down to the social organization of childcare. The state itself presents different faces and different outcomes in its various activities. This complex panorama makes it difficult to identify a 'care regime' (in Sainsbury's terms) or a single 'care diamond' (as in Razavi's approach). Instead, I refer to the 'political and social organization of care'. This concept is used to allude to the dynamic configuration of care services provided by different institutions, and the way in which households and their members benefit from them. My key argument is that in Argentina social policies themselves may reproduce class inequalities among women (by assigning different responsibilities and benefits to mothers from different socio-economic groups) as well as children (by making different kinds, and qualities, of care services available to different social groups, instead of promoting genuinely 'equal opportunities'). In this light, childcare appears to be a realm in which both gender and class inequalities are reproduced, making it a useful focus for the analysis of a welfare model that has undergone rapid change in recent years.

The article is structured as follows. In order to contextualize the analysis, the first section contains a brief description of the processes of socio-economic and political change in Argentina, their impact on people's capacity to access paid work and decent livelihoods, and the implications for care arrangements. This is followed by an examination of the political and social organization of childcare, exploring not only the State's policies and criteria for eligibility but also their outcomes for different social groups. The third section begins with an analysis of employment-related childcare services and their impact on gender and social stratification. It then goes on to explore the kind of provisioning that the State, markets and communities provide through pre-school schemes and social assistance care services. Analysing the facilities' coverage among different ages and social groups allows me to highlight the uneven capacity of available services to defamilialize childcare. These findings are complemented with an examination of the caring role assigned to poor women, whether by default or by design, through Poverty Reduction Strategies, before reaching a conclusion on the structuring of the political and social organization of care in contemporary Argentina.

STRUCTURAL CHANGE IN ARGENTINA

Argentina was largely considered a 'pioneer' in Latin America for developing a social protection system that combined both public and corporate institutions. The welfare model that was in place during a good portion of the twentieth century has been described as a 'stratified regime' based on the principle of universality (Barrientos, 2004; Filgueira, 2005). Indeed, while primary education was extensively provided by the public sector, healthcare and retirement schemes reflected a more complex provision model. The effectiveness of the social security institutions depended on the power of unions, which oversaw a large proportion of pension schemes (Huber and Stephens, 2000). Healthcare services were delivered by the public system and corporate institutions (*obras sociales*), the latter managed by trade unions and covering only formal wage earners and, by extension, their family dependants. Hence, far from being universal, the model tended to stratify the beneficiaries on the basis of their position on the occupational and social ladder, and their gender. Regarding the latter, social rights reflected the male-breadwinner family model, which meant that some women were indirect beneficiaries of corporate health and pension schemes as 'dependants' of their male partners. As for those women who had children and were employed in the formal labour market — and were thus in a similar position to their male counterparts — labour regulations continued to assign to them (and not to men) the responsibility for the fulfilment of family care needs. Even during the 'golden years' of Argentine social policy, the family's primary role in the provision of care and in the daily reproduction of the labour force was firmly maintained, with implications for women's autonomy and gender relations.

Eventually, continuous financial constraints in the state's social institutions undermined their capacity to provide stable and efficient social services and cash transfers. The model was dramatically shattered under the military dictatorship of the 1970s. The 'anti-labour offensive' ushered in a process of labour deregulation, a loss in real wages and a major erosion of social benefits (Cortés and Marshall, 1999).[1] Historical fluctuations in social protection were deepened by the debt crisis in the 1980s. New corrosive shifts began with the opening up of the economy in the early 1990s under Carlos Menem's government, determined to reform social policy and to make it compatible with the principles of economic liberalization.

Structural measures during the 1990s included the deregulation of labour codes, the privatization of social security and an extensive reform of the education system. The Argentine State itself became precarious, and undertook a process of targeting of services, with major drawbacks in social

---

1. Policies to decentralize financial responsibility for education and health were implemented through the country's highly diverse provinces. These measures began to erode the quality of social services, while creating obstacles to their access.

terms. One of the major effects of neoliberal policies in the 1990s was the increasing casualization of labour market conditions, with high unemployment and poverty levels, and a large number of 'additional' workers who were being incorporated into the labour force, among them women (Beccaria, 2001). In addition, the new distributive matrix proved to be profoundly unequal, shaping a society with high levels of poverty and sharp social polarization.[2] In fact, the relatively isolated 'pockets of poverty' that had spotted the Argentine landscape before the military coup (amounting to just 4 per cent of the urban population in 1974), had by 2006 expanded to include one out of every five households, one in four individuals, and nearly one out of every two children, with major regional differences. The regressive impact of these reforms was borne, at a very high cost, by families and communities, especially by the women within them.

Within the context of structural reforms, the entry of new workers into the labour market became one of the principal coping strategies available to households. The feminization of the labour force reduced the historically high gender gaps in economic activity rates (Cerrutti, 2000).[3] As a result, the 'male breadwinner–female housewife and carer' model was deeply altered. Between 1980 and 2001, available data show that the incidence of such households in Greater Buenos Aires (the most modern and densely populated region of the country) fell from 74.5 per cent to 53.7 per cent, while the 'two-earner' model (i.e. households where both adult men and women are working) saw a rise from 25.5 per cent to 45.3 per cent (Wainerman, 2007). In spite of this trend, much of the care work was, and still is, assigned to women within the context of the household. Furthermore, household income has an influence on the amount of time parents devote to childcare: time use data show that poor mothers (but not poor fathers) allocate *more* time to childcare compared to their better-off counterparts (Esquivel, 2009).

At the same time, women's greater autonomy and longer life expectancy brought changes in conjugal models and reproductive practices, reflected in the increasing prevalence of consensual unions, higher divorce rates, and a rise in the average age at which women have their first child. All of these factors affected the formation of households (Jelin, 1998). Despite these general trends, there are significant disparities among the poorest and the wealthiest households regarding their size and composition, which in turn have an impact on the responsibilities and work burdens of adult women and men. Smaller households where single persons and couples without children reside are overrepresented in the wealthiest segments (accounting

---

2. In 1974, households in the highest income decile accounted for 26.9 per cent of all income, whereas by 1999 their share had gone up to 33.9 per cent. The share of total income in deciles 1 to 3 dropped from 11.4 per cent to 8.2 per cent over the same period (Altimir and Beccaria, 1999).

3. Data for the fourth quarter of 2006 showed that the rate of female activity was 48.7 per cent, demonstrating continued participation in the labour market by women, though at a lower rate than men (73.3 per cent) (INDEC, 2006).

for 50 per cent of households from the fifth quintile). On the other hand, the high proportion of larger households as a response to the economic privations that lower income sectors have experienced reflects a strategy that allows the pooling of resources to meet particular needs such as shelter and care for children while adults seek work.[4] Finally, the much higher prevalence of single-parent households among the poorest sectors (double the rate of the wealthiest households — 20.6 per cent and 10.1 per cent respectively), shows the pauperization of households belonging to the less educated sectors in which women are not only responsible for the generation of income but also for housework and care of dependants (UNFPA, 2009). In this sense, when analysing the 'feminization of poverty', it is important to consider women's poverty in the broader context of gender relations as well as to contemplate the multiple dimensions of privation (not only examining income levels but also access to resources and rights together with inputs of time dedicated to reproductive labour). Such an analysis captures what Sylvia Chant refers to as the 'feminization of responsibility and obligation' (Chant, 2006).

With respect to childcare services, structural reforms affected both employment-related facilities and pre-school schemes. The implementation of employment-related crèches had never been extensively enforced in Argentina, and access to such facilities was in fact thwarted by labour market deregulation and informality. Regarding the education system, the reform institutionalized by the 1993 Federal Education Act (Law 24.195) had complex ripple effects. Not only did it change the structure and funding of education, it also made school attendance mandatory for children from the age of five.[5] Including children of this age group in the formal education system at a time when many provinces were subjected to severe fiscal constraints (given the country's decentralized federal system), resulted in contradictory outcomes. That is, while coverage of five-year-olds was expanded, the inclusion of younger children in pre-school was neglected, especially in the poorest provinces. Given the deficit of state-run childcare services, community crèches and 'kindergartens' began to spread during the 1990s in order to meet care needs of the lowest income groups. Run by social and community organizations, they usually relied on the 'caring mothers' of the community. Occasionally, the poorest sectors would resort to cheap, privately run

---

4. Own calculations based on EPH-INDEC (INDEC, 2006) show that multi-generation and other extended-family households represent more than 25 per cent of households in the lowest quintile, but slightly above 11 per cent in the highest quintile. Smaller households reflect not only a process of ageing and increasing autonomy and individualization but also the postponement of childbearing by young couples.

5. The Federal Education Act established ten years of compulsory education. It also deepened the decentralization process that had begun in previous years: teachers' salaries, infrastructure and the system's management and administration remained the responsibility of the provinces (Anlló and Cetrángolo, 2007).

care options where possible (related, for the most part, to ecclesiastical institutions). Indeed, private childcare facilities also proliferated during those years. Propelled by a widespread belief in the 'efficiency' and 'better quality' of private management, as opposed to public administration, these centres bourgeoned in order to meet the care demands of middle and upper classes mainly, filling the void left by care provided by the state.

The aforementioned processes have resulted in a widening of the gap between women in poor sectors and those in middle- and high-income households. With a greater cultural capital and a smaller number of children, women from middle and upper social strata generally have greater possibilities of reconciling market work and family responsibilities by defamilializing care, either because they have better access to different kinds of institutionalized (public or private) care services, or because they can afford to hire domestic helpers (or indeed combining the two). By contrast, women from lower-income sectors have fewer alternatives: they can stay at home and care for their children, they can take part in communitarian experiences in order to secure food and services for their children, or they can join the labour market juggling to get their children cared for.

THE POLITICAL ORGANIZATION OF CHILDCARE IN A NEW CONTEXT

The limits of the neoliberal model emerged in 2001–02 through a crisis that was economically cataclysmic for households in Argentina. Unemployment reached 21.5 per cent of the economically active population, and more than half of the population found themselves living under the poverty line (Beccaria et al., 2005). In the political sphere, the crisis produced the spectacle of five different presidents in a single week. Ultimately, Eduardo Duhalde became the stable interim president and took emergency measures to contain social protest and deal with unprecedented unemployment rates. With the launch of the Unemployed Heads of Households Plan (Plan Jefes y Jefas, or PJJHD), cash transfer programmes began to constitute a major building block of the State's new social orientation.

The recovery of the economy which began in 2003 ushered in an annual increase in GDP of more than 8 per cent over six consecutive years. New policy shifts were introduced by President Néstor Kirchner (2003–07), and both poverty and unemployment declined due to high rates of economic growth. The successive governments of Néstor Kirchner and Cristina Fernández de Kirchner (2007 to date) attempted to re-cast a labour-based approach to social policy, as exemplified by the reinstatement of collective bargaining and the renationalization of pension funds. These developments, however, have involved mainly formal wage earners and traditional labour institutions and unions (e.g. General Confederation of Workers, CGT), thus failing to incorporate new political actors and the issues they strive for (Etchemendy and Collier, 2007).[6] They have also failed to protect the rights (among them maternity leave and care services) for those working informally. With respect to pensions, however, a 'moratorium' was implemented, establishing a catch-up payment plan which made it possible for more than one million beneficiaries to join the rolls. This measure allowed people of retirement age who did not meet the minimum thirty years of cumulative contributions to be eligible for pensions. In addition, the retirement regime for housewives was reformed, making around one million women eligible for pensions since 2005.[7]

At the same time, income transfers became a — if not *the* — fundamental policy instrument for the alleviation of poverty for poor, low-income households with children under eighteen. The poverty reduction strategy put in place as of 2004 aimed to replace the Unemployed Heads of Households Plan with the Families for Social Inclusion Programme, and with the propagation of community kitchens through the National Food Plan. Instead of addressing 'female heads of households', the new programmes picked 'mothers' as the main beneficiaries. As shall be seen, these policies did not truly incorporate a gender perspective, but rather reflected a stereotypical view of women prevalent in social policy planning.

Within this context, organized demands for work and family reconciliation policies and childcare services as part of a gender equality agenda did not come high on the political agenda. On the one hand, this omission may be explained by the weakening of the National Women's Council (the policy machinery within the state responsible for women's issues) during the presidencies of Nestor Kirchner and Cristina Fernández de Kirchner. In fact, the Council has been demoted over the last few years, and has remained under the authority of the Social Development Ministry whose political perspectives are not particularly supportive of gender equality. On the other hand, women's movements hardly brought up the issue of care as part of the feminist agenda, perhaps a reflection of the fact that their claims in the last decades have been primarily focused on sexual and reproductive rights and gender-based violence.

Despite the relative lack of visibility of the issue of childcare, two recent developments are worth mentioning. First, increasing efforts have been made to promote educational opportunities for children. These efforts have implied a legal recognition of the responsibility and jurisdiction (although not the obligation) of the education system in serving children from the age

---

6. Such as the Congress of Workers of Argentina (CTA) which also represents informal and unemployed workers and social organizations.

7. Official estimates of the impact of pension reforms are hard to obtain. For an in-depth study of the consequences and outcomes of recent pension reforms, see Arza (2009). Her estimations suggest that largely as a result of the 'moratorium', between 2005 and 2009, coverage of men (at their statutory retirement age of sixty-five) increased from 74 to 85 per cent, and the coverage of women (at their statutory retirement age of sixty) from 56 to 81 per cent.

of forty-five days. Second, the legalization of the so-called Child Development Centres represents an attempt to cater for the needs of children under four years from socially deprived backgrounds who have no access to the education system, in effect regulating a pre-existing communitarian childcare strategy. These improvements reflect and deepen a longstanding ideological tension between pedagogical and 'assistentialist' approaches to childcare, and the sectors, institutions and actors which should take responsibility for its provision.

Regarding early education, progressive measures were taken with the passing of two strategic pieces of legislation in 2006. The Educational Funding Act (Law 26.075) sought to extend investment in education, science and technology and to contain the continuous salary demands of the strong trade unions in this sector, aiming to reach 6 per cent of GDP by 2010.[8] Further steps were taken when Early Education was recognized by the 2006 National Education Act (Law 26.206) as a 'Special Pedagogic Unit' divided into two categories: that of crèches (for children between forty-five days and two years of age), and that of kindergartens (ages three to five). In spite of this advance and of the fact that the state was obliged to 'universalize' educational services for four-year-olds, attendance remained compulsory only for the five-year-old cycle.

During the process of negotiating the law, different perspectives on the role of the state *vis-à-vis* families emerged in relation to care and early education.[9] Significantly, none of the actors involved in the debate argued for the expansion of initial education as a way to widen access to care. It became clear that the issues under discussion involved multiple economic and pedagogical dimensions, but also ideological perspectives. The national government's motivations underpinning the passing of the new Education Act included the wish to enhance children's school performance at primary and secondary levels and to promote the social integration of all children.[10] Experts from the teachers' trade union (CTERA) supported the universalization of the three- and four-year-old cycles. They favoured the expansion of access to pre-school education as a way of raising children's opportunities, rather than to fulfil the care needs of 'parents'. In a corporatist defence of the 'professionalism' of education *vis-à-vis* the 'familialism' of care (and clearly demoting the latter) they claimed that the fulfilment of care needs through educational institutions reinforced an 'assistentialist'

---

8. The law establishes as a priority objective the 100 per cent enrolment of five-year-olds, as well as the goal of 'ensuring the growing incorporation of children three and four years of age, with priority given to the most disadvantaged social sectors' (Law 26.075, Article 2).
9. This analysis is based on original field research, carried out in 2009 with the collaboration of Lovisa Ericson.
10. The political decision was to prioritize strategies to retain adolescents in secondary school — which is a serious problem in Argentina — rather than to promote early childcare services. As a result, secondary school actually became compulsory according to the 2006 law.

view of the education system. Opposition parties recommended either making the education of three- and four-year-olds compulsory, or making it mandatory for four-year-olds while trying to universalize provisions for three-year-olds (but without making it compulsory). But they all faced strong opposition when presenting those ideas to the fiscally challenged provincial governments.

Upholding traditional family values, the most conservative sectors sought to restrict state intervention in early childcare provision. They argued that the State should not intervene in an area that was traditionally seen as the responsibility of the family. The Catholic Church played a key role in this debate. It resisted the idea that education may start at the age of forty-five days, and managed to re-instate into the new law an article that was part of the 1993 Educational Law, stating that 'the family is the main unit responsible for the rearing of their children' (Law 26.206, Art. 6). This assertion was also shared by many provincial representatives since it provided some justification for the lack of public sector provision for the non-compulsory cycles, thus alleviating their responsibility in the establishment of crèches and kindergartens.

The legislative silence regarding childcare as an objective in itself is eloquent: evidently, the caring role of kindergartens is still not widely seen by the State and other public actors as one of their main objectives or positive externalities, and it has not been given priority in the public agenda. This void reflects not only an ideological tension but also a budgetary problem. Providing kindergartens for children up to three years old is particularly onerous, since they require more personnel than classrooms for four- and five-year-olds, as well as more expensive infrastructure. Predictably — given the cast of actors — what was also largely missing from the discussion was the (old) feminist argument that the expansion of initial education can simultaneously facilitate women's options and life choices and children's well-being. Indeed, with very few exceptions, childcare was widely understood as a private issue: a primary responsibility of 'the' family (purportedly homogeneous), which should resort to the market or to the community when familial care is unavailable.

In addition, and reflecting a new shift in the historical tension between educational and social development sectors regarding early childhood education, a new bill was passed in 2007. This law was aimed at establishing the so-called 'Child Development Centres' or CEDIS (National Law 26.233), targeting services to poor children under four years of age. The Act states that CEDIS may be run by the state or by non-governmental organizations. They must 'integrate families in order to strengthen parenting capacities as well as children's development, exerting a preventive, promoting and reparative role' (Art. 9). These institutions are not conceived as universal providers of childcare for the population they target. According to educational experts gathered in CTERA, the political subtext behind this measure was to empower the Social Development Ministry at the local level, ultimately

Table 1. Main Care Giver of Children Aged 0–5 Not Attending Early Education, by per capita Household Income Quartile, Country Total, 2004

	25% Poorest	25% Lower-Middle	25% Upper-Middle	25% Wealthiest	Total
Mother	82.5	82.9	66.2	77.3	80.4
Father	5.5	3	5.1	3.0	4.6
Other family members or neighbours	1.8	2.7	9	4.0	3.0
Paid domestic worker	0.0	0.2	6.4	14.3	1.6
Siblings under 15	1.9	0.6	0	0.6	1.2
Siblings over 15	8.2	10	13.2	0.7	8.9
Other	0.1	0.5	0.1	0.1	0.2
Total	100.0	100.0	100.0	100.0	100.0

Source: author's calculations, based on EANNA (2004).

reinforcing the clientelistic logic of targeted social assistance, in contrast to the promotion of universal enrolment and rights through the educational sector.

Ultimately, the fact is that when public services are out of reach, the burden of childcare remains in the private sphere. The principal care giver for over 80 per cent of children not attending childcare facilities is the mother, compared to the 4.6 per cent who are being cared for by the father (Table 1). An analysis of these averages, however, shows that children from the poorest, middle and wealthiest social groups who do not attend kindergarten or crèches are cared for differently.

In upper middle-class households, where dual-earner couples are concentrated, mothers play a relatively smaller role in primary childcare than mothers in other strata. Here, 13.2 per cent of the youngest children are cared for all or most of the time by siblings who are over fifteen years of age (most likely sisters); 5.1 per cent are cared for by fathers, and 9 per cent by other family members (such as grandmothers). In wealthier families, only 4 per cent of children are cared for by other family members or by neighbours. In this sector, the market plays a more significant role than family networks, and while mothers are also the primary carers, paid domestic workers care for 14.3 per cent of pre-school children. Indeed, privatizing care by hiring domestic workers is one of the principal strategies women from the upper classes resort to for commodifying their labour. This strategy is also used to delay the entrance of children to a crèche or kindergarten up to the age of two or three, keeping them cared for within the home while both parents engage in paid work. The downside of this situation is that even though domestic workers play a fundamental part in the organization of care in these households, their wages continue to be very low and the levels of informality in this highly feminized occupation expose lower-income women employed in this sector to the risks of unregulated and unprotected work (Esquivel, 2010). In contrast, in the poorest and lower middle-class households, care remains in the familial sphere, as the role of siblings (most likely sisters) is the second alternative to maternal care. Thus, poor women's ability to enter the labour market largely hinges on the availability of public offerings and family networks, and, to a lesser extent, community services.

In sum, a deep fragmentation of social policies is nowadays the constitutive mark of the Argentine welfare 'model', which in fact expresses competing logics that filter down to the political and social organization of childcare, clearly affecting household care arrangements. From a rights-based approach, efforts are made both to encourage labour registration and to provide educational opportunities for children. From a social assistance perspective, programmes seem to be confined to the neoliberal logic of targeting services while providing income transfers for the poorest. The impact of such a mixed model on the provision and quality of childcare can only be determined by a cross-sectoral analysis that examines both the logic underpinning the policies and its effects.

CHILDCARE AS WOMEN WORKERS' RIGHTS

Historically, labour regulation brought up the first attempt to reconcile women's family responsibilities with their participation in the labour force. This process started in Argentina in 1907, and was particularly dynamic during the first decades of the twentieth century. The main gains of this era included: a) the protection of women's work during pregnancy and its aftermath; b) the recognition of maternity leave; and c) the provision of childcare facilities at the workplace under particular circumstances (Pautassi et al., 2004).

The relevant legal norms were highly specific in terms of gender, allocating distinct rights and responsibilities to men and women, and strengthening an institutional framework that reinforced a strong male-breadwinner family model (Lewis and Ostner, 1991). While men were the right-holders entitled to 'family allowances', health insurance and social security on behalf of their families, women workers were entitled to other types of rights, related to their roles as mothers and care givers, reflecting a strong maternalistic perspective (Nari, 2004).

Almost a hundred years after this legal framework was developed, the relevant norms and devices regarding employment-related childcare provision are still based not only on female stereotypes of motherhood but also on male stereotypes which largely ignore men as potential family care givers (Faur, 2006). For instance, while maternity leave entitlement in the private sector amounts to ninety days, paternity leave in the same sector is only two days. Although marginal differences can be discerned among sectors, and some workers are entitled to longer parental leave, it is clear that parental leave is

Table 2. *Parental Leave for Mothers and Fathers in Selected Sectors/Activities, 2007*

		Mother	Father
Private sector	Private sector (Law 20744)	90 days	2 days
Public sector	National Level	100 days	5 days
	Municipalities of the Province of Buenos Aires	90 days	1 day
	City of Buenos Aires	105 days	3 days
Special statutes	Teachers of the Province of Buenos Aires	135 days	5 days
	Teachers of the City of Buenos Aires	165 days	10 days
	Domestic workers	0 days	—

Source: compiled by author on the basis of legislation currently in force.

of limited duration and a gender-differentiated logic remains in place (see Table 2). Needless to say, this pattern differs markedly from that of some European social democratic regimes, which not only recognize paid leave for both the father and the mother that lasts around one year, but also tend to promote the involvement of fathers in childrearing (Ellingsaeter, 1999; Sainsbury, 1996).

Besides subsidized leave, Argentine labour regulations oblige businesses or organizations employing fifty women or more to provide daycare centres, but no such rights are guaranteed for working fathers. This institutional scaffolding reinforces the view that women are the ones who bear the primary responsibility for child rearing, transforming them into priority subjects for the reconciliation of work and family responsibilities.

Regarding implementation, while paid leave is almost fully guaranteed for salaried workers in the formal sector, the right to childcare services exists only on paper, due to the historical absence of regulatory structures to implement existing legislation in this area. In addition, since this benefit is legally reserved for mothers, the few corporations that provide daycare centres offer them exclusively to their female workers. More importantly, the provision of employment-based crèches is not necessarily enforced, and largely depends on collective bargaining arrangements, with very different results across sectors, resulting in a context that has been defined as one of 'segmented neocorporatism' (Etchemendy and Collier, 2007).[11]

For those who are actually protected by labour regulations (formal salaried workers), the likelihood of defamilializing childcare through these devices is highly unequal. As shown in Table 2, differences in legislation are seen depending on whether the employer is the state or a private actor, and even vary from one province to another (as each province has its own legal

---

11. For instance, public sector employees have better access to daycare centres than workers in the private sector (Berger and Szretter, 2002).

system).[12] Those who perform jobs that are highly protected and those who are represented by stronger trade unions (e.g. teachers and public employees) have better access to parental leave and childcare services, whereas domestic workers, because of a special statute that regulates their work, have no right to parental leave, even when they work 'on the books'.[13] The absence of rights for this category of worker has a particularly detrimental impact on poorly educated and underprivileged women, who make up the bulk of domestic workers, accounting for 17.1 per cent of all employed women (INDEC, 2006).[14]

Above and beyond this, it should be noted that employment-related childcare is only guaranteed for those working in the formal sector of the economy. In this sense, access to maternity leave and work-related infant care services are areas that have been adversely affected by labour market deregulation and informality, which has expanded under the structural reforms of recent decades. Despite the political will to recast a labour-based social policy approach since 2004, informal employment in 2006 accounted for over 40 per cent of the employed population aged over eighteen, with a rate of 47.5 per cent for women compared to 38.1 per cent for men (INDEC, 2006).[15]

To summarize, as far as employment-related childcare rights are concerned, we can identify both a deep stratification amongst formal employees and a pervasive fragmentation that leaves informal workers unprotected. Even among formal workers, legislation tends to perpetuate inequalities depending on the sector and type of activity carried out. Additionally, the gender segregation of the labour market tends to relegate women, especially those with lower educational credentials, to informal jobs. The resulting picture is one of complex interaction between state regulations, gendered social relations, class and labour markets as far as workers' childcare benefits are concerned. The question that necessarily follows is: what happens to those who fall outside the formal labour market? How does public policy respond to their care needs?

---

12. The Law of Labour Contracts (Law No. 20744) is applicable to salaried workers, with the exception of national, provincial and municipal public administration employees, agrarian workers and domestic workers and teachers, who are covered by special statutes. The 1999 Law of National Public Employment (Law No. 24164) and the Decree 214/2006 regulate employment in the public sector at the national level. Public employees in different jurisdictions are governed by particular laws, not unlike education which has its own norms in each province. The totality of labour regulations is complemented with agreements reached through collective bargaining.
13. Although a large campaign to regulate domestic work was launched in 2005, more than 90 per cent of domestic employees remain informally employed.
14. Based on EPH-INDEC, third quarter of 2006, data on employed persons 14 years and older (INDEC, 2006).
15. Based on EPH-INDEC, third quarter of 2006 (INDEC, 2006).

CHILDCARE AS A CHILD'S RIGHT

Where parents cannot access care services through their employment, they rely on other channels such as public services, market services and/or community networks. To a certain extent, different kinds of formal and informal facilities are available for the youngest children (up to five years old). These include: a) early education services, run by the State education sector and private providers; b) Childhood Development Centres (CEDIS), focusing on poor children and mainly provided by the Ministry of Social Development, in association with social organizations and poor families, at subnational levels; and c) community crèches run by civil society organizations. Are we witnessing a process aimed at universalizing rights of early childcare?

This section examines the design and coverage of kindergartens and Childhood Development Centres. Focusing on the supply of state-run services, it points out that the two main types of services respond to different regulations and institutional logics and have different eligibility criteria and outcomes. In addition, kindergartens and CEDIS cover different proportions and segments of the population. Overall, the diversification of services deepens the existing inequalities among children.

Kindergarten: A Caring Institution?

Making education for five-year-olds mandatory in 1993 resulted in a vast expansion of coverage, transferring part of the care responsibility hitherto assigned to families to public institutions. In 2006, the national rate of enrolment for this cycle was close to 90 per cent. But since the service provided in public schools depends entirely on the funding capacities and policy priorities of each province, a great disparity remains in the coverage of children in non-compulsory cycles: barely 60 per cent of four-year-olds and only 30 per cent of three-year-olds attend nursery schools (MECYT, 2007).

Providing access to kindergartens and educational crèches is probably the most comprehensive and equalizing strategy for guaranteeing equality of opportunity to parents as care givers and children as recipients of care. It enhances the possibility of defamilializing care for children whilst educating them. While access to educational services from an early age can narrow the huge gaps between the wealthiest and poorest children, the supply of full-time, state-run pre-schools may also directly affect women's ability to enter and remain in the labour market, and hence the household's ability to increase its income level.

Despite legal advances and political debates, the country's early education system shows important biases in investment and expansion of early education, which have in turn furthered inequalities. The problem is more acute at those levels of the system that are not mandatory, mainly for children under three. As may be seen, the differences in early education coverage are associated not only with the age of children, but also with differences between jurisdictions.

In the wealthiest jurisdictions, where the State and private sectors have invested more heavily (such as in the City and the Province of Buenos Aires), more services are available for the youngest children. In many of the poorest jurisdictions, in contrast, only the mandatory services are available. Information on the percentage of total enrolment of five-year-olds clearly shows that in eleven out of the twenty-four provinces, over 70 per cent of enrolment is in this mandatory cycle. At the same time, roughly 75 per cent of enrolment in programmes for three-year-olds is concentrated in the province of Buenos Aires, and slightly over 10 per cent in the City of Buenos Aires. However, other jurisdictions show extremely low levels of enrolment at the educational crèches and at the three- and four-year-old level, reflecting the sharp inequalities masked by the general enrolment data and national averages (Faur, 2009).

Undoubtedly, problems in access particularly affect the youngest children from the country's poorest regions and households. As shown in Figure 1, attendance rates for children under five reveal major differences and correlate strongly with per capita household income. Although there is only a small gap between the attendance of poor and wealthier children in the five-year-old category (which has been made mandatory and where public services have expanded), the attendance of three-year-olds among the wealthiest

Figure 1. Attendance Rates in Large Cities, by Age and per capita Household Income, first half of 2006

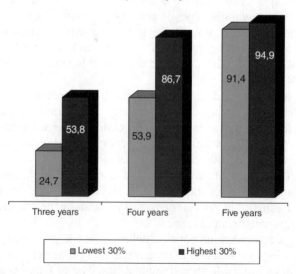

Source: author's calculations, based on EPH-INDEC (INDEC, 2006).

30 per cent of households is more than double that of children from poorer households, with only one in four attending. At the four-year-old level, enrolment of the poor increases but still the gap remains significant.

Finally, nursery schools (for children between forty-five days and two years old) have been relegated to a more informal status than that of kindergartens. Given a highly tenuous position in law, the supply of crèches is still very limited in the country overall, with an enrolment that scarcely reaches 43,000 children up to two years of age (contrasting the more than 1.3 million boys and girls enrolled at three- to five-year-old cycles). Besides, while 70 per cent of the country's pre-school enrolment (from three to five years) is covered by the state, as much as 66 per cent of national enrolment for the earliest cycle (forty-five days to two years old) pertains to the private sector and, accordingly, users must pay to gain access, impeding the defamilialization of childcare for the poorest segments of society (Faur, 2009).[16] Insufficient free public provision (especially of full-time services) restricts poor women's possibilities of commodifying their labour, since the fees charged by private institutions represent a significant portion of the household budget among these groups (Faur, 2011).[17]

Moreover, pre-school and kindergarten schedules often clash with standard working hours, this being perhaps the most significant difference with employment-related crèches. Practically no jurisdiction in the country exceeds 2 per cent enrolment in full-day programmes (i.e. providing 7.5 hours of care per day). Thus, the majority of Argentine children who attend early education centres do so for no more than 3.3 hours per day. Of particular interest is the fact that the City of Buenos Aires is the only jurisdiction in the country that supplies a relatively large proportion of state-run, full-time kindergartens, as Figure 2 shows. In fact, 18 per cent of early education enrolment, and as much as 30 per cent of state-managed enrolment is full-day. Nevertheless, as the supply of state-run services has not expanded to keep pace with demand, those who are unable to get a place or to afford fee-paying private services face long waiting lists for access to a state-run crèche or kindergarten (Faur, 2009, 2011).[18]

Thus, even in the wealthiest jurisdiction of the country — the City of Buenos Aires (CABA), with its diversified and relatively dense network of kindergartens, crèches, and relatively high rate of full-day

---

16. Based on data from the National Directorate of Information and Evaluation of Educational Quality, provided by the National Ministry of Education, Annual Figures, 2006.
17. Qualitative research conducted in the poorest neighborhoods of the City of Buenos Aires shows that private education facilities for these age groups charge high fees for poor families who strive to gain access to a free-of-charge crèche or kindergarten in the public sector (see Faur, 2009, 2010).
18. Recently, the deficit of public early education offerings led to collective legal action (by the Civil Association for Equality and Justice, ACIJ), alleging a violation of the right to education, autonomy, equal treatment and non-discrimination in the City of Buenos Aires. This strategy has placed parental claims for childcare at the judicial level.

Figure 2. Children Attending Early Education Centres, 2006

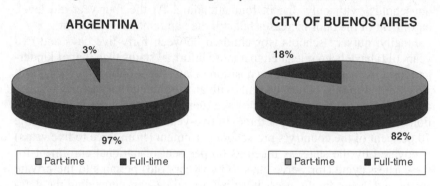

Source: author's calculations, based on MECYT (2007).

programmes — care institutions fall short. A deficit in the supply, in turn, (re)creates inequality in access. Throughout the country, the highest percentages of children not attending care services are concentrated in lower-income households.

Childhood Development Centres: The Focus on Poor Children

In order to accommodate the care needs of children from poor homes, part of the State's recent strategy has been to establish the so-called Child Development Centres, or CEDIS. These are not managed by educational authorities but by other State entities, such as the Ministry of Social Development, sometimes through agreements with community organizations and the families themselves. They neither intend to provide universal coverage of children under four, nor do they try to guarantee access to all poor children. These services are less institutionally structured than kindergartens, since they are not integrated into the official education system, and children attending them are not counted in the enrolment data cited above. Personnel for these 'centres' are not required to be teachers, as is the case in kindergartens, and many are social workers or 'carer mothers'.

The main goal of CEDIS appears to be to accommodate a small proportion of those who cannot access formal facilities, to regulate a pre-existing community and state intervention (that extended during the 1980s and 1990s), and to legitimate the involvement of the National Ministry of Social Development. This programme clearly represents a relatively minor investment (of money and dedication) on the part of the public sector.

Though data at a national level are not available, a systematization of this 'experience' carried out by UNICEF (2005) shows a highly heterogeneous picture across the country, both in terms of coverage and in the methodological approaches of CEDIS. Reviewing data valid for the wealthiest city in the country is also relevant: the alternative crèches can only take about 2,000 children in CABA, scarcely 2 per cent of the total enrolment in the city's pre-schools and 1 per cent of children under four. The resulting long waiting lists for space in CEDIS are proof of how difficult it is for the poorest families to defamilialize childcare: their possibilities, in contrast to those of middle and high income sectors, are seriously constrained.[19]

In short, we may say that these programmes carry the mark of neoliberal compensatory policies, focusing their contributions on the poor, providing limited coverage and exhibiting lower quality compared to mainstream educational services. It is also worth noting that the role of civil society actors in such programmes cannot be considered as independent of the state. Where community actors are involved, either in providing facilities (as in the case of the jointly managed care institutions) or through the use of women from the community to provide the various services, it reinforces the idea that the poor must 'participate' in supplying services if they are to enjoy access to them. This romanticized notion ends up aggravating inequality, since by focusing on poor children the state legitimizes the fragmentation of care services, failing to achieve universal high quality coverage.

Thus, a tension exists between the institutional realms of education and care. On legal grounds, kindergartens and nursery schools have a greater number of provisions that protect children and their qualified teachers, while CEDIS and community crèches operate under a flexible framework that performs poorly on both counts. This tension, however, goes far beyond the regulatory realm: it has roots in a historical and cultural (false) dichotomy that casts 'caring' as different from, and opposed to, 'educating', and is underpinned no doubt by a subtle gender sub-text. While 'professional' teachers try hard to differentiate themselves from 'maternalistic' carers, parents demand from teachers that they care for their children, and carers from CEDIS see themselves as 'second mothers' to those they care for (Faur, 2011). The result is a diverse and heterogeneous plurality not only of actors but also of expectations, demands, interests and strategies displayed in order to fulfil childcare needs. The bottom line is that these different provisions cannot guarantee equal access to and quality of services for early childhood. Does this framework then institutionalize inequality among children from different socio-economic backgrounds?

Maternalism for the Poor? A Glance at Poverty Reduction Strategies

Even though poverty reduction programmes do not actually provide public care services for children in Argentina, analysing the role these programmes assign to women sheds light on how assumptions about who should

---

19. Information based on special tabulations valid for 2008, given to the author at her request by the CABA's Ministry of Social Development.

provide childcare in an underprivileged household shape policy design, thus impacting on the social organization of care. In other words, such analysis helps to illuminate the question: do these policies encourage and support poor women's capacity to reconcile participation in the labour market with family responsibilities?

Two such means-tested programmes are especially relevant for this purpose, due to their focus on poor households with children, their emphasis on women and their extensive coverage. Covering some 1.8 million households by 2007, they are the Unemployed Heads of Household Plan (PJJHD or *Plan Jefes y Jefas*), mentioned above, and the Families for Social Inclusion Programme (or Families Programme for short).[20] Their principal aims are to ensure a minimum income for the household, to encourage children to stay in school, as well as to promote routine medical visits for children and pregnant women.

These aims corresponded to prevalent blueprints for conditional cash transfer programmes that have mushroomed in Latin-American countries. Promoted by international financial institutions, these schemes rapidly developed in the region throughout the last decade, reproducing the same strategy to address poverty in different contexts (Tabbush, 2009). Some of the main features in their design were the introduction of notions of 'co-responsibility', 'participation' and 'empowerment' of beneficiaries, which had been 'part of mainstream thinking in the 1990s' (Molyneux, 2007). Beyond their discursive construction, co-responsibility and participation were to be realized by demanding the performance of certain tasks from beneficiaries in exchange for programme benefits (*contraprestaciones*). None of them, however, make explicit reference to the more general problem of caring for children under five while simultaneously holding down a job.

By targeting the poorest households, these cash transfer programmes contributed to creating a diversified welfare regime, quite unlike 'ideal types' in welfare regime analysis. In fact, they introduced a degree of complexity into the Argentine social protection system, by layering old and new approaches. Making women the primary recipients of transfers because of their more 'altruistic' use of money and claiming to 'empower' them, advocates of the schemes seem to have disregarded the implications that conditionalities have on women's autonomy and rights. In this respect, by assigning poor women the bulk of caring responsibilities in exchange for benefits, one could ask whether the state is facilitating work and family reconciliation, or curtailing the commodification of women's labour in the market place?

---

20. In December 2009, a new policy, the Universal Child Allowance, was launched. The beneficiaries of this policy are children whose parents are: i) unregistered workers, ii) low-earning employees, iii) self-employed workers or iv) excluded from the labour market. This conditional cash transfer has effectively put an end to the Families Programme, since it involves more cash and has expanded the pool of potential beneficiaries. Whether the Universal Child Allowance initiative marks the end of targeted poverty reduction policies is yet to be seen, but that question is beyond the scope of this paper.

Plan Jefes y Jefas

The Unemployed Heads of Household Plan was launched in 2002, in the context of the acute socio-economic crisis in which poverty levels peaked at 57 per cent of the population. The programme targeted the unemployed heads of households (regardless of gender) who are responsible for a child under eighteen years of age or caring for a disabled child or a pregnant spouse. The conditional cash transfer method was massively used for the first time in Argentine social policy by this Plan. Attempting to merge the different social programmes into one plan with broad coverage, it absorbed most of the country's existing employment programmes, especially those run by the national government. In exchange for the cash benefits provided,[21] recipients were expected to perform some community work, assigned at the local level.

In the first months of its implementation, the plan reached over one million beneficiaries, and within a year it had reached over two million recipients, 60 per cent of whom were women. Beyond this figure, the plan had a notable symbolic effect in gender terms. It explicitly included in its title 'unemployed male and *female* heads of household', acknowledging that some households are headed by women, not only mothers and wives but also potential workers, and eligible in their own right for a social programme that recognizes them as such. In fact, almost half of female beneficiaries were spouses and a significant proportion of the women were economically inactive (i.e. out of the workforce) (Cortés et al., 2004). However, the design and implementation of the PJJHD lacked a cohesive approach to gender social relations. Beneficiaries' work commitments were assigned at the local level and thus included a wide spectrum of activities, depending on local conditions. While the work performed by women mainly represented care responsibilities at the community level, men worked primarily in construction or maintenance of local or community facilities, a division of labour that reinforced deeply-rooted gender stereotypes.

As of May 2003, entry to the plan was no longer permitted and coverage declined each year thereafter. Since then, beneficiaries have left the plan, but none have joined. Notably, as the number of beneficiaries declined, the proportion of women increased. In the second quarter of 2002, women represented 63 per cent of beneficiaries; in 2004, 67.7 per cent; and in the fourth quarter of 2006, 72 per cent.[22] This fact can be explained in the light of a set of concurrent factors. On the one hand, the economic recovery that took place between 2004 and 2006 was prompted by traditionally masculine sectors of the economy (like construction and manufacturing). This

---

21. Subsidies have been 150 ARS (approximately US$ 39) per month since 2002.
22. According to the figures of the Ministry of Labour, Employment and Social Security, the programme's beneficiaries numbered over 1.6 million in September 2004, and had fallen to slightly over 1.2 million by September 2006. (Website of MTEySS, visited in 2007.)

meant that non-qualified women had less employment opportunities than men. Added to this, the lack of care facilities also contributed to curbing women's participation in the labour market. Furthermore, employment for women in the lowest income quintiles did not seem to have helped women climb out of poverty during that period (Cortés and Groisman, 2008). This situation was evaluated by the PJJHD managers as proof of poor women's 'unemployable' condition. This discriminating classification links work opportunities to personal abilities rather than to a set of enabling structures that play a fundamental role in women's labour force participation (Campos et al., 2007).

Finally, the PJJHD did not offer women or their families any type of childcare assistance or service. The educational requirement for children began at the age of five, when school attendance becomes mandatory. No strategy was implemented to cover care or educational needs of younger children in state-run facilities. Thus, pre-school care remained invisible, the assumption being that families, and especially mothers, are the ones responsible for its provision. The negligence of care needs also contributed to limit poor women's opportunities, choices and rights.

Families Programme: From 'Heads of Household' to 'Mothers'

In 2004, in the context of improved social and employment conditions throughout the country, another cash transfer programme named Families for Social Inclusion was launched. The aim was to incorporate a substantial number of PJJHD's female beneficiaries into the Families Programme. Specifically, the hope was that PJJHD beneficiaries classified as 'unemployable' would be encouraged to 'migrate' to the Families Programme.[23]

The official beneficiaries of the Programme are women in their capacity as mothers. Instead of a work commitment in exchange for benefits (which was a central feature of the *Jefas* programme), the Families Programme requirements only included the schooling and health of the children of beneficiaries receiving the subsidy.[24] Thus the state provides income while the recipients demonstrate care in exchange — care that is part of attending to the education and health needs of their children, or that takes the form of domestic work, transforming resources into services. With this new shift, the symbolic progress achieved earlier by the PJJHD in recognizing women as potential workers underwent a setback. The Families Programme once

---

23. National Executive Branch Decree 1506/04.
24. By 2007, it served 539,000 households, according to the Ministry of Social Development. The benefit consists of a monthly transfer calculated in relation to the size of the family, with a minimum benefit of ARS 185 (US$ 49) per month per child or pregnant woman, and ARS 30 (US$ 8) for each additional child, up to a maximum of six children at ARS 305 (US$ 80), according to the Ministry of Social Development Resolution 693 of 2007. See Campos et al. (2007).

again addressed poor women solely in their capacity as mothers and carers. This is not merely a semantic issue: the identification of motherhood with cash transfers may in fact help crystallize such an association. Unlike the PJJHD, the Families Programme includes care considerations. That is, the programme implicitly recognizes that women's domestic work is a significant input into family and child welfare. Since childcare services for the youngest and the poorest remain insufficient — as seen above — the Families Programme addresses this particular issue by transferring a small cash stipend to mothers so as to enable them to stay at home and care for their family. In doing so, however, a paradoxical feature of the approach becomes apparent: the recognition, indeed reinforcement, of traditional gender roles associated with domesticity forecloses the search for equality and life options that would give women greater autonomy.

The 'maternalist' orientation of these programmes is clear. Their unvarying appeal to mothers' responsibility and to the need for commitment, as prerequisites for obtaining the minimum resources needed for subsistence from the State, reflects a traditional perspective re-packaged into a modern criterion for eligibility for social assistance — conditional cash transfer programmes. In line with Chant's considerations, the analysis of these plans confirms that anti-poverty strategies reinforce and intensify women's domestic tasks and obligations, making them responsible for coping with the burden of poverty and survival (Chant, 2006).

In sum, far from promoting work and family reconciliation, the gender subtext of these programmes resolves the conflict between employment and care in the most traditional way: they tend to re-familialize, naturalize and feminize childcare, reinforcing its social undervaluation. This approach contributes to reproducing a system in which care work clashes with market work. Paradoxically, while many countries are discussing how to strengthen social policies to make it possible for women to 'reconcile' work and family obligations, anti-poverty programmes delivered in Argentina appear to be grounded in a culturalist view of gender as 'complementary roles' which reifies motherhood. For poor women, this means either having to do voluntary work to keep their children in some form of community care, or fully familializing care in return for the transfers that social programmes offer them.

CONCLUDING REMARKS

The Argentine system manifests a complex configuration in which the roles and responsibilities of the different pillars of the welfare system overlap and interconnect in the social organization of care. Although gradually emerging, the issue of care still appears as a marginal component of each of the policies implemented in this highly diverse system. As a result, the supply of care services provided by different institutions affects care arrangements in households differently depending on geographic location, occupational status and socio-economic position of its members. This contribution has shown the fragmentation and lack of coordination among different levels of government for the implementation of social policies that, either by action or omission, govern the way in which childcare is provided by different institutions.

First, employment-based care benefits — such as paid parental leave and workplace crèches — not only cover less than half the working population, but also segment benefits by gender and scale them by occupational status, thereby protecting some groups (such as public employees and teachers) while leaving others (informal workers, including domestic workers) without any kind of benefit. Second, the state's educational services for children under three are still limited throughout the country. The younger the child, the more families need to resort to family care or to private establishments. Third, the strategy of establishing so-called 'Child Development Centres', focused on underprivileged households, effectively legitimates a double standard through the supply of different kinds of services to different social groups. Yet these scarcely cover the emerging demand, and thus carry the mark of neoliberal compensatory policies. The outcome is a three-tier care provision system featuring not only a public–private divide, but also a further divide within the public sector, in terms of the quality of care provision. Finally, poverty reduction strategies reinforce care in its most maternalist form, providing incentives for the re-familialization of care among women beneficiaries of the programme, and hindering poor women's employment opportunities.

Despite recent attempts to undo the neoliberal path, our analysis of policies suggests that these are hardly able to structure an 'equal opportunities' model for social protection. The current labour market is unable to replicate the 'golden years' of the Argentinean welfare state (given the large proportion of workers who continue to be informally employed), and therefore social protection benefits accessible through the labour contract remain out of reach for the mass of workers who are informally employed and among whom women predominate. In the education sector, the inclusion of five-year-olds within the mandatory pre-school cycle has represented an important step forward, practically achieving universal enrolment for this age group. However, other educational policy priorities (such as adolescent inclusion and retention within the system) and the lack of consensus among the different provinces on the extension of early childhood education, have resulted in the postponement of the universalization of services for three- and four-year-olds, as well as limited provision of state-run services for children under two. Finally, compensatory type policies have tended to focus on the delivery of targeted cash allowances rather than the universal provision of state-run services (or a combination of both). Thus, they have deepened and re-packaged an 'assistentialist' model of social protection, which reinforces the reproduction of gender and class inequalities.

This analysis of the organization of care thus reflects that Argentina today does not have either a strictly 'informal' (Barrientos, 2004) or 'stratified universal' (Filgueira, 2005) welfare regime, but rather an intricate mix of these different models, showing different faces of the state through highly fragmented social policies. Some state provisions are universal and available to all citizens; others are clearly means tested and, to a certain extent, accessible to the most disadvantaged social groups. Still other benefits depend on formal labour market participation, while the rest are directly privatized. The implication of such a welfare 'model' on care arrangements can hardly be seen as homogeneous. Each of the policies we have analysed here assumes and somehow creates a different profile of the beneficiary, not only reproducing a fragmented welfare system but also affecting poor women's prospects of joining the labour market and overcoming poverty.

Thus, while state and employer provisions cover part of the demand from mid to lower socio-economic segments of society, the rest of this demand is covered by the market, through educational services and privatized care (including domestic service). The role of families and communities continues to be dominant in the provision of care for the poorest, who face serious obstacles in obtaining a broad range of services, among them childcare services, to ensure their overall well-being. The higher-income households have access to overlapping options, while maternalism is particularly promoted through the Poverty Reduction Programmes. These diverse responses translate into a high level of privatization for the most privileged, and a high level of familialization in the case of lower-income households, thereby widening the gap between women from different socio-economic groups.

As a result, in Argentina, we cannot speak about a homogeneous 'care regime' or a single 'care diamond' with a uniform and somehow predictable configuration, which seems more appropriate for European countries, where state policies and institutions are significantly more stable and path dependent. It is precisely for this reason that I refer to these arrangements in terms of a *political and social organization of care*, one which is constantly developing through the interventions of public and private offerings, and which has different shapes and outcomes across social class.

REFERENCES

Altimir, O. and L. Beccaria (1999) 'Distribución del Ingreso en Argentina' ['Income Distribution in Argentina']. Economic Reform Series, No. 40. Santiago de Chile: ECLAC.

Anlló, G. and O. Cetrángolo (2007) 'Políticas Sociales en Argentina: Viejos Problemas, Nuevos Desafíos' ['Social Policies in Argentina: Old Problems, New Challenges'], in B. Kosacoff (ed.) *Crisis, Recuperación y Nuevos Dilemas. La Economía Argentina 2002–2007* [*Crisis, Recovery and New Dilemmas. The Argentinean Economy 2002–2007*], pp. 395–426. Santiago de Chile: ECLAC.

Arza, C. (2009) 'Back to the State: Pension Fund Nationalization in Argentina'. Working Paper No. 73. Buenos Aires: CIEPP.

Barrientos, A. (2004) 'Latin America: Towards a Liberal-informal Welfare Regime', in I. Gough and G. Wood (eds) *Insecurity and Welfare Regimes in Asia, Africa and Latin America: Social Policy in Development Contexts*, pp. 121–68. Cambridge: Cambridge University Press.

Beccaria, L. (2001) 'Empleo e Integración Social' ['Employment and Social Integration']. Buenos Aires: Fondo de Cultura Económica [Economic Culture Fund].

Beccaria, L., V. Esquivel and R. Maurizio (2005) 'Empleos, Salario y Equidad durante la Recuperación Reciente en la Argentina' ['Employment, Salaries and Equity during Recent Recovery in Argentina'], *Desarrollo Económico* 45(178): 235–62.

Berger, S. and H. Szretter (2002) 'Costos laborales de hombres y mujeres. El caso de Argentina' ['Male and Female Labour Costs. The Case of Argentina'], in L. Abramos and R. Todaro (eds) *Cuestionando un mito: Costos laborales de hombres y mujeres en América Latina [Questioning a Myth. Labour Costs of Men and Women in Latin America]*, pp. 51–113. Lima: International Labour Organization.

Campos, L., E. Faur and P. Pautassi (2007) 'Familias por la Inclusión Social. Entre el Discurso de Derechos y la práctica Asistencial' ['Families for Social Inclusion. Among Rights Discourse and Paternalistic Practice']. Research and Analysis Collection. Buenos Aires: CELS.

Cerrutti, M. (2000) 'Economic Reform, Structural Adjustment and Female Labour Force Participation in Buenos Aires, Argentina', *World Development* 28(5): 879–91.

Cortés, R. and F. Groisman (2008) 'Hogares, Empleo y Pobreza en Argentina: ¿estructuras Persistentes?' ['Households, Employment and Poverty in Argentina. Pre-existing Structures?'], in Jorge Granda Aguilar *Pobreza, Exclusión y Desigualdad [Poverty, Exclusion and Inequality]*, pp. 33–49. Quito: Ecuador.

Cortés, R. and A. Marshall (1999) 'Estrategia Económica Instituciones y Negociación política en la Reforma social de los 90' ['Economic Strategy, Institutions and Political Negotiation in the 1990s Social Reform'], *Desarrollo Económico* 39(154): 195–214.

Cortés, R., F. Groisman and A. Hoszowski (2004) 'Transiciones Ocupacionales: el caso del plan Jefes y Jefas' ['Occupational Transitions: The Case of the Unemployed Head of Households Plan'], *Argentina: Realidad Económica* 202: 11–28.

Chant, S. (2006) 'How Can We Make the "Feminisation of Poverty" More Policy-relevant? Towards a "Feminisation of Responsibility and Obligation"?', in L. Mora and M.J. Moreno (eds) *Social Cohesion, Reconciliation Policies and Public Budgeting: A Gender Approach*, pp. 201–33. Mexico City: United Nations Population Fund-GTZ.

Daly, M. (2001) *Care Work: The Quest for Security*. Geneva: International Labour Office.

Daly, M. and J. Lewis (2000) 'The Concept of Social Care and the Analysis of Contemporary Welfare States', *The British Journal of Sociology* 51(2): 281–98.

EANNA (2004) 'Encuesta de Actividades de Niños, Niñas y Adolescentes' ['National Survey of Child and Adolescent Activities']. Buenos Aires: Ministry of Labour, Employment and Social Security.

Ellingsaeter, A.L. (1999) 'Dual Breadwinners between State and Market', in R. Crompton (ed.) *Restructuring Gender Relations and Employment. The Decline of the Male Breadwinner*, pp. 40–59. New York: Oxford University Press.

Esping-Andersen, G. (1990) *The Three Worlds of Welfare Capitalism*. Princeton, NJ: Princeton University Press.

Esquivel, V. (2009) 'Time Use in the City of Buenos Aires. Measuring, Analysing and Valuing Unpaid Care Work'. Doctoral dissertation, School of Advanced Studies, University of London.

Etchemendy, S. and R.B. Collier (2007) 'Down But Not Out: Union Resurgence and Segmented Neocorporatism in Argentina (2003–2007)', *Politics & Society* 35(3): 363–401.

Faur, E. (2006) 'Gender and Family–Work Reconciliation. Labour Legislation and Male Subjectivities in Latin America', in L. Mora and M. J. Moreno (eds) *Social Cohesion, Reconciliation Policies and Public Budgeting. A Gender Approach*, pp. 127–50. Mexico City: United Nations Population Fund-GTZ.

Faur, E. (2009) 'Organización Social del Cuidado Infantil en Ciudad de Buenos Aires. El rol de las Instituciones Públicas y Privada 2005–2008' ['The Social Organization of Childcare in the City of Buenos Aires. The Role of Public and Private Institutions 2005–2008']. PhD dissertation. Buenos Aires: FLACSO (Latin American Faculty for Social Sciences).

Faur, E. (2010) 'Desencuentros entre oferta y demanda de servicios de cuidado en Buenos Aires Lógicas en Tensión' ['Missmatches between Care Services Supply and Demand in Buenos Aires. Logics in Tension'], *Revista de Ciencias Sociales* 23(27): 68–81. Special Issue, *Usos del tiempo, cuidados y bienestar. Desafíos para Uruguay y la Región [Time Uses, Care and Welfare. Challenges for Uruguay and the Region]*.

Filgueira, F. (2005) 'Welfare and Democracy in Latin America: The Development, Crisis and Aftermath of Universal, Dual and Exclusionary Social Status'. Working document. Geneva: United Nations Research Institute for Social Development.

Huber, E. and J. Stephens (2000) 'The Political Economy of Pension Reform: Latin America in Comparative Perspective'. Geneva: United Nations Research Institute for Social Development.

Instituto Nacional de Estadística y Censos (INDEC) (2006) 'Encuesta Permanente de Hogares (EPH)' ['Permanent Household Survey']. http://www.indec.mecon.ar/dbindec/login.asp (accessed 16 September 2009).

Jelin, E. (1998). 'Pan y afectos. La transformación de las familias' ['Bread and Affection. The Transformation of Families']. Buenos Aires: Fondo de Cultura Económica.

Lewis, J. and I. Ostner (1991) 'Gender and the Evolution of European Social Policies'. Paper presented at the CES workshop on Emergent Supranational Social Policy: The EC's Social Dimension in Comparative Perspective, Center for European Studies, Harvard University (15–17 November).

Lister, R. (1994) 'She Has Other Duties: Women, Citizenship and Social Security', in S. Baldwin and J. Falkingham (eds) *Social Security and Social Change: New Challenges to the Beveridge Model*, pp. 31–44. London: Harvester Wheatsheaf.

Ministerio de Educación, Ciencia y Tecnología (MECYT) [Ministry of Education, Science & Technology] (2007) 'El nivel inicial en la última década: desafíos para la universalización *Boletín DiNIECE* No. 2, Año 2' ['Preschool Level in the Last Decade: Challenges for its Universalization', DINIECE Bulletin No. 2, Year 2']. Buenos Aires: DiNIECE – MECyT.

Molyneux, M. (2007) 'Change and Continuity in Social Protection in Latin America. Mothers at the Service of the State?'. Gender and Development Paper No. 1. Geneva: United Nations Research Institute for Social Development.

Nari, M. (2004) *Políticas de maternidad y maternalismo político [Maternity Policies and Political Maternalism]*. Buenos Aires: Editorial Biblos.

O'Connor, J. (1993) 'Gender, Class and Citizenship in the Comparative Analysis of Welfare Regimes: Theoretical and Methodological Issues', *British Journal of Sociology* 44(3): 501–18.

Orloff, A.S. (1993) 'Gender and the Social Rights of Citizenship State Policies and Gender Relations in Comparative Research', *American Sociological Review* 58(3): 303–28.

Pautassi, L., E. Faur and N. Gherardi (2004) 'Legislación Laboral en Seis países latinoamericanos: Avances y omisiones para una mayor equid ad' ['Labour Legislation in Six Latin American Countries: Advances and Omissions for Further Equity']. ECLAC Women and Development Series No. 56. Santiago de Chile: ECLAC.

Razavi, S. (2007) 'The Political and Social Economy of Care: An Issues Paper'. Geneva: United Nations Research Institute for Social Development.

Sainsbury, D. (1996) *Gender, Equality and Welfare States*. Cambridge: Cambridge University Press.

Tabbush, C. (2009) 'Gender, Citizenship and New Approaches to Poverty Relief: The Case of Argentine CCT Strategies', in S. Razavi (ed.) *The Gendered Impacts of Liberalization:*

Towards Embedded Liberalism?, pp. 488–526. London and New York: Routledge/UNRISD Series in Gender and Development.

UNFPA (2009) 'Situación de la población en la Argentina' ['Population Situation in Argentina']. Buenos Aires: United Nations Population Fund.

Wainerman, C. (2007) 'Conyugalidad y paternidad. ¿Una revolución estancada?'['Married Life and Paternity. A Stalled Revolution?'], in M.A. Gutierrez (ed.) *Género, familias y trabajo: rupturas y continuidades. Desafíos para la investigación política* [*Gender, Families and Work: Disruptions and Continuities. Challenges for Political Research*], pp. 179–222. Buenos Aires: CLACSO-Libros.

6

Who Cares in Nicaragua? A Care Regime in an Exclusionary Social Policy Context

Juliana Martínez Franzoni and Koen Voorend

INTRODUCTION

Policies of economic liberalization and structural adjustment during the 1990s have increased the burden of unpaid work assumed by Latin American women, particularly in countries with historically strong social policy regimes which have experienced State retrenchment during the last three decades, as is the case in the Southern Cone countries (Molyneux, 2000).[1] Has neoliberal restructuring had a similar impact on women's unpaid work in countries with more familialist social policy regimes? This contribution will explore this question by focusing on Nicaragua, a country that went from a liberal to a revolutionary regime and back to a (neo)liberal regime in less than thirty years. It provides an interesting case study for understanding certain continuities in the gender dimensions of the care regime which stand apart from economic and political transformations.

Nicaragua is the second poorest country in the Western Hemisphere. Gross domestic product (GDP) is exceptionally low (US$ 958 per capita) and remittances from family members who have emigrated to the United States or Costa Rica are a primary source of national income (World Bank, 2008a). Some 20 per cent of individuals are illiterate, 80 per cent of the economically active population are classified as vulnerable workers, and 70 per cent of the population lives below the poverty line (ECLAC, 2007a). Furthermore, the country is very vulnerable to natural disasters such as hurricanes and earthquakes (IDB, 2008).

Within this complex reality, families are known to play a key role in the survival strategies of the majority of the population. Furthermore, family networks often rely heavily on mothers, daughters and other female family members, and are not necessarily shaped by marriage or partnership between

We are deeply grateful to Shahra Razavi, guest editor of this special issue, to Silke Staab, and to the anonymous referees, for their generous and patient comments on numerous drafts of this article. We wish to acknowledge the input of the interviewees and thank them for their time and insights, as well as the Nicaraguan researcher Carmen Largaespada-Fredersdoff for conducting these interviews and helping us reconstruct the formation of social policy in Nicaragua. We are responsible for any errors and omissions.

1. Following O'Connor et al. (1999), we understand social policy regimes as institutionalized patterns in state social provision that establish systematic relations between the state and social structures. The outcomes capture a broad range of interventions that go well beyond state transfers and services.

Seen, Heard and Counted, First Edition. Edited by Shahra Razavi.
Chapters © 2012 The Institute of Social Studies. Book compilation © 2012 Blackwell Publishing Ltd.

women and men (Largaespada-Fredersdoff, 2006a, 2006b). In this sense, Nicaragua does not fit the traditional welfare regime literature from the North which is largely premised on the idea of a heterosexual couple (either through marriage or cohabitation). In fact, in the North, social provision against social risks has historically been accompanied by the reproduction of traditional gender roles, based on the model of the male provider and female care giver (Fraser, 1994; Orloff, 1996, 2009; Sainsbury, 1996).

This normative underpinning does not hold in the case of Nicaragua. While women are central in the productive and reproductive work of the family, close to 40 per cent of households are managed by women without a male partner or spouse (ECLAC, 2007a). Like many countries in Latin America, Nicaragua has seen a significant increase in the number of female-headed households (Canales, 2004; Rendón, 2004) as a result of growing trends of migration and informality, labour flexibilization and underemployment. At the same time, it also has one of the highest proportions of extended family households in Latin America (34 per cent), along with Honduras and Venezuela (Barahona, 2006). What is unusual about Nicaragua is that, here, extended families are a widespread phenomenon not only in rural, but also in urban areas. Some studies suggest that their prevalence increased between 1993 and 2001, particularly in rural areas, in what has been described as the 'accordion effect' or the tendency by families to come together and separate depending on the availability of resources (Agurto and Guido, 2001). Family support networks become 'a central resource in the process of social reproduction of individuals and their families: they allow access to other resources (education, work, income, health), [and] they play a decisive role in carrying out certain daily activities (care of children, domestic work, care for the sick...)' (Ariza and Oliveira, 2004: 26, own translation). In Nicaragua, then, these networks are more important than traditional notions of the nuclear family would seem to suggest.

In this 'familialistic' context,[2] did neoliberal public policy between the 1990s and 2006 increase the demand placed on female unpaid work, as it did in the Southern Cone countries? To answer this question, we compare the nature of the Nicaraguan care regime between 1990 and 2006 with the legacies of the Sandinista revolution (1979–1990). Our findings suggest that the argument that structural adjustment increased women's high care burden may need to be more nuanced in the Nicaraguan context. In both the Sandinista and the neoliberal period, albeit for different reasons, the care regime was highly and explicitly dependent on unpaid work of mostly women. Also, women's unpaid contribution has been, and continues to be, central for the viability of many public social programmes. That is, despite major economic, political and policy shifts, the role of female, unpaid work remained central throughout both periods.

---

2. A familialistic welfare regime is defined as one that 'assigns a maximum of welfare obligations to the households' (Esping-Andersen, 1999: 45).

Unpaid work includes two distinct components: first, unpaid domestic and care work that is largely performed by women and often mediated through family and kinship relations; and second, a more ambiguous category of work, widely referred to as 'community' or 'voluntary'[3] work which may be mediated by community relations or performed in the context of public social programmes as a condition for accessing their services. The two components share some characteristics. Neither involves direct monetary reward (although 'stipends' may be offered for some forms of 'community/ voluntary' work), nor are they included in the system of national accounts (SNA). Moreover, their analysis involves similar conceptual, methodological and measurement problems (Benería, 1999). Both reflect larger societal arrangements — rather than being based on isolated individual decisions — particularly the degree to which states expect engagement or 'participation' from their citizens (Anheier and Salamon, 2001). There are also significant differences: community work is very often part of an organized programme, whereas unpaid domestic work is not; beneficiaries of the latter are members of the immediate household or family, whereas the former mostly targets people outside the family (Benería, 1999). There are nevertheless close connections between the two which makes it difficult to draw boundaries between them (ibid.). As will be shown below, this is also the case with community work in Nicaragua's social programmes, which is far from 'voluntary' and more akin to being a conditionality for accessing public social programmes. In this sense women's 'voluntary' work may be seen as an extension of their unpaid domestic and care work to secure the well-being and care of their dependants.

In characterizing Nicaragua's care regime we start by presenting some general features of the social policy regime. In the following section we address the principal components of the care regime, namely, education, healthcare, social protection and care services, and analyse their similarities and differences. The final section presents some concluding remarks about the nature of Nicaragua's care regime, its policy implications and prospects for change.

NICARAGUA'S EXCLUSIONARY SOCIAL POLICY REGIME

In Nicaragua, unlike the rest of Latin America, the first half of the 1980s witnessed a considerable expansion in the provision of education, healthcare and care services in the immediate aftermath of the Sandinista revolution (Chávez Metoyer, 1999). Underpinning this expansion was a universalist

---

3. This is, however, a somewhat misleading label. As in the case of unpaid domestic and care work, community work is embedded in societal expectations and norms which override individual choice. In addition, as we will discuss below, much 'voluntary' work is basically mandatory for the women whose children access social services.

vision, in which social services were to be made available to all citizens through the workings of a strong, centralized State. In reality, such expansion in service provisioning was only possible through the mobilization and organization of volunteers.[4] Most of the volunteers were women: 'The Sandinistas' women's organization, the Association of Nicaraguan Women (AMNLAE) mobilized large numbers of young women as teachers for the Literacy Crusade, with their mothers for logistical support. When that was over, many of the same women participated in vaccination campaigns and nutrition hygiene, and preventative medicine brigades' (Chinchilla, 1990: 376).

Childcare services were not available on a significant scale until the second half of the 1980s, when the economy relied on a massive incorporation of women into the labour force (Molyneux, 1985). At this point, the goal of establishing universal social policies remained intact, but social spending dropped considerably due to the combination of a badly needed adjustment policy and the Contra war. In this context, many women who had volunteered for the provision of social services joined the Popular Militias (Chinchilla, 1990). In the 1990s, however, the earlier policy vision was sharply reversed as governments inspired by neoliberal ideas came to power, promoting decentralization and the targeting of services, along with higher levels of commodification through the imposition of co-payments and user charges as a condition for accessing public social services, as well as the expansion of private provision.

Today, Nicaragua's education system has a public sector, financed by public revenues, and a private sector financed through out-of-pocket payments. Its healthcare system combines social security, which funds pensions and healthcare services, with private sector and public and community services, creating a highly stratified and uncoordinated system (Mesa-Lago, 2008). Although the pension system has a private component, coverage is negligible, with huge gaps in protection in many cases. Education, healthcare and pensions are supplemented by social assistance programmes which are implemented by many different institutions. Of particular relevance are cash transfers and nutrition and childcare programmes, which are designed to mitigate poverty and provide care services.

In many Latin American countries, public policy was transformed during the first half of the twentieth century in response to social demands articulated by organized labour (Collier and Collier, 2002). This was not the case in Nicaragua. As a result, Nicaragua's social policy regime was termed 'exclusionary' (Filgueira, 1998), that is, a social state in which only a small and privileged part of the population has access to social protection, even before the wave of neoliberal reforms swept the region. In various ways, the role

---

4. The National Literacy Campaign is the best-known example, but volunteer work played a similar role in other sectors such as healthcare and childcare.

of the State was, and continues to be, secondary to the very significant role played by families in both subsistence and social protection. First, funding is extremely limited and only basic services, such as primary healthcare, are provided. Second, in the division of responsibility between the State and the family/community, the latter bears most of the burden. Third, distinctions between market, public and family allocation of resources are blurred by the overwhelming role that unpaid work plays across all three, leading Martínez Franzoni (2008) to classify Nicaragua as an 'informal' welfare regime. Not only is the State's role in welfare arrangements limited (Martínez Franzoni, 2008; Mesa Lago, 2008), but most of the existing public programmes also require beneficiaries, their families and communities, to contribute via what is often referred to as 'voluntary work' (*trabajo voluntario*) and, in some cases, through co-payments. Nearly all social programmes, including those that are formally universal, are in practice targeted to the poor; however, given that the poor comprise the majority of the population, coverage is in fact rather limited. For example, between 1998 and 2005, pre-school provision for children under six years of age stagnated at around 17 per cent of eligible children. And while both primary and secondary school enrolment increased in the same period, the latter reached only 43 per cent of the population in 2006 (Gershberg, 1999).

In general, Nicaragua's social policy regime has relatively little influence on care arrangements, which instead largely rely on social practices that are unrelated to the State and its policies. Nevertheless, it is important to understand the role and relative importance of State institutions if the overwhelming reliance on the family is ever to be changed. Moreover, in a context such as Nicaragua's, with relatively underdeveloped care services, we should not only focus on those institutions with explicit care goals (such as childcare centres), but also on other institutions that may not have been specifically designed to cater to care needs, but which in reality play an important role in its provisioning, such as primary schools.

Social Spending

During the 1990s, trends in social spending across Latin America reflected the 'Washington Consensus': social policy was to be rearranged around privatization, decentralization and the targeting of all social expenditure. The State's role was to be limited to compensating for market 'failures', promoting individual risk management and encouraging the market-based allocation of resources (Molyneux, 2007). Yet, the prevailing international paradigm had different outcomes in very diverse national contexts as the adoption of this general recipe was conditioned by how it was filtered domestically.

Ideally, to study Nicaragua's social spending, time-series data would be needed to allow us to compare the 1990s with the 1980s. However, in 1990,

Figure 1. *Public Social Spending as percentage of GDP, 1990–2006*

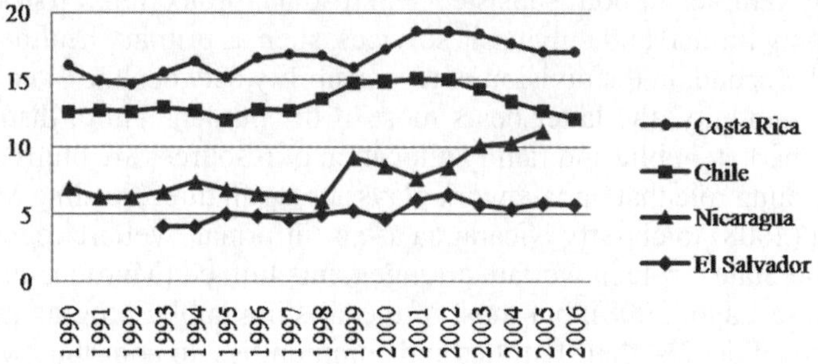

Source: ECLAC (2007b).

Nicaragua was emerging from a devastating and asymmetric war against the United States, which means that the data for the 1980s is patchy and unreliable. For this analysis we therefore use data sets that begin in 1990. In general, when we make claims based on available data, it should be borne in mind that the statistical base line is 1990, that is, the year in which the Contra war ended and the neoliberal administration took over from the Sandinistas.

In the period 1990 to 2005, under post-war rebuilding and democratization, public social expenditure increased from 6.9 to 11.2 per cent of GDP, with the increase becoming sharper in 1998. More specifically, expenditure dropped during the first half of the 1990s (under the Barrios de Chamorro government), remained constant during the second half of the decade (the Alemán government), and then increased again in 2001 (with the Bolaños government) when Nicaragua joined the debt forgiveness initiative for Highly Indebted Poor Countries (HIPC) and received support to cope with the devastating effects of Hurricane Mitch. As a percentage of GDP, Nicaragua's entire investment in social policy is comparable to what Costa Rica spends on one specific sector alone (e.g. education). While in terms of social spending as a percentage of GDP Nicaragua performs better than certain other countries in the region, like El Salvador (see Figure 1), because Nicaragua's GDP is so small, social spending in absolute terms is the lowest of all Central American countries.

Nicaragua's educational spending, for example, is among the lowest in Latin America. The gap between Nicaragua and countries with State welfare regimes is enormous; Costa Rica spent US$ 250 per capita on education in 2006, compared to Nicaragua's US$ 45 per capita. But even compared with El Salvador, another country with an exclusionary social policy regime, the gap is significant: in the same year, El Salvador's per capita spending on education (US$ 79) was considerably higher than that of Nicaragua (ECLAC, 2009).

Overall, Nicaragua's annual per capita social spending more than doubled between 1990 and 2005, from US$ 45 to US$ 95 (see Figure 2). Priority has

Figure 2. *Nicaragua: Evolution of per capital Public Social Spending*
(in 2000 dollars), 1990–2006

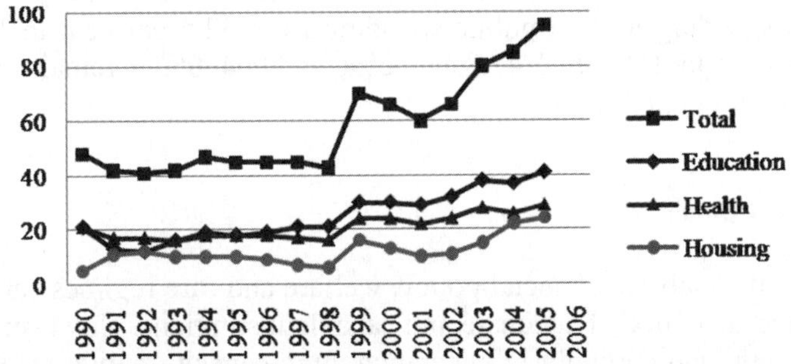

Source: ECLAC (2007b).

been given to education and health, which were allocated similar levels of funding, while housing has traditionally received less. The lack of data on social security is not a coincidence; it reflects the persistent lack of social protection for risks such as old age, disability and death, despite the current pay-as-you-go pension system.[5] The marginal role of the State in social provisioning becomes clear if we compare public social expenditure per person with the contributions of the family and international cooperation. For example, in 2005, remittances made up 6.1 per cent of GDP, which translated into a per capita average of US$ 95 and US$ 52 *per month* in urban and rural areas respectively (Proyecto Estado de la Región, 2008). These remittances are, of course, not all spent on social services, but according to the Proyecto Estado de la Región (2008), almost half is spent on medicine, housing and education. Similarly, close to US$ 132 per capita came into the country in the form of foreign direct assistance in 2006 (World Bank, 2008b). When these figures are placed alongside those on public social expenditure they show the relatively small role played by the State in sustaining livelihoods compared to the much larger contribution of family networks and international cooperation.

In terms of public per capita social spending on health, there has been considerable stagnation, with only a slight increase in 2005 (US$ 29) over 1990 (US$ 21). The biggest changes have occurred in education and housing expenditure, which increased by US$ 20 and US$ 19 per capita, respectively. These trends in per capita social spending are important to keep in mind

---

5. Those who contribute to the pension plan are given the option, although they are not automatically obliged, to contribute to health insurance, but only when there are social security healthcare services available in the area where they live. Thus, some individuals have relatively comprehensive coverage for disability, old age, life and occupational risk, as well as healthcare, while others have only limited coverage (Rodríguez, 2005). There was an attempt to replace the pay-as-you-go regime by an individual capitalization regime, and legislation was passed to that effect, but it was never enforced.

when assessing the effectiveness of the large number of public social programmes described in the following section. Despite overall increases in social expenditure between 1990 and 2005, and a rise in the percentage of social spending in total public spending from 32.5 per cent in 1990 to 40.2 per cent in 1994 and 41.8 per cent in 2004–05, it remains low in comparative regional terms.

Institutional Changes

In the North, analyses of social policy, welfare and care regimes can safely assume the existence of adequate and capable institutions. However, in the global South, and certainly in Nicaragua, high-capacity public institutions for the implementation of social policies are often lacking. In Nicaragua, the period under review was rife with insecurity, instability and change. The ability of the State to implement proposals was repeatedly undermined by the lack of organizational, technical and financial capabilities (Medellín Torres, 2004). In addition, the precarious nature and instability of institutions was exacerbated by the demands of external actors involved in shaping social policy, which often came in the form of conditionalities attached to funding.

During the 1980s, the Sandinista government had created the Ministry of Social Welfare which was in charge of implementing social policies and programmes during the revolution. The Ministry, however, lacked financial sustainability and in 1983 its functions were transferred to the Social Security Institute, which then became the Nicaraguan Institute of Social Security and Welfare (INSSBI) (Largaespada-Fredersdorff, 2006a). With the advent of peace, the government faced demands for land, work, food and housing, especially from former combatants from both sides of the conflict (Sandinistas and Contra forces).[6] In order to successfully demobilize these groups, a response to their demands was prioritized in the political agenda. In 1993, the government launched the so-called 'Social Agenda', which included universal education and healthcare services, along with targeted measures to reach vulnerable groups such as war veterans and, very specifically, orphan children who were malnourished and poor.

Both the new administration and the Sandinista opposition considered community involvement — inherited from the 1980s — to be part and

---

6. In contrast to the El Salvadoran and Guatemalan civil wars, Nicaragua's war did not end with a negotiated settlement but with an election that was won by the political party that was supported by the armed opposition. The Chamorro government therefore had no formal obligations to militants on either side to ensure demobilization. By 1992, conditions were so bad that many of the Contras had rearmed themselves. However, the government was able to appease the Contras primarily through land distribution and weapons repurchase (Armony, 1997).

parcel of all social policy, albeit for different reasons. For the Barrios administration, the priority of the Social Agenda was decentralization which implied rapid and radical institutional reforms in the education and health sectors. Given the financial constraints and the public sector retrenchment which were conditions of structural adjustment loans from the International Monetary Fund, community involvement was seen as vital. For the Sandinistas, on the other hand, community involvement had a far more political character and was driven by the legacies of the revolution which required 'mobilization from below'. Several accounts show the importance of participation in the Sandinista concept of democracy; the bottom-up involvement and participation of community members in the collective allocation of resources was central to their policies (Hoyt, 1997; Luciak, 1995; Molyneux, 1985, Prevost, 2000; Serra, 1993). Hoyt (1997: 3) argues that 'the major contribution of the Sandinista revolution for Latin America was to bring together in practice and in theory representative, participatory, and economic aspects of democracy'. Brown (2003) describes the same three pillars: representative democracy (i.e. the popular election of governments); participatory or 'mass' democracy (i.e. a substantial citizen participation in the regime's activities); and economic democracy (i.e. a more equitable distribution of the means of production and wealth).

Of most relevance for this paper is participatory democracy, which entailed establishing 'popular institutions that would build democracy from below through the construction of neighbourhood, gender, or functional grass roots, mass organizations. These new organizations were to be the primary mechanism for popular empowerment' (Prevost, 2000: 279). On the one hand, these policy measures had positive effects on childcare, family health, housing and food provision, which 'not surprisingly elicited a positive response from the women affected by them' (Molyneux, 1985: 249). On the other hand, the time demands of this participation of women in politics and social programmes often created tensions with the demands of providing for their families (Chinchilla, 1990).

The gains in women's participation in political activity occurred in the context of a very traditional, male-dominated society (Molyneux, 1985; Prevost, 2000) — a traditionalism that reached the inner circles of Sandinista government officials. In addition, the strong influence of the Catholic Church proved a sizeable limitation to reforms that improved women's position in the family and political and economic life (Molyneux, 1985; Prevost, 2000). The conservative wing of the Catholic Church was indeed a 'formidable opponent' because of its 'extensive institutional presence, forms of organization, access to the media, and base within a substantial section of the population' (Molyneux, 1985: 243). While many consider that the Sandinistas' promise of emancipation was never delivered (Molyneux, 1985), by 1990 'women had indeed emerged . . . as much greater players in Nicaraguan society than ever before' (Prevost, 2000: 284).

Kampwirth (1997) shows how, in Nicaragua after 1990, changes in social policies promoted by neoliberal governments largely depended on the political convictions held by the heads of specific social ministries, and whether they decided to fight for (as in the case of the Ministry of Health) or abandon (as in the Ministry of Social Welfare) 'the gains of the Sandinistas in the context of now tighter budgets' (Brown, 2003: 111, review of Kampwirth, 1997).[7] While some programmes and institutions were eliminated, the neoliberal governments generally avoided making major changes in popular and effective social programmes (Kampwirth, 1997). This in practice meant that social policy continued to be heavily influenced by Catholic values, and that within many social programmes community participation and 'voluntary' work remained a central pillar — albeit motivated by a concern with cost efficiency and public sector retrenchment rather than any interest in promoting political participation.

During the Alemán government (1997–2002), social policy reflected the technocratic adoption of social investment ideas (Jenson, 2008) prevalent in the region. Through direct 'social investment' for the development of 'human capital', social policy aimed to eradicate extreme poverty as quickly as possible, and to efficiently and equitably increase the coverage and quality of public services. The new priorities did not necessarily entail interrupting previous programmes, although several new ones were put in place. Community participation was officially established as a matter of public policy; the government was to enable the rights and duties of the population while civil society was to have a larger role in managing, funding and implementing social policy. In addition, the government banned any collaboration between Sandinista organizations and State institutions, in particular in the health sector — although the ban was quickly rescinded with the threat of a dengue epidemic and the devastation of Hurricane Mitch, when all available help was needed.

Again reflective of the government's responsiveness to international forces and norms, in 1998, Nicaragua sanctioned the Code of Children's Rights and Obligations (Asamblea Nacional de la República de Nicaragua, 1997), which conceived of children as full right-bearers, and defined the respective obligations of the State, the family and the community towards them.[8] Similarly, in 1999 the government established the Ministry of the Family (MIFAMILIA), although it left no doubt that its adoption of some elements of the global

---

7. For instance, 'the minister of social welfare Simeón Rizo, who saw social welfare as a tool of a "totalitarian" welfare state, eliminated his ministry entirely and replaced it with an agency designed to channel funds only to NGOs that worked with children. In contrast, the Health Ministry incorporated the views of many FSLN community health workers, avoided mass or ideologically motivated layoffs, received input from former [Sandinista] health ministers . . . , and generally avoided making major changes in Nicaragua's most popular and effective social service ministry' (Brown, 2003: 111).
8. The Code seemed to be responding directly to the 1989 International Convention on the Rights of the Child.

agenda for gender equality was not going to upset its broader commitment to the heterosexual family as the unit of reproduction, giving 'greater importance to the nucleus of the family, the husband and wife, both basic elements in the education of the children' (Max Padilla quoted in Ramírez González, n.d.).

In 2001, the Enhanced Economic Growth and Poverty Reduction Strategy (Estrategia Reforzada de Crecimiento Económico y Reducción de Pobreza, or ERCERP), provided yet another framework for social policy, under the HIPC initiative. This framework rested on four pillars: economic growth with job creation through expanded production and support to rural areas (and the agricultural sector); social investment based on a human development approach; social protection of the most vulnerable population; and good governance and institutional strengthening. A review of this programme in 2003 led to a longer-term strategy with the National Development Plan announced by the Bolaños administration (2002–2007). For the first time, Nicaraguan social policy formally had a long-term vision (up to 2050), including medium-term goals and estimated costs. During this administration, the contribution of voluntary health personnel was officially recognized through the payment of stipends (a cash payment intended to cover the commuting expenses of the volunteer to the worksite) or other perks (like T-shirts and caps), mainly provided by non-governmental organizations.

In short, Nicaraguan levels of public social spending remain very low and clearly inadequate to address the country's pressing social needs. Despite some increase in levels of public expenditure allocated to the social sectors, the government has not been able to meet the high levels of demand for education, access to safe drinking water, electricity and social services. That said, the country has made progress in reshaping and expanding the remit of public policy, albeit under a clearly different policy paradigm than the one promoted by the Sandinista revolution. This progress is reflected, for example, in the considerable expansion in both the coverage of primary education and the proportion of children completing primary school. At the same time, in the period under review, the expansion of the State's social services has been very dependent on family participation. This participation, as we have shown, was neither new nor unique to the neoliberal policies of the time: participation had been central during the Sandinista era when community involvement 'from below' was widely promoted as a central feature of democratic state–society relations.

Molyneux (1988) shows that in Nicaragua, the Sandinistas' rise to power initiated a period during which considerable efforts were made:

> to promote improvements in women's socio-economic position: women have seen an extension of their rights within the family and in the workplace through legal reform; they have been more involved in the political life of the country than ever before; and they have been encouraged to participate in the defence and development efforts, entering various kinds of economic activity in large numbers. (Molyneux, 1988: 116)

Indeed, on Women's Day 1987, the Sandinistas made their 'first program-matic statement on the situation of women' (Chinchilla, 1990: 370) which represented a 'historic commitment the FSLN made to combating discrimi-nation against women' (ibid.: 371). While women experienced some degree of empowerment as the Sandinistas embraced selected elements of the fem-inist agenda, for example their focus on women's 'double shift' and the need for women's self-organization, they also tried to maintain cordial rela-tions with those in their alliance who advocated a more traditional position on women and the family. This was reflected in the Sandinista silence on the contested questions of birth control, sex education and abortion, and in the statement that 'the family is the basic unit of society and guarantees social reproduction not only from the biological point of view, but also of the principles and values of society' (FSLN, 1987 cited in Chinchilla, 1990: 371).

The Sandinista silence, however, was much more benign for gender equal-ity than the fierce 're-traditionalization' of women's roles pursued by the neoliberal governments in the 1990s (Mann, 2005). These governments 'continued to shore up the turn towards conservative familialism in policies of reproduction and sexuality . . . and began to roll back the more progres-sive measures by dismantling the INIM [National Institute for Nicaraguan Women] and further integrating Christianity into state policies' (ibid.: 27). More specifically, the Catholic Church, 'the oldest and most influential ethi-cal tradition in the Latin American region' which 'provides a basic script for men's and women's proper roles, the function and nature of marriage and the family, and the significance of reproduction' (Htun, 2003: 30–31) justifies the nuclear family based on a strict and allegedly traditional sexual division of labour. This has been the argument behind state reforms pursued since 1990: to explicitly revitalize the traditional nuclear family. However, this nuclear family has never been a major part of reality for most Nicaraguans, among whom it is commonplace that people live together without getting married, that women have children with more than one man and outside of wedlock, and that a large proportion of families are headed by women (Chávez Metoyer, 1999).

The policies towards the family of the neoliberal, but at the same time Catholic, governments of the 1990s reflected conservative views of the family and of women in their role as care givers. This was evident in the establishment of the Ministry of the Family as an umbrella agency for chil-dren and women's affairs. Feeney (1997: 1) describes how '[t]he right wing in Nicaragua, particularly an especially conservative brand of Catholicism' pushed for the establishment of this Ministry. The women's movement voiced concerns about the traditional definition of the family and the role of women which the Ministry adopted, 'describing women's role in the family in a very limited fashion, based on conservative traditions not necessarily relevant to some women's lives' (ibid.). Not surprisingly, this conservative view of the family has been reflected directly in the policies formulated by the Ministry of the Family, as well as other ministries, that together have shaped the institutional framework for care, to which we now turn.

NICARAGUA'S CARE REGIME

In this section we describe the institutional blueprint for childcare, focusing on primary education, pre-school education and care programmes, and other aspects of Nicaragua's care regime, such as the conditional cash transfer programme. It is important to note that these programmes rank second to unpaid care mediated through household and family relations, which constitutes the most significant component of care giving in Nicaragua. Despite methodological difficulties in capturing this work, the first section provides a brief insight into unpaid care arrangements, using data from the time use section of the 1998 National Standard of Living Survey; this is followed by an analysis of the institutional care framework.

Unpaid Care Work

It should come as no surprise that women have much higher participation rates in, and devote much more time to, unpaid care activities than men. These gender gaps exist in both urban and rural areas, but time use data suggest that rural women devote relatively more time to such work, given the larger size of rural households and the fewer amenities and services available, like clean water and electricity (Espinosa, 2009). Moreover, in line with general trends in most other countries, Nicaraguan women, particularly urban ones, have increasingly entered the labour market, while assuming a disproportionate share of unpaid care work. It is noteworthy that men tend to do a relatively larger amount of unpaid care work when they are older and retire or do fewer hours of paid work, whereas women assume a relatively larger amount of unpaid care work when they are at the peak of their labour capacity. Hence, the gender gaps in unpaid work are larger during the reproductive years and in families with young children: 'The presence of children under 6 in the household leads to a reinforcement or resumption of traditional gender roles, as women reduce their participation in paid work to devote more time to unpaid care work, whereas men do the opposite' (ibid.: 18).

Using multivariate analysis and an econometric model based on time use data, Espinosa estimates that 'women account for approximately 79 per cent of the value of unpaid care work and 87 per cent of the value of care of persons' (ibid.: 24), and, using the same model, that the value of unpaid care work is equivalent to about 31 per cent of Nicaragua's GDP. Despite the central importance of unpaid care work, especially by women, in Nicaragua's care regime, it is also important to understand formal arrangements through state policy, if care is ever to be taken out of the private realm and into the public (Hernes, 1987).

The Institutional Care Framework

Primary and Secondary Education

Primary and secondary education services were expanded in 1990 with increases in public spending. Primary education coverage increased from around 73 per cent for the period 1985–90 to 90 per cent in 2006; enrolment in secondary schools rose from 18 per cent in 1985 to 43 per cent in 2006 (ECLAC, 2007a). An important aspect of Nicaragua's formal education system is that, in addition to external loans, many resources are supplied by the unpaid work of families, such as in school management and food preparation. Family participation in the implementation of public educational programmes has been a constant factor over the last couple of decades. In terms of school management, Nicaragua underwent one of the most radical decentralization reforms in Latin America during this period, allegedly based on the Chilean model:

> Its autonomous schools programme implements a system of school-based management with local school-site councils that have a voting majority of parents and allocate resources that are derived in part from fees charged to parents. Nowhere in Latin America have parents officially been given so much responsibility, and nowhere have they been asked to directly provide such a large proportion of school resources. (Gershberg, 1999: 8)

Indeed, in the context of acute budgetary constraints, the government decreased the State's involvement in 1992 and promoted the educational model entitled 'Self Help' (Ministry of Education, 1990), following Latin American regional trends of reducing the size and functions of the State. Administration was decentralized to the schools, and the central government assumed 'facilitation' tasks, such as regulating the schools' operation, defining the basic programme content, and establishing quality standards for the selection of material, qualifying teachers and school infrastructure.

However, according to the authorities at the time, the Chilean-inspired reforms were impulsive and lacked external resources during the first two years.[9] As a result, existing resources needed to be more efficiently utilized, and community input into the maintenance and improvement of facilities needed to be increased. Autonomous schools were free to solicit 'voluntary' contributions from parents and to carry out fundraising activities.[10] Resource constraints were thereby addressed and solutions that encouraged shared responsibility among various stakeholders linked to each school, notably the families, were explored. Among the positive outcomes were greater

---

9. Interview with Humberto Belli, Education Minister during the Chamorro Administration and the first half of the Alemán administration. Interview by Carmen Largaespada, Managua (28 April 2008).
10. The possibility of asking for voluntary contributions, which were in fact co-payments, was abandoned soon after (at least on paper), as they excluded the lower-income population.

involvement and more responsibility on the part of parents. On the more negative side, however, was the considerable amount of time that teachers and parents, mostly mothers, had to devote to fundraising aimed at improving school conditions and staff wages. Compared to the majority of countries which have school systems in which parents are expected to participate not as volunteers, but only as beneficiaries, parents' involvement with school management activities is much higher in Nicaragua (Greenwood and Hickman, 1991).

Another weakness of school autonomy was the absence of timely and adequate supervision, as well as effective mechanisms to verify information and reports provided by the autonomous centres. The high degree of autonomy that the schools were given, together with their dependence on transfers received from the central government, and the economic and social constraints faced by the education sector in general, led to questionable practices. For example, autonomous centres were known to alter records, reporting an inflated number of enrolments in order to obtain more transfers from the government.[11] Decentralization and school autonomy also had major implications for teacher–school labour relations. Rather than being part of the national payroll, teachers were hired by a decentralized, parent-run commission, with 'full hiring and firing power'.[12] This new recruitment method led to tensions with the unions and the Sandinista opposition, whose support bases were unionized workers.

Childcare Programmes

Since the 1980s, various pre-school programmes have been implemented to cater for children between three and five years of age. The 1980s also saw the creation of the flagship care programme of the Sandinista period, Children's Development Centres (CDIs, to use their Spanish acronym), which accommodated children from birth up to five years of age. The pre-school programmes and the CDIs share a similar history: they were created and expanded during the revolutionary period, with a significant role for direct family and community involvement in service delivery.[13] In most cases, the force behind family and community participation came, and continues to come, from women. Puar (1996: 80) argues that 'along with their roles as reproducers, Nicaraguan women must cope with two additional duties:

---

11. Interview with Elisabeth Espinosa, the General Director of Security and Evaluation of the Social Sector in the Secretary of Social Action in the Alemán Administration. During the Bolaños administration she was an expert on social protection in the Technical Secretary of the Presidency. Interview by Carmen Largaespada, Managua (26 April 2008).
12. Interview with Elisabeth Espinosa (see footnote 11).
13. Interview with Juan José Morales, former director of National Pre-school Education from the second half of the 1990s until March 2008. Interview by Carmen Largaespada, Managua (24 April 2008).

Table 1. *Coverage of Care Centres among Children below Six Years of Age by Type of Centre and Year (absolute numbers and percentages)*

Care centre	1998		2001		2005	
	Children	%	Children	%	Children	%
Infant care (CDIs)	6,926	1%	7,075	1%	5,010	1%
Children's lunchrooms	...	...	10,746	1%	17,206	3%
Pre-school	128,205	16%	128,875	17%	116,028	18%
Primary school	16,723	2%	20,456	3%	5,585	1%
Do not attend	635,521	81%	595,628	78%	509,958	78%
Not accounted for	...	...	213	0%	89	0%
Total	**787,374**	**100%**	**762,993**	**100%**	**653,875**	**100%**

those of producer and of community manager', the latter being seen as a natural extension of their domestic duties. Montaño (2003) argues that this female participation is especially important in initiatives fighting poverty. The concept of 'feminization' has special significance in the Latin American context in general, and in Nicaragua in particular, where women are over-represented in the fight against poverty. Referring to Nicaragua as one of the countries that illustrates her point, Montaño argues that 'there are countless programmes executed by the government, NGOs and development agencies, in which female presence is crucial' (ibid.: 363, own translation).

As such, care programmes combine both formal and informal modes of care. The CDIs were created by the Sandinista government as part of the social security system, rather than under social assistance,[14] and served as many as 37,000 children. But with the change of government in 1990, the number of CDIs declined considerably (exactly how much is unclear because of lack of data), and with it the number of children they served (see Table 1). Although pre-school coverage increased and diversified in the 1990s with the participation of civil society organizations as new actors alongside parents and communities, Table 1 shows that their relative importance in coverage did not vary much over the period 1998–2005. The pre-school, CDI and primary school coverage of children under six stayed relatively constant in that period, at around 17 per cent, 1 per cent and 2 per cent, respectively.

Table 2 gives an overview of the CDIs and all the pre-school programmes. The neoliberal period saw the creation of several different programmes. The Day-care Centres Programme, created in 1993 for children under six years of age, offered early childhood stimulation, pre-school education and food prepared by female volunteers from the community. The programme also provided supplementary education and healthcare activities. In 1994, nearly 90,000 children were reportedly being served by these Day-care

---

14. Ten years later, child and adolescent care was separated from social security because of a change in the conception of the government's responsibilities for people's well-being.

Table 2. Overview of the Pre-school Programmes and the CDI Programme Implemented in Nicaragua

Period	Programme	Year	Responsible Agency	Objective
Sandinista	National Action Plan of the Main Project from Primary Education 1983–1986	1980s	Ministry of Education	Provide pre-school education for children between 0 and 6 years old.
	Children's Development Centres (CDIs)	1980s	Social Security and Welfare Institute	Provide care and education for children from birth until 5 years of age
Neoliberal	Non-School Pre-school Education Centres (CEPNE)	1980s	Social and community organization that remained after the National Literacy Crusade of 1980, with Van Leer Foundation and the Ministry of Education	Assistance to educators, improvement of educational infrastructure, with donations of food and furniture etc.
	Day-care Centres	1993	Nicaraguan Fund for Children and Youth	Early childhood stimulation, pre-school education, and food
	Learn Project	1995	Government (Ministry of Education) with a loan from the World Bank	Technical assistance, supply of materials and financial support to educators in formal and community pre-schools.
	Programme of Comprehensive Care for Nicaraguan Children (PAININ)	1996	Nicaraguan Fund for Children and Families (FONIF – later the Ministry of Family) with technical assistance from the IDB.	Continuation of Learn Project, assumed the recruitment of educators for community pre-schools

Source: authors' own elaboration.

Centres — more than double the number served by the CDIs. In the mid-1990s, the Programme of Comprehensive Care for Nicaraguan Children (PAININ) was launched as an adaptation of the Learn Project of 1995. It aimed to look after poor children under six years of age in rural and marginal urban areas. Although it did not impact on the rates of coverage at the national level, the programme served nearly 100,000 children between 2002 and 2005, which meant that approximately 30 per cent of children in vulnerable conditions[15] in the sixty-seven priority municipalities were covered.

These programmes share several features that we will show to be characteristic of the Nicaraguan care regime. First, while there seems to be more continuity in the CDI programmes as compared to pre-school programmes, both share a heavy reliance on unpaid family and especially female work, albeit for different reasons. The Sandinistas' CDIs, at least at their inception, used to rely on community involvement to preserve their revolutionary ideals. The CDIs have changed considerably since the 1980s, and one could argue that the concept 'revolutionary' no longer resonates in the current, largely neoliberal setting. That said, the CDIs nevertheless continue to carry a largely symbolic meaning for the beneficiary population and the larger public.[16] The programmes of the 1990s, on the other hand, included family involvement as a means of cutting programme costs.

A good example of this is the PAININ programme, in which the demand for volunteer work of parents has been formalized in public policy plans. While assessments of this programme have been mostly positive in terms of its impacts on child health and development, evaluations also document the vital role of families and communities in its success: providing support networks and eliciting community and 'volunteer' work have been key in building infrastructure[17] and providing food. Given the low levels of public accountability in the field of social policy, such 'participation' seems to be indicative of the exploitation of existing forms of familialism and the further feminization of the care and welfare systems, rather than reflecting the effective realization of citizen participation. Although the costs of social programmes are reduced considerably, it is highly questionable whether this volunteer support is appropriate in a context where families, especially women, already face multiple demands on their time in the form of wage earning, care -giving and voluntary work in other State social programmes.

---

15. Defined in terms of exposure to malnutrition and inadequate schooling due to a lack of (pre-school) services.
16. This was made evident in the four focus groups we conducted in the capital city of Managua and in Estelí as part of our research. Although the CDIs currently reach only about 1 per cent of children under six years of age, most of our informants pointed to them as a successful and relevant component of Nicaraguan public care policy.
17. This includes the construction of wells and latrines, remodelling of buildings, provision of land, and contributions of construction labour and materials.

Second, these programmes have also been very dependent on external sources of funding from international organizations and/or NGOs and are, partly because of this, characterized by high levels of discontinuity. International agencies and NGOs typically work on a short- or medium-term project basis, and therefore their agendas will only partially coincide with those of the government. This in itself is not a problem, but when government programmes are dependent on NGO funding and their agendas, it may lead to discontinuity in implementation and inconsistencies across programmes, as happened in Nicaragua, especially in the 1990s. This could help explain why public perceptions regarding CDIs are more positive than perceptions concerning current programmes such as PAININ, despite the fact that the latter provide higher coverage.

Care Practices in Other Programmes

The fact that these features are not limited to childcare programmes can be demonstrated by examining school food programmes, healthcare services and conditional cash transfer programmes. All three are very important for care and all are highly dependent on family and community participation.

First, school food programmes help families with a basic need: as part of their survival strategy, low-income families often reduce food consumption, which in turn increases the risk of malnutrition. When food is provided by the school or care centre, part of the family's basic needs is (temporarily) provided for and school enrolment rates can also increase (Chacón, 2005). All food programmes implemented in Nicaragua since the 1980s were aimed at reducing the risk of malnutrition, improving (poor) children's diets and increasing school attendance. The most important programme during the Sandinista period was the Community Kitchens for Children (which ceased operation during the Bolaños administration), while the neoliberal period saw several different programmes, including the School Glass of Milk Programme (1992 to the late 1990s, and resumed in 2003) and the School Biscuits Programme (started in 1994).

Similar to the pre-school programmes, most of the school food programmes have been highly dependent on external sources of funding. As in other Latin American countries, a Social Investment Fund, FISE, was created in 1994 with USAID as its principal donor, and with partial funding from the Inter American Development Bank (IADB). Its purpose was to fund development and other programmes and projects to cushion the social effects of structural adjustment policies. Specifically, it responded to 'the necessity to create a programme of public investment that generates new jobs and restores the national infrastructure at the end of the war' (Envío, 1990). The FISE was extended in 1999, and Ortega's Sandinista government maintained the fund under the name 'the new FISE'.

This dependency of programmes on external sources of funding has, on occasion, led to conflicting interests. For example, the 1995 programme, the Construction and Operational Sustainability of Lunchrooms, funded under FISE, aimed at providing all community pre-schools with food and all children's lunchrooms with pre-school education. Under this programme, lunchrooms were created within community pre-schools. As a result, many parents withdrew their children from formal pre-schools and enrolled them in community pre-schools which were able to provide food. Furthermore, as with the pre-school and childcare programmes, these programmes too show a high level of reliance on voluntary work, often by the mothers of the targeted children.

While the healthcare sector has not institutionalized community and family participation to the extent that the CDIs, pre-school and food programmes have, family co-payments nevertheless play an important part in financing the low-coverage and low-quality healthcare services that are offered. Health services in Nicaragua are characterized by a high degree of stratification between the private sector, public services, services provided by social security, and community services.[18] In theory private sector care is mainly financed through 'out-of-pocket' payments, public services through the national budget, social security services through contributions, and community services through a combination of external resources and volunteer work. However, in practice, the distinctions are not always clear: families contribute half of the total annual expenditure on healthcare out-of-pocket, and co-payments (either as doctors' fees or for the purchase of medicines or laboratory exams) are common when accessing health services, even for public and social security services (Rodríguez, 2005).

Finally, in Nicaragua's conditional cash transfer programme, the Social Protection Network (RPS), family participation was again crucial. In 1999, Nicaragua adopted the conditional cash transfer (CCT) approach that was strongly promoted in the region by the World Bank. Its programme — 'exemplary but short-lived' (Moore, 2009) — was implemented during two consecutive government administrations, Alemán (1997–2002) and Bolaños (2002–2006) but discontinued thereafter. It provided cash transfers to households in extreme poverty.[19] Similar to other countries in the region, transfers were conditional; in this case, they were conditional on school attendance of children under twelve years of age, and on children under three years of age undergoing health checks (growth monitoring, weight and development).

---

18. There is no information on those covered by private insurers and HMOs (health maintenance organizations), though we know these represent a small proportion of the total (Rodríguez, 2005).
19. The idea of implementing direct transfers had existed since 1997, although at that time they were meant for poor farmers in order to capitalize on their assets (Largaespada-Fredersdorff, 2006a).

Although the RPS has received positive evaluations in terms of its impact on children's access to education and health services,[20] its scope was nevertheless limited and it failed to secure adequate public investment for strengthening public services (in health and education, but especially in care services). It also became clear that the RPS was built on the same principle of family participation that pervades other social programmes. A report by IFPRI (2001) captures this idea in its title, 'My Family Breaking the Poverty Cycle' (IFPRI, 2001, own translation), and it becomes particularly clear when looking at the evaluations in terms of gender relations. There is some consensus in the literature that the fact that the cash transfer is made directly to women can have some positive effects in terms of women's self-esteem and economic autonomy. However, evaluations do not agree on the effect the conditional cash transfer can have on gender equality. First, there is the concern that the RPS perpetuated traditional gender roles by reinforcing women's role as the natural 'carers' while excluding men from such activities (Bradshaw and Quirós Viquez, 2008; Fredersdoff-Largaespada, 2006b). Second, there is the argument that transfers which go to women do not necessarily lead to increases in their control over household resources, given the skewed power relations between the recipient women and the *promotoras* of the programme. These *promotoras* guided the women 'at all stages of the programme, including accompanying women to receive their cash transfer' (Bradshaw and Quirós Viquez, 2008: 838), in many cases even monitoring purchases. Bradshaw and Quirós Viquez argue that '[t]he role of the *Promotoras* in the RPS casts some doubt on the autonomy of the women in the programme' (ibid.). Finally, the transfers are said to increase women's workloads because of the conditionalities that come with the CCT programme (Regalia and Castro, 2007). However, while the programme did perpetuate a vision of full-time mother/carer, the reality is that a significant proportion of households in Nicaragua are headed by women and lack a permanent male presence, and for many, therefore, there is no immediate alternative to combining care giving with primary breadwinning.

Our analysis of Nicaragua's care regime shows that the role of the State in care is very small as compared to the role played by highly familialized arrangements. First, social provisions for care by the State are lacking, and given Nicaraguans' generally low capacity to commodify care, the family remains central in care arrangements. Second, the different social programmes that do exist depend heavily on family and community participation and, third, these cut across all social programmes directly or indirectly related to care, perhaps even in the healthcare sector. On more than one occasion, this reliance on 'family and community participation' has even been formalized

---

20. The RPS programme is probably one of the most extensively evaluated programmes in the history of Nicaragua. Evaluations have included quasi-experimental studies. One of the most cited studies was funded by the World Bank and conducted by IFPRI and academics from various universities (Maluccio and Flores, 2005).

in official programme designs, as in the case of PAININ in the mid-1990s, or more recently in the country's CCT programme. Fourth, as discussed above, when the neoliberal governments started implementing their policies in the 1990s, the care programmes' high dependence on families and communities was not a new feature. What was substantially different was the motivation for community involvement during the neoliberal administrations as compared to the Sandinista revolution. In the revolutionary era, individuals and families were expected to participate in social care programmes as a means of upholding the revolutionary legacy, through bottom-up involvement and community participation. In practice, this implied a high degree of feminization and familialization of care, and low effective degrees of decommodification through State programmes. In the later period, care programmes continued to depend heavily on unpaid (mostly female) work, but this participation was more clearly motivated by fiscal constraints in the context of structural adjustment policies.

Finally, the care programmes share a high level of discontinuity, in part due to their dependence on external sources of funding. This is especially true in the case of the neoliberal period, when the already weak presence of the State came under pressure through policies that promoted decentralization and the targeting of services. In relative terms the Sandinistas' CDIs have done better in this sense, which may also help explain their popularity among Nicaraguans, despite the fact that later programmes have achieved higher levels of coverage.

SO WHO CARES?

Since the 1990s, neoliberal governments have promoted social programmes under an exclusionary vision of targeted social policy: economic growth would automatically lead to more equal distribution. Decentralization was the main policy mechanism, which in turn underlined the role of the family (especially mothers), participation and community organizations (such as school boards). It also decreased the number of State employees and weakened their capabilities, creating a high degree of job instability among social service workers, especially among women working in jobs associated with care (such as nurses, teachers and cooks). Social policy was mainly organized through projects (rather than specific policies) each with distinct objectives and implementation cycles and principally funded through private loans from multilateral banks and donations. This mode of organization led to instability and discontinuity, lack of coordination and duplication of activities and initiatives.

However, our study has shown that in Nicaragua the central role of community involvement in social policy preceded economic liberalization. Of course, the down-sizing of government promoted by structural adjustment policies has not been favourable to the burden of responsibility that

Nicaraguan women have had to carry. But this burden is also explained by other, more structural factors. First, Nicaragua is characterized by a heavy long-term reliance on solidarity as a means of confronting crises, coupled with social endorsement of community interventions in care, in particular among households and communities with meagre economic resources. Second, the appeal of the Sandinista opposition to govern 'from below' and to defend the revolutionary achievements strongly endorses community involvement. Third, even when political parties disagreed with community participation they supported it when faced with epidemics or natural disasters, both of which were prevalent in the country during this period.

Nicaragua is thus one of many countries in which 'social services have come to rely heavily on "voluntary" or "community" work — very often a short-hand for unpaid or underpaid work' (Razavi and Staab, 2010: 10). In much the same way as conditional cash transfers — the current star programmes of social policy — 'voluntary' work could be considered a conditionality for accessing the benefits of the social programmes. Of course, this 'voluntarism' is interesting to the government in terms of cost saving, but is questionable in a context of extensive poverty and structurally high unemployment, and places extra demands on the already overburdened women of Nicaragua.

Despite the increasing role of the State after the war, Nicaraguan social policy remains very limited, both in fiscal terms and in its institutional structure. The social policy regime is further weakened by an ineffective State bureaucracy and the high level of dependence on non-governmental organizations and parent associations, which assume some of the strategic functions of the State. In order to mitigate the lack of resources, social policy is supported by external resources (increasingly loans rather than grants) from international organizations, which in turn define often inconsistent priorities that do not support public institutional strengthening. Consequently, the State's social programmes lack resources, are insecure, unstable and offer poor services.

Parent associations, NGOs and other forms of local organization play an important role in compensating for the absence (or weakness) of State policies. The care regime is highly dependent on unpaid, predominantly female work. Mothers, who have often not finished primary school themselves, are managing educational institutions. These same mothers are also expected to generate income, care for their children, and be volunteer cooks or *brigadistas* in the existing care centres. For over three decades, this reliance on women's unpaid work has been a constant feature across all sectors of the care regime, from health and nutrition, to social protection and education. It has remained basically unchanged, despite dramatic swings in political ideology and changes in ruling political parties. The argument often made about Latin American countries with more developed social policy regimes — that structural adjustment policies increased women's unpaid work, particularly related to care — may not be all that appropriate when applied to the Nicaraguan care regime, where female unpaid work constituted one of the main pillars of the care regime long before the neoliberal wave hit the country.

The challenges for policy making are multiple. There is a pressing need to address the high degrees of familialization and, more challenging still, feminization of the care regime. The first is a necessary but not a sufficient condition for the second. Shifting care work out of the family has not, even in the most 'successful' cases, reduced its feminization. Sweden is a good example; there, significant policy measures have been taken to shift care out of the family domain, but public employees in care occupations are still predominantly women and the country has one of the most gender-segmented labour markets in the world (Charles, 1992; Sainsbury, 1996).

In addition, while in countries with formal labour markets commodified care work has been relatively well paid and well protected, this is not often the case in developing countries with considerable informal labour markets. In Nicaragua (as in many other low-income countries), where so much of care work is unpaid and highly feminized, having a strategy for providing some care through public policy could provide some respite to family carers. Up to now, the discontinuities in Nicaragua's social policy and its high levels of dependence on external resources and the agendas of international cooperation have made it extremely difficult to systematically address the needs of women, families and care. One critical question is whether unpaid female work can be turned into paid decent work, even if this work is primarily done by women.[21] For this to happen, it would be necessary to break with the 'traditional' paradigms that guide Nicaraguan social policy, through which women in their role as mothers are naturally held responsible for care. This would also imply challenging the Catholic dogma of the family that has shaped policy, particularly during the neoliberal period. Instead of assuming that women care, social policy should start to care about women.

REFERENCES

Agurto, S. and A. Guido (2001) 'Mujeres: pilares fundamentales de la economía nicaragüense' ['Women: Fundamental Pillars of Nicaragua's Economy']. Managua: FIDEG.

Anheier, H. and L. Salamon (2001) 'Volunteering in Cross-national Perspective: Initial Comparisons'. Civil Society Working Paper 10. London: Centre for Civil Society, London School of Economics.

Ariza, M. and O. de Oliveira (2004) 'Universo familiar y procesos demográficos' ['Family Universe and Demographic Processes'], in M. Ariza and O. de Oliveira *Imágenes de la familia en el cambio de siglo* [*Images of the Family at the Turn of the Century*], pp. 9–45. Mexico: UNAM-IIS.

21. This would also entail a considerable restructuring of labour markets to ensure that the service economy in general, but care services in particular, can play a key role under the productive regime, thereby creating more favourable conditions for women to participate in both.

Armony, A. (1997) 'The Former Contras', in T.W. Walker (ed.) *Nicaragua without Illusions: Regime Transition and Structural Adjustment in the 1990s*, pp. 203–18. Wilmington, DE: Scholarly Resources.

Asamblea Nacional de la República de Nicaragua (1997) 'Ley 290. Ley de organización, competencia y procedimientos del Poder Ejecutivo' ['Law on the Organization, Competencies and Procedures of the Executive Power']. *La Gaceta*, No. 102, 3 June. Managua.

Barahona, M. (2006) 'Familias, hogares, dinámica demográfica, vulnerabilidad y pobreza en Nicaragua' ['Families, Households, Demographic Dynamics and Poverty in Nicaragua']. ECLAC Population and Development series, No. 69. Managua: CELADE/UNFPA.

Benería, L. (1999) 'The Enduring Debate over Unpaid Labour', *International Labour Review* 138(3): 287–309.

Bradshaw, S. and A. Quirós Víquez (2008) 'Women Beneficiaries or Women Bearing the Cost? A Gendered Analysis of the Red de Protección Social in Nicaragua', *Development and Change* 39(5): 823–44.

Brown, D. (2003) 'The Sandinista Legacy in Nicaragua', *Latin American Perspectives* 30(3): 106–12.

Canales, A. (2004) 'Vivir del Norte: Perfil socio-demográfico de los hogares receptores de remesas en una región de alta migración' ['Making a Living of the North: Socio-demographic Profile of Remittances-recipient Homes in a Region of High Migration'] in M. Ariza and O. de Oliveira *Imágenes de la familia en el cambio de siglo* [*Images of the Family at the Turn of the Century*], pp. 321–55. México: UNAM-IIS.

Chacón, J. (2005) 'Merienda escolar garantizada' ['Guaranteed School Snack'], *La Prensa* 29 June. http://www.laprensa.com.ni/archivo/2005/junio/29/nacionales/nacionales-20050629–01.html (accessed 29 November 2008).

Charles, M. (1992) 'Cross-National Variation in Occupational Sex Segregation', *American Sociological Review* 57(4): 483–502.

Chávez Metoyer, C. (1999) *Women and the State in Post-Sandinista Nicaragua*. London: Lynne Rienner.

Chinchilla, N.S. (1990) 'Revolutionary Popular Feminism in Nicaragua: Articulating Class, Gender, and National Sovereignty', *Gender and Society* 4(3) Special Issue: Women and Development in the Third World: 370–97.

Collier, Ruth and David Collier (2002) *Shaping the Political Arena: Critical Junctures, the Labour Movement, and Regimen Dynamics in Latin America*. Notre Dame, IN: University of Notre Dame Press.

ECLAC (2007a) *Social Panorama of Latin America 2007*. Santiago de Chile: ECLAC.

ECLAC (2007b) 'CEPALSTAT'. Online database http://www.eclac.org/estadisticas/ (accessed on various occasions in November and December 2008).

ECLAC (2009) *Social Panorama of Latin America 2009*. Santiago de Chile: ECLAC.

Envío (1990) 'El FISE: la respuesta de AID al desempleo' ['The FISE: AID's Response to Unemployment']. Revista Envío, 116. http://www.envio.org.ni/articulo/674 (accessed 30 June 2010)

Esping-Andersen, G. (1999) *Social Foundations of Postindustrial Economies*. New York: Oxford University Press.

Espinosa, I. (2009) 'The Case of Nicaragua', in Debbie Budlender (ed.) *Time Use Studies and Unpaid Care Work*, pp. 171–96. New York: Routledge/UNRISD Research in Gender and Development.

Feeney, M. (1997) 'Legislating Morality in the "New" Nicaragua'. CEPAD Report. Council of Evangelical Churches of Nicaragua. http://www.geocities.com/CapitolHill/1336/familia.html (accessed 29 September 2009).

Filgueira, F. (1998) 'El nuevo modelo de prestaciones sociales en América Latina: residualismo y ciudadanía estratificada' ['The New Model of Social Provision in Latin America: Residualism and Stratified Citizenship'], in Bryan Roberts (ed.) *Ciudadanía y política social* [*Citizenship and Social Policy*], pp. 71–116. San José, Costa Rica: FLACSO/SSRC.

Fraser, N. (1994) 'After the Family Wage: Gender Equity and the Welfare State', *Political Theory* 22(4): 591–618.

FSLN (1987) 'El FSLN y la mujer en la revolucion popular Sandinista' ['The FSLN and Women in the Sandinista Popular Revolution']. Managua: *Editorial Vanguardia*, 8 March. (Excerpts in English in *The Militant*, 22 May 1987.)

Gershberg, A. (1999) 'Decentralization, Citizen Participation and the Role of the State: The Autonomous School Programme in Nicaragua', *Latin American Perspectives* 26: 8–38.

Greenwood, G. and C. Hickman (1991) 'Research and Practice in Parent Involvement: Implications for Teacher Education', *The Elementary School Journal* 91(3): 279–88. (Special Issue, *Educational Partnerships: Home-School Community*.)

Hernes, H. (1987) 'Women and the Welfare State: The Transition from Private to Public Dependence', in Anne Showstack Sasoon (ed.) *Women and the State*, pp. 72–92. London: Hutchinson.

Hoyt, K. (1997) *The Many Faces of Sandinista Democracy*. Athens, OH: Ohio University Press.

Htun, M. (2003) *Sex and the State. Abortion, Divorce, and the Family Under Latin American Dictatorships and Democracies*. Cambridge: Cambridge University Press.

IDB (2008) 'Nicaragua. IDB Country Strategy with Nicaragua 2008–2012'. Washington, DC: Inter-American Development Bank.

IFPRI (2001) *Red de Protección Social. Mi Familia Rompiendo el Ciclo de Pobreza* [*Social Protection Network: Families Breaking the Cycle of Poverty*]. Washington, DC: International Food Policy Research Institute.

INEC/INIDE (various years) 'Encuesta Nacional de Hogares sobre Medición de Nivel de Vida' ['Survey of the National Standard of Living']. Managua: INEC (now INIDE — Instituto Nacional de Información de Desarrollo).

Jenson, J. (2008) 'Writing Women Out, Folding Gender In: The European Union "Modernises" Social Policy', *Social Politics* 15(2): 131–53.

Kampwirth, K. (1997) 'Social Policy', in T.W. Walker (ed.) *Nicaragua without Illusions: Regime Transition and Structural Adjustment in the 1990s*, pp. 115–30. Wilmington, DE: Scholarly Resources.

Largaespada-Fredersdorff, C. (2006a) 'Nicaragua: Red de Protección Social y Sistema de Atención a Crisis' ['Nicaragua: Social Protection Network and Crisis Support System'], in E. Cohen and R. Franco (eds) *Transferencias con corresponsabilidad. Una mirada latinoamericana* [*Co-responsibility Transfers. A Latin American Perspective*], pp. 321–61. Mexico City: SEDESOL-FLACSO.

Largaespada-Fredersdorff, C. (2006b) 'Igualdad de género, pobreza, políticas de conciliación entre los ámbitos productivo y reproductivo. Un estudio de caso sobre Nicaragua' ['Gender Equality, Poverty, Policies of Productive and Reproductive Work Reconciliation. A Case Study of Nicaragua']. Prepared for the UNFPA-GTZ regional project on Fiscal Policy with a Gender Focus.

Luciak, I. (1995) *The Sandinista Legacy: Lessons from a Political Economy in Transition*. Gainesville, FL: University Press of Florida.

Maluccio, J. and R. Flores (2005) *Impact Evaluation of a Conditional Cash Transfer Program. The Nicaraguan Red de Protección Social*. Research Report 141. Washington, DC: International Food Policy Research Institute.

Mann, E. (2005) 'Familialism in Nicaragua. Reproductive and Sexual Policy Regime, 1979–2002'. Paper prepared for the 2005 meeting of the ISA Research Committee 19, Chicago, Illinois (8–10 September).

Martínez Franzoni, J. (2008) *Domesticar la incertidumbre en América Latina: mercados laborales, política social y familias* [*Domesticating Uncertainty in Latin America: Labour Markets, Social Policy and Families*]. San José: Editorial de la UCR.

Medellín Torres, P. (2004) 'La política de las políticas públicas: propuesta teórica y metodológica para el estudio de las políticas públicas en países de frágil institucionalidad' ['The Politics of

Public Policies: A Theoretical and Methodological Proposal for the Study of Public Policies in Countries with Fragile Institutions']. Working Paper 'Serie Políticas Sociales' No. 93. Santiago de Chile: ECLAC.

Mesa-Lago, C. (2008) *Reassembling Social Security: A Survey of Pensions and Healthcare Reforms in Latin America*. Oxford: Oxford University Press.

Ministry of Education (1990) 'Líneas de Políticas y Medidas Educativas. Plan Operativo MED 1990–1996' ['Policy Guidelines and Educational Measures: Operational Plan MED 1990–1996']. Managua: Ministry of Education.

Molyneux, M. (1985) 'Mobilization without Emancipation? Women's Interests, the State, and Revolution in Nicaragua', *Feminist Studies* 11(2): 227–54.

Molyneux, M. (1988) 'The Politics of Abortion in Nicaragua: Revolutionary Pragmatism, or Feminism in the Realm of Necessity?', *Feminist Review* 29: 114–32.

Molyneux, M. (2000) 'State and Gender in Latin America', in E. Dore and M. Molyneux (eds) *Hidden Histories of Gender and the State in Latin America*, pp. 33–81. Durham, NC: Duke University Press.

Molyneux, M. (2007) 'Change and Continuity in Social Protection in Latin America: Mothers at the Service of the State?'. Gender and Development Programme Paper No. 1. Geneva: UNRISD.

Montaño, S. (2003) 'Políticas para el empoderamiento de las mujeres como estrategia de lucha contra la pobreza' ['Policies for Women's Empowerment as a Strategy to Tackle Poverty'], in R. Atria and S. Marcelo (eds) *Capital social y reducción de la pobreza en América Latina y el Caribe: en busca de un nuevo paradigma* [*Social Capital and Poverty Reduction in Latin America and the Caribbean: In Search of a New Paradigm*], pp. 361–77. Santiago de Chile: ECLAC.

Moore, C. (2009) 'Nicaragua's Red de Protección Social: An Exemplary but Short-lived Conditional Cash Transfer Programme'. Country Study No. 17. Brasilia: International Policy Centre for Inclusive Growth, United Nations Development Programme.

O'Connor, J., A.S. Orloff and S. Shaver (1999) *States, Markets, Families: Gender, Liberalism and Social Policy in Australia, Canada, Great Britain and the United States*. New York: Cambridge University Press.

Orloff, A.S. (1996) 'Gender and the Welfare State'. Institute for Research on Poverty Discussion Paper No. 1082–96. Madison, WI: University of Wisconsin – Madison.

Orloff, A.S. (2009) 'Farewell to Maternalism? State Policies, Feminist Politics and Mothers' Employment in Europe and North America'. PowerPoint presentation at the NCoE NordWel Summerschool 2009, Bergen, Norway (8–11 June).

Prevost, G. (2000) 'Political Policy: The Sandinista Revolution and Democratization', *International Journal of Economic Development* 2(2): 275–302.

Proyecto Estado de la Región (2008) 'Informe Estado de la Región en Desarrollo Humano Sostenible' ['Report on the State of Sustainable Human Development in the Region']. San José: Proyecto Estado de la Nación.

Puar, J.K. (1996) 'Nicaraguan Women, Resistance, and the Politics of Aid', in H. Afshar (ed.) *Women and Politics in the Third World*, pp. 73–92. London: Routledge.

Ramírez González, X. (n.d.) 'Interview with Max Padilla'. *Revista Páginas Verdes*, Report No. 44. Managua. http://www.euram.com.ni/pverdes/Entrevista/max_padilla.htm.

Razavi, S. and S. Staab (2010) 'Underpaid and Overburdened: A Cross-national Perspective on Care Workers', *International Labour Review* 149(4): 407–22.

Regalia, F. and L. Castro (2007) 'Performance-based Incentives for Health: Demand- and Supply-Side Incentives in the Nicaraguan Red De Proteccion Social'. Center for Global Development Working Paper No. 119. SSRN. http://ssrn.com/abstract=1003251

Rendón, T. (2004) 'El mercado laboral y la división intrafamiliar del trabajo' ['The Labour Market and the Intra-family Division of Labour'], in M. Ariza and O. de Oliveira (eds) *Imágenes de la familia en el cambio de siglo* [*Images of the Family at the Turn of the Century*], pp. 49–87. México: UNAM-IIS.

Rodríguez, A. (2005) *La reforma de salud en Nicaragua* [*Health Reform in Nicaragua*]. Santiago de Chile: ECLAC/GTZ.

Sainsbury, D. (1996) 'Introduction', in D. Sainsbury (ed.) *Gender, Equality and Welfare States*, pp. 1–11. Cambridge: Cambridge University Press.

Serra, L. (1993) 'Democracy in Times of War and Socialist Crisis: Reflections Stemming from the Sandinista Revolution', *Latin American Perspectives* 20(2): 21–44.

World Bank (2008a) 'Nicaragua', in *Migration and Remittances Factbook 2008*, pp. 171. Washington, DC: The World Bank, Development Prospects Group.

World Bank (2008b) *World Development Report 2008. Agriculture for Development*. Washington, DC: The World Bank.

7

A Perfect Storm? Welfare, Care, Gender and Generations in Uruguay

Fernando Filgueira, Magdalena Gutiérrez and Jorge Papadópulos

INTRODUCTION

Compared to other countries in Latin America, Uruguay has a mature welfare state; it also spends more on maintaining its welfare state than almost any other country in the region in terms of gross domestic product (GDP). Yet it is an old and rigid system which has become less and less capable of confronting social risk. The central reason for the decline of the welfare state is the fact that while both family structures and labour markets have changed dramatically in Uruguay, the welfare state system has remained unchanged, based on the continental Bismarckian model with its contributory bias for financing and entitlements, its emphasis on cash transfers and its orientation toward the nuclear, male-breadwinner family model. In this sense, Uruguay constitutes a test case for the challenges facing welfare states in the context of three major changes in the social structure that bring the issue of social protection and care to centre stage: women's increasing labour force participation, changes in family arrangements, and an ageing population.

As the relationship between social risk distribution and state response becomes delinked in Uruguay, it is inevitable that the welfare regime — made up of the state, market and families — faces multiple tensions and fails to achieve optimal balance in terms of the present and future welfare of the population. Markets and families have undergone a number of major transformations. Structural unemployment and precarious labour relations have become regular features of labour markets (Amarante and Arim, 2005; Amarante and Espino, 2007; Kaztman et al., 2003; UNDP, 2002); cohabiting couples and single-parent, female-headed households are part of the fast changing landscape of family arrangements (Cabella, 2007; Filgueira, 1996; Filgueira and Peri, 2004; Paredes, 2003); and an ageing population is adding complexity and further challenges to the reform of the welfare state.

A welfare state model based on formal employment and its occupational categories, oriented to the male breadwinner and assuming a nuclear bi-parental household, is radically dissociated from this new risk structure. True, this model has guaranteed basic protection for the elderly with stable

The authors would like to thank Shahra Razavi, Silke Staab, and the anonymous referees of the journal for helpful comments on earlier drafts of this paper.

Seen, Heard and Counted, First Edition. Edited by Shahra Razavi.
Chapters © 2012 The Institute of Social Studies. Book compilation © 2012 Blackwell Publishing Ltd.

careers (mostly male). But because of its past achievements and the powerful stakeholders it has created in an ageing society, it has left young people, children and women bereft of robust state protection for their particular risks. In Uruguay, the state response to the transformation of the quantity, quality and distribution of social risks has been slow, fragmented and until 2005 — with the exception of education and tentative attempts at family allowances — plainly wrong.

URUGUAY'S SOCIAL CRISES AND THE LACK OF STATE RESPONSE

The basic principles underpinning the Uruguayan welfare architecture of the 1960s were relatively simple and mirrored a Bismarckian/Southern European social model. They comprised:

- a pension regime and a social insurance system based on formal labour market employment along occupational categories, oriented toward the male breadwinner, as well as residual policies for non-formal workers;
- a healthcare system built along similar lines, with residual policies for those outside the formal labour market;
- heavy reliance on the family as the major and central unit of protection, with a family model along traditional patriarchal lines: stable, two-parent, with one male breadwinner and one female carer.

This system of social protection was not without problems, but it rested on two basic tenets that were reasonable in terms of the social realities of that period: full employment for male heads of households in formal labour markets, and relatively stable marital patterns. The social context, however, has changed dramatically since the 1960s, both with respect to the labour market and in terms of household and family arrangements.

In 1967 the open unemployment rate for male adults in Uruguay was relatively low.[1] Furthermore, in 1970, urban employment was largely formal, given the weight of industrial and state-based sectors. However, the extent of state and industrial employment underwent significant decline over the next thirty years. Unemployment for the male population rose to an average of 8 per cent in the 1980s and 12 per cent in the 1990s, reaching almost 14 per cent in 1999. Informality also rose to an estimated 10 per cent in 1981 and to almost 26 per cent in the year 2000 (INE-UNIFEM-UDELAR, 2008).

---

1. Data from a 1967 household survey in Montevideo show a 3 per cent rate of unemployment for male heads of households and less than 5 per cent for all male adults (Filgueira and Gelber, 2005). Data were not available for the whole of the country since no household surveys were carried out for Uruguay as a whole at that time. However, the unemployment rate in Montevideo was probably similar to other urban centres, which in 1967 collectively represented around 90 per cent of the Uruguayan population.

Table 1. Economic Participation Rates by Sex (per cent)

	Total	Men	Women
1970	48.2	72.2	27.6
1980	55.7	75.1	39.5
1990	59.5	74.5	47.4
2000	61.3	72.1	52.5

Source: Filgueira et al. (2005).

In addition to this increasingly unstable and precarious labour market, there is evidence of a major transformation in those joining the ranks of the labour force. The labour force participation rate of women in 1970 was less than 28 per cent. In the year 2000 it was over 50 per cent (see Table 1). In the 1960s and 1970s, most women drew their income from family arrangements in which they worked as unpaid care givers, while males were the market breadwinners. Although there are no data available regarding the distribution of care responsibilities for the 1960s and 1970s, it is quite clear that the male breadwinner/female carer arrangement was the most common one. This was based not only on a labour market that provided relatively full employment with 'family wages' for men, but also on a state that complemented the family wage with a social wage anchored in a strong system of family allowances, which, for lower-income families, represented up to 20 per cent of total income. Yet this system of family allowances was based on formal labour market participation of at least one family member. In other words, protection was provided for women and children, as long as the two basic tenets of the model were upheld: formal employment and a stable legal family arrangement based on marriage.

While traditional stable patriarchal family arrangements are rightly seen as a form of domination, they nevertheless constitute — with all the relevant caveats — a form of (patriarchal) protection. For a woman, the predominant way of accessing income and social protection provided by the state was to be legally married. Survivors' pensions, family allowances and healthcare access depended to a large extent on being married, or on having been married (in the case of widows), to a formally employed male. This side of the social equation also underwent drastic changes. Between 1973 and 1983 the number of marriages per adult member of the population fell at the rate of 2 per cent annually. It then stabilized until 1990, before dropping again. But what was more important was that marriages survived for shorter lengths of time, and the rate of divorce rose steeply. In 1961 there were 1,800 divorces: by the 1990s this number had jumped to more than 8,300 per year (Filgueira, 1996). If both marriages and divorces are considered, they reflect a true revolution in the family (Filgueira, 1996). While in 1961, there was one divorce for every twelve marriages, by 1991 that ratio was one divorce per 2.8 marriages. There was also a marked increase in cohabitation (*uniones libres* or *concubinato*), which in 1994 accounted for 22.7 per cent of all couples for the population aged 15 to 29 years in Montevideo, and 24.3 per cent of all couples in the rest of the country. In the 1970s and 1980s, by contrast, this figure was only 13 per cent for Montevideo. Births out of wedlock also increased dramatically. From 1961 to 1990, the number tripled among those between 15 and 19 years of age, and doubled among other age groups. Finally, the rate of remarriage also rose, increasing the number of 'reassembled' families.

With respect to the labour market, especially, these changes took place largely because the old social model could not be upheld any longer. The real wage in Uruguay was cut to half of its value between 1960 and 1980, and had only recovered to 60 per cent of its 1960 value by 1994. The entry of women into the labour market was in many ways inevitable, as the family wage had ceased to be adequate. It is critical to understand that the pattern of incorporation — particularly of middle- and lower-income women in the labour market in the 1970s and early 1980s — was based upon a productive model that maximized the possibility of a 'double shift', with women shouldering both a second wage and the burden of care. As Suzana Prates (1983) showed in her analyses of the textile and leather industries, the new export-oriented model of the 1970s and 1980s was based largely on the massive inclusion of women in the outsourcing of production, where they could work at home for large export firms, finishing clothes and shoes. Other forms of outsourcing dominated manufacturing and some service economies.

The upper middle classes and the more educated sectors of society underwent a similar process, both in terms of women's participation in the labour market and new family arrangements, but for them the shift was based more on secular cultural processes of emancipation which had been incorporated into the political agenda in the 1960s. Women from the higher socio-economic strata had greater cultural and material capital to soften this transition. Yet, because the welfare model and the labour market also punished non-traditional arrangements and offered fewer devices to reconcile work and family, the final result of these processes was a major decrease in fertility rates for this sector and a marked postponement of childbearing. This was not the case among lower strata families, where reproductive behaviour did not change to the same extent.

In contrast with the transformed landscape in markets and families during this period, no major changes took place in the pension, healthcare or education systems. No pre-school system was developed, nor was an extended school period implemented. No access to healthcare based on citizenship, maternal or reproductive status was put in place and no system of cash transfers, independent of formal labour market participation and marriage, was set up. As the labour market situation deteriorated, family arrangements became less stable and welfare policies failed to improve, women became the last resource for family income. Not surprisingly children — the primary recipients of care — also suffered from this delinking of risk, care demands and the state system of social protection.

The ageing of the population should also be seen as a major challenge for the financial sustainability of the welfare state and for the economies of care. Uruguay was among the first of the Latin American countries to close the demographic window of opportunity: dependency ratios are no longer going down. Since the 1970s these demographic changes have produced fiscal problems for the social security system. The end of the demographic bonus not only affects the fiscal sustainability of the cash transfer system, it is also squeezing increasing amounts of time out of the active population and families that were already stretched. We will come back to this issue later.

THE THREE WORLDS OF SOCIAL RISK AND CARE IN URUGUAY

Gillian Pascall offers the following short but insightful description of the male breadwinner model:

> Male breadwinner regimes make women dependent within marriage/cohabitation especially when they have young children. Women's labor market participation has increased widely across many different welfare regimes, but where the male breadwinner regime is strong, women are likely to bear high costs in unpaid work, to work part-time and to have broken career patterns. This exposes them to much lower levels of lifetime earnings than men and to insecurity and poverty on relationship breakdown. . . . Lone mothers fit the model awkwardly and have tended to be treated either as mothers or as workers. (Pascall, 2006)

This description requires a class specification, which is crucial for understanding the challenges that middle-income countries with high levels of inequality face. It is at the lower end of the income distribution that the persistence of the male breadwinner model — in spite of its slow decay in reality — has the most damaging impact. As can be seen from Table 2, it is among the poor and the less well-off that the higher prevalence of female-headed households and cohabitation can be found. The marriage and fertility patterns of the middle and upper classes, as well as their participation in the labour market, are distinctly different: they marry or enter into cohabitation later, they postpone childbearing, and tend to have one or two children at most. They also tend to be well educated and enter the labour market before marrying and having children. While this does not guarantee autonomy and freedom from patriarchal forces, it definitely provides these women with better social and economic opportunities than if they had married young, with few educational credentials, had children early and either not entered the labour market at all, or done so in precarious ways. When the data on fertility and fertility differentials are combined with family arrangements, education and labour market participation, it is clear that this pattern is consistent in the better educated and well-off segments of society, but not in the lower-income urban sectors.

The lower-income urban segments of Uruguayan society present a configuration of relatively high and early fertility, with women either living

Table 2. Selected Indicators of Fertility, Market Participation and Family Arrangements by Social Strata for Women (circa 2000)

	Lower income and/or education	Medium income and/or education	Higher income and/or education
Median age of women at first child[a]	20	23	29
Rate of economic participation of women with children of 5 years or younger[c] (%)	48	61	82
Rate of employment of women with children of 5 years or younger[b] (%)	32	50	79
Women who are mothers by 19 years of age[a] (%)	37	16.2	2
Women managing households on their own with children of 14 years or younger[c] (%)	20.7	16.6	8.1
Women cohabiting with men in bi-parental arrangements with children of 14 years or younger[c] (%)	32	17	7.7
Women 24–30 years who have formed new households[d] (%)	69	48.1	45
Women 24–30 years who live with partners[d] (%)	66	45	34
Women 24–30 years who are mothers[d] (%)	81	36	14.5
Women 24–30 years who are active in the labour market[d] (%)	58	85	85

Sources:
[a] Varela et al. (2008).
[b] Kaztman and Filgueira (2001).
[c] Household Survey 2001 (National Institute of Statistics, 2008).
[d] Ciganda (2008).

on their own with their children or cohabiting with partners, with lower rates of economic activity and employment, and early emancipation patterns[2] from youth to adulthood (see Table 2). This constellation poses major challenges for the welfare of women and children. The provisioning of

---

2. Emancipation patterns refer to the time and timing of transition from youth to adulthood. Finishing education, entering the labour market, forming a new family, having children and leaving the parental household are typical events in this transition. The timing of each event and the intervals between them vary across countries, gender and social strata (Filgueira, 1998; Filgueira et al., 2001).

care in these social groups is based overwhelmingly on the family, and on women's unpaid work, as access to either robust state services or quality services through the market is not feasible. It is particularly interesting to analyse how this burden of care interacts with the capacity to enter the labour market. Entry into the labour market presents a major challenge for women with low educational credentials who also have young children (0–5 years old). When children grow up and enter school, the effect of childbearing on economic participation and employment does not disappear but becomes less salient. This reality is also present among women with middle levels of education, but with a less steep curve by age of children; it is non-existent, however, in the case of highly educated women (Filgueira et al., 2005). This is probably the clearest evidence of the difficulties women in lower- and middle-income groups face in balancing work and family. The adaptive behaviour of the middle sectors tends to be through the post-ponement of childbearing, while among the lower-income strata it is not the fertility rates that are adjusted, but the labour market prospects. Examining similar data over time (Table 3) allows for additional observations. First, the difference in employment rates and activity rates between income quintiles has widened among women who have young children (0–5 years old). Second, the gap in terms of the unemployment rate has also increased markedly.

This breakdown of the breadwinner model and its stratified nature mirrors a broader trend towards the stratification of welfare, protection and care.

Table 3. Labour Market Participation and Employment of Women from Bi-parental Households with Children (0–5 years), according to Income (per cent)

	1990				
	1st quintile	2nd quintile	3rd quintile	4th quintile	5th quintile
Employed	30.7	43.7	61.9	78.1	69.9
Unemployed	7.4	7.2	4.8	4.2	3.2
Inactive	61.9	49.1	33.3	17.7	26.9
	2005				
	1st quintile	2nd quintile	3rd quintile	4th quintile	5th quintile
Employed	33.6	57.8	75.2	83.1	87.4
Unemployed	16.6	8.0	6.5	5.2	2.2
Inactive	49.8	34.1	18.3	11.7	10.4

Note: the category 'inactive' includes women who perform unpaid work and care work.
Source: authors' elaboration based on microdata from Household Surveys 1990 and 2005 (National Institute of Statistics, 2008).

Based on a cluster analysis of household data, we see that there were — and to a large extent still are — three parallel 'worlds', or ways of producing and reproducing risk and care in Uruguay.

- A vulnerable Uruguay, where poverty is widespread, informality in the labour market extensive, child poverty prevalent, and exclusion from strong social protection systems the norm. This Uruguay relies for care provision and risk protection on a weakened universal part of the social state, and on families and community. In this Uruguay, most of the reproductive basis of the country rests on the shoulders of women, along with most of the burden of care for children.
- The remnants of the 'old' corporatist and public Uruguay, increasingly vulnerable, with a high percentage of elderly people and organized middle sectors of society, defensive in nature, with low fertility and late emancipation patterns among the young.
- The private Uruguay, comprising upper middle classes and upper classes, with a highly educated population, also showing late patterns of emancipation to adult life and fertility, and relying heavily on the market for healthcare and education.

There is a political-economic explanation of how this came to be, and it is important to highlight the differential position of women from different strata in this rather perverse game of privatization, corporatist decay and increased vulnerability of lower-income groups. Uruguay emerged from the authoritarian regime with an import-substitution industrialization (ISI) model and welfare state that was injured but not dead. The elderly, women included, pushed the new democracy for the improvement of pension benefits, which they considered to be vital. Widows from the old welfare and ISI model concentrated on receiving what the patriarchal welfare model had promised all along: protection in old age because of their status as spouses of former formal workers. Upper middle class and upper class sectors that had benefited from the authoritarian model of development sought market solutions for reconciling work and care. The women who had the most leverage to put these issues on the government's agenda were more concerned with other central gender issues, such as reproductive rights. Finally, in the vulnerable sectors, both women and men remained weak in organizational terms. With weakened trade unions and a predominantly service-based economy with increasingly informal and precarious employment, the issue of work and care, or of a welfare response to this problem, slipped from the agenda. This configuration of interests and power led to politics and policies that allowed patterns of stratification to become patterns of segmentation. Uruguay's already high level of inequality, in comparative terms, was heightened further, with patterns of inequality that were not only expressed in differences in income but also spilled over into different and unequal worlds of welfare and ill-fare along generational and gender lines.

Table 4. Basic Socio-economic Profile

	Average age	Probability for non-poverty	Per capita income (constant *pesos*)	Household educational level[a]
Corporatist cluster	52.9	83.1	4,610.2	5.1
Vulnerable cluster	22.6	48.3	2,479.3	7.8
Private cluster	36.3	96.4	9,202.7	13.4
Total	36.2	73.9	5,213.3	8.7

Note:
[a]includes average years of education of head of household and spouse.
Source: authors' elaboration based on microdata from Household Survey 2001 (National Institute of Statistics, 2008).

This segmentation of Uruguayan society is illustrated by a cluster analysis which included variables such as the age of individuals, the income level of the household, the economic activity status of the head of the household, and the educational achievement of the head of the household.[3] This cluster analysis identifies a country divided into three tiers with differentiated profiles according to the selected variables. The different social worlds that coexist in Uruguay have contrasting levels of welfare and assets, as well as age structure (see Table 4). The private Uruguay is the least likely to have households which fall below the poverty line and the highest combined educational achievement among adults. It is also a rather young Uruguay, with an average age of thirty-six years. The vulnerable Uruguay has the youngest population; households are more likely to be poor; educational attainments are low, but not the lowest, among adults. The lowest educational attainment can be found in the older, basically non-poor Uruguay, where education did not go much beyond primary school or, at the most, junior high school.

The sources of welfare and risk for these three social groups are clearly different. Approximately 65 per cent of the members of the private Uruguay generate income; 70 per cent of corporatist Uruguay receives some type

---

3. The cluster analysis can be seen in detail in Filgueira et al. (2005). It was performed based on standardized variables that included interval, dichotomous and ordinal variables standardized in their variance for the purpose of such cluster analyses. Based on an iterative model of Euclidean Distances individuals were clustered based on attributes that were both individual and household based. They included the age of the individual, the per capita household income, the activity of the household head and the educational achievement of the household head. Cluster values were then attached to each individual case and further analyses regarding the means and percentages of other variables were considered and conveyed. The cluster analysis showed discriminant capacity in all its base variables. The strong correlation between clusters and income levels was expected, but the clusters showed important overlaps between income levels. Age, educational achievement of the household, and especially the type/condition of economic activity of the household, provided additional clustering criteria.

Table 5. Access to Health Benefits according to Cluster (per cent)

	Private emergency and primary healthcare	Mutual aid or private healthcare
Corporatist Uruguay	32.6	53.8
Vulnerable Uruguay	17.4	33.0
Private Uruguay	62.1	84.0
Total	36.0	55.2

Source: authors' elaboration based on microdata from Household Survey 2001 (National Institute of Statistics, 2008).

of income; and only 44 per cent of vulnerable Uruguay receives any type of income. Unemployment is highest in vulnerable Uruguay, and lowest in privatized Uruguay. Another feature which clearly separates the three groupings is what we call *decommodification* of income sources. In this sense, corporatist Uruguay is different from the rest, with 62 per cent of those who receive an income or obtain cash transfers doing so from the state, either via pensions or (as salaries) through public employment. The decommodification rate is high, too, in private Uruguay, due mostly to public sector jobs rather than pensions. Finally, in vulnerable Uruguay, only 26 percent of income comes directly from the state.

Another clearly identifiable feature is the differentiated ways in which these groups access social goods and services (see Table 5). One group has access to education and health services largely through the systems of corporatist solidarity, sheltered by the state or the systems of universal solidarity, as in the case of public education. But there is another group, increasingly private and privatized, whose basic access to these goods and services relies on its purchasing power. Public health is the most time-consuming to access; mutual aid societies or MAS (a cooperative form of insurance) rank second; while purely private alternatives are the easiest and fastest to access. Furthermore, paying a private, mobile and primary healthcare provider is a central strategy for diminishing the time and human cost of healthcare access and healthcare at home by members of the family. As can be seen in Table 5, privatized Uruguay buys time-saving healthcare in the market; corporatist Uruguay gets its healthcare both from the market and the state; and vulnerable Uruguayans have to rely mostly on the state-provided services, which are most demanding in terms of time taken to access services.

A similar pattern, but with a more clear-cut difference in favour of private Uruguay, can be seen in the sphere of education. In most cases private education in Uruguay provides six to seven hours of schooling per day, with sports, languages and academic support all provided within school hours. On the other hand, for children who attend public primary schools, only 7 per cent get such extended time in school. It is also worth noting that both corporatist and vulnerable clusters have a high drop-out rate from high

Figure 1. Proportion of Households with Women aged 19 to 44, who have no Children in the 0 to 14 Age Group

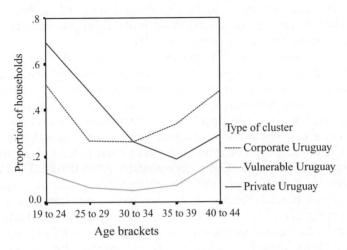

school, placing additional burdens and suggesting a failure of care in teenage years (Filgueira et al., 2005).

The differences between these three social worlds are revealed not only in terms of income, occupational group and access to social goods and services, but also by the differences in reproductive behaviour and emancipation patterns of young people (see Figures 1 and 2). In the vulnerable cluster

Figure 2. Emancipation from Household of Origin, by Age in Accumulated Frequencies

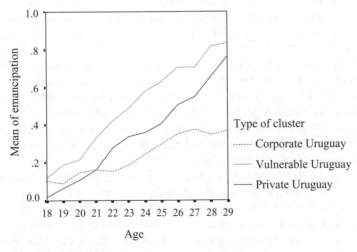

Source: Filgueira et al. (2005).

women tend to begin their reproductive life early and tend to have more children than the other social groups. Those who fall within the corporatist cluster delay emancipation and fertility much longer, while those in the private cluster steer a middle course in terms of fertility, number of children and age at emancipation (Filgueira et al., 2005).

The private cluster clearly leans towards the model of a dual-earner family that buys care in the market, invests heavily in education and postpones (but does undertake) emancipation, marriage and reproduction. The vulnerable part of the country, however, does not postpone emancipation, marriage or reproduction. It relies mostly on the state for basic services and on the family for additional care requirements and social protection. It does not invest in education and has the lowest ratio of income earners to family members. In other words, care and work are not reconciled, but rather divorced, with clear consequences in term of social mobility and welfare. Finally, the corporatist section of society relies heavily on the state, buys a very limited amount of services in the market (probably due to an inability to pay), and adapts by attempting a dual-earner strategy that requires pooling together generations and having fewer children. Market, family and state solutions to care needs are all present in Uruguay, and they tend to cluster around these three social worlds, clearly exposing the inability of the Uruguayan social model to deal with the new constellation of family, markets and age.

THE HOUSEHOLD ECONOMY OF CARE AND PROTECTION IN URUGUAY

In much of the earlier literature on gender and households it was *assumed* that households place an inordinate burden of responsibility for their welfare, care and reproduction on the shoulders of women, but there were little systematic data to support this view. The pioneering works by Aguirre (2003, 2005), Batthyány (2004), Batthyány, Alesina and Brunet (2007) and Batthyány, Cabrera and Scuro (2007) in Uruguay have provided, for the first time, an empirical picture that supports this assumption. The first relevant, but by no means surprising, piece of information is the enormous amount of time that is spent on unpaid work (see Figure 3). This is consistent with some of the estimates of contribution to real GDP, when work time that is not exchanged for a wage is counted as part of the GDP (Salvador, 2008). Looking at data by sex illustrates, in turn, the important role played by women in the unpaid economy, and the diminished amount of time that women are, as a consequence, able to allocate to paid work.

The average time spent by women on the provision of unpaid care and other types of domestic work adds up to almost a full-time paid position in the labour market (36.3 hours per week) (INE-UNIFEM-UDELAR, 2008). As expected, unpaid work tends to be concentrated in households with children, and especially in households with children under four years of

Figure 3. Time Allocated to Paid and Unpaid Work in Population 14 Years and Older (as percentage of all time); General and Specific for Men and Women

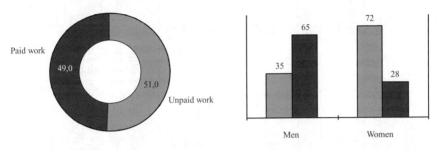

Source: INE-UNIFEM-UDELAR (2008).

age. This cut-off point has a simple explanation. Uruguay has advanced toward the universalization of education based on the public provision of pre-school services for children aged four years and above, leaving an important proportion of younger children in the care of either family or market-based solutions (see Table 6).

The gender gap in hours of unpaid work is particularly wide when children are young (six years or less) and the family is in the early stages of parent-hood; in this case women dedicate an average of 57 hours a week to unpaid work, against 22 hours for men. As the children grow up, women reduce their unpaid work to an average of 45.8 hours, while men limit their input to 15.3 hours (INE-UNIFEM-UDELAR, 2008). If we look at it from a lifecycle perspective, combined with stratification, the data show how fertility, mar-ket access to care and gendered division of labour affect the distribution of care (see Figure 4). Young women (21–30 years) from the lowest income quintile spend an average of 8 hours a day doing unpaid work, while men in the same quintile and age bracket spend 2 or less hours in unpaid work. Meanwhile women in the highest income quintile peak in terms of unpaid work at later ages and only reach an average of between 4 and 5 hours. Men in the richest quintile are more or less consistent with their poorer gender peers; although they seem to contribute slightly more hours of unpaid work, they never work without pay for more than 3 hours (Figure 4). Thus with regard to household chores and provision of care, men always contribute fewer hours of unpaid work than women, but the gap in the poorest quintile is almost 6 hours a day, while in the richest quintile it is approximately 3 hours a day.

In a context where the prevalence of female-headed households is increas-ing, women are entering the labour market, and there are persistent fertility differentials, the picture above leaves no room for doubt. When it comes to the care of children and unpaid work in the household, women — and

Table 6. Population Coverage of Children aged 0 to 5 years by both Formal and Non-formal Education, 2006–2007

	0 to 1 year		2 years		3 years		4 years		5 years + older	
	Number	%	Number	%	Number	%	Number	%	Number	%
Formal education										
Public	0	0.0	34	0.2	5,317	21.8	33,699	75.1	42,783	82.6
Private	1,207	15.8	3,677	24.0	5,273	21.6	6,815	15.2	7,831	15.1
Non-formal education										
Private and other[a]	3,269	42.9	5,737	37.4	6,395	26.2	3,131	7.0	1,142	2.2
CAIF (daily)	3,142	41.2	5,892	38.4	7,430	30.4	1,245	2.8	33	0.1
Total	7,618	100.0	15,340	100.0	24,415	100.0	44,890	100.0	51,789	100.0
Total population	97,114		48,342		48,886		50,039		51,454	
Coverage (%)	7.8		31.7		49.9		89.7		100.7	

Notes:

Formal early education is provided by public institutions recognized and regulated by the National Public Education Administration (ANEP).

Non-formal education is provided by private or third sector institutions (like the Early Childhood and Family Care Centres/CAIF) which are under the aegis of the Ministry of Culture (MEC). ANEP, and not MEC, is responsible for the recognition of formality in education.

[a]92 per cent are private institutions and the rest are services provided by different public institutions like the Montevideo municipality and others.

Source: Cerutti (2006), based on information provided by the Ministry of Education (Estadísticas Educativas) and INE (Proyecciones de Población).

Figure 4. Average Hours per Day Spent in Unpaid Work, by Age and Income Quintile

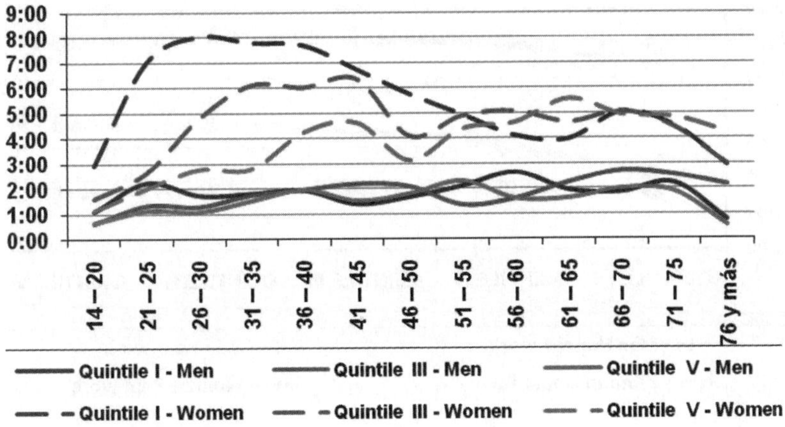

Source: ECLAC (2009).

especially lower-income women — perform the bulk of the work. The absence of extended school hours in the public system and the only marginal development of early and accessible childcare services, leaves just two options for meeting the demand for care and unpaid work. These are the family (which means women) and the market (which means domestic service and out-of-household market solutions). For lower-income women, who cannot access market solutions, this in turn implies a severe limitation on their capacity to engage in paid work, thus curbing their financial autonomy and increasing their vulnerability. The data on unpaid and paid work by quintiles and sex (shown in Figure 5) are precise in showing this configuration.

In a country that shows a secular trend toward less stable bi-parental family arrangements and increased divorce rates, the configuration depicted in Figure 5 implies that women — and especially lower-income women — have lost out to a traditional patriarchal division of labour and a decaying model of stable nuclear families. In addition, these same women, whose continuous involvement in paid work is already compromised by their other commitments, also have a greater likelihood of being alone in old age, with no retirement benefits. In an ageing population, the problem of gendered differentials in labour market histories and protection will become larger in the near future.

In Uruguay, there is already a problem with regard to the elderly. This is not (yet) so much the result of a lack of cash benefits/pensions for their retirement, but of a lack of social services and care provision for them. While the pension system in Uruguay covers both men and women almost universally — even though women receive lower levels of transfer than

Figure 5. Paid and Unpaid Work in Average Hours per Day, by Sex and Income Quintiles

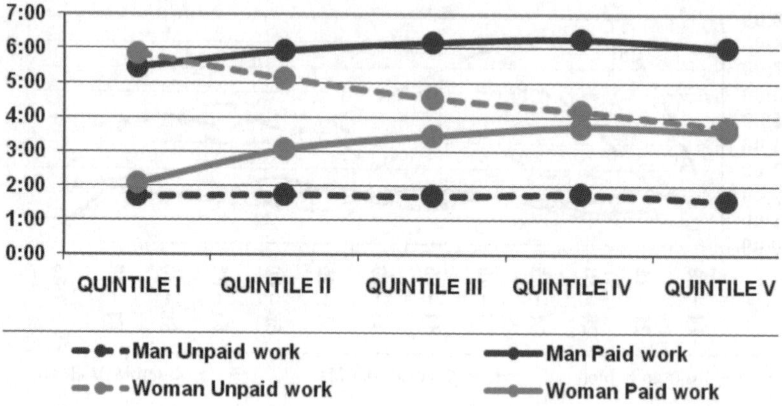

- ● - Man Unpaid work   ━●━ Man Paid work
- ● - Woman Unpaid work   ━●━ Woman Paid work

Source: ECLAC (2009).

men — the system of care for the elderly needs to be developed almost from scratch. From a care perspective it is important to note that the percentage of the very old (i.e. those above 75 years of age), who are more prone to disability, is increasing rapidly, from 3.4 per cent of the total population in 1975 to 5.2 per cent in 2005, and projected to reach 6.7 per cent by 2025 (Papadópulos, 2008).

If the public cash transfer system has felt the impact of this trend, the private spheres of family and markets have also been affected by it. At present, almost 170,000 people aged 60 years and older are covered by some form of private care service, called company services. They are not permanent and are of very uneven quality; they basically provide a service (company) focused mainly on the elderly and the disabled, including cleaning, providing medicine, helping the elderly with issues of basic mobility, and supporting their physical ailments, such as diminished sight, and mental disability. The lack of a robust system of public care in this area has allowed for a marked increase in these types of enterprise, which usually operate at low cost, paid as insurance, and not on the basis of 'use and pay'. This system is working for the moment because the ratio of insured to actual recipients is high. As the very elderly population increases, this rate will deteriorate.

Thus, the transformation of labour markets, family arrangements and demographic trends, together with the household economies of care and unpaid work, has torn apart earlier generational and gender contracts. In the process, it has redistributed risk, vulnerability and workload, not only in ways that are biased in gender and generational terms, but also in a deeply regressive manner as far as social class is concerned.

RECENT SOCIAL REFORMS: CAUSE FOR MODERATE OPTIMISM?

Four areas of policy reform, one from the 1990s and three from the post-2005 period, suggest a more responsive state of affairs than this article has so far portrayed: education reform in 1995, healthcare reform between 2006 and 2009, social security reform in 2008/9 and the family allowance reform of 2008. In particular, the arrival in government of the Left in 2005 signalled a new agenda for social policy reform that combined an orientation towards child welfare and, to a lesser extent, some elements of the feminist or gender-sensitive agenda. The Left brought to the table the social movements that have always been its main source of support (trade unions, as well as student, human rights and cooperative movements) but also gave more space and voice to some of the new social movements (feminist and environmental).

Reforms in the Education Sector

Four concrete policy initiatives within the education sector are worth high-lighting: the creation of full-time schools in lower-income neighbourhoods; the expansion of public pre-school education services aimed at universal coverage of children aged four and five years old; the expansion of break-fast and lunch services to cover almost all schools in lower-income areas; and the creation of 'community teachers' who travel to low-income homes and provide support to both children and their families. Another initiative, which started as early as 1985 and picked up speed later, was the cre-ation of a number of Centres for the Assistance of Families and Infants (Centro de Atención Integral a la Infancia y Familia — CAIF) outside of the formal educational system, which children up to four years old could attend on a daily or weekly basis.

Although these are encouraging trends, the biggest deficit of the education system in Uruguay is not at either the primary or pre-school level, but at the level of high school. Uruguay has one of the best completion rates at the primary school level in Latin America and one of the worst completion rates at the secondary level. The secondary school system — designed for middle and upper middle classes — suffers from a range of problems, including organizational weaknesses, lack of resources and, in contrast to primary schools, the complete absence of any services such as food programmes, after-school activities, extended time in school, health check-ups, and so on (ANEP, 2005).

Health Sector Reforms

Until 2006, Uruguay's healthcare system was defined by a marked strat-ification in access and quality between the public, the private mutual aid societies (MAS),[4] and the purely private system. Mobile care[5] and house call services had become a rare commodity, prompting the expansion of private emergency mobile healthcare units[6] (EMU) that provided house calls as an additional service to public healthcare or the MAS, for those who could afford it.

The new National Integrated System of Healthcare (SNIS) put in place in 2006 has succeeded in bringing major changes. With new financial contributions made by the state, the recent healthcare reform includes employees and employers and all children who have at least one parent who is formally employed.[7] Those who retired after the start of the reform are also eligible and can choose a MAS of their liking. Spouses are not yet included unless, of course, they themselves are formally employed. Finally, those who are not able to opt into the new system — and this would include the non-employed, informal workers, those already retired, and children whose parents are either informally employed or not employed — will remain in the public system. Recent data (Pereira et al., 2005) show the clear impact of the reform in terms of the incorporation of adults and, especially, children into the new system. It is also important to note that the reform of health and social insurance has reduced the burden on the public system by reducing the level of demand and by making more money available per person (ibid.).

Family Allowances

In their original form, family allowances were not, at least in countries with a familialistic care regime, aimed at gender equality. Rather, they sought to increase fertility and both reinforce and recognize women's roles as care givers and household caretakers in the framework of stable patriarchal arrangements. Yet this type of transfer has become another possible instrument for pursuing gender equality and reconciling work and family life, in at least three ways. First, it provides an income that allows families to purchase services in the market, thus deflecting part of the burden of care from women. Second, it usually delinks eligibility from formal male employment and

---

4. Mutual Aid Societies (MAS) were already in existence at the start of the century as cooperative, voluntary, risk-pooling systems that charged a private fee and had their own facilities. In the 1970s, the state created the Directorate of State Health Services (DISSE). This was a mandatory health insurance scheme for private formal workers whereby part of their salary was retained (plus employee and state contributions) and passed along to a MAS of the beneficiary's choice. This insurance scheme did not include the children or spouse of the beneficiary. People could still join a MAS by paying for it themselves.
5. Mobile care refers to mobile primary and emergency care units staffed by a doctor and a nurse who pay house calls.
6. Initially the units provided only emergency services, but now provide additional services.
7. Before the reform, parents had to pay to include their children in a MAS, otherwise the children would be entitled only to public healthcare facilities and services.

makes it conditional on income level — when it is not universal — and on the school attendance of children and adolescents, thereby providing an incentive to use other state services that reduce the unpaid care burden of women.[8] Finally, if the allowance is high enough, it reduces women's financial dependence on others, and provides a fallback position, especially in cases of divorce and separation, irrespective of women's labour market status and civil situation.

In the 1940s, Uruguay became the first Latin American country to adopt a system to complement family wages in the framework of a traditional continental European conservative and familialistic welfare regime. Eligibility for the family wage complement was based on the formal employment of the male, combined with the presence of a wife and child(ren). By the 1980s, the cash benefit had deteriorated to such an extent that reform was needed; however, the first reform narrowly targeted the benefit and sought to improve its value, but included only formal workers. Some other reforms thereafter sought to improve coverage, and included the extension of this entitlement to female-headed households with children, irrespective of the mother's labour market status. In 2006 the government undertook a broader reform of the system, keeping it targeted but in more generous terms (all households below the poverty line), increasing its value and making it open to all adults in households with children, irrespective of the adults' link to employment (Amarante and Arim, 2005).

With this reform, the number of beneficiaries doubled between 1995 and 2009, while the average benefit also almost doubled in value. The benefits are still low but by no means insignificant. They amount to US$ 30 per month for one child below twelve years of age and US$ 40 for children above that age and in high school, up to a total of nearly US$ 60 for a family with two children, and slightly higher for those with more children. For receipt of this allowance, the per capita income of poor families has a ceiling of US$ 240 per month, while the mean per capita income of poor households hovers around US$ 180. When fiscal space becomes available, the government intends to increase the amount of the benefit, as well as the proportion of the population covered (Arim et al., 2009).

Pension and Retirement Benefits

Uruguay's pension and retirement system covers more than 550,000 persons in a population of slightly more than 3.2 million. It is heavily financed from general revenue, since contributions from employees, employers and the state can no longer foot the bill. Almost 4.5 per cent of GDP goes to cover the deficit in the system (Alegre and Filgueira, 2009).

---

8. Although it is true that in many cases it also links these benefits to joint medical check-ups of mother and child, thus re-linking gender and the role of care taker.

Despite this enormous fiscal effort, Uruguay has an underdeveloped system of elderly care, in part precisely because it has an over-inflated and fiscally voracious pension system. This does not mean that retirement benefits are adequate. Many retirement benefits provide an income that is barely above the official poverty line. But other retirement benefits — especially those of the military, police, bank employees, professionals, and the upper levels of industry and commerce — are generous. This implies that the less well-off are partially footing the bill for a system from which they are unlikely to benefit when they are old. They will have to be satisfied with access to lower benefits in means-tested, non-contributory pensions. This bias in the pension system carries the implicit conviction that the issue of the elderly is not a question of providing public care services, but rather of private capacity to pay for them in the market. The large number of pensioners who today cannot access care services — such as health and social care or community services — suggests that a publicly organized system of supply for these services is badly needed.

In addition, the traditional contributory pay-as-you-go system includes a compulsory private accounts pillar. Yet this pillar only really accommodates the middle classes and those above them, and not the lower middle classes and those below them. This is not only a problem of income inequality; it also includes a gender bias. Women who enter and leave the workforce and those in the informal sector are the ones who will have the greatest difficulty in reaching the years of contributions needed for retirement benefits. Hence, the future of pensions in Uruguay will be segmented along class and gender lines. The reform of 2008 has lowered the number of years of contributions needed (from thirty-five to thirty) and has also lowered the replacement rates for those pensions. Still this change does not solve the problem of approximately 30 per cent of the population, who, according to most recent estimates based on data from labour market histories, will not have enough stable contributions to reach old age with retirement benefits (Bucheli et al., 2006).

The Politics of Reform

In order to understand why the state began to address some of these issues — albeit belatedly and often inconsistently — in the 1990s, and more proactively after 2005, three convergent political and policy processes have to be taken into account.

First, it is important to analyse the role of women and the feminist movement in Uruguay. From its beginnings in the 1980s, the feminist agenda was initially neglected, but gradually made inroads over the years. In the trade union movement, for example, the women's movement was able to push through a 'mandatory representation guarantee' by which women had to be represented in collective bargaining. Women from the lower-income sectors, supported by part of the feminist intelligentsia, were able to place the issue of domestic violence on the public agenda, and a Comisaría de las Mujeres (Commissioner for Women) was created to deal with cases of domestic violence. The Plenario de las Mujeres (PLEMU), the first umbrella organization for women's NGOs,[9] survived the restoration of traditional politics in 1985 and started to gain momentum toward the mid-1990s. A broader alliance that included women from almost all classes pushed forward a bill on reproductive rights. Female political leaders and intellectuals created a women's parliamentary alliance and worked toward the creation of a Women's Institute that is now attempting to become a ministry. While the issues of work and care were not central to the feminist agenda, they did at least start to become part of that broader public agenda (Batthyány, Alesina and Brunet, 2007).

A second critical process was the growing consensus emerging among political elites, policy makers and the academic community regarding the demographic, labour and generational challenges that Uruguay faced. The notions of 'infantilization of poverty' and a generational welfare imbalance were widespread in the press and in public debate. The claim that 50 per cent of all children were born below the poverty line became common knowledge (Filgueira et al., 2005). The appearance of CAIF centres and the expansion of pre-schools for four- and five-year-olds were policy responses to this growing consensus. The need to reinforce the system of family allowances was another element in the policy response to a shared diagnostic. Women's entry into the labour market was also increasingly seen as a necessary strategy for sustaining a financially crippled social security system. In general, it is probably fair to say that the shift in policy, which recognizes the transformed landscape of family and labour markets, has been more concerned with the welfare of children than with the welfare of women. But this concern has spurred some changes that point in the right direction.

The triumph of the Left in the 2004 national elections was the final ingredient that enabled a more robust attempt to address the issues of care, work, gender and inequality. The crisis of 2002 had destroyed the country's social fabric. The Left pledged an emergency social plan, and created a Social Development Ministry to launch it. This Ministry deals with non-formal workers and with women and children, because that is where poverty is predominant. The Left, which belonged to the old trade union tradition and had always talked of a return to 'paradise lost', found itself on a steep learning curve when it was confronted with the reality of poverty in Uruguay. *La pobreza tiene cara de mujer y la pobreza tiene cara de niño* ('poverty has the face of a woman, and poverty has the face of a child') became the motto of the Ministry. In understanding the survival strategies of lower-income women and coming to terms with a transformed family landscape, the administration has had to accept that the old welfare architecture was not a solution, but in fact part of the problem.

---

9. Though PLEMU was not a full-fledged federation of the different expressions of the women's movement, it brought together the most important ones.

A final, but by no means unimportant, development that emerged from the Left's victory was the presence of women in decision-making positions: several ministries were now in the hands of women. At least three factors might help explain this. First, the feminist agenda, while still resisted — or even mocked in a male-dominated milieu — had much more legitimacy within the Left than it did in the Centre and Centre-Right parties in Uruguay. Second, some of these women were from the heavily feminized labour segments (education and health) where they had entered politics through trade union activism. Workers in these two sectors were also traditionally supporters of the Left. Finally, the human rights movement that first fought against the dictatorship and then kept up the struggle, trying to bring to justice those who had violated human rights during the dictatorship, was both dominated by the Left and much more feminized in its leadership than either the trade unions or the political parties. These factors together might have contributed to the increased presence of women in visible positions, which in turn opened a space for certain elements of the feminist agenda.

CONCLUSION

The issues of care, use of time and unpaid work have landed squarely on the academic and policy-making agendas of most of the OECD countries. To a lesser extent, they are also making their presence felt in emerging and developing countries. In the case of Uruguay, as in several other countries of the Southern Cone, processes of social and economic change have pushed the question of care onto the public agenda. These challenges can be summed up in very simple terms: family transformation, the ageing of the population, women's full entry into the labour force, high levels of inequality, increased inheritance of social disadvantage, with its effect on the intergenerational reproduction of poverty, and labour market deterioration.

In Uruguay, these processes have caused increased inequality, leading to the segmentation of society into three distinct worlds where welfare and ill-fare assume different patterns and logics, as this contribution has shown. Private, state-based and family-based forms of protection dominate these three worlds. Those in what we have called the 'vulnerable sector' of this three-tiered Uruguay are left with inadequate state protection and have to fend for themselves, while the 'corporate' Uruguay hangs by a thread to a system based on the legacies of the old welfare state. In doing so they assume defensive adaptive modes of survival with low fertility and late and stagnant emancipation patterns from youth to adulthood. Meanwhile, the 'private' Uruguay becomes increasingly disaffected and unwilling to support — politically or fiscally — the public services and protections. While the dominance of the Washington Consensus and processes of globalization and liberalization go a long way to explaining the trend towards heightened inequality, we have argued that the fuel behind this three-tiered society lies somewhere else. The persistence of a patriarchal and elderly-oriented model of the social state that cannot recognize changing family patterns, women's diversified roles and increased child vulnerability, a labour market that discriminates along gender lines and does not recognize the double role of women as carers and breadwinners, and families that sustain a division of labour in the private sphere without acknowledging the drastic changes of this same division of labour in the public sphere, are not just the ingredients of an unfair gender and generational contract, but also the central culprits of an increasingly segmented social reality.

A welfare state in a relatively resource-poor and fiscally constrained country such as Uruguay has to face the triple challenge of an ageing population — which diverts money from much-needed cash transfers, educational and care services for children and families with children — a changed family composition and a labour market that puts increasing strains on families, and especially women, to juggle work, family and care. When this takes place in a welfare state which has been modelled on the continental corporatist European style, the case tells a fascinating story. Moving toward a welfare mix of family, markets and state that is more socially responsive and at the same time sustainable is proving to be a challenging task. It has taken twenty years for an increasingly irrelevant family allowance system to start moving in the right direction. Healthcare reform has taken one step forward, but if it does not find a solution for the sustainable incorporation of the elderly and women, it might very well take two steps back. Pension reform is struggling to come to terms with the fact that the system as it stands is unfair, inefficient and, in the long term, unsustainable. Yet little has been heard about elderly care, and all efforts seem to be aimed at maintaining a contributory system with pay-as-you-go and private account pillars that are male-oriented and linked to the formal labour market. They may survive, but it is our deep conviction that, as they stand, they are part of the problem rather than part of the solution.

There are no easy fixes for the dilemmas posed throughout this paper. But whether it is because we care about gender equality, or because we are concerned about income and generational equality, it seems clear that far more courageous and often politically painful responses have to be considered. The reforms undertaken so far in education, pensions, family allowances and healthcare have both positive and negative aspects, but given the magnitude of the challenges, they will not be enough to get us where we need to be in the near future.

REFERENCES

Aguirre, R. (2003) *Género, Ciudadanía Social y Trabajo* [*Gender, Social Citizenship and Work*].
    Montevideo: Universidad de la República, Departamento de Sociología.
Aguirre, R. (2005) *Uso del Tiempo y Trabajo No Remunerado* [*Time Use and Unpaid Work*].
    Montevideo: UNIFEM-Universidad de la República.
Alegre, P. and F. Filgueira (2009) 'Assessment of a Hybrid Reform Path: Social and Labour
    Policies in Uruguay, 1985–2005', *International Labour Review* 148: 316–35.

Amarante, V. and R. Arim (2005) 'Las políticas sociales de protección a la infancia' ['Social Policies for Childhood Protection'], in UNICEF *Inversión en la Infancia en Uruguay. Análisis del Gasto Público Social: Tendencias y Desafíos* [*Childhood Investment in Uruguay. An Analysis of Social Public Expenditure: Trends and Challenges*], pp. 13–82. Montevideo: UNICEF.

Amarante, V. and A. Espino (2007) 'Informalidad y Protección Social en Uruguay: Elementos para una Discusión Conceptual y Metodológica' ['Informality and Social Protection in Uruguay: Issues for a Conceptual and Methodological Discussion']. Instituto de Economía Working Paper 1/07. Montevideo: Universidad de la República, Facultad de Ciencias Económicas.

ANEP (Gerencia de Evaluación e Investigación Educativa) (2005) 'Panorama de la Educación en Uruguay. Una década de transformaciones, 1992–2004' ['Educational Panorama of Uruguay. A Decade of Transformations, 1992–2004']. Montevideo: ANEP.

Arim R., G. Cruces and A. Vigorito (2009) 'Programas sociales y transferencias de ingresos en Uruguay: los beneficios no contributivos y las alternativas para su extensión' ['Social Programs and Cash Transfers in Uruguay']. Santiago de Chile: ECLAC.

Batthyány, K. (2004) *Cuidado Infantil y Trabajo: ¿Un Desafío Exclusivamente Femenino?; Una Mirada desde el Género y la Ciudadanía Social* [*Childcare and Work: An Exclusively Feminine Challenge? A View from Gender and Social Citizenship Perspective*]. Montevideo: CINTERFOR/OIT.

Batthyány, K., L. Alesina and N. Brunet (2007) 'Género y Cuidados Familiares. ¿Quién se hace cargo del cuidado y la atención de los adultos mayores en Montevideo?' ['Gender and Family Care. Who Takes Care of the Elderly Population in Montevideo?']. Research Project I+D CSIC–UDELAR. Montevideo: Facultad de Ciencias Sociales, Departamento de Sociología-UNFPA.

Batthyány, K., M. Cabrera and L. Scuro (2007) *Encuesta Nacional de Hogares Ampliada 2006: Perspectiva de Género* [*Extended National Household Survey 2006: A Gender Perspective*]. Informe Temático, May. Montevideo: INE-UNDP-UNFPA.

Bucheli, M., N. Ferreira-Coimbra, A. Forteza and I. Rossi (2006) 'El acceso a la jubilación o pensión en Uruguay: ¿cuántos y quiénes lo lograrían?' ['Access to Pensions in Uruguay: Who Will Make It?']. Unidad de Estudios Especiales. Montevide: ECLAC.

Cabella, W. (2007) 'El cambio familiar en Uruguay: una breve reseña de las tendencias recientes'. ['Family Change in Uruguay: A Review of Recent Trends']. Serie divulgación. Montevideo: UNFPA.

Cerutti, A. (2006) 'Centros de Atención Integral a la Primera Infancia y la Familia: Una Primera Mirada al Plan CAIF'. Paper prepared for the debate of the 'Red Género y Familia' (Gender and Family Network), Montevideo (October). (Mimeo.)

Ciganda, D. (2008) 'Jóvenes en transición hacia la Vida Adulta: ¿el orden de los factores no altera el resultado?' ['Transition to Adulthood: Is the Result Independent from the Order of Factors?'], in C. Varela Petito (ed.) *Demografía de una sociedad en transición. La población uruguaya a inicios del siglo XX* [*Demography of a Society in Transition: The Uruguayan Population at the Start of the Twentieth Century*], pp. 69–82. Montevideo: UNFPA/Programa de Población Universidad de la Republica.

ECLAC (2009) *Social Panorama of Latin America*. Santiago de Chile: ECLAC.

Filgueira, C. (1996) *Sobre Revoluciones Ocultas: Las Transformaciones de la Familia en el Uruguay* [*On Hidden Revolutions: Transformations of the Family in Uruguay*]. Montevideo: ECLAC.

Filgueira, C. (1998) *Emancipación Juvenil: Trayectorias y Destinos* [*Youth Emancipation: Paths and Destinies*]. Montevideo: ECLAC.

Filgueira, C. and A. Peri (2004) 'América Latina. Los rostros de la pobreza y sus causas determinantes' ['Latin America: The Faces of Poverty and its Causes']. Serie Población y Desarrollo. Santiago de Chile: ECLAC.

Filgueira, C., F. Filgueira and A. Fuentes (2001) 'Critical Choices at a Critical Age: Youth Emancipation Paths and School Attainment in Latin America'. Working Paper R-432. Washington, DC: IADB.

Filgueira, F. and D. Gelber (2005) 'La Informalidad en Uruguay: ¿Un Mecanismo de Adaptación del Trabajo o del Capital?' ['Informality in Uruguay: An Adaptation Mechanism of Work or of Capital?']. Monitor Social del Uruguay IPES Working Paper No. 5. Montevideo: IPES.

Filgueira, F., F. Rodríguez, C. Rafaniello, S. Lijtenstein and P. Alegre (2005) 'Estructura de riesgo y arquitectura de protección social en el Uruguay actual: Crónica de un divorcio anunciado' ['Risk Structure and Current Social Protection Architecture in Uruguay: Chronicle of a Divorce Foretold'], in F. Filgueira and D. Gelber (eds) *Dilemas Sociales y Alternativas Distributivas en el Uruguay* [*Social Dilemmas and Alternative Distribution Choices in Uruguay*], pp. 7–42. (Thematic issue of *Revista PRISMA*).

INE-UNIFEM-UDELAR (2008) 'Uso del Tiempo y Trabajo No Remunerado en el Uruguay. Módulo de la Encuesta Continua de Hogares, 2007' ['Time Use and Unpaid Work in Uruguay. Based on the Permanent Household Survey, 2007']. Montevideo: INE-UNIFEM-UDELAR.

Kaztman, R. and F. Filgueira (2001) 'Panorama de la Infancia y de la Familia en Uruguay' ['Panorama of Childhood and the Family in Uruguay']. Programa de Investigación sobre Integración, Pobreza y Exclusión Social (IPES). Montevideo: Universidad Católica del Uruguay, Faculty of Social Sciences and Comunication.

Kaztman, R. et al. (2003) 'La Ciudad Fragmentada: Mercado, Territorio y Marginalidad en Montevideo' ['The Fragmented City: Market, Territory and Marginality in Montevideo']. CSUIM Working Paper # 02-UR-01. Austin, TX: University of Texas, Austin.

National Institute of Statistics (INE) (2008) 'Household Surveys from 1980 to 2000'. http://www.ine.gub.uy/biblioteca/publicaciones2008.asp#ECH

Papadópulos, J. (2008) 'Por una Política de Cuidados en una Nueva Arquitectura del Bienestar' ['For a Care Policy as Part of a New Welfare Architecture']. Paper presented at the 'Red Género y Familia' (Gender and Family Network), Montevideo (October).

Paredes, M. (2003) 'Los cambios en la familia en Uruguay: ¿Hacia una segunda transición demográfica?' ['Changes in the Family in Uruguay: Towards a Second Demographic Transition?'], in UDELAR-UNICEF *Nuevas Formas de Familia* [*New Family Forms*], pp. 73–101. Montevideo: UDELAR- UNICEF.

Pascall, G. (2006) 'Male Breadwinner Model', in *International Encyclopedia of Social Policy*. http://cw.routledge.com/ref/socialpolicy/male.html

Pereira, J., L. Monteiro and D. Gelber (2005) 'Cambios estructurales y nueva configuración de riesgos: desbalances e inequidades en el sistema de salud uruguayo' ['Structural Changes and New Risk Configurations: Inequities in the Uruguayan Health System'], in F. Filgueira and D. Gelber (eds) *Dilemas Sociales y Alternativas Distributivas en el Uruguay* [*Social Dilemmas and Alternative Distribution Choices in Uruguay*], pp. 141–68. (Thematic issue of *Revista PRISMA*).

Prates, S. (1983) 'Cuando el Sector Formal Organiza el Trabajo Informal: Las Trabajadores del Calzado en el Uruguay' ['When the Formal Sector Organizes Informal Work: Shoe Industry Workers in Uruguay']. Working Paper No. 60. Montevideo: CIESU.

Salvador, S. (2008) 'La Valorización del Trabajo no Remunerado en el Uruguay' ['Putting Value on Non-paid Work in Uruguay']. Working Paper. Montevideo: INE-UNIFEM-CIEDUR.

United Nations Development Programme (2002) *Desarrollo Humano en Uruguay 2001.* [*Human Development in Uruguay 2001*]. Montevideo: UNPD-ECLAC.

Varela, C., R. Pollero and A. Fostik (2008) 'La fecundidad: evolución y diferenciales en el comportamiento reproductivo' ['Fertility: Evolution and Differentials in Reproductive Behaviour'], in C. Varela Petito (ed.) *Demografía de una sociedad en transición: la Población uruguaya a inicios del siglo XXI* [*Demography of a Society in Transition: The Uruguayan Population at the Start of the Twentieth Century*], pp. 36–68. Montevideo: Trilce.

8

Stratified Familialism: The Care Regime in India through the Lens of Childcare

Rajni Palriwala and Neetha N.

INTRODUCTION

The care regime in India is fuzzy and rests on a series of contradictions. It is an ad hoc summation of informal and stratified practices of (in)security and care. These practices come together on the basis of a fragile institution of family and an ideology of gendered familialism. These frame a discourse that obscures and justifies absences in state actions and governance and tie into a market that is embedded in social and economic inequalities.

In explicating this, three features of India's political economy and social policies, which feed into each other, have first to be elaborated. Each of these features either contradicts what has become political common sense or is paradoxical in itself. The first pertains to economic trends and employment patterns. The relatively high rates of GDP growth and the expansion of an educated and service sector-based middle class in the last two decades are tied into an overwhelming and increasing predominance of unorganized/informal work, such that socio-economic inequalities have grown. Economic trends, as context, shape the pre-conditions within which care takes place as well as the demand for and delivery of care. In shaping the distribution of work, livelihoods, wealth and poverty, this feature influences the time availability and flexibility of individuals/households and the possibilities of purchasing the time of others. It also delineates the provision of commoditized care giving. The second paradox is that India's elaborate list of social programmes adds up to a residual welfare regime. This feature, too, is part of the context shaping the instrumentalities of care and also delineates the possibilities of state provisioning of care. Running through state policy, valuations and possibilities of giving and accessing care can be discerned, at times in an explicit discourse, at times implied. This brings us to the third feature and paradox: the hiatus between the public rhetoric of women's empowerment and the gendered familialism (elaborated later) of public policy, which reiterates care as a familial and female responsibility.

This article is based on various reports of the India study in the UNRISD project on 'The Political and Social Economy of Care', in particular Palriwala and Neetha (2009a). We would like to thank all members of the UNRISD project, especially Shahra Razavi and Silke Staab, for continuing discussions and comments, and the anonymous referees for comments on an earlier draft of this paper.

Seen, Heard and Counted, First Edition. Edited by Shahra Razavi.
Chapters © 2012 The Institute of Social Studies. Book compilation © 2012 Blackwell Publishing Ltd.

Elaborating these features together is vital to unpacking the state–market–family–society dynamics that produce care practices in India. These dynamics and the range of childcare practices from the viewpoint of the care giver — which have been largely ignored or touched on in only a general manner in earlier discussions — are the central foci of this article.[1] It builds on the view that social and economic policies and a welfare regime rest on an implicit conceptualization of care and its practices (Jenson, 1997), the latter in turn affected by the orientation and possibilities which these policies create, reinforce or foreclose. It also emphasizes that an explication of care cannot be limited to the dyad of individuals who give and receive care; the structural and institutional context is decisive. Despite the neoliberal turn and the lack of an explicit care policy, the state is directly and indirectly critical. The notion of the 'care diamond' (Razavi, 2007) provides an entry point in delineating the range of institutions in and through which everyday care practices are organized. In pulling together the various strands of the care diamond, what emerges are the differentiations, informalities, and uncertainties in care giving and receiving. The ideology and discourse of gendered familialism, which assume a uniform practice of care by women within the family, obscure this differentiation and the actualities of a stratified familialism, which we elaborate in the conclusion.

INFORMAL WORK IN A GROWING ECONOMY

Turning to the first of the features mentioned above — the economic context of care provisioning — one notes the sharp acceleration in India's GDP growth rate in the 1980s and 1990s, after the institutionalization of the neoliberal agenda. It increased from around 3 per cent per annum in the 1970s to 5.9 per cent over the period 1991–2005 (Nayyar, 2006). The tertiary sector, particularly services, led this growth, such that its share expanded from 31.9 per cent of GDP in 1970–71 to around 54 per cent in 2005–06 (Government of India, 2006). Assertions that an emphasis on this sector would improve the quantity and quality of employment, lead to a decline in

---

1. As well as official reports and statistics, research papers — both quantitative and qualitative — and other secondary material, this study drew on fieldwork in which care and gender were concerns. The fieldwork sites were in Sikar and Dholpur (Rajasthan), Morena (Madhya Pradesh), Fatehgarh Saheb (Punjab), NOIDA (UP), Delhi, Rohtak (Haryana), and Vellore and Tiruppur (Tamil Nadu). The fieldwork included rural and urban sites and was conducted at various times over the last decade (other than in Sikar). In 2007, life histories specifically focused on care practices were collected in a village in Rohtak and in Vellore; primary school teachers and *anganwadi* workers and helpers were interviewed; and a survey of domestic workers was conducted in Rohtak town and of *anganwadis* in one block in rural Rohtak. Policy makers were also interviewed. A wide range of oral communications and discussions are also drawn on. In this paper we name the person, institution, or area only where a point is very specific to that source.

poverty levels, and enhance standards of living are not found to hold true, especially for women.

Workforce participation rates (WPR) since 1984 have declined for rural women and fluctuated for men and urban women, with an upward trend only in 2004–05.[2] The WPR for urban women remains as low as 16.6 per cent as against 55 per cent for men, even when subsidiary workers are included. Despite diversification, agriculture, which constitutes the bulk of the primary sector, remains predominant in employment (especially for women), as seen in Table 1, and is also significant in urban areas.[3] The growing employment in the service sector is very heterogeneous in income and benefits, job expansion, skills, and productivity. Formal employment has stagnated, while informal work increased from 89 per cent of the total workforce in 1989 to 92.4 per cent in 2004–05. Between 1999–2000 and 2004–05 the net employment increase has been in informal employment (Figure 1), even as the share of the informal sector in total GDP reduced by about 5.5 percentage points in aggregate (NCEUS, 2007). Thus, not only have the hopes of betterment in employment not been met, there is a rise in social and economic inequalities, including rural–urban inequality, demonstrated in various studies (see e.g., Dev and Ravi, 2007; Patnaik, 2006; Sen and Himanshu, 2004).

By definition, informal employment is marked by a lack of social security benefits and the absence of unionization and is also characterized by long hours and low and irregular wages/income, especially for women. The low wages of the highly informal work they find, in whichever sector they work, is one indication that it is poverty and distress that drives most women into the labour market. As we will draw out later, the increase in low-paid, casual, home-based, 'putting out' work and unremunerative self-employment for women in the 1990s (Chandrasekhar and Ghosh, 2006) is not only in keeping with economic policy, but also with the gendered familialism and male breadwinner model undergirding social policy.

Although less than 7 per cent of female employment was in the tertiary sector in 2004–05, a closer look is important in understanding the market provision of care, which is a growth sector. Employment in education, long seen as acceptable for women, has risen and accounts for 38 per cent of women workers in this sector. The proportion of women workers in retail trade, hotels and restaurants, and personal and community services, has also increased (Palriwala and Neetha, 2008). The last category contains the sub-category of 'private households with employed persons', which includes domestic workers, watchmen, gardeners, etc. The number of women working as housemaids/servants has nearly quadrupled. The share of this category in the total service employment of women has more than doubled between 1999

---

2. India has not seen the feminization of the workforce noted for other economies.
3. The female shares of employment in both the secondary and service sectors have fluctuated, but in 2004–05 were close to the shares seen in 1983.

Table 1. *Broad Sectoral Distribution and Shares of Male and Female Workers (Usual Principal and Subsidiary Status—UPSS) (per cent)*

Sector	Male				Female			
	1983	1993–94	1999–2000	2004–05	1983	1993–94	1999–2000	2004–05
Primary	62.3 (60.00)	58.3 (60.81)	54.9 (61.56)	51.54 (59.23)	81.1 (40.00)	77.8 (39.19)	76.2 (38.44)	74.16 (40.77)
Secondary	15.0 (70.09)	16.8 (76.14)	17.8 (77.03)	11.98 (69.02)	12.5 (29.91)	10.9 (23.86)	11.8 (22.97)	11.24 (30.98)
Tertiary	22.7 (82.97)	24.6 (81.84)	27.3 (83.49)	36.48 (83.93)	9.1 (17.03)	11.4 (18.16)	12.0 (16.51)	14.60 (16.07)
Total	100 (65.53)	100 (67.37)	100 (68.97)	100 (67.64)	100 (34.47)	100 (32.63)	100 (31.03)	100 (32.36)

Note: Figures in parentheses refer to sex-wise share in total employment in the given sector.
Source: NSSO Employment and Unemployment Data, various rounds.

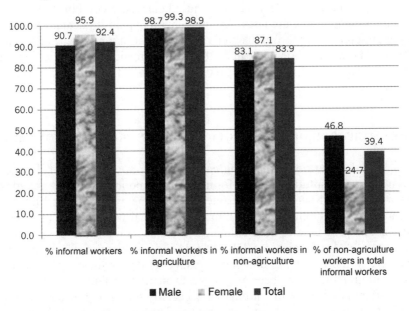

Figure 1. Workers in Formal and Informal Employment (2004–05)

Source: Computed from NCEUS (2007: Appendix A1.2).

and 2004 from 11.8 per cent to 27.1 per cent, further feminizing this category of workers (Palriwala and Neetha, 2009b).[4] The broad characteristics of domestic workers that emerge from the NSSO 2004–05 data are that they are employed largely in urban areas, are mostly married or widowed women (73.1 per cent), illiterate or without any formal schooling (60 per cent), a large chunk falls in the age group 21–40 years (48 per cent) and the total includes 33.4 per cent Scheduled Castes (SCs). Micro-studies and our fieldwork suggest that a large proportion of domestic workers are migrants (Kaur, 2006; Moghe, 2006; Neetha, 2003).[5] There is a regular inflow from particular rural pockets, linked to rural–urban inequalities. Many women are migrating alone, leaving their children with their kin, while they undertake paid care work in elite, urban households. We see here the emergence of local care chains.[6]

In sum, women's labour is far from being defamilialized, is limited in its commodification, and easily segues into unpaid care work, which through the common sense gendering of work and family, continues to be asserted

4. Some of this increase may be due to greater recognition and hence better enumeration of domestic service.
5. The proportion of migrants among domestic workers cannot be estimated as the NSSO employment data do not give migration status.
6. The national counterpart of the global care chains suggested by Hochschild (2000).

as women's responsibility. Hours and patterns of some of the new paid work opportunities enable women of varied classes to combine paid work — such as teaching or domestic service — with unpaid childcare, returning when children are back from school or working at or near their homes and children. However, time that can be devoted to unpaid care is shrinking for growing numbers of women. We return to this point in our discussion on stratified familialism.

THE PATCHWORK OF SOCIAL POLICY AND THE PRIVATIZING OF CARE

The second dimension structuring care practices is composed of the programmes and institutions which form the social policy regime. A paradox that is embedded here is that despite the very many detailed and diverse social policy programmes, India remains a residual welfare state (Titmuss, 1958). The programmes outlined below are also in line with Gough's description (2004) of a piecemeal, haphazard and reactive process. With anti-poverty, welfare, equality and social justice as the variously stated ends, these programmes have been responses to market or family 'failures' or have offered assistance to marginal or especially 'deserving' social groups. While there is a large body of work that has focused on the trends in India's social policy and programmes,[7] internal incongruities (other than the lack of implementation) have rarely been elaborated, the implications of gendered ideologies and the absence of care concerns have not been integrated,[8] and their link to informal, private and familial systems of care have not been analysed. These incongruities make formal systems ad hoc, informal, and fuzzy.[9]

---

7. Only a few of these studies and discussions can be mentioned here. Some studies focus on specific programmes or initiatives pertaining to a particular social category, while others look at social policy and funding in general with varying levels of empirical detail (Dev and Mooij, 2005; Sen and Rajasekhar, 2009). They examine the implications of the economic reforms, identifying insecurities associated with shifts in employment and labour (Srivastava, 2009), poverty and growing inequalities (Dev, 2008), and continuities in social exclusion and marginalization (Thorat, 2009; Wazir, 2009). Some have been framed in a discussion of the contending principles and bases of entitlement which do or should enliven social policy (Chhachhi, 2009), including universal social protection versus targeted programmes (Saith, 2009; Srivastava, 2009), paternalism, freedoms and rights in a context of globalization (Standing, 2009), or promotional and protective aspects of social security (Sen and Rajasekhar, 2009). Besides the seminal works by Sen (1982) and Dreze and Sen (1995), which look at the relationship between development, democracy and state economic policy and the huge body of work on poverty, inequality and development, studies which look specifically at the relationship between politics, redistribution and poverty reduction (e.g. Kohli, 2007) are also important.

8. Sen and Rajasekhar (2009) and Chhachhi (2009) are among the few that focus on the gender dimensions of social policy, the latter also raising the issue of care.

9. Abhijit Sen, Member of the Planning Commission, suggested in an interview in 2007 that welfare policy became fuzzy long before the neoliberal turn, from the early 1970s, even as the anti-poverty rhetoric increased.

As is well known, with the reforms from the end of the 1980s, GDP growth, the market, and a push to curtail state expenditures in social programmes became the overarching principles of state policy. Key to policy redesign were arguments that individual/familial responsibility and civil society initiatives should be facilitated as against state responsibilities. With privatization, there was a shift from universal to targeted programmes and the possibility of simultaneous market and family 'failures' was played down. Importantly, though much of social policy in India falls within the purview of provincial governments, the balance of jurisdiction and fiscal powers lies with the central government. With the help of a centralized bureaucratic service this has meant that centrally advocated neoliberal reforms could be pushed across the country.

Thus, social sector expenditure declined (as a percentage of GDP) in the early 1990s (Figure 2), rose in the late 1990s, and subsequently fluctuated with a substantial climb in the period 2008–09. 'Social security and welfare' includes a range of non-universal, discretionary schemes for 'deserving sections' as well as the Integrated Child Development Scheme (ICDS) discussed later. The small upward movements over the last decade are a result of patronage politics (which the growing informal economy enhances), the

Figure 2. Expenditure on Social Sector as a Proportion of Gross Domestic Product (GDP)

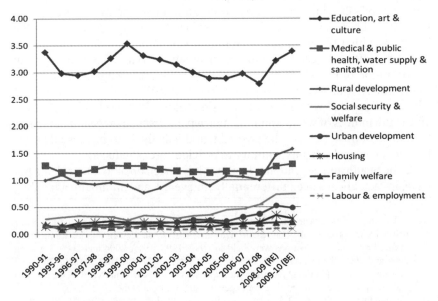

Note: For GDP upto 2003–04, base year is 1999–2000; for GDP from 2004–05 onwards, base year is 2004–05.
Source: Computed from Ministry of Finance *Public Finance Statistics* (various years), and Reserve Bank of India *Handbook of Statistics on Indian Economy* (various years).

compulsions of social constituencies, electoral concerns[10] and alliances, and social and political mobilizations at the local and national levels, rather than a value commitment to welfare on the part of the governments in power.

In the following sub-sections, social policy and the welfare regime in India are discussed through a cluster of features that encompass the frequent shifts in policy language. These features are internally contradictory and the resultant social policy is difficult to pin down neatly. In negotiating livelihoods and the residual, patchwork welfare regime, care practices are constructed, enhanced, or diminished, often in a makeshift manner. Some aspects of social policy, such as those pertaining to primary schooling and health, directly relate to care. Others have an indirect implication for care, through their effects on acquiring the means for care, on the cost of care, on the likelihood that people will choose to give care, and whom they will give care to. Due to these implications, the latter have also to be outlined in setting out the social policy context for care.

Limiting Universality

The one universal welfare measure that was accessed by large sections of the poor, the lower middle class and others was the public distribution system (PDS). Under the PDS, specific grains and 'basic needs' items were sold at fixed prices through 'fair price' shops to ration-card holders. This was the government's flagship anti-poverty programme, tacitly premised on a right to food. With liberalization, the PDS was replaced by a targeted system — the TPDS — with differential pricing for those classified 'Below Poverty Line' and 'Above Poverty Line'. There is considerable variation between states in the operation of the TPDS and in evaluations by official agencies, scholars (Dev, 2008), and women's organizations (AIDWA, 2008). Scholars and activists argue that with errors of omission (of needy households), nutrition and health indices of women and children have worsened or the improvement has slowed down.[11] It may be posited that this is likely to increase the care burden, even as the family's ability to provide care is reduced.

Public health and educational facilities have been open to all residents but have, in fact, always been differentially, unevenly, and minimally available,

---

10. A looming election year influences government budgets in recognition of the effects of patronage and social policy on results. This is evident if, on viewing Figure 2, one keeps in mind that general elections were held in 1996, 1998, 1999, 2004 and 2009. Between 2004 and 2009, the central government's dependence on the Left and pressures of social movements were additional factors in the expansion of the ICDS and NREGA (see below) and the upward trend in social sector expenditure. See also Kohli (2007).

11. Though there is a paucity of data regarding intra-household distribution, qualitative studies have indicated the gender differential (against women) in the basics of survival — nutrition and access to health services, especially at maternity. The prevalence of anaemia among women and children is widespread and has risen, including among pregnant women. It is higher among Scheduled Caste and Scheduled Tribe women than among other women (Bose, 2006; IIPS and MI, 2007).

a situation that has been exacerbated with privatization. Large sections of the poor often could not access public facilities due to their non-availability or the immediate loss of wages or of family workers that accessing a facility (such as schooling) entailed. The middle classes and elite have always turned to private facilities, with a few exceptions. Thus, those who run the government have had little stake in ensuring and improving public facilities, though they access the 'islands of excellence'[12] within them. This orientation has undoubtedly also has much to do with the dearth of public crèches and day-care for children.

The health system is critical to the social and political economy of care and has been a standard index for evaluating a welfare regime from the time of the Beveridge Plan. From the start, the public health system was marked by low funding, poor spread into rural areas, paucity of staff, and substandard facilities (Duggal and Gangolli, 2005). The dominance of out-of-pocket expenses in healthcare in India, particularly in out-patient treatment, stands out internationally (see Gough, 2004, for a comparative view). In addition, as population control became a principal 'development' strategy of the Indian state, allocations for health, especially of women and children, were increasingly in family planning programmes — euphemistically named 'family welfare'. This made even the poor wary of public health facilities.

This has been accentuated since the end of the 1980s with the push for privatization. In 1997, far more than half of hospitals and dispensaries, but less than half of beds, were in the private sector, the latter expanding hugely since then. Most doctors are private practitioners and form the single largest category of health services utilized (Duggal and Gangolli, 2005: 7). Imposition of user fees within public health institutions and the rising costs of medicine following market deregulation have pushed people towards the private sector and reduced access to healthcare among the poor (Priya, 2005).

The shortage of nurses is severe,[13] related to the lack and quality of training institutions, low wages, bad working conditions, low social status, and migration of trained nurses to Europe and the USA. The last feature is another strand in the global care chain. The lack of affordable medical treatment and professional nurses means that the care of the ill, and not just of the chronically sick, falls on family members (usually women and girls), or else the sick, such as girl children, are denied any treatment that has to be paid for (John et al., 2008). Not only has the decline in infant and child mortality rates slowed, nearly 25 per cent of deaths of under-fives per year globally are in India and maternal mortality rates are scandalously high (Ved and Dua, 2005). Clearly, families and informal systems are unable to provide the required care.

Primary schooling is of particular import to the social and political economy of childcare. While pedagogical aims may be the principle, with formal

---

12. Particularly in higher education and specialized medical treatment.
13. Only in four states are the number of nurses above the very low recommendation of the Bhore Committee of 150 per 100,000 population (Gangolli et al., 2005: S-14).

schooling some basic care of children shifts from the domestic to the public domain. Schooling is also the minimal programme expected in any public welfare system. In India, the education budget did not match the requirements of universalization. Though higher in absolute terms than in earlier decades, it declined with fluctuations, as a percentage of GDP after 1990. Central taxes earmarked for education increased from 2004–05, but expenditures by states declined. Primary education gained over secondary and higher education, in part due to new and varied primary education programmes (Palriwala and Neetha, 2009a). The latter focused on literacy in different age and social groups and pushed non-formal education, such that children were retained for only short hours in the non-domestic setting, if at all. Even today, a small but significant percentage of habitations and populations do not have an easily accessed primary school, and/or the basic infrastructure and teaching staff are inadequate (Borooah, 2007: 391; Planning Commission, 2008b), even though a large number of trained teachers are unemployed. These are factors in the lower enrolments reported for rural areas, for girls, for the upper-primary level and among poorer religious and caste groups as against urban areas, boys, the lower-primary level and better-off castes (Planning Commission, 2008b).

Yet, over the last twenty-five years, enrolment in elementary education has substantially improved and the drop-out rate has declined, especially for girls (Palriwala and Neetha, 2008). A major factor has been the introduction of the Mid-Day Meal (MDM) scheme, a programme partly initiated to promote access, retention and nutritional care of primary school children (Rajivan, 2006; Ramachandran et al., 2003). Following actions by civil society organizations, the MDM was designated as a universal provision in all government and government-aided primary schools in 2001. The orientation of the government and the preferences of much of the middle class during this period, however, were to encourage private schools. The significance of the MDM scheme and public education and their role in household strategies is seen in the fact that despite the rapid growth of private schools since the 1990s, the poor and lower middle classes continued to enrol their children preponderantly in government schools (Tilak and Sudarshan, 2007).[14]

Care and Primary Schooling

The lack of facilities and activities to engage children in school lead to truancy and lower attendance rates evident in low levels of learning (ASER, 2011). In addition, illness, migration for work, and labour requirements at home, especially during the peak agricultural seasons, are among the reasons

---

14. According to the provisional Annual Status of Education Report, 2010, rural enrolment of the 6–14 age group is now over 96 per cent. Over 24 per cent are enrolled in private schools, a big jump in just five years. Private enrolment is higher for boys and in the southern states (see ASER, 2011).

given by parents for lack of enrolment or attendance (Ramachandran et al., 2003).[15] If children do not attend school regularly, the pedagogical aims of schooling cannot be fulfilled and care/custodial functions cannot be made a public responsibility.

While the long distances between home and school accentuate local concerns over the sexual and physical safety of girls and affect their enrolment, demands of domestic and familial care work on daughters are also critical.[16] Poor and labouring families in which all adult members are in paid work turn to 'older' daughters to care for younger children and complete chores around the home. The absence of functioning and quality crèches and day-care centres leave them with little choice. The early imposition of the gendered division of labour in domestic and care responsibilities in the lifecycle of girls can lead to lack of time in keeping up with school work and their eventual dropping-out, even if they are not explicitly withdrawn due to marriage or domestic work norms. Fees, as in private education, compound the loss of care labour and further discourage schooling for girls. The MDM scheme and various incentive schemes, like the provision of free uniforms, textbooks and scholarships to poor children and girls, can only partially counter the demands of care and domestic labour made on daughters.

Early Childhood Education and the Integrated Child Development Scheme

Child welfare and child development have been a leitmotif in women-related social policy, as we will discuss again later, which in conjunction with anti-poverty concerns were translated into child nutrition programmes. After setting up a small network of child centres under the Central Social Welfare Board from the 1950s, the government provided financial assistance to NGOs for running crèches for children of 'ailing and working mothers'[17] from 1975. This was a limited scheme (Swaminathan, n.d.); it expanded after being renamed the Rajiv Gandhi National Creche Scheme in 2005–06, but still covered only about half a million children (Government of India, n.d.: 64).

From the 1990s and particularly over the last decade, the Integrated Child Development Scheme (ICDS) has grown into the largest child nutrition programme in the world. It is organized through community-based centres called *anganwadis*. The number of centres and beneficiaries has steadily increased to cover more than 26 per cent of children aged 0–6 (Supreme Court

---

15. Ghosh (2001) surmises non-attendance on observing the lower degree of participation in education in the current weekly status as against the participation by the usual status definitions in the 55th round of the NSS. Ramachandran et al. (2003) found irregularity of attendance to be particularly the case for first generation learners and children of poor families and cite similar findings from the larger survey by Jha and Jhingran (2002).
16. See Nambissan (1996), Probe Team (1999), Sen (2009). Our field data from Haryana also showed sibling care as an important reason for girls dropping out from school.
17. Who work in the informal/unorganized sector.

Commissioners, 2005). Functioning of the centres and of the supplementary nutrition programme is very uneven between states (Dreze, 2006), but it has been suggested that the ICDS is a major factor in the decline in child mortality rates (Kaul, 2002). However, even in Tamil Nadu, Puducherry and Kerala, which are said to have the best programmes (Dreze, 2006; Rajivan, 2006) and where the centres are open for the longest hours, their timings do not suit the demands of day-care and working mothers. The proportion of children below the age of three who remain at the centres is particularly negligible (Gragnolati et al., 2006; Ramachandran et al., 2003).

Like crèche services, pre-primary education and early childhood educa-tion (ECE) facilities, which inevitably become partial substitutes for unpaid, domestic childcare, have not been a government priority.[18] The enrolment of children in the age group 3–6 in public initiatives that had a component of ECE rose from 15 per cent in 1989 to just under 21 per cent in 2004 (Government of India, n.d.: 63).[19] Rather than developing an alternative net-work of childcare centres, the proposal was to transmute the *anganwadis* of the ICDS into a nutrition-cum-crèche-cum-pre-school programme, empha-sized also in the Tenth Plan. This proposal has still not been realized, not least due to arguments of some ICDS supporters that it should be a programme for home-based nutritional supplements (Supreme Court Commissioners, 2005).

The 86th Constitutional Amendment in 2002 changed the right to free and compulsory education from 0–14 years to 6–14 years. Swaminathan (2001: para 4) argues that this freed 'the government of taking responsibility for care and development of children before school age' and left early childhood education to the family. In this, both the family's right and the child's right to formal early childhood care and education were abrogated.

Exclusive Social Protection and Ad Hoc Workfare

A range of social protection entitlements are available to those in formal, particularly public, employment, making the latter much sought after. These entitlements are significant in ensuring resources that facilitate the giving and receiving of care. Thus, paid medical leave, pensions, and termination benefits enable the needs of the sick and the elderly to be met, including that of physical care. Paid maternal childcare leave, recently extended to a total of two and a half years to be taken at any time before the child turns eighteen, allows for the care of infants and children, as well as of the mothers. Public employees are allowed a variety of leave, designated as earned, paid,

---

18. Only 1.3 per cent of the total union budget was spent on the ICDS, the crèche scheme and child health combined (cited in Working Group on Children under Six, 2007).
19. Various, rather confusing, data are given. Another figure in the same document suggests an enrolment of 36 per cent in 2005.

half-paid or unpaid, without any threat to their jobs. Thus, people covered by social protection measures tied to formal employment are more likely to receive care and are able to make time to give non-routine care.

Not only does formal employment, to which these measures are linked, form a very small part of the economy, the government has placed curbs on permanent recruitment in the public sector. Most importantly, it bypasses its own regulatory framework through the segmentation of its employees into permanent, contract, and voluntary workers. Increasingly, governments are hiring only contract staff, who are not given the benefits mentioned above.[20] Publicly-funded organizations have also been directed to follow suit. This move is taken the furthest in institutions directly relating to care, such as in Sarva Shiksha Abhiyan schools, the Integrated Child Development Scheme, and the Rural Health Mission. Most field-level workers are women with their own familial care responsibilities, but are designated as 'volunteers' on stipends.

In addition, the few social protection measures that are applicable to the private sector increasingly go unmonitored. Several studies have shown that laws related to minimum wages, equal remuneration, regulation of hours of work, and maternity benefits are not implemented (Mazumdar, 2006). The double accounting[21] of employee registration and wages (since applicability of labour laws is tied to the number of employees) and the refusal to hire married women with young children have a specific bearing on women workers and their care responsibilities. The regulation violated most easily and on which there is perhaps the least noise and visibility is that related to the provision of crèches and day-care centres.

The array of cash transfer programmes would at first sight appear to fill part of the gap left by the exclusivity of social protection entitlements tied to formal employment. These cover a range of needs and include the Indira Awas Yojna (for housing), the National Old Age Pension, widow/disabled pension, maternity benefits (Janani Suraksha Yojana), and rural educational scholarships. Though most of these schemes are not directly about care,[22] they (as with some of the entitlements linked to formal employment) can play a role in providing money to buy care inputs and assist in the giving of care. However, not only are these programmes targeted, the benefit amounts are very low, as is coverage (Srivastava, 2009). Indeed, these schemes are not funded to cover all members of the targeted groups, even when a comparatively low poverty line is the main eligibility criterion, nor are they designed to do so. Schemes for informal workers, whether for medical care or

---

20. Though a Karnataka High Court judgement makes this illegal.
21. Employers keep one register to show the labour inspector on the rare chance that he visits and a second for their own accounts. Trade unions working in and around Delhi discovered this in a number of medium-sized factories.
22. See Razavi and other authors in this volume on cash transfers.

pensions, require contributions from them, but migration and their abysmally low wages make it difficult for them to be regular in their payments, with unpaid women 'helpers' in an even more difficult situation.[23] Thus, those who are primary carers have the least access to social protection. Knowledge regarding schemes is also low (Dev, 2008), placing claimants at the mercy of bureaucrats, politicians, and 'brokers' at various levels. The long and complicated process that individuals have to go through to avail of the benefits makes it even more daunting, especially for poor, illiterate women with care responsibilities.[24]

A constant refitting of earlier schemes combined with insufficient budgetary allocations is evident in the various workfare programmes, which constitute an important component of anti-poverty programmes in India. Their premise is that market and 'developmental' failures are bound to be temporary, such that stop-gap arrangements to plug crises are sufficient and efficient. Only with the National Rural Employment Guarantee Act (NREGA) has there been an expansion. This programme carries an annual guarantee of 100 days of casual, manual work within a 5 km radius to each rural household that enrols, at a minimum wage and with specifically listed worksite and welfare facilities. Compared to its predecessors the NREGA is radical, but a brief look shows continuity in the care and gender outlook of government policy. Unrealistically high, piece-rate productivity norms make women, the handicapped and the elderly unwelcome members of work-teams. The maximum of 100 days work per household can create conflict for separated/divorced women who live in their natal homes. Yet, female labour days formed 44 per cent of the total (all-India) days logged (Hirway, 2008). Despite their specification in law and their presence in public discourse subsequent to the debate on NREGA, childcare facilities at worksites are almost completely absent (Hirway, 2008; ISWDS, 2006).

The discussion above not only points to the well-known gap between promise and concrete activity in government social programmes, but to the internal contradictions that make this almost inevitable. We suggest that these gaps are not accidental or a result merely of the lack of a larger political vision. Rather, there is a deliberate fuzziness in policy that helps to obscure underlying continuities and structural contradictions that the state does not wish to address. It also suggests that state thinking on gender, care, and the family, which we elaborate in the next section, is central to such policy designs and to the implementation of social programmes.

---

23. The NCEUS proposals on social security for the unorganized/informal sector have not taken these problems into account (Neetha, 2006). Some of the schemes suggested are contributory (Unorganized Workers' Social Security Act 2008, Rastriya Swastiya Bima Yojana or National Health Insurance Scheme), such that unpaid women 'helpers' are excluded in the design itself.
24. This was evident in the lack of success in attempts by AIDWA, Delhi, to assist widows in resettlement colonies and working class areas to access the widows' pension scheme.

GENDERED FAMILIALISM AND CARE IN POLICY
THINKING AND DISCOURSE

The modes of (non-)recognition of care rest on two further elements that imbue policy thinking in India. One is *familialism* — the assumption that the state need not deal with people as citizens with individual rights, but may deal with them as members of family and community networks (see also Chhachhi, 2009). Familialism draws on the idea that the family is essentially good and that any internal inequalities and power dynamics enable the functioning of this necessary social unit (à la Parsons). Despite public bemoaning among the urban, middle class of the decline of the joint family, it also supposes the continuing prevalence of extended kin ties, which demographic figures do not completely belie. Family 'failures' are taken to be the exception, the pathological, as against the socially normal mode of life, or a trend which can and should be reversed. It is thence assumed that familial relationships form a security and care net that people can and will turn to.

The second element is the *gendered* qualifier — women's place is in the home. A theme often heard in public discourse is that it is against tradition and undesirable for women to go out to work, all the more so if familial care responsibilities are to be met. Versions of this are reflected in policy. The male breadwinner model is vital to the idea and practice of familialism. Women are viewed as dependent family members and mothers rather than as economically independent workers or citizens.[25] That paid work does not define women's lives is not without foundation. Women's low employment rates and informal work have been discussed earlier. Furthermore, the romanticization of the family as essentially good draws a veil on the gender inequalities embedded in it. Legally and socially recognized violence is cast as an aberration[26] rather than structural, or an exaggeration on the part of women's groups, to be redressed without the divisions and allocations of work and resources within the family being questioned.

Constitutional equality and women's rights to education, employment and property, along with the vote, raised by women's organizations during the national movement, were legislated soon after Independence. However, an

---

25. This is evident from patterns of funding and from reading official documents in their entirety. The parts of any one document can in themselves mislead as they are padded with long expositions of views from domestic and international women's movements that, however, remain at the level of rhetoric. For instance, the introductory chapter of the Eleventh Five Year Plan begins with an acknowledgement of women's agency and their specific rights and needs, but many women-specific issues and needs are clubbed together under women and child development, with women's role in the latter being the primary focus. See Planning Commission (2008a, 2008b).

26. Many gender/women related issues are cast as an excisable 'social evil' in official statements and in various court judgements related to dowry or domestic violence. See Agnihotri and Palriwala (2001); Kapur and Crossman (1996).

equation of women's, children's, and family interests meant that notions of child welfare and child development were taken as the framework for women's development.[27] The first women-specific programmes were measures such as the Mahila Mandals (women's groups) designed to teach poor and rural women to be good mothers (Mehra, 1983) or schemes to help destitute women (assumed to be women without husbands or adult sons) (Palriwala, 2002). Special provisions for women (toilets, rest rooms) in some labour laws as well as rules regarding crèches were not the result of a conscious policy decision to promote women's employment and, as indicated earlier, have often not been complied with — much in keeping with the picture in many developed, capitalist countries.

From the 1970s, women's organizations and the Committee on the Status of Women in India (CSWI) argued that women's rights as independent citizens and as workers had to be expanded. In that discussion, women's contribution to GDP was highlighted, leading to the official recognition of women's 'productive potential' in the Seventh Five Year Plan (1985). This plan also suggested that women's earnings were a surer way to improve the conditions of poor families (and children); women's informal, income-earning work was to be a path out of poverty. Income-generation programmes for women of different occupational categories, including agricultural workers, farmers, traders, and artisans were introduced. These programmes were meant to enable women to earn a *supplementary* income, preferably from home-based, self-employed, or informal work, furthering their engagement in semi-marketized, semi-monetized, and non-contractual subsistence activities.

With liberalization, the language changed with only a slight shift in policy. Women were to be empowered by transforming self-employment into entrepreneurship through micro-credit and the formation of NGO-aided Self Help Groups. The continuing sub-text of most programmes has been that women's 'employment' should be informal or home-based, so as to enable them to combine paid work and their care responsibilities in the domestic domain.[28] Maternity and other benefits (including leave provisions that enable care-giving) need not and have not been extended to them. This thrust remains even as voices in public discourse, including feminist ones, argue that the predominance of the informal sector is inevitable. With the language of women's empowerment, the noticeable increase in school enrolment, and the visibility given to the employment of young women in new occupations, state policy is caught in apparent contradictions. While the Tenth Plan noted the need for day-care and women's participation in workfare programmes grew noticeably, childcare facilities continue to be meagre and

---

27. At that time, this was not of course unique to India, even while legal rights for women put it at the forefront in a global comparison.
28. See note 25.

poorly funded. Indeed, the notion that only 'ailing and working' mothers need crèches remains entrenched with little cognizance that childcare can be a deterrent to women's entry into paid work. One finds that in most of the discussions on the ICDS and the Indian state's child policy, women's rights to crèches or any sort of formal childcare services does not even enter the discourse. Governmentalities around gender and care have not been shaken, whether by the advocacy of women's paid work, assertions of growth in that sector, or talk of women's empowerment.

This suggests that care policies in India are shaped in a social, employment and wage policy discourse imbued by *gendered familialism*. This has meant that women's paid work is accepted but not encouraged and its full complement remains unacknowledged. This is evident in the persistence of gender disparity in wages and further declines in women's real wages after 1999–2000 (NSSO). It is assumed that women will undertake the care of the old, the sick, men, and children. It is not acknowledged that poverty and the absence of alternative livelihoods may require them to invest long hours in low-income earning work, such that care tasks have to be abbreviated or neglected. Simultaneously, paid care workers are devalued, as reflected in the dearth of childcare facilities, low wages for most categories of carers, and the lack of labour legislation for the growing number of domestic and personal service workers.

Gendered familialism reiterates that care work is a private responsibility, women's responsibility, and is embedded in familial relations, thereby defining the pool of carers and care receivers. It is not only a refusal to recognize care as a public responsibility, but an inability to comprehend that women have to combine paid work with their care responsibilities, especially in childcare, and may have difficulties in doing so. It thereby also limits women's abilities to acquire the resources necessary to enable care.

THE CARE DIAMOND: FAMILIAL, GENDERED AND INFORMAL SYSTEMS OF CARE

In drawing out the implications and outcomes for care of economic trends, social policy and state discourse, it is clear that the family is the primary institution in which care takes place and women and girls are the primary and predominant carers. This section outlines care practices at the points of the care diamond, starting with the family-household, and suggests the range of informal practices and strategies adopted by families and women, as they draw on various circles of support, including the state and the market. Professional and paid carers are also predominantly women and informal workers, even within formal institutions. The latter are limited in range and number, and are also 'informalized' through the deficiencies described when discussing social policy.

Unpaid Childcare Practices in Families

The patterns that emerge from the analysis of the Time Utilization Survey (TUS) data[29] (see Neetha and Palriwala, 2008) are more or less in keeping with what we would expect from the discussions so far, with one exception: the time spent on direct care of persons,[30] including childcare, is low across the board. Thus, of the various components of unpaid care work, women spent by far the greatest part of their time on household maintenance and shopping for their own household rather than on person care, whether on children, the sick, or the elderly. While this possibly points to a care deficit, it is also linked to the social value given to care labour. The survey probably did not capture the full extent of familial and women's time spent on care, since much of the latter can be, and is, undertaken along with other tasks.[31] With the gendered naturalization of care work and the devaluation of what it entails, unpaid childcare may not be recognized even by the carer, especially as the Indian survey prioritized SNA (System of National Accounts) work. In particular, the extent of low intensity 'presence' and availability that person care requires is often acknowledged only in a crisis.

The TUS data indicate that the proportion of men engaged in care work is small and the gender gap in unpaid care work, especially direct childcare, is very large. Engagement in unpaid care work was significant across all categories of women, whether or not they participated in paid work. More urban men participated in unpaid care work (50.7 per cent) than rural men (45.7 per cent), possibly related to a smaller proportion of extended households and kin in urban contexts. This variation may also be linked to differences in the doing and the recording of unpaid care work with sharper distinctions between paid and unpaid work in urban contexts and the greater simultaneity of activities in rural areas; 73.5 per cent of rural women combined SNA and Extended SNA as against 41.5 per cent in urban areas. Thus,

---

29. This survey was conducted by the CSO in 1998–99 and covered 18,591 households spread over six states. Although it was conducted as a pilot survey, this is the only nationally representative survey of time use available for India. The analysis here is based on the aggregate data of all the six states. The state and region-wise commonalities and differences are complex, such that any meaningful discussion would demand a separate paper.
30. Direct care of persons includes physical care of children, the sick, elderly and disabled; teaching, training and instruction to own children; accompanying children to places such as the school, primary health care centre (PHC), doctor, etc.; supervising adults and children needing care, with or without other activities; and travel related to care of children and adults.
31. Time use surveys have devised the full minute measure which adds up the time spent on simultaneous activities as if they had been undertaken separately. This measure showed higher values for all categories of care work compared to the 24 hour calculation, confirming the prevalence of simultaneity in care work. However, the difference was small, suggestive of underreporting and misreporting of multiple activities (for details see Neetha and Palriwala, 2008).

despite the greater participation by men, the male–female difference in time spent in unpaid care work was slightly larger in urban areas where women spent about 6.1 hours daily on unpaid care work in contrast to 5.5 hours spent by rural women and 1.2 hours by men in both rural and urban areas.

Women in informal work, for wages or in unpaid employment in family enterprises, and those with less education recorded more time spent on care work, including direct childcare, than did women working in the formal sector, in remunerated employment, and with higher education. Apparently, work in family enterprises and the unorganized sector, whether it is in the fields, at the loom, or in the forest, can be interwoven with domestic and care work. Mothers carry their children with them, though they may be no more than a presence in the child's immediate environ.[32] Where women were in formal employment, families had to make other arrangements.

Men and women in the high expenditure class tended to spend less time in direct childcare than did those of middle or low expenditure classes. However, time spent on direct childcare by the middle expenditure class was marginally above that of low income categories. The middle expenditure class best fits the ideology of gendered familialism; the larger proportion of women in this cateogry would not be in paid employment and a substantial proportion would not have studied beyond high school. Among the urban middle classes, grandparents may temporarily join the household to help with care in the first year after a child's birth. In both rural and urban working class neighbourhoods, children may be left with kin or neighbours or even left on their own, on the assumption that in an emergency neighbours will take charge or contact the parents at their nearby worksites (Palriwala and Neetha, 2009b). While these represent extreme cases, they also indicate that the compulsion to work among the income-poor can mean that women's paid work, possibly as carers in middle class and elite households, leads to a care deficit in their own. These employed women and their families cannot afford or do not avail of non-domestic care facilities even if they exist.

Women's and men's time in childcare are higher in the absence of a spouse, in the oldest age group, and in larger households, except in the largest size category. It decreases with the presence of older children. It is relevant to note that although the average household size has decreased since 1981, the decrease in the percentage of households with more than one married couple is marginal — from 20.2 per cent in 1981 to 19.6 per cent in 2001 (Household Tables in Registrar General, 1981; 2001). An additional and substantial proportion of households include kin beyond the nuclear family of parents and unmarried children (Palriwala and Neetha, 2008). As per Census figures, the absolute numbers of children and elderly not living with other kin or in non-institutional households are not small, but their

---

32. Our field data (see note 1) informs the discussion throughout this section.

proportions are. The practice of care work by older family members and of sibling care is part of everyday life — a practice which is reinforced by official gendered familialism. Mothers are viewed as the principal child carer, assisted by their 'older' children if any, particularly daughters, and older kin. Such kin are more likely to be present in the household or neighbourhood in rural rather than in urban locations, enabling a reduction in the time rural women spend in direct childcare. At least one marriage is nigh universal in India, especially for women; though rising, average age at marriage remains low and a substantial proportion of women become mothers before the age of eighteen (Registrar General, 2001; IIPS and MI, 2007). This means that as daughters, sisters, and mothers, women become care givers at an early age.

State-mandated Day-care Amenities and Crèches

There is a lack of crèches even in legally mandated worksites, private or public, such as the NREGA sites mentioned earlier. Studies indicate that where worksite services exist, they tend to be of poor quality and insufficiently staffed (Palriwala and Neetha, 2009a). Due to this and/or the difficulties faced in commuting with young children in cities with crowded and inadequate public transport, workers may not use worksite crèches (Datta, n.d.; Datta and Konantambigi, 2007). Generally, mothers of infants exit paid work, mostly without recourse to maternity benefits, or make other familial/community arrangements; there is a very low percentage of women among the formal, professional, and high-income workers, who can access commercial services. In accordance with labour laws, a few corporate groups (such as Glaxo and Port Trust Chennai) are running model crèches or pre-schools for their employees (Swaminathan, n.d.). In some cases, as with the ICICI bank, concerns are raised about the restricted coverage, resources and lack of user participation in the management of the facilities.

As discussed earlier, the ICDS was to expand into crèche and early childhood education activities. However, except in states such as Kerala, Tamil Nadu, and Puducherry, the short opening hours and lack of facilities, including space, teaching materials and workers — especially those trained to care for young children — mean that *anganwadis* are not used by parents of infants and young children for day-care or pre-school. Parents do not trust that care will be provided. Children are bored and do not want to stay at the centres. In many parts of the country, children come to the centres only at meal times and *anganwadis* are viewed as food kitchens rather than crèches. The quality of facilities and the irregular functioning of the centres are critical factors in the low enrolment and even lower attendance of children. Rather than highlighting these features, opinions that Indian parents are *culturally* disinclined to leave their children in extra-familial care are asserted to argue against the expansion of crèche services in the ICDS.

Another critical factor in the poor quality of day-care and ECE in the ICDS is the informalization of ICDS field staff. As indicated earlier, the workers are treated as part-time, 'volunteer social workers' on a stipend, though their hours and workload have been increasing over the years. As well as the work directly related to the *anganwadi* centres and supplementary nutrition and immunization related tasks, a constantly expanding list of record-keeping duties is being assigned to them. Since they work within the community, they are considered a cheap conduit for a range of government programmes (Gragnolati et al., 2006), the latest being the formation of Self Help Groups. The assumption among administrators appears to be that *anganwadi* workers have free time since childcare is taken to be light, intermittent work, easy and natural for women. Thus, the time of *anganwadi* workers and helpers is constantly being diverted away from care or pre-school education, for which their training is in any case insufficient. The small stipend or honorarium[33] also reinforces the idea that not only is care work undemanding and unskilled, it is to be measured in 'moral' rather than economic terms (Palriwala and Neetha, 2010).

Voluntary Sector Provisioning

The 1980s and 1990s had seen a vast growth of the voluntary or NGO sector, but not in crèches or ECE, even when activities were focused on working women or education. Mobile Crèches was the first and perhaps only NGO to specifically work in this area, with its innovative attempt to set up crèches at construction sites where women worked. Subsequently, other organizations, such as SEWA, started day-care projects. These initiatives, with different models and varying degrees of success, draw on multiple sources of funding, national as well as international — government, employers, private donors, the community, and users — to provide day-care to children of poor, working class families (Palriwala and Neetha, 2009a). There are also occasional examples of 'community' crèches initiated by middle class workers in formal institutions (such as the Tata Institute of Social Sciences, Mumbai). The Forum for Crèche and Child Care Services (FORCES), a network of organizations and individuals, was formed in 1989 as a centralized platform to mobilize and lobby on the issue of childcare.

However, no all-India survey has been undertaken of NGO initiatives in crèche or ECE services and the information and data available on numbers or characteristics are extremely unreliable. Part of the problem in estimating the coverage is that it is often difficult to draw a line between private,

---

33. Though there have been revisions in the amount in recent years, the total honorarium, which differs across states, remains lower than the pay of private primary school teachers, which is a comparable occupational category in terms of working hours, job profile and educational levels. See Palriwala and Neetha (2009b) for detailed discussions.

market-based ventures and not-for-profit initiatives, where the former may be given the garb of an NGO[34] or where employers provide services which are legally mandated, but presented as part of a corporate social responsibility initiative. The Working Group on Development of Children for the Eleventh Five Year Plan (2007–2012) indicates the very wide variation in the estimates of the number of children between three and six who are enrolled in NGO-provided early childhood education: between 3 and 20 million (Government of India, n.d.). The responses to a Solution Exchange (2010) query put to the Gender Community and the Maternal and Child Health Community indicate that most NGO initiatives were focused on children, who, for varied reasons, were 'parentless', especially where children below the age of two were concerned, rather than day-care and crèches for children in general. Extracting from the experiences documented in various case studies, it is clearly difficult to maintain crèches that are affordable and yet provide services at the required level without some state support, funds from employers, or external donations (Palriwala and Neetha, 2009a). Thus, while this sector can play an important role in providing innovative models and in lobbying for a care policy that recognizes the need for institutional day-care for children, it is not likely to be able to satisfy the huge need on its own.

Market and Private Initiatives

Private day-care centres range from the more formalized, commercial ventures to those run by women in their own homes and catering to middle class, working mothers who live nearby (Datta, 1995). The bulk of private crèches and pre-schools are outside public monitoring and accountability with very variable quality, especially given the paucity of trained crèche workers and pre-school teachers. The Eleventh Plan Working Group on Development of Children noted that there were no accurate figures for enrolment in private sector ventures, but estimated that it stood at around 10 million children in the age group 3–6 (Government of India, n.d.: 64). Rough surveys indicate that pre-primary education centres range from expensive, elite ventures to those available to lower middle class families. Even substandard facilities are able to continue due to the low costs and the sheer demand in an environment where education is the main hope and channel for economic mobility.

Rather than using crèches, whether informal or formal, many urban parents employ domestic workers and nannies. As noted earlier, hired domestic

---

34. While doing fieldwork in Delhi, one of the authors was approached by some people with a request that she certify that she knew of them as a local NGO involved in educational activities so that they could apply for governmental funding.

workers are predominantly women and their numbers are growing. They are mostly employed to take on domestic tasks other than childcare or with childcare as only one of their tasks. The demand is from the elite and the new middle class, not only where women are going out to paid work, but also as a result of the continuing elaboration of domestic and care work and as a status marker. Micro-studies suggest that the bulk of workers are live-out, part-time workers rather than live-in, full-time ones. Wages are both piece-rate and monthly, on a par with those for unskilled labour, varying with locality within the same town/city and with specific tasks. Workers tend to change their work neighbourhood only if they move house. In Rohtak, Haryana, domestic workers sought part-time work close to their own residences. This enabled them to come home during the day to tend to their own children and then return to their employers' houses. Further, task-based employment in multiple households allowed them to add or subtract tasks or employers to suit the changing cash and care demands of their families (Palriwala and Neetha, 2009b). Despite this, children of part-time workers may be withdrawn from or not enrolled in school to help their mothers with unpaid care work (see note 16).

There has been a recent upsurge in 'placement' agencies/individuals supplying migrant, full-time, live-in domestic workers, especially in metropolitan cities: the number is estimated to be between 800 and 1,000 in the capital city of Delhi (Neetha, 2009). Large numbers of young women are recruited through networks of agents from tribal areas in the states of Jharkand, Chattisgarh, Orissa, and West Bengal to be 'placed' in employer households. Remittances from these workers are often the only source of cash income for their family-households in their place of origin, important for the support of children whom the married workers leave behind in the care of kin. While these young women facilitate care, paid work, and leisure in the urban households of their employers, the effects of their migration and their remittances on their family-households and their children in their place of origin have not been systematically studied.

From the above, it can be inferred that despite the hegemonic character of gendered familialism and the predominance of familial and informal care practices, childcare strategies are differentiated. This is crucial in pinning the care regime together; this is the last aspect that we discuss.

STRATIFIED FAMILIALISM AND THE CARE DEFICIT

The care diamond in India rests on a labour/care regime in which care work is socially and economically devalued and constrains women in paid work. Women across the board carry a larger burden of care and many feel the strain. The institutional context, including state economic and social policies and the political economy of livelihoods not only stratifies families, it also produces differential care practices. However, this stratification is not in clearly demarcated layers. At one end are those who have the possibility to retain familial carers at home and supplement them with paid and other institutional carers and, at the other, are those who are neither able to retain family members at home nor fill the care gap through formal institutions.

The first dimension of stratified familialism and care is in terms of the quantity and quality of family care that can be and is given. Among poor and labouring households, where mothers are engaged in paid work, in or away from the home, care is abbreviated and children have to care for themselves. In contrast to this, among the elite and middle classes, changing concepts of childcare have expanded the requirements of adult attention to children; 'good' care now includes multiple, organized activities as modern, progressive, and an 'investment' in the child's future. This very elaboration of care requirements makes others' practices appear as a care deficit. The high infant and child mortality rates among the poor are blamed on, among other factors, the ignorance and negligence of familial carers of children, rather than on the structures which compel them to be absent for long hours in the search for subsistence.[35]

The second dimension of the care deficit and of stratified care is to be seen in the access to formal care and the costs of paid care. Public crèches and pre-schools are not widely available and institutional arrangements such as maternity leave are not available to the bulk of women who are informal workers, often self-employed or unpaid workers in familial enterprises. These workers cannot afford commercial facilities. State-mandated workplace childcare facilities are lacking even for those in the formal sector, who otherwise have a right to a range of social benefits. Quality facilities are not cheap or easy to organize and short-term profits often take precedence, especially when the social responsibility for and productivity pay-offs of care are not recognized. This is particularly true given that the elite, and many who run the state, are able to ensure the presence of the mother at home and/or access expensive, commercial amenities.

However, the elite and middle classes often prefer private, hired individual services that enable the care of infants at home. Their ability to replace and supplement both familial and institutional carers through such services reinforces the idea of familial care. Where new opportunities and high earnings are the stimulus for women's paid work, it is largely new

---

35. This theme has a long history and examples can be cited from the critique of women jute workers in the colonial period (Sen, 1999) to the design of the Mahila Mandals to teach poor women to be better nutritionists and mothers (Mehra, 1983). Its contemporary presence in official documents is more subtle (see note 25), although government personnel at various levels, as well as 'social' volunteers, suggest it fairly clearly at various fora. It is seen in the continuing emphasis on schemes and programmes — government-based or government-funded — to 'educate' poor women about nutrition and hygiene and breastfeeding, the advocacy of conditional maternity benefits, and of treating day-care and crèches as an add-on and a welfare issue with low priority rather than central to the problem.

private care provision through nannies that are tapped during infancy, rather than institutional facilities. Thus, these classes are able to draw on multiple care options. In this we see a third dimension of the stratified familialism in care.

This also points to the local care chains mentioned earlier and to a final aspect of stratified familialism — a stratification in the range of kin and unpaid care available, and the extent to which these can be drawn on. We have seen that care work is pooled within families (largely by women) across urban and rural locations, classes, regions, and castes. However, those most successful at maintaining large households and living near kin are non-migrant, middle and upper class, and rural households, categories which may overlap. They are more able to maintain the exchanges that enable long-term reciprocity and immediate help, can more easily call on kin, and are likely to have kin who will more readily provide assistance. The urban poor, especially migrants, are less able to live near kin or maintain large households. Furthermore, in poor and labouring households, all members need to earn, even if at very low income levels, often supplementing familial care in elite households at the cost of a deficit in their own. Their kin may also have no time given the pressures of their own livelihood and care responsibilities. Poverty makes immediate assistance difficult and places the long-term reciprocity of kinship networks in constant jeopardy, even if the work and exchanges to maintain them are not set aside.

In conclusion, although there are differences between various states and the central government in social policy, all tend to assume familial, gendered, and informal systems of care. While some feminist groups and organizations have voiced the demand for maternity leave and childcare, it has not been a concerted focus of the women's movement in India — perhaps in reaction to the maternalistic thread in 'pro-women' policies and the traditionalist assertion that mothering is women's primary responsibility and the basis of her social status (Palriwala, 2002). Care has entered public discourse and government policy inadvertently as pressure has built up to improve nutrition levels and lower infant and child mortality rates (ICDS), and enhance 'human resources' through education (ECE and schooling), or as part of the international discourse on care for the elderly. In effect, there is a continuing official denial of the time and skill requirements in practices and responsibilities of childcare — and indeed in care for the sick and the elderly — which works in conjunction with the non-recognition of women's multi-layered work lives and the fragility of familial lives in India. The encouragement of the informal sector appears to enable women's presence as unpaid familial carers and strengthens assumptions regarding the availability of such care. Not only do the informal practices of women and children become the means by which social life is held together; gendered familialism and the practices of stratified familialism and care in fact play a central role in the working of state economic and social policies in India.

REFERENCES

Agnihotri, I. and R. Palriwala (2001) 'Tradition, the Family and the State: Politics of the Women's Movement in the Eighties', in *Gender and Nation*, pp. 167–211. Delhi: Nehru Museum and Library.

All India Democratic Women's Association (2008) 'Memo to the Planning Commission, with Annexure' (submitted on 19 April). New Delhi: All India Democratic Women's Association.

ASER (2011) 'ASER 2010. Is the Right to Education Merely a Right to Schooling?'. Press Release 14 January. http://images2.asercentre.org/aserreports/ASER_2010_PRESS_RELEASE. pdf (accessed 23 January 2011).

Borooah, V.K. (2007) 'Births, Infants and Children: An Econometric Portrait of Women and Children in India', in A. Shariff and M. Krishnaraj (ed.) *States, Markets and Inequalities: Human Development in Rural India*, pp. 373–423. New Delhi: Orient Longman.

Bose, A. (2006) 'Falling Fertility and Rising Anaemia?', *Economic and Political Weekly* 41(37): 3923–6.

Chandrashekhar, C.P. and J. Ghosh (2006) 'Working More for Less'. *Macroscan.* http://www.macroscan.org/fet/nov06/fet281106Working_More.htm (accessed 28 November 2006).

Chhachhi, A. (2009) 'Ensuring Democratic Citizenship: A Gender Perspective on Contending Pathways for Socio-Economic Security in South Asia', *Indian Journal of Human Development* 2(1): 133–64.

Datta, V. (n.d) 'Reaching the Unreached: Early Childhood Care and Education Interventions in India'. Unpublished mimeo.

Datta, V. (1995) *Home Away from Home: Family Day Care in Bombay*. Suraksha Series 1. Chennai: M.S. Swaminathan Research Foundation.

Datta, V. and R.M. Konantambigi (eds) (2007) *Day Care for Young Children in India: Issues and Prospects*. New Delhi: Concept Publishing Company.

Dev, S.M. (2008) *Inclusive Growth in India: Agriculture, Poverty and Human Development*. New Delhi: Oxford University Press.

Dev, S.M. and J. Mooij (2005) 'Patterns in Social Sector Expenditure: Pre-and Post-reform Periods', in K.S. Parikh and R. Radhakrishna (eds) *India Development Report 2004–2005*, pp. 96–111. New Delhi: Oxford University Press.

Dev, S.M. and C. Ravi (2007) 'Poverty and Inequality: All India and States 1983–2005', *Economic and Political Weekly* 42(6): 509–21.

Dreze, J. (2006) 'Universalisation with Quality: ICDS in a Rights Perspective', *Economic and Political Weekly* 41(34): 3706–15.

Dreze, J. and A. Sen (1995) *India: Economic Development and Social Opportunity*. Delhi: Oxford University Press.

Duggal, R. and L.V. Gangolli (2005) 'Introduction to Review of Healthcare in India', in L.V. Gangolli, R. Duggal and A. Shukla (eds) *Review of Healthcare in India*, pp. 3–18. Mumbai: Centre for Enquiry into Health and Allied Themes (Cehat).

Gangolli, L.V., R. Duggal and A. Shukla (eds) (2005) *Review of Healthcare in India*. Mumbai: Centre for Enquiry into Health and Allied Themes (Cehat).

Ghosh, J. (2001) 'Rural Employment in the 1990s'. *Macroscan.* http://www.macroscan.org/fet/jul01/print/prnt240701Rural_Employment.htm (accessed 24 July 2007).

Gough, I. (2004) 'Welfare Regimes in Development Contexts: A Global and Regional Analysis', in Ian Gough and Geof Wood (eds) *Insecurity and Welfare Regimes in Asia, Africa and Latin America: Social Policy in Development Contexts*, pp. 15–48. Cambridge: Cambridge University Press.

Government of India (n.d.) 'Working Group on Development of Children for the Eleventh Five Year Plan (2007–2012): A Report'. New Delhi: Ministry of Women and Child Development.

Government of India (2006) *Economic Survey of India (2005–2006)*. New Delhi: Ministry of Finance.

Gragnolati, M., C. Boedenkamp, M. Dasgupta, Y.K. Lee and M. Sekhar (2006) 'ICDS and Persistent Undernutrition: Strategies to Enhance the Impact', *Economic and Political Weekly* 41(12): 1193–1201.

Hirway, I. (2008) 'Plan for Long Term', *The Indian Express* 2 February (New Delhi).

Hochschild, A.R. (2000) 'The Nanny Chain,' *The American Prospect* 11(4) Online, 30 November. http://www.prospect.org/cs/articles?article = the_nanny_chain (last accessed 29 June 2011).

Indian School of Women's Development and Studies (ISWDS) (2006) *Monitoring and Evaluation of National Rural Employment Guarantee Scheme with Special Focus on Gender Issues*. New Delhi: Indian School of Women's Development and Studies.

International Institute for Population Sciences (IIPS) and Macro International (MI) (2007) *National Family Health Survey (NFHS-3), 2005–06*: India. Mumbai: IIPS.

Jenson, J. (1997) 'Who Cares? Gender and Welfare Regimes', *Social Politics* 4(2): 182–7.

Jha, J. and D. Jhingran (2002) *Elementary Education for the Poorest and Other Deprived Groups*. New Delhi: Centre for Policy Research.

John, M.E., R. Kaur, R. Palriwala, S. Raju and A. Sagar (2008) *Planning Families, Planning Gender: Adverse Sex Ratio in Select Districts of Madhya Pradesh, Himachal Pradesh, Rajasthan, Haryana, Punjab*. Bangalore: Books for Change.

Kapur, R. and B. Cossman (1996) *Subversive Sites: Feminist Engagements with Law in India*. Delhi: Sage.

Kaul, V. (2002) 'Early Childhood Care and Education', in R. Govinda (ed.) *India Education Report: A Profile of Basic Education*, pp. 23–34. New Delhi: Oxford University Press.

Kaur, R. (2006) 'Migrating for Work: Rewriting Gender Relations', in Sadhna Arya and Anupama Roy (eds) *Poverty, Gender and Migration*, pp. 192–213. Delhi: Sage.

Kohli, A. (2007) 'State and Redistributive Development in India'. Background paper prepared for the UNRISD Report *Combating Poverty and Inequality*. Geneva: UNRISD.

Mazumdar, I. (2006) *Women Workers and Globalization: Emergent Contradictions in India*. Calcutta: Stree.

Mehra, R. (1983) 'Rural Development Programmes: Neglect of Women', in R. Mehra and K. Saradamoni *Women and Rural Transformation: Two Studies*, pp. 3–31. New Delhi: Concept Publishing Company.

Ministry of Finance (various years) *Public Finance Statistics*. New Delhi: Ministry of Finance, Government of India.

Moghe, K. (2006) 'Shouldering the Double Burden: Experiences of Organizing Domestic Workers in Pune City'. Paper presented in the Seminar on Globalization and the Women's Movement. Centre for Women's Development Studies, New Delhi (20–22 January 2006).

Nambissan, G. (1996) 'Equity in Education? The Schooling of Dalit Children in India'. Discussion Paper No. 15, Studies on Human Development in India. New Delhi: UNDP.

National Commission for Enterprises in the Unorganised Sector (NCEUS) (2007) 'Report on the Conditions of Work and Promotion of Livelihoods in the Unorganised Sector'. Delhi: Dolphin Printo Graphics. http://www.nceus.gov.in/Condition_of_workers_sep_2007.pdf (accessed 30 November 2007).

Nayyar, D. (2006) 'Economic Growth in Independent India: Lumbering Elephant or Rising Tiger', *Economic and Political Weekly* 41(6): 1451–8.

Neetha, N. (2003) 'Migration, Social Networking and Employment: A Study of Domestic Workers in Delhi'. NLI Research Study Series No. 37. NOIDA: V.V. Giri National Labour Institute.

Neetha, N. (2006)'"Invisibility" Continues? Social Security and Unpaid Women Workers', *Economic and Political Weekly* 41(32): 3497–9.

Neetha N. (2009) 'Placement Agencies for Domestic Workers: Issues of Regulation and Promoting Decent Work'. Paper presented at the National Consultation with the Civil Society on Domestic Workers Issues, International Labour Organization, New Delhi.

Neetha, N. and R. Palriwala (2008) 'Analysis of the Time Use Data'. India Research Report 2 for the Political and Social Economy of Care Project. Geneva: UNRISD.

NSSO (various years) 'Employment and Unemployment Data'. New Delhi: National Sample Survey Organization.

Palriwala, R. (2002)'Rhetorics of Motherhood: Politics, Policy, and Family Ideologies in India', in K. Sharma, L. Sarkar and L. Kasturi (eds) *Between Tradition, Counter-Tradition and Heresy*, pp. 247–70. Delhi: Rainbow Publications.

Palriwala, R. and N. Neetha (2008) 'The Context: Economic, Demographic and Social Trends'. India Research Report 1 for the Political and Social Economy of Care Project. Geneva: UNRISD.

Palriwala, R. and N. Neetha (2009a) 'The Care Diamond: State Social Policy and the Market'. India Research Report 3 for the Political and Social Economy of Care Project. Geneva: UNRISD.

Palriwala, R. and N. Neetha (2009b) 'Paid Care Workers: Domestic Workers and Anganwadi Workers'. India Research Report 4 for the Political and Social Economy of Care Project. Geneva: UNRISD.

Palriwala, R. and N. Neetha (2010) 'Care Practices and Care Bargains: Paid Domestic Workers and Anganwadi Workers in India', *International Labour Review* 149(4). http://onlinelibrary. wiley.com/doi/10.1111/j.1564–913X.2010.00101.x/pdf

Patnaik, U. (2006) 'The Republic of Hunger'. *Macroscan* 21 April. http://www.macroscan. org/the/poverty/apr04/pov210404Republic_Hunger.htm (accessed 2 December 2007).

Planning Commission (2008a) *Eleventh Five Year Plan (2007–2012): Inclusive Growth*. Volume I. New Delhi: Oxford University Press.

Planning Commission (2008b) *Eleventh Five Year Plan (2007–2012): Social Sector*. Volume II. New Delhi: Oxford University Press.

Priya, Ritu (2005) 'Public Health Services in India: A Historical Perspective', in L.V. Gangolli, R. Duggal and A. Shukla (eds) *Review of Healthcare in India*, pp. 41–73. Mumbai: Centre for Enquiry into Health and Allied Themes (Cehat).

Probe Team (1999) *The Public Report on Basic Education in India*. New Delhi: Oxford University Press.

Rajivan, A.K. (2006) 'Tamil Nadu: ICDS with a Difference', *Economic and Political Weekly* 41(34): 3684–8.

Ramachandran, V., K. Jandhyala and A. Saihjee (2003) 'Through the Life Cycle of Children: Factors that Facilitate/Impede Successful Primary School Completion', *Economic and Political Weekly* 38(47): 4994–5002.

Razavi, S. (2007) 'The Political and Social Economy of Care: Conceptual Issues, Research Questions and Policy Options'. Gender and Development Programme Paper No. 3. Geneva: UNRISD.

Registrar General (1981) *Census of India (1981)*. New Delhi: Registrar General.

Registrar General (2001) *Census of India (2001)*. New Delhi: Registrar General.

Reserve Bank of India (various years) *Handbook of Statistics on Indian Economy*. New Delhi: Reserve Bank of India.

Saith, A. (2009) 'Towards Universalizing Socio-economic Security: Strategic Elements of a Policy Framework', *Indian Journal of Human Development* 2(1): 9–38.

Sen, A. (1982) *Poverty and Famines: An Essay on Entitlement and Deprivation*. Delhi: Oxford University Press.

Sen, Abhijit and Himanshu (2004) 'Poverty and Inequality in India II', *Economic and Political Weekly* 39(39): 4248–63.

Sen, G. and D. Rajasekhar (2009) 'Social Protection in India: Policies, Experiences, Challenges'. Poverty Reduction and Policy Regimes programme. Geneva: UNRISD.

Sen, R. (2009) 'Education for Women's Empowerment: An Evaluation of the Government Run Schemes to Educate the Girl Child'. CCS Working Paper No. 183. New Delhi: Centre for Civil Society.

Sen, S. (1999) *Women and Labour in Late Colonial India: The West Bengal Jute Industry.* Cambridge: Cambridge University Press.

Solution Exchange (2010) 'United Nations Country Team in India'. Solution Exchange Service for the Gender Community and the Maternal and Child Health Community in India, Consolidated Reply issued 20 April 2010 on 'Initiatives and Models for Supporting Gender Sensitive Child Care Services – Examples'. ftp://ftp.solutionexchange.net.in/public/gen/cr/cr-se- gen-mch-05021001.pdf

Srivastava, R. (2009) 'Towards Universal Social Protection in India in a Rights-based Paradigm', *Indian Journal of Human Development* 2(1): 111–32.

Standing, G. (2009) 'Reviving Egalitarianism in the Global Transformation: Building Occupational Security', *Indian Journal of Human Development* 2(1): 39–62.

Supreme Court Commissioners (2005) 'Sixth Report in the Writ Petition (Civil) 196 Of 2001 PUCL Vs. Union of India & Others'. http://www.righttofoodindia.org/icds/icds_comrs_reports.html (accessed 20 April 2008).

Swaminathan, M. (n.d.) 'Crèches: At the Workplace or Residence? Not EITHER/OR but BOTH'. Unpublished mimeo.

Swaminathan, M. (2001) 'Delegitimising Childhood', *The Hindu* 7 October. http://www.hindu.com/thehindu/2001/10/07/stories/1307061d.htm (accessed 15 May 2008).

Thorat, S. (2009) 'Social Exclusion in the Indian Context: Theoretical Basis of Inclusive Policies', *Indian Journal of Human Development* 2(1): 165–81.

Tilak, J.B.G. and R.M. Sudarshan (2007) 'Private Schooling in Rural India', in A. Shariff and M. Krishnaraj (eds) *States, Markets and Inequalities: Human Development in Rural India,* pp. 269–327. New Delhi: Orient Longman.

Titmuss, R. (1958) *Essays on the Welfare State.* London: Allen and Unwin.

Ved, R.R. and A.S. Dua (2005) 'Review of Women and Children's Health in India: Focus on Safe Motherhood', in *Burden of Disease in India. National Commission on Macroeconomics and Health* (Background Papers), pp. 85–111. New Delhi: Ministry of Health and Family Welfare.

Wazir, R. (2009) 'Newly Emerging Needs of Children: Towards Widening the Policy Agenda in South Asia', *Indian Journal of Human Development* 2(1): 183–202.

Working Group for Children Under Six (2007) 'Strategies for Children Under Six: Abbreviated Report Presented to the Planning Commission', *Economic and Political Weekly* 42(52): 87–101.

9

Putting Two and Two Together? Early Childhood Education, Mothers' Employment and Care Service Expansion in Chile and Mexico

Silke Staab and Roberto Gerhard

INTRODUCTION

While demands for public childcare support have been part and parcel of women's movements' struggles for gender equality since the early twentieth century, three developments have spurred recent state interest and activity in the area of childcare. Concerns about demographic change and declining birth rates, the quality of 'human capital' as a factor of economic competitiveness, and the desire to create new employment opportunities in the service sector have propelled childcare issues onto the agenda of a wide range of developed economies. They have triggered policy changes in different areas, including parental leave, working time regulations, cash benefits, early childhood education and care services. At the same time, women have been targeted by social and work/family reconciliation policies in order to reduce welfare dependency and poverty risk among low-income and/or single-earner families as well as to increase the sustainability of social security systems. Care responsibilities have come to be recognized as an obstacle to achieving these goals.

These ideas have found their way into policy discourses and practices of the Global South where they have mixed with concerns specific to the development context, such as persistent poverty, inequality and development. In Latin America, the 'rediscovery' of the social (Mkandawire, 2004) has been accompanied by a range of care-related policy innovations, including conditional cash transfer schemes, different modalities for early childhood education and care (ECEC) services, and the introduction of child-rearing credits in pension schemes. Because women have traditionally carried the main responsibility for child rearing and childcare, the dynamics of women's paid and unpaid work are central in these policies which, in turn, have important implications for the overall burden that falls back on women.

Feminist research has long interrogated the gender dimensions of 'new' and 'old' social policies, different entitlements for men and women, as well as the kind of family models and social norms that underpin access to welfare benefits. This is also true for the analysis of new social assistance measures.

The authors are indebted to Elena Gaia and Shahra Razavi for valuable comments on earlier versions of this article. Helpful feedback was also provided by two anonymous referees. Any errors remain our own.

Seen, Heard and Counted, First Edition. Edited by Shahra Razavi.
Chapters © 2012 The Institute of Social Studies. Book compilation © 2012 Blackwell Publishing Ltd.

Indeed, much scholarly attention has focused on the gender implications of conditional cash transfers (CCTs) which have proliferated in the region, and which in some countries, such as Brazil and Mexico, cover a significant share of the population.[1] Positive effects on child well-being notwithstanding, CCTs have been viewed critically by feminist scholars who fear that stipends combined with care conditionalities reinforce traditional gender roles and add to the total workload of poor women whose (paid and unpaid) input into household survival has diversified and intensified in many developing countries (Chant, 2008). A major critique of these programmes has been their failure to provide long-term strategies for women's economic security through job training and childcare provision (Molyneux, 2007; Tabbush, 2009).

Childcare service expansion is qualitatively different from these programmes as it is explicitly aimed at (or implicitly facilitates) the *commodification* of female labour and the *de-familialization* of care. Over recent years, a number of middle-income countries, including Chile, Mexico and Uruguay, have increased the availability of ECEC services. The fact that these developments have received little scholarly attention so far leaves the (surely unintended) impression that Latin American social policy is unalterably stuck on a familialist track, when in fact national and regional trends are likely to be more varied.

This contribution looks at recent efforts to expand ECEC services in Chile and Mexico. Although concerns over low female labour force participation and child welfare have emerged on both countries' political agendas, their approaches to service expansion differ significantly. In general terms, the Mexican programme kick-starts and subsidizes home- and community-based care provision with a training component for childminders, while the Chilean programme emphasizes the expansion of professional ECEC services provided in public institutions. Through a comparison of the two programmes, this study shows that differences in policy design have important implications in terms of the opportunities the programmes are able to create for women and children from low-income families and the prospects for mitigating — or indeed entrenching — gender and class inequalities.

The pairing of Chile and Mexico offers strong parallels as well as contrasts. While both countries depend to a large extent on exports, growth has been more stable and sustained in Chile compared to Mexico, whose economy has suffered from recurrent crises. Thus, the Chilean GDP grew at an average of 5 per cent during the 1990s. Poverty has declined steadily from almost 40 per cent in 1990 to under 14 per cent in 2006 (ECLAC, 2008). Meanwhile, the growth rate of the Mexican economy stagnated at an accumulated 1.3 per cent throughout the 1990s, and poverty rates have been falling more slowly, from almost 50 per cent in 1989 to around 30 per cent in 2006. In

---

1. Gender analyses of CCTs include: Bradshaw (2008); Molyneux (2007); Serrano (2005); Tabbush (2009).

the aftermath of the 1994 crisis, poverty rates rose dramatically, but then continued to fall.

Like many other Latin American countries, Chile and Mexico underwent market reforms during the 1980s and 1990s, including trade liberalization, (partial or complete) privatization of social insurance, and increased private sector participation in social services (Teichman, 2001). The reforms accentuated already high levels of social inequality. As has been repeatedly argued, poor women shouldered a disproportionate burden of structural adjustment, making up both for a decline in male earnings and for the waning of public social services following fiscal retrenchment (Molyneux, 2000).

Since their transition to democracy (albeit from very different forms of authoritarianism),[2] Chile and Mexico have tried to address 'social deficits' by experimenting with new social programmes. Some, including the respective cash transfer schemes, *Chile Solidario* and *Progresa/Oportunidades,* have become influential blueprints in the region. More recently, both countries have actively expanded ECEC services for children up to four years. Given the pace at which cash transfer schemes have proliferated in the region, it is not impossible that these two cases will spur a discussion on options for the expansion of ECEC services in Latin America. The alternatives embodied by the Chilean and the Mexican programme thus merit a closer examination.

The rest of this article is structured as follows: the first section sets the scene by providing evidence on how transformations in demographic, household and employment structures have nurtured the demand for extra-familial childcare alternatives. The following two sections then trace the development of ECEC services in the two countries under study. After a brief overview of policies since the mid-1990s, these sections will provide more detailed accounts of two recent programmes: the Federal Day-Care Programme for Working Mothers (*Programa Guarderías y Estancias Infantiles*) in Mexico, launched in 2007, and the ECEC service component of *Chile Crece Contigo* through which childcare has been extended in Chile since 2006. Commonalities and differences in the design of the programmes and their likely implications for gender equality, equal access to quality care and sustainability of childcare programmes will be discussed. Since both programmes are rather recent, a proper evaluation cannot be carried out in this paper; rather, we will look at policy design, the assumptions underlying the programmes in terms of the organization of care, and their potential and limitations for reducing gender and social inequalities. The fourth section ventures some hypotheses as to why the two countries may have chosen such different responses to address similar problems.

---

2. Chile started the transition from military dictatorship to electoral democracy in 1989. In Mexico, the Partido Revolucionario Institucional (PRI) lost its majority in Congress in 1997 for the first time since it came to power in the 1930s. The year 2000, when the conservative Partido Acción Nacional (PAN) won the Mexican presidency, marked the unequivocal end of what Mario Vargas Llosa labelled 'the perfect dictatorship'.

CHANGING PATTERNS OF HOUSEHOLD AND
EMPLOYMENT STRUCTURES

State responses to childcare needs in many middle-income countries have at least partly been triggered by changes in employment, household and demographic structures which, in turn, have modified the parameters of care giving over the past two to three decades. Across Latin America, women's entry into the workforce has intensified, family structures have been transformed, and demographic and socio-cultural changes have created new demands for care. As a result, nuclear male-breadwinner families are an ever less common phenomenon: only one-fifth of households in the region followed this traditional model by the mid-2000s (Arriagada, 2007). Chile and Mexico are no exception.

In both countries, women's participation in the paid economy has picked up, reaching 43 per cent (Chile) and 48 per cent (Mexico) in 2006, although this is still low compared to the OECD average of 57.5 per cent (OECD, 2008). Women from lower-income households are less likely to participate in the labour force than women from higher-income households, while men's labour force participation shows less variation across income groups (Colina, 2008; Mideplan, 2006). In Chile, single mothers from the lowest income quintile are also much more likely to be unemployed than those from the highest income group (10 per cent vs 2 per cent in 2006) (Mideplan, 2006) — and the rate has increased for the former and declined for the latter since 1990, thus widening the gap. These patterns partly explain the high poverty rates among female-headed households in Chile[3] as well as the government's emphasis on promoting employment and access to welfare services for single mothers in the years after the democratic transition (Badía Ibañez, 2002).

In both countries, significant proportions of the labour force are in informal employment, and women are over-represented in precarious work. This has implications for welfare and care entitlements linked to employment status, such as maternity leave, company-based childcare provision as it (formally) exists in Chile or childcare provision tied to social security as is the case in Mexico. Other forms of childcare service provision — such as those currently pursued by both countries — are thus of utmost importance for a large proportion of households, particularly for women with low educational credentials and little work experience, whose potential labour market earnings are unlikely to compensate for the 'opportunity costs' of alternative childcare arrangements.

Gender gaps in earnings are significant with female labour market earnings reaching 72 per cent and 64 per cent of male earnings in Chile and Mexico in 2006. At the same time, female earnings are the main source of income for a sizeable 28 per cent of households in both countries (Cepalstat, 2005).

---

3. Poverty rates for female-headed households were 18 per cent in 2006, compared to 14 per cent national average (ECLAC, 2008).

As one might expect, the share of households in which a woman is the main earner is particularly high among single-parent households. In sync with the regional trend, the share of this household form has increased in recent decades, and most of these households are headed by women. Women are also the main earners in many extended or composed households, both of which have become more common. Not surprisingly then, female labour force participation is actually *desired* by both governments and forms an integral part of their strategies to fuel economic growth and reduce poverty.

In a nutshell, the transformation of household and family structures, the growth in female labour force participation and the increasing reliance of households on female earnings have put a squeeze on time available for unpaid childcare and increased the need for childcare services that support women in their quest to combine employment with the childcare tasks that are still largely assigned to them. And, slowly but surely, governments have been responding.

EARLY CHILDHOOD EDUCATION AND CARE SERVICES IN MEXICO

The development of ECEC services in Mexico can be broadly divided into three periods, with a different institution entering the scene in each: (i) the Mexican Institute for Social Security (IMSS) from the mid-1970s,[4] focusing on day-care for the children of mothers working in formal employment; (ii) the Ministry of Public Education from the early 2000s, when pre-school education was made mandatory for all three- to five-year-olds; and (iii) the Ministry of Social Development (Sedesol) since 2007, when the most recent day-care programme was put in place to target children of mothers who are informally employed. This programme is targeted at low-income households.

Access to institutional childcare for children aged forty-three days to four years was established as a right of working mothers in the formal sector in 1973. It is a contribution-based entitlement, provided by IMSS and financed by a 1 per cent across-the-board payroll deduction. Expansion of service provision, however, was sluggish until the mid-1990s, when IMSS was running 487 centres nationwide. These centres offered day-care for less than 60,000 children, corresponding to around 5 per cent of the eligible population (Knaul and Parker, 1996). Low coverage can partly be attributed to the fact that IMSS has witnessed a continuous decline in revenue since the early 1980s and is struggling with a combination of falling real wages, increasing informalization of the labour force and declining government subsidies (Brachet-Márquez, 2007).

---

4. Services for civil servants were provided by the Institute for Social Security and Services for Public Employees (ISSSTE).

In 1997, IMSS decided to expand services through outsourcing agreements with employers, community organizations and individual families. These new providers would offer company-, neighbourhood- and home-based day-care funded and regulated by IMSS. The cost difference between the outsourced modality (*guarderías subrogadas*) and the previous model (*guarderías ordinarias*) was tremendous, with monthly per-centre costs plummeting by around 75 per cent.[5] By 2007, only 8.6 per cent of the day-care centres were still run by IMSS. Within a decade, the number of centres tripled, and coverage rose to over 200,000 children — almost 20 per cent of the target group (children of formal sector workers aged forty-three days to four years). However, IMSS was a long way from fulfilling formal sector demand, and doubts were raised about quality standards due to underfunding (Leal, 2006).

Reservations about safety were tragically confirmed by a fire in an outsourced facility in Hermosillo, Sonora, in 2009, where the lack of proper emergency exits left forty-nine children dead and another seventy-five severely injured. While it would be unfair to judge all outsourced day-care centres on the basis of this accident, the results of a Supreme Court investigation following the event did reveal a widespread state of disarray in the contracting, operating and monitoring procedures regarding the outsourced day-care facilities.[6] The report, together with sustained pressure from the parents of the affected children, led to the design of a new law which stipulates a set of minimum safety standards across publicly financed day-care institutions (including those of the new *Estancias* programme outlined below) and legally mandates regular inspection and monitoring. It was approved by the Mexican Senate in April 2011 and, at the time of writing (May 2011), is awaiting approval by the Chamber of Deputies.

In 2002, pre-school education was made mandatory for all children aged three to five. This educational policy — tailored to children's rather than their (working) parents' needs and independent of the latter's employment status — has universal aspirations, and its achievements have been significant. Since the reform, overall pre-school coverage has increased from 50 to 80 per cent. By 2007–08, universal coverage of four- and five-year-olds had been achieved, while coverage of three-year-olds had more than doubled from 15 to 34 per cent (Presidencia, 2008). Most pre-schools are public and run only half-day programmes, limiting the extent to which they can free working parents from their childcare responsibilities.

---

5. Communication with the National Coordinator of the IMSS Day-Care Centres, 26 March 2009.
6. Thus, only 14 of the 1480 outsourcing contracts reviewed by the Supreme Court fully complied with the documentation requirements and only a few met the legal requirements to offer the service. Half of the centres had not gone through the process of approval of adequate safety measures (Comisión Investigadora, 2010).

A third childcare programme was introduced in 2007, focusing on women workers' access to childcare rather than early education. The Federal Day-Care Programme for Working Mothers (*Programa Guarderías y Estancias Infantiles*, or *Estancias* for short) started operating shortly after Felipe Calderón became President in December 2006. It was designed to fill the gaps left by IMSS activities, by expanding childcare services for working mothers without access to social security-based services. It forms part of a larger national strategy to reduce poverty and inequality, within which women's role as earners is seen as crucial (Presidencia, 2007). The programme's specific contribution to these broader goals is the subsidized provision of day-care services for children from the age of one to three years and eleven months from low-income households (below six minimum wages per month), who have no access to social security-based daycare. This is meant to allow the participating mother to work, study or look for a job. The objective is to offer day-care places to half a million children by 2012 (corresponding to 5 per cent of children in this age group, based on 2005 census data).

Rather than expanding the role of public institutions in the provision of care, the programme creates a 'quasi-market' for home-based day-care services through supply-side incentives and demand-side subsidies. Thus, Sedesol offers a lump sum of 35,000 Mexican pesos (MXN)[7] to individuals or civil society organizations interested in opening and running a day-care centre at their individual home or community centre, to help them adapt and furnish their facilities according to the requirements. To qualify for the grant, the potential service provider does not need any formal training or previous experience (except to have completed secondary education). However, candidates have to pass a psychological test and participate in training courses regarding programme rules and the basics of childcare. By 2009, 3,446 care givers had received a childcare certificate. After completing this process, potential providers are granted a month's time to recruit 'clients' to reach the minimum enrolment target of ten children who fulfil the targeting requirements of the programme. Once the centre starts operating, it has to provide day-care services for at least one year, for eight hours a day, five days a week. According to the rules and regulations, the person running the centre has to hire at least one assistant per eight children. All operational costs have to be covered through the public subsidy plus a fee charged to parents.

In order to enrol their children and receive the state subsidy, mothers must be working, looking for a job or studying, their household income must be below the threshold of six minimum wages per month, and they must not have access to day-care services provided by IMSS. As well as meeting the same criteria, fathers who wish to apply for the service must also be single. Since 2009, the subsidy has been provided on a two-step scale which decreases with rising household income. The maximum subsidy

7. US$ 1 = 13.06 MXN (rate according to Banco de México, December 2009).

is 700 MXN per month per child. The subsidy is paid directly to the day-care centre (rather than to the mother who enrols her children). According to Sedesol (2008), the average day-care centre had enrolled thirty-four children at an average cost of 1,031 MXN[8] per month per child (including the state subsidy). For the average care giver, this scenario resulted in a revenue of 34,680 MXN per month from which operational costs of the centre had to be deducted, including the provision of two hot meals and a snack per day as well as the salary of one childcare assistant per eight children. The assistant's salary is subject to the primary care giver's discretion and was an average of 2,050 MXN per month in 2007. There is evidence that not all centres are 'profitable', i.e. providing primary care givers with sufficient income, a scenario that seems to have been anticipated by Sedesol which expected community action and 'solidarity' to kick in in these cases (Pereznieto and Campos, 2010: 40)

For parents, the co-payment means that they get the day-care service at a lower cost, but not for free. According to Sedesol, the average co-payment is 355 MXN[9] (roughly 22.5 per cent of the monthly minimum wage) with individual amounts depending on the subsidy received by the household. The vast majority of enrolled children belong to the lowest income group (receiving the highest subsidy of 700 MXN). On an aggregate basis, this means that 65 per cent of the operational costs of the programme are borne by the state and 35 per cent by parents.

In terms of quantity, the achievements of the programme have been re-markable. Within one year, it had stimulated the creation of over 5,000 day-care centres, reaching more than 200,000 children (Sedesol, 2007). In 2008, another 3,000 day-care centres were created, and coverage rose to more than 244,000 children and around 222,000 mothers (Sedesol, 2008). Within two years, the programme had already outnumbered the capacity of IMSS's centres built up over a thirty-year period and by the end of 2010 there were more than 9,000 *estancias* in operation (Pereznieto and Campos, 2010). By 2008 it was the single most important provider of childcare for children under the age of four, running 84 per cent of all centres and cover-ing 56 per cent of enrolled children. Furthermore, the government claims to have created jobs for over 46,000 women through the programme, including as primary care givers and as their assistants (ibid.). While the numbers are impressive, the quality of these jobs is questionable, since care givers and their assistants are self-employed and thus lacking social security benefits.

The programme has been criticized for providing a low-quality service to low-income families (Milenio, 2008; Zaragoza, 2007). Not only do Sedesol centres operate on a much lower budget than IMSS centres, quality standards are also poorer. Based on official data provided by the different institutions,

---

8. Since exact information was hard to come by, the 1,031 MXN is an approximation. For further details see Staab and Gerhard (2010).
9. Communication with Sedesol, 16 June 2009.

we calculated that the Sedesol programme accounted for 26 per cent of the total annual budget for childcare services, covering more than half of the enrolled population, while the IMSS budget accounts for 74 per cent, covering around 41 per cent of the enrolled population. The monthly cost per child at Sedesol centres was less than 25 per cent that of centres directly managed by IMSS and almost 40 per cent lower than that of the centres IMSS had contracted out to other providers.

While lower costs are not equivalent to lower quality, differences are extreme and likely to entail trade-offs in terms of staff, infrastructure and equipment as well as care workers' working condition and wages (implying a downgrading of skills and qualifications). Child–staff ratios specified for centres run by IMSS or ISSSTE are significantly higher than those for Sedesol centres. Further, IMSS requires a first degree in pedagogy, childcare, nutrition, early education or pre-school education to qualify to be a care giver (IMSS, 2009), while Sedesol merely asks for complete secondary education. An interesting detail in this context is that a large number of primary care givers actually seem to be quite well educated. In a survey carried out in 2007, almost 60 per cent of primary care givers claimed to hold either university or technical degrees (GEA–ISA, 2007).[10]

Calderón stressed in several speeches that the programme intended to create jobs for unemployed care professionals (educators, teachers, social workers etc.). Considering the employment conditions outlined above, this casts serious doubts on the proper recognition and compensation of professional care work in the Mexican context. Rather, it points toward a strategy for saving labour costs and avoiding public sector unions which have important leverage over educational policies in the country (Ornelas, 2008). After Partido de Acción Nacional (PAN) won the presidency in 2000, and as a result of the corporatist legacy, the teachers' union became an important and independent political actor. It practically co-governs the educational system through a strong presence in the related Congressional commissions, as well as among educational authorities at the federal and state levels (Santibañez, 2008). It would thus be unsurprising if the PAN administration wanted to avoid the involvement of the Ministry of Education and the teachers' union.

Despite these reservations, the programme implies a significant state commitment to defamilialization. While the budget allocated to the programme in 2009 (2,522 million MXN) was a fraction of the cash transfer scheme *Oportunidades* (24,460 million MXN), *Estancias* did rank among the larger social development programmes after *Oportunidades*, *70 y más* (11,976 million MXN) and *Habitat* (2,745 million MXN). It is also worth noting that a number of surveys have found high levels of satisfaction among programme

10. Some public universities in Mexico also provide the last three years of high school education. Thus, university figures may capture some of these students who are not university graduates in the common sense. We are grateful to an anonymous referee for pointing this out.

beneficiaries who stressed, among other things, the positive impact on their ability to find more stable jobs (Pereznieto and Campos, 2010).

EARLY CHILDHOOD EDUCATION AND CARE SERVICES IN CHILE

The Chilean approach to ECEC services has been closely tied to the Ministry of Education (Mineduc) and educational goals seem to have a greater historical importance than in Mexico, even for the younger age groups. ECEC services are structured according to age groups: (i) the crèche level (eighty-four days to two years); (ii) the intermediate level (two to three years); and (iii) the transitional level (four to five years). While some services are targeted to 'vulnerable' groups and executed by specialized institutions, most of them are overseen by Mineduc. In contrast to Mexico, the private sector plays a much larger role in education due to far-reaching reforms carried out under military rule (1973–1989).

Since the mid-1990s, the transitional level has been considered part of the educational system. In contrast to Mexico, pre-school education is not mandatory for any age group. Though coverage has increased steadily since 1992, Chile has moved more slowly toward universal coverage for this age group than Mexico, reaching 74 per cent in 2009.[11] Services are provided by five main institutions, mirroring the primary and secondary educational system, which was municipalized and opened up to private sector participation under military rule. In 2006, truly public (municipal) schools accounted for 30 per cent of enrolment, subsidized private schools for another 36 per cent, while purely private schools catered to 12 per cent. The remaining 21 per cent was absorbed by two semi-public institutions (National Council of Kindergartens/JUNJI and Fundación Integra) bound to Mineduc. As in the rest of the educational system, segmentation along the lines of household income looms large with respect to coverage and the type of institution children attend. While the richest quintile sent 94 per cent of children from this age group to pre-school — half of whom are enrolled in private schools — coverage in the first quintile was 81 per cent and largely concentrated in public institutions.

At the intermediate level, coverage has been rather stagnant, and institutional childcare for infants at the crèche level was practically insignificant until 2003. The institutional setting for the crèche and intermediate levels shows a stronger tendency towards public and purely private providers than the transitional level. The private subsidized variant is much less significant (17 per cent as of 2006). Two institutions play a particularly important role: centres run or accredited by JUNJI, a government body, and centres run by Fundación Integra, a private non-profit foundation that belongs to the

---

11. These and all the following coverage figures are based on data from the triennial household survey CASEN (Mideplan, 1990; 1996; 2003; 2006; 2009).

Presidency's network of foundations. Both are linked to Mineduc through annual agreements. Their centres are free of charge for children from households belonging to the first two income quintiles. Together, they absorb more than half of the enrolment in the younger age group. Purely private providers account for almost 20 per cent of enrolment.

During the Lagos administration (2000–2006), the lack of childcare services formed part of a public debate over the country's low female employment rates, and the conflict between work and family responsibilities was seen as one of its major causes. The deficiencies of available childcare service regulations for working women—such as the obligation of employers to provide work-based crèches in companies with more than twenty female employees—were increasingly subject to criticism: they reached only a limited proportion of women who were formally employed in larger companies, were rarely complied with, weakly enforced, and acted as a disincentive to female employment (Valenzuela, 2000).

In 2004, Lagos called on the national women's ministry (*Servicio Nacional de la Mujer*, SERNAM) to come up with proposals for childcare provision as a way of facilitating women's participation in paid employment.[12] As a response SERNAM launched the so-called *comunicentros*. Similar to the Mexican *estancias*, the *comunicentros* were based on the idea of taking advantage of and supporting already existing informal community-based childcare through a subsidy per child paid to a home-based care giver. The programme was piloted in three municipalities, but seems to have vanished into thin air after the 2006 elections, as the new administration concentrated its efforts on scaling up the availability of institutional childcare in public crèches and kindergartens. Whether this was due to a lack of success of the pilot project or political priority setting after the 2006 election remains unclear. It seems, however, that the Ministries of Education and Finance pooled efforts to push for the expansion of formal institutional ECEC. Educational authorities had criticized the lack of attention to quality education, suggesting that it would be preferable to direct these funds to increasing institutional coverage through JUNJI (Honorato Barrueto, 2006).

With the Bachelet administration (2006–2010) the expansion of ECEC services became a policy priority. Following the recommendations of a Presidential Advisory Board, the government launched *Chile Crece Contigo* (Chile Grows with You), an integrated child protection scheme, in October 2006. Its goals included guaranteed access to crèches and kindergartens for all children under four from the two poorest income quintiles, and universal pre-school coverage for four- and five-year-olds (Mideplan, 2007). The policy passed Congress in 2009, establishing free access to crèche and kindergarten services as a right for children from low-income families.

---

12. At this point in time, the Ministry of Education was only in charge of pre-school education for four- and five-year-olds.

JUNJI and Fundación Integra act as implementing institutions; almost all the new places at the crèche and intermediate level have been created by these two institutions. Modalities include centres run by both institutions as well as subsidies to centres run by municipalities and non-profit organizations. Subsidies to market providers — which dominate at the transitional, primary and secondary school level — are not part of the expansion strategy. This could have been an attempt to avoid the kind of fragmentation associated with the country's larger educational system, reshaped and buttressed under authoritarian rule and inherited by the democratic regime. This system is still highly segmented, with public schools absorbing more than half of the country's poorest students, while (high-quality and fee-based) private schools cater to the wealthiest segment. The fact that coverage of children under the age of four was extremely low before the reforms arguably increased the government's room for manoeuvre in shaping the institutional setting in which services would be provided. It is possible that the government used this leeway to strengthen the role of public institutions — in contrast to the larger educational system where powerful private-sector interests have been a major obstacle to equity-oriented reforms.

According to official sources, the number of public crèches increased from around 700 in March 2006 to more than 4,000 by the end of 2009 (Ortiz, 2009). The number of available places for children up to two years has more than quintupled from around 14,000 in 2005 to 61,000 in 2008, and was estimated to reach 85,000 by March 2010. As to the intermediate level (two- to three-year-olds), JUNJI has almost doubled the number of crèches since 2005 (ibid.). Between 2003 and 2009, coverage among children from the two lowest income quintiles grew by about 7 per cent, faster than during the preceding seven-year period (when it grew by 3–4 per cent).

Although JUNJI's expansion has almost exclusively taken place through agreements with third parties (mostly municipalities), more than three-quarters of the kindergartens and more than half of the crèches are still directly administered by the institution (JUNJI, 2008). Similarly, Fundación Integra provides ECEC both through its own centres and through agreements that delegate administration to non-profit providers (community, faith-based and non-governmental organizations) conditional on compliance with Integra's curricular standards. According to official sources, Integra enrolled around 74,000 children in 954 centres in 2006, the majority of which (90 per cent) were centres run by the foundation (Ministerio de Hacienda, 2008).

Contrasting sharply with the Mexican case, educators in public or accredited crèches and kindergartens are required to have a five-year university degree in early education. Support staff involved in the direct care of infants are required to hold a technical degree in early education from an institution recognized by the Chilean state. JUNJI and Integra employed around 16,000 workers in 2006–07. JUNJI workers are public employees and their salaries are negotiated alongside salaries for other public sector workers. Around three-quarters are employed on a fixed-term basis, while the remaining staff have permanent posts (Ministerio de Hacienda, 2008). There have been concerns, however, regarding the modality under which JUNJI carries out the current expansion of crèches (that is, through agreements with municipalities). While staff in municipal crèches are considered public employees — and therefore entitled to the same kind of benefits — there have been complaints about them receiving significantly lower salaries than their colleagues working in centres directly administered by JUNJI.

While their employment status is likely to be better than that of self-employed care givers in Mexico, the salaries of early childhood educators are among the lowest in the educational sector. Professional pre-school educators who graduated in 2005 and 2006 earned an average of 360,000 Chilean pesos (CLP)[13] in their first year (around 20 per cent less than primary school teachers). This is very low when compared to graduates from professional careers of similar duration, both care-related, such as nurses (732,000 CLP), and non-care related, such as accountants (700,000 CLP) or construction engineers (622,000 CLP). After five years, the average salary of pre-school teachers who had graduated in 2000 and 2001 had increased by only 11 per cent, showing that neither higher education nor work experience are valued highly in this educational group.[14]

Regarding working conditions (and quality), there is evidence that crèches and kindergartens run by Integra and JUNJI are under-staffed, and that this situation is more severe in Integra establishments. In 2006, less than two thirds of JUNJI's centres and less than half of Integra's complied with the Mineduc staff coefficient (Ministerio de Hacienda, 2008). Turnover rates among staff are high among Integra workers (around 30 per cent), but relatively low at JUNJI (less than 3 per cent).

While the main rationale of the recent expansion was to guarantee children from disadvantaged households a 'fair start', strategies did not completely lose sight of working parents' needs. Indeed, the majority of children attending JUNJI and Integra centres at the crèche and intermediate level are enrolled in full-day programmes (from 08.30 to 16.30), and there are efforts to offer extended schedules until 19.30. Similar to the Mexican case, however, the availability of full-time programmes is much lower at the transitional level (particularly at private subsidized schools). While at the crèche and intermediate level, over half of enrolled children were in full-time care in 2006, this share dropped to 25 per cent for four- and five-year-olds.

SIMILARITIES, DIFFERENCES AND IMPLICATIONS OF POLICY DESIGN

Table 1 presents an overview of some of the basic characteristics of the programmes. Generally speaking, Mexico's *Estancias* programme subsidizes

---

13. US$ 1 = 506.43 CLP (rate according to Banco Central de Chile, December 2009).
14. Futuro Laboral database (www.futurolaboral.cl). All salaries are gross salaries.

Table 1. Overview of Programme Characteristics

	Programa Guarderías y Estancias Infantiles, Mexico	**Programa de Salas Cunas y Jardines Infantiles, Chile**
Executing entity	Secretaria de Desarrollo Social (Sedesol)	Ministry of Education (Mineduc)
Objectives	Reduce the poverty risk of households by enabling mothers with young children to work; Create employment through the expansion of childcare services	Promote child development and equal opportunities for children from low-income/ vulnerable families; Enable parental employment
Main beneficiary	Mother (if a working father is the only care giver, then he can be the beneficiary)	Child
Basis of entitlement	Targeted: Households with a monthly income of less than six minimum wages (approx. 14% of all households)	Targeted: Lowest two income quintiles until 2010; Lowest three income quintiles as of 2011
Other conditions of access	Mother must be working or looking for work; Mother must have no access to social-security based childcare services upon registration	Mother must be working, studying or looking for work for the child to have free access to crèche services (up to two years) and full-day kindergarten (two to three years); No further requirements for access to part-time kindergarten
Delivery mechanism	State subsidies to home-based provision	Public or semi-public institutions
Financing mechanism	State: General revenue (average 65%)	State: General revenue
	Households: Co-payments on sliding scales (average 35%)	Free of charge for the first two quintiles (2010)/three quintiles (from 2011)
Professionalization	Low (no specific qualifications for care givers required)	High (care givers are pre-school or early education teachers with university or technical degrees)
Quality (child-to-staff ratio as specified by programme rules)	One primary care giver per centre; One assistant per eight children	*Professional* educators Up to two years: 1:40 children Two to three years: 1:48 children *Technical* assistants Up to two years: 1:6 children Two years: 1:12 children Three years: 1:16 children

Source: authors' elaboration based on official documents.

community- and home-based day-care to facilitate the employment of low-income mothers without pursuing explicit educational aims. Poor women (rather than children) are the programme's target group. While female employment activation has definitely been pursued by the Chilean government and the expansion of childcare has been perceived as crucial for its achievement, it is only a secondary objective. Rather, the Chilean programme has primarily been couched as a strategy to invest in the capabilities and equalize the opportunities of children from low-income families. Indeed, the title *Chile Crece Contigo* echoes well-known narratives about 'social investment' (Jenson and Saint-Martin, 2003; Lister, 2003). Children (rather than women) are the main beneficiaries of the programme and have, in fact, been granted the *right* to a crèche and kindergarten place.

In Chile, service delivery is being developed in ways that combine educational objectives with working parents' needs through professionalized institutional care and working-time adjusted service hours. While overall Mexican ECEC policies have tried to address female labour force participation as well as children's access to early education, none of the programmes has ever pursued these goals in tandem. While IMSS childcare services never prioritized educational goals,[15] the absence of educational concerns is even stronger in the recent Sedesol programme which has lowered the standards and regulations compared to the IMSS centres. Overall, the differentiation between the provision of early education and care as well as the diversity of institutional arrangements within the (non-educational) care sector have brought about an extremely segmented system of public childcare services in Mexico, where quality is bound to differ greatly from one institutional arrangement to another. In Chile, segmentation seems to be more pronounced across the public/private divide than among public programmes themselves.

The education/care divide also produces substantial discontinuities. In Mexico, some working mothers may have access to full-day childcare for children aged up to three, but once the children enter pre-school, half-day programmes are the norm. At the same time, childcare services have few educational components with the potential to prepare children for pre- and primary school. Efforts are being made to move towards an integrated system that works for both children and working parents in Chile, but, as in Mexico, the pre-school system is still dominated by half-day enrolment.

In terms of the basis for entitlement, research on developed welfare regimes suggests that universal provisioning is more likely to lead to redistributive and financially viable services of equal quality than targeting, because it fosters the 'willingness to pay' through taxation and the 'willingness to stay' in public schemes among wealthier segments (Korpi and Palme, 1998). Hence, quality can be maintained at high levels. Neither Mexico nor Chile offers a universal entitlement to ECEC services and both apply

---

15. Communication with the National Coordinator of the IMSS Day-Care Centres, 26 March 2009.

means-testing as a targeting mechanism. Yet, there are significant differences in the scope and legal enshrinement of benefits. Thus, the Chilean programme targets a much broader public (40 per cent of households until 2010; 60 per cent of households from 2011 onwards) compared to the Mexican programme, which targets households with a monthly income of less than six minimum wages (approximately 14 per cent of households). The latter remains largely residual and is less likely (and in fact does not intend) to attract middle-income sectors, whereas the Chilean programme has begun to reach out to middle-income groups. Whether the Chilean programme can move further towards universalization will depend on the extent to which financial backing, service quality, professionalism and — very importantly — political will can be maintained.[16]

Besides means-testing, the rules of both countries' programmes stipulate that the beneficiary mother must be working or looking for work or studying in order to have access to full-day childcare. In Chile, no such requirements are established for access to part-time care. Further, *Chile Crece Contigo* has been enshrined in a law which defines the right to a crèche and kindergarten place for the target group. No such move has been made in Mexico for children under the age of three. *Estancias* is a unilateral offer by the state which can be withdrawn at any time and depends to a significant extent on the 'market' response to public subsidies. Thus, the state does not decide or influence where childcare centres are established, but leaves this up to the forces of demand and supply.[17] The absence of a rights-based entitlement also differentiates the *Estancias* programme from the social security-based service provision through IMSS where access to childcare is — albeit stratified along the lines of labour market status — the right of working mothers.

Programme financing comes mainly out of general revenue. In contrast to the Chilean programme, however, the Mexican programme holds on to the co-responsibility component — a pet concept of the 'New Poverty Agenda' according to which beneficiaries of social services should not be mere recipients of state 'hand-outs', but should shoulder part of the costs to be paid in money or kind. Thus, parents, however poor, are expected to make a co-payment for the childcare services they receive. In Chile, on the other hand, ECEC services are offered free of charge to lower-income households.

The different delivery mechanisms have important implications for the speed and sustainability of expansion as well as for service quality. On the quantitative side, the Mexican programme has increased the availability

---

16. This is uncertain in the current context, considering that the centre-left coalition Concertación lost the 2010 elections to the conservative Alianza por Chile. Unfortunately, the negotiations of the 2011 budget demonstrated that the further construction of crèches was not a priority for the Piñera administration (Cámara de Diputados, 2010).

17. The fact that more than two-thirds of the childcare centres are located in less marginalized neighbourhoods and only 6 per cent are located in neighbourhoods with high levels of marginalization (Pereznieto and Campos, 2010) may be an expression of this lack of coordination.

of childcare places at an impressive speed. While expansion has moved more slowly in Chile, it seems more promising with regard to sustainability. Not least, the construction of new crèches implies important investments in public infrastructure and more public employment (although see footnote 16 above). The Mexican programme, on the other hand, subsidizes the remodelling of private housing, tying the grant to the operation of a childcare centre for one year. Thereafter, the centre can, theoretically, be closed down.

While care quality is generally difficult to assess, professionalization of childcare is lower in the Mexican programme, which seems to be based on the assumption that childcare doesn't require any particular skills (beyond secondary education). The Chilean policy, in contrast, emphasizes professional care, even for the very young. This does not imply, however, that there are no quality-related problems in the Chilean case. As we have seen, child-to-staff ratios are rather low and rarely complied with in practice. In fact, the overall ratio may be more favourable in the Mexican programme where, according to the programme rules, there must be at least one assistant care giver per eight children.[18] On the other hand, children of very different ages (from one to four years) need to be cared for simultaneously by one person, so that specific activities suitable for each age group may be more difficult to organize.

Childcare service expansion also creates employment opportunities which in turn are often taken up by women. While this is not an explicit goal stated in the programme rules, the Mexican government has portrayed *Estancias* as the 'biggest employment programme for women in Mexico' (Calderón, 2009), claiming to have created thousands of jobs for (previously unemployed or 'inactive') women. As 'care-entrepreneurs' running small childcare businesses, primary carers are largely self-employed, with no access to social protection, and there have been complaints about subsidies being too low for the carers to comply with the programme rules and earn a decent wage at the same time (Levy, 2008; Zaragoza, 2007). The wages and working conditions of the assistants that the primary carers are required to employ are even more dubious. Moreover, care givers are not connected in any meaningful way that would allow them to organize around their entitlements and the conditions under which childcare is provided. This seems particularly contradictory in a context where trade unions in education (including pre-school) are comparatively strong and able to impose their demands. While ECEC jobs are far from being adequately recognized and compensated in Chile, most care givers are publicly employed and the prospects for collective bargaining are more favourable.[19] Important challenges remain in increasing the valuation

---

18. Unfortunately, we have no evidence on compliance with this rule.
19. Of course, this must be taken with a grain of salt in a context that is characterized by a severe overall disempowerment of trade unions whose bargaining position *vis-à-vis* employers has not been significantly strengthened since the return to democracy.

of childcare work as well as in equalizing entitlements and pay across the institutions involved in the new programme.

Both governments have engaged in powerful communication strategies to foster support for their respective programmes. The Mexican programme has mostly been framed as helping (poor) women to engage in paid work without having to worry about the whereabouts of their children or leave them in potentially dangerous arrangements in order to earn a living. The maternalist ideal is extended to include paid work and appeals to working mothers' 'heroism' as worthy of public support. A recurrent theme in Calerdón's speeches is that working mothers are the 'pillars of the Mexican household... who with their work and care pull their families through' and should be supported in their quest for 'harmonizing their family and work activities, and of course to improve their life quality as women and also that of their children' (Calderón, 2007a). However, framing the day-care programme in a politically acceptable way can become quite a balancing act in the face of the strong conservative currents within PAN itself, as the following quote shows:

> And one of the things that most hindered women from finding work is the fact that they had to take care of their children, and it's good that children can be taken care of by their mothers. It's good that we can foster the value of the family, the affection of the mother, the affection of the father as well; but especially the bond between the mother and her children. But also, it's good that we can open spaces so that the mother can work. (Calderón, 2009; authors' translation)

In Chile, the expansion of ECEC services has featured prominently in Bachelet's speeches where it has been framed mainly as a way of creating of 'equal opportunities from the cradle' for children from low-income families. Although presidential discourses mention childcare services as a means of facilitating mothers' employment, they essentially focus on their value as an educational policy and institutional childcare is continually presented as being 'good' for children. The careful calibration of professional and maternal concern is well captured in the following extract of a Bachelet speech:

> You have heard me say this many times and I have said that — *as a woman, as a mother, but also as a paediatrician* — I am convinced that initial education is fundamental, that all the efforts in primary, secondary and later, of course, tertiary education won't be enough if we arrive late. And one way to be on time is to start at the youngest age. Therefore, and because we fight against inequality as of the cradle and we give mothers the opportunity to work, we will vigorously continue the crèche programme. (Bachelet, 2007: 15; authors' translation, emphasis added)

Despite their distinctive focus, both governments are struggling to find frames that reconcile offers of defamilialization with traditional views about women's duty as mothers and primary care givers. While mothers' employment is being portrayed as crucial for their children and families in Mexico, the benefits of institutional care and education for children are at the centre of official discourses in Chile. The fact that enabling women to work in order to increase *their* economic security and autonomy is not a major consideration in either case goes to show how difficult it is to move away from maternalist ideals in both countries. How far the programmes promote the development and well-being of small children remains to be seen.

ACCOUNTING FOR DIFFERENT DEVELOPMENTS: SOME HYPOTHESES

Why have the two countries chosen such different routes to expand early childhood education and care services? We suggest that a combination of institutional legacies, overall frameworks for social policy and politics have made particular modes of ECEC service provision more attractive to governments and have shaped the ways in which similar objectives are translated into different policies. The following are hypotheses, rather than waterproof research findings, intended to provide a starting point for future research on the contemporary politics of (child)care, an area that has not received much scholarly attention so far.

Firstly, institutional legacies and blueprints within which the expansion of publicly funded childcare services takes place seem to matter whether educational goals (for young children) or care needs (of working parents) are addressed separately or together. In Chile, the creation of JUNJI in 1970 was the product of both a growing interest in the early stimulation of children and the struggle of women activists from different party backgrounds for women workers' right to childcare (JUNJI, 2005). From the beginning, the institution was linked to Mineduc, and although it was moved to the Ministry of Domestic Affairs' Division for Social and Community Organizations during the military dictatorship, it was reintegrated into Mineduc upon the return to democracy. In Mexico, IMSS's mission was to address working mothers' needs for custody rather than to serve educational objectives, and it is this model that served as a blueprint for the new programme. Political calculations may have also played a role in keeping education and care separated. As mentioned earlier, the teachers' union has lent crucial support to the rapid expansion of pre-schooling since 2002 in Mexico. Anecdotal evidence suggests that Sedesol has been careful not to frame the programme as a first step on the educational ladder in order to avoid the involvement of the teachers' union which holds important political leverage over the educational system and its policies.[20]

At the same time, the Chilean programme shows that blueprints emanating from previous arrangements are not carved in stone. The fact that state-subsidized private delivery—a common strategy for childcare expansion in other countries such as Argentina and the Republic of Korea

20. Personal communication with programme manager, October 2008.

(see Faur and Peng, this volume) — was not considered in Chile may reflect the government's reluctance to replicate a model which in the broader educational arena has led to far-reaching segmentation and social inequality. Since services at the crèche and intermediate levels are basically being created from scratch, the leverage over institutional shape was arguably greater than at the transitional level, where coverage was more advanced and the subsidized private variant an established fact.

Secondly, the Mexican day-care programme mirrors general trends in the country's social protection policies according to which sectoral ministries produce watered-down versions of IMSS's social protection schemes for workers who are not covered by social security (Levy, 2009). Since 2004, for example, the Ministry of Health has run a voluntary health insurance scheme (*Seguro Popular*) for informal sector workers, which offers less comprehensive benefits than IMSS. With the conditional cash transfer scheme *Oportunidades*, the day-care programme shares the characteristic that benefits are not based on social rights, but provided as assistance measures that can be withdrawn any time.

In Chile, the decision to go for publicly provided professionalized childcare rather than home- or community-based day-care mirrors the social protection strategy pursued by the Lagos and Bachelet administrations and their emphasis on improving the quality of social services and extending existing protection mechanisms to previously excluded or disadvantaged groups (rather than creating parallel programmes as in the Mexican case). In health, for example, Plan AUGE (launched in 2004) defined a number of health conditions to be universally covered by the public system regardless of age, gender, race, insurance status and income (Gideon, 2006). The pension reform (approved in 2008) introduced a series of changes in order to improve coverage and efficiency of the existing system of individual accounts.

Thirdly, decisions over change and continuity in institutional arrangements are embedded in the political context of each country. Previous studies on gender politics in Latin America have shown that the potential of redistributive and gender-progressive policies depends to a significant extent on the political inclination of the ruling majority along the Left–Right as well as the secular–religious spectrum (Huber et al., 2009; Macaulay, 2006). There are significant differences between Chile and Mexico across both dimensions. In Chile, *Concertación* — a Centre–Left party coalition — ruled the country between 1990 and 2010. The first two presidents following the return to democracy came from the Christian-Democratic Party (PDC) and it has been argued that PDC's social conservatism has slowed down (and, in some cases, impeded) the advancement in key women's rights issues (Baldez, 2001). The two consecutive presidents — Ricardo Lagos (2000–2006) and Michelle Bachelet (2006–2010) — came from the (historically secular) Socialist Party. There seems to be some agreement that particularly under the Bachelet administration women's rights and gender equality were key themes and that 'changes have been symbolic as well as material' (Rios Tobar, 2007: 28).

The political context in Mexico is quite different. While the 2000 national elections ended over seventy years of one-party rule, it was not a Centre–Left party coalition that emerged from this transition, but a pro-Church, pro-business party (PAN) that very much adhered to the conservative Catholic doctrine with regard to women, sexuality and the family. Two early incidents illustrate PAN's unfortunate start on gender issues. First, while President Vicente Fox strengthened the independence and increased the resources of the Mexican women's machinery, he appointed an avowedly anti-abortionist to head the institution rather than one of the candidates backed by feminist organizations. Second, in a speech entitled 'What Mexico expects of its women', delivered in March 2001, the Secretary of Labour depicted the 'natural order' of women's position at the centre of the family and held that work outside the home undermined this sacred duty (Magally, 2001). The statement spurred widespread disapproval, and with the new day-care programme, the government of Felipe Calderón (2006 to date) seems to have moved slightly closer to the reality of working women. The discourse of the 'necessary evil' of women's work outside the home has been nuanced, and now appeals to cultural representations of the self-sacrificing 'supermadre' who works — not for herself, but for her family, children and community.

As Franceschet and Macdonald (2004) show, the countries' political trajectories, and democratic transitions in particular, have also shaped different types of women's movements, including different demands and possibilities to liaise with the state in policy making. In Chile, massive opposition to the military regime fostered cross-class alliances among organized women and with other political actors. The widely diffused slogan 'democracy in the country and in the home' illustrates that the gender division of labour was an important part of the movements' agenda. Although many of these cross-class linkages have faded today, the women's movement gained political voice during the transition and part of its membership built strong links with parties through double militancy.

Similar cross-class unity and political alliance building was never achieved among organized women in Mexico (Franceschet and Macdonald, 2004: 8) where top-down corporatist rule either co-opted movements or marginalized them from the policy process. The fact that corporatist rule was followed by a Centre–Right government with extremely conservative stances on gender issues, meant that the scope for influencing the state in policy making remained limited. Feminist scholarship has long emphasized the drawbacks of women's movements' links with the state and political parties in Chile, pointing to feminists' marginalization within parties, the loss of autonomy and linkages to their support base as well as the political fragmentation of movements (Chuchryk, 1994). In contrast to Mexico, however, these linkages have increased the footing and presence of feminist policy entrepreneurs in parties, the legislature and the national women's machinery from where they have spearheaded policy proposals for gender equality (Haas, 2006). While in both countries the recent childcare service expansion seems to be largely a top-down phenomenon, it is not impossible that these linkages have allowed Chilean feminists to shape policy proposals for care more directly than their Mexican sisters.

Given the rather unfavourable conditions in Mexico, why would a conservative government launch a childcare services programme at all? Here too, political circumstances may have come into play. Indeed, the issue of childcare services came up during the 2006 presidential elections, with several candidates promising measures to address the double burden faced by mothers. Following the close election results, the Calderón government was under considerable legitimacy pressures to comply with campaign promises, one of which had been the expansion of childcare services. In this context the new government certainly had an interest in the fast roll-out of the day-care programme and the rapid visibility of its results, which may have influenced policy choice: professionalized institutional care would have not only been more costly, but also slower in increasing coverage.[21]

FINAL REMARKS

Over the last decade, ECEC policies have become more prominent on the policy agendas of several Latin American countries. As the cases of Chile and Mexico show, policy options are not restricted to cash transfers, but increasingly include a concern for pre-school and childcare service provision. Both countries have significantly expanded the availability of ECEC facilities and places over the last years. These are notable and laudable developments in a context where conservative views about women's roles still feature prominently.

However, despite the convergence around concerns over the promotion of child welfare and female employment, the programmes differ markedly in scope and character. This article has mentioned a series of factors that may have shaped different policy designs, including institutional legacies, the overall dominant approach to social policy and the political context. This is an area where future research could make a fruitful contribution, exploring cross-country variations in the ways care concerns have entered the political arena and the roles that different actors and institutions have played in the design of specific programme choices.

In our view, programme design is not only a reflection of how much policy makers 'care' about the needs of low-income women and their children,

---

21. Calderón — aware of the critics who have pointed to the limitations of the programme — frequently uses the quantity/quality dichotomy in his speeches, underlining that investments in public infrastructure would have led to inefficiency and that employing public servants would have slowed down the process of expansion due to union power, among others (e.g. Calderón, 2007b; 2008; 2009).

but also shapes the kind of opportunities that ECEC services can create for them. In this sense, the integration of education and care into one system (as in the Chilean case) seems more promising. While free crèche and kindergarten places are targeted to children from lower-income families, they come closer to a unified system of public childcare. In Mexico, bureaucratic fragmentation prevails — between pre-school education (Ministry of Education), insurance-based (IMSS/ISSTE) and targeted day-care (Sedesol) — and risks entrenching existing inequalities, mainly along the lines of labour market status, and producing discontinuities across age groups. As we have seen, the separation of (pre-school) education and care into different programmes also creates a highly fragmented workforce: some workers are qualified and well organized, while others have little formal training and few entitlements. Thus, Mexico seems to be moving away from the model of an integrated childcare workforce with a 'core' profession through a diversification of service offers, while efforts are being made in Chile to integrate and unify the public ECEC system.

Despite these differences, the programmes share four features which in our view are symptomatic for care-related policy making in the region. First, the commodification of care through ECEC services has not changed the fact that it is carried out by women. The low value accorded to what is still largely regarded as 'women's work' is evident in both cases. In Chile, where services are professionalized and pre-school teachers relatively well organized, salaries are nevertheless low compared to other jobs requiring similar qualifications. In Mexico, childcare workers join the ranks of the self-employed without access to social security and protection. Although the highly decentralized and individualized mode of service provision is likely to hamper the employment prospects of workers, it would not be impossible to improve this situation within the modality of home-based day-care, for example, by creating links among childcare providers, promoting national organization and increasing workers' access to basic social rights.

Second, the absence of men from policy debates around childcare is striking. Since it is hardly possible (nor particularly desirable) to commodify all unpaid care work, a large amount of it remains to be done even when full-time quality ECEC services are available. There has been little improvement in public policies aimed at a more equal intra-household division of caring labour, at least formally by including fathers among the eligible population for childcare services or parental leave. Parental leave remains short and is still restricted to mothers. In Chile, fathers have been entitled to four days of leave after childbirth since 2005 — a regulation that may have some symbolic value, but falls short of substantially changing gendered norms and practices in child rearing.[22]

---

22. A reform of maternity/parental leave regulations is currently being debated in the Chilean Congress.

Third, there is little discussion about the kinds of jobs available to women from low-income (and often low educational) backgrounds, despite the fact that the extent to which recent policy innovations will increase women's economic security critically depends on the kind of employment opportunities the countries' growth models generate. This is indicative of post-Washington Consensus frameworks, which have rehabilitated social policy, but stop short of recognizing the interrelated character of 'the social' and 'the economic' and consequently ignore the need to integrate social and macroeconomic policy making into coherent strategies that take into account both production and social reproduction (Elson, 2004). Thus, while the expansion of ECEC services certainly contributes to reducing women's burdens of unpaid childcare, it does not in and of itself resolve gender inequalities. More and better policies are needed to improve women's status and end discrimination on the labour market, including the promotion of women's participation in stable and productive employment, the enforcement of anti-discrimination laws, and the investment in training opportunities (Mesa-Lago, 2008).

Fourth, both programmes commit (at best) to the strengthening of 'equal opportunities' for children and women from low-income households. This is deeply problematic in the face of the extreme social inequalities prevalent in both countries. The Chilean programme reflects the desire to make specific groups of children (from low-income backgrounds) 'fit to compete' rather than creating an educational environment where children of different social classes can mix. At the same time, extending ECEC to these groups is certainly not enough to level the playing field, as long as the rest of the educational system remains unchanged.[23] While Mexico's cash transfer programme *Oportunidades* has similar ambitions of social investment, the country's childcare service system seems to reproduce existing inequalities rather than mitigating them. Given the low-cost and loosely regulated character of the *Estancias* programme, the extent to which it is driven by a desire to encourage children's development at all is questionable.

Increasing policy attention to childcare services can provide an enormous opportunity for promoting children's and women's social and economic rights in highly unequal contexts. As this study has shown, however, the devil is in the details of programme design. The extent to which childcare services can enhance gender equality and child development depends crucially on the state's commitment to these goals, underpinned by sufficient financial resources and the effective regulation of quality.

REFERENCES

Arriagada, I. (2007) 'Transformaciones Familiares y Políticas de Bienestar en América Latina' ['Family Transformations and Welfare Policies in Latin America'], in I. Arriagada (ed.) *Familias y Políticas Públicas en América Latina: Una Historia de Desencuentros* [*Families*

---

23. See Staab (2010) for a more detailed discussion.

and Public Policies in Latin America: A History of Estrangement], pp. 125–52. Santiago de Chile: CEPAL.

Bachelet, M. (2007) 'Mensaje Presidencial 2007 (21 de mayo)' ['Presidential Address 2007 (21 May)']. www.gobiernodechile.cl/viewEjeSocial.aspx?idarticulo=23439& idSeccionPadre=119 (accessed 28 September 2008).

Badía Ibañez, M. (2002) 'Gender and Development Policy in Chile: The Aid Programme to Female Heads of Households', in L. Haagh and C. Helgø (eds) *Social Policy Reform and Market Governance in Latin America*, pp. 77–100. Basingstoke: Palgrave Macmillan.

Baldez, L. (2001) 'Coalition Politics and the Limits of State Feminism in Chile', *Women and Politics* 22(4): 1–36.

Brachet-Márquez, V. (2007) 'Las Reformas de los Sistemas de Salud y Seguridad Social en México' ['Reforms in Health and Social Security Systems in Mexico'], in V. Brachet-Márquez (ed.) *Salud Pública y Regímenes de Pensiones en la Era Neoliberal: Argentina, Brasil, Chile y México (1980–2000) [Public Health and Pension Regimes in the Neoliberal Era: Argentina, Brazil, Chile and Mexico (1980–2000)]*, pp. 291–348. Mexico City: El Colegio de México.

Bradshaw, S. (2008) 'From Structural Adjustment to Social Adjustment: A Gendered Analysis of Conditional Cash Transfer Programmes in Mexico and Nicaragua', *Global Social Policy* 8(2): 188–207.

Calderón, F. (2007a) 'Discurso: El Presidente Calderón en el Anuncio del Sistema Nacional de Guarderías y Estancias Infantiles' ['Speech: President Calderón Announces the National System of Childcare Centres']. www.presidencia.gob.mx/prensa/discursos/?contenido=30143 (accessed 9 June 2009).

Calderón, F. (2007b) 'Discurso: El Presidente Calderón en la Inauguración de la Estancia Infantil 3000' ['Speech: President Calderón at the Inauguration of Childcare Centre Number 3000']. www.presidencia.gob.mx/prensa/?contenido=31141 (accessed 20 September 2009).

Calderón, F. (2008) 'Discurso: El Presidente Calderón en el Evento Más Oportunidades para las Mujeres' ['Speech: President Calderón at the Event More Opportunities for Women']. www.presidencia.gob.mx/prensa/?contenido=36729 (accessed 23 September 2009).

Calderón, F. (2009) 'Discurso: El Presidente Calderón en el Evento por el Día Internacional de la Mujer' ['Speech: President Calderón at the Event celebrating International Women's Day']. www.presidencia.gob.mx/prensa/?contenido=42912 (accessed 9 June 2009).

Cámara de Diputados (2010) 'Diputados DC Critican Drástica Reducción de Presupuesto para Educación Técnica y Preescolar' ['Christian-Democrat Deputies Criticize the Drastic Reduction in the Budget for Technical and Pre-school Education'], *Noticas del Congreso*, 20 October. http://www.camara.cl/prensa/noticias_detalle.aspx?prmid=40285 (accessed 20 October 2010).

Cepalstat (2005) 'Estadísticas e Indicadores Sociales' ['Social Statistics and Indicators']. http://websie.eclac.cl/sisgen/ConsultaIntegrada.asp (accessed 20 September 2009).

Chant, S. (2008) 'The "Feminisation of Poverty" and the "Feminisation" of Anti-Poverty Programmes: Room for Revision?' *Journal of Development Studies* 44(2): 165–197.

Chuchryk, P. (1994) 'From Dictatorship to Democracy: The Women's Movement in Chile', in J. Jaquette (ed.) *The Women's Movement in Latin America: Participation and Democracy*, pp. 65–107. Boulder, CO: Westview Press.

Colina, L. (2008) *Economía Productiva y Reproductiva en México: Un Llamado a la Conciliación [Productive and Reproductive Economy in Mexico: A Call for Conciliation]*. Mexico City: CEPAL.

Comisión Investigadora (2010) 'Informe Preliminar sobre el Ejercicio de la Facultad de Investigación 1/2009' ['Preliminary Report on the Proceedings of Investigation 1/2009']. Mexico City: Comisión Investigadora de los hechos acontecidos el cinco de junio del dos mil nueve en la guardería ABC de Hermosillo [Investigative Commission on the events of 5 June 2009 in the Childcare Centre ABC in Hermosillo]. http://www.scjn.gob.mx/documents/informe_preliminar_comision_abc.pdf (accessed 16 May 2011).

ECLAC (2008) *Social Panorama of Latin America 2007*. Santiago de Chile: ECLAC.

Elson, D. (2004) 'Social Policy and Macroeconomic Performance: Integrating "the Economic" and "the Social"', in T. Mkandawire (ed.) *Social Policy in a Development Context*, pp. 63–79. Basingstoke: Palgrave in assoc with UNRISD.

Franceschet, S. and L. Macdonald (2004) 'Hard Times for Citizenship: Women's Movements in Chile and Mexico', *Citizenship Studies* 8(1): 3–23.

GEA-ISA (2007) 'First Survey Conducted on Care Providers and Beneficiaries in 2007'. México City: Grupo de Economistas y Asociados-Investigaciones Sociales Aplicadas.

Gideon, J. (2006) 'Accessing Economic and Social Rights under Neoliberalism: Gender and Rights in Chile', *Third World Quarterly* 27(7): 1269–83.

Haas, L. (2006) 'The Rules of the Game: Feminist Policymaking in Chile', *Politica* 046: 199–225.

Honorato Barrueto, G. (2006) '¿Qué Mano Mece la Cuna? Los Peligros de una Educación Parvularia sin Control' ['Whose Hand Rocks the Cradle? The Risks of a Kindergarten Education without Control']. Report presented to the Department of Communication, Universidad del Desarrollo, to apply to the academic rank of graduate in social communication and to the professional title of journalist. www.udd.cl/prontus_facultades/site/artic/20060111/asocfile/tesis_la_mano_que_mece_la_cuna_1_.pdf (accessed 5 December 2008).

Huber, E., J.D. Stephens, D. Bradley, S. Moller and F. Nielsen (2009) 'The Politics of Women's Economic Independence', *Social Politics* 16(1): 1–39.

Instituto Mexicano de Seguridad Social (IMSS) (2009) *Información sobre el Perfil de las Cuidadoras del IMSS* [*Information on the Profile of IMSS Care-takers*]. Mexico City: IMSS, Coordinación de Guarderías.

Jenson, J. and D. Saint-Martin (2003) 'New Routes to Social Cohesion? Citizenship and The Social Investment State', *Canadian Journal of Sociology* 28: 77–99.

Junta Nacional de Jardines Infantiles (JUNJI) (2005) *30 Años Trabajando por los Niño y Niñas de Chile* [*30 Years Working for the Children of Chile*]. Santiago de Chile: Gobierno de Chile and JUNJI.

Junta Nacional de Jardines Infantiles (JUNJI) (2008) *Balance de Gestion Integral, Año 2007* [*Complete Management Balance 2007*]. Santiago de Chile: JUNJI.

Knaul, F. and S. Parker (1996) 'Cuidado Infantil y Empleo Femenino en México: Evidencia Descriptiva y Consideraciones sobre Las Políticas' ['Childcare and Female Employment in Mexico: Descriptive Evidence and Policy Considerations'], *Estudios Demográficos y Urbanos* 11(3): 577–607.

Korpi, W. and J. Palme (1998) 'The Paradox of Redistribution and Strategies of Equality: Welfare State Institutions, Inequality, and Poverty in the Western Countries', *American Sociological Review* 63(5): 661–87.

Leal, G. (2006) 'Guarderías IMSS: "Crecer" sin Calidad?' ['"Growth" without Quality?'], *La Jornada* 18 November.

Levy, S. (2008) 'Se Subsidia la Informalidad' ['Informality Is Being Subsidized'], *Enfoque*: *Reforma* 7 September.

Levy, S. (2009) 'Entrevista con Santiago Levy: Buenas Intenciones, Malos Resultados' ['Interview with Santiago Levy: Good Intentions, Bad Outcomes'], *Nexos* 1 February.

Lister, R. (2003) 'Investing in the Citizen-Workers of the Future: Transformations in Citizenship and the State under New Labour', *Social Policy and Administration* 37(5): 427–43.

Macaulay, F. (2006) *Gender Politics in Brazil and Chile: The Role of Parties in National and Local Policymaking*. Basingstoke: Palgrave Macmillan.

Magally, S. (2001) 'Las Mujeres Deben Preferir la Misión de Ser el Corazón de una Familia Sólida: Carlos Abascal' ['Women Should Prefer the Mission to be the Heart of a Solid Family: Carlos Abascal'], *Comunicación e Información de la Mujer (CIMAC)*. www.cimac.org.mx/noticias/01mar/01032104.html (accessed 24 September 2009).

Mesa-Lago, C. (2008) 'Social Insurance (Pension and Health), Labour Markets and Coverage in Latin America'. Programme on Social Policy and Development Paper No. 36. Geneva: UNRISD.

Milenio (2008) 'Estancias Infantiles de Calderón: Improvisación y Fines Electoreros' ['Calderón's Estancias Infantiles: Improvisation and Electoral Objectives'], *Milenio* 25 May. http://impreso.milenio.com/node/8065659 (accessed 14 May 2011).

Ministerio de Hacienda (2008) 'Evaluación Comprehensiva del Gasto. Junta Nacional de Jardines Infantiles (JUNJI), Fundación Integra y Programa de Educación Preescolar de la Subsecretaria de la Educación' ['Comprehensive Spending Evaluation. National Council of Kindergartens (JUNJI), Fundación Integra and Preschool Education Programme of the Subsecretariat for Education']. Santiago de Chile: Ministerio de Hacienda, Dirección de Presupuestos.

Ministerio de Planificación (Mideplan) (2007) 'Chile Crece Contigo — Sistema de Proteccion Integral a la Infancia. Dossier Informativo para Encargados Comunicacionales de Ministerios, Servicios, Gobiernos Regionales y Municipalidades' ['Chile Grows With You — System of Comprehensive Childhood Protection. Informative Dossier for Communication Officers at Ministries, Services, Regional Governments and Municipalities']. www.crececontigo.cl/download.php?c=upfiles/materiales&a=4753efa82a60e_Dossier_info rmativo_CHCC.pdf (accessed 15 June 2008).

Ministerio de Planificación (Mideplan) (1990) (1996) (2003) (2006) (2009) 'Encuesta de Caracterización Socioeconómica (CASEN)' ['Survey of Socioeconomic Characteristics']. www.mideplan.ch/casen

Mkandawire, T. (2004) 'Social Policy in a Development Context: Introduction', in T. Mkandawire (ed.) *Social Policy in a Development Context*, pp. 1–31. Basingtoke: Palgrave in assoc with UNRISD.

Molyneux, M. (2000) 'Twentieth-century State Formations in Latin America', in E. Dore and M. Molyneux (eds) *Hidden Histories of Gender and the State in Latin America*, pp. 33–81. Durham, NC: Duke University Press.

Molyneux, M. (2007) 'Change and Continuity in Social Protection in Latin America: Mothers at the Service of the State?'. Programme on Gender and Development Paper No. 1. Geneva: UNRISD.

Organization for Economic Cooperation and Development (2008) *OECD Employment Outlook*. Paris: OECD.

Ornelas, C. (2008) 'El SNTE, Elba Esther Gordillo y el Gobierno de Calderón' ['The SNTE, Elba Esther Gordillo and the Calderón Government'], *Revista Mexicana de Investigacion Educativa* 13(37): 445–69.

Ortiz, M.E. (2009) 'Cuenta Pública Junji Gestión 2006–2009' ['Public Account Junji Management 2006–2009']. http://www.junji.cl/junjijoomla/index.php?option=com_remository&Itemid=176&func=startdown&id=78 (accessed 28 September 2009).

Pereznieto, P. and M. Campos (2010) *Gendered Risks, Poverty and Vulnerability in Mexico: Contributions of the Estancias Infantiles para Apoyar a Madres Trabajadoras Programme*. London: Overseas Development Institute.

Presidencia (2007) 'Plan Nacional de Desarrollo 2007–2012' ['National Development Plan 2007–2012']. Mexico City: Poder Ejecutivo Federal.

Presidencia (2008) 'Vivir Mejor: Política Social del Gobierno Federal' ['Live Better: The Federal Government's Social Policy']. Mexico City: Federal Government of Mexico.

Rios Tobar, M. (2007) 'Chilean Feminism and Social Democracy from the Democratic Transition to Bachelet', *NACLA Report on the Americas* (April): 25–9.

Santibañez, L. (2008) 'Reforma Educativa: El papel del SNTE' ['Education Reform: The Role of SNTE'], *Revista Mexicana de Investigación Educativa* 13(37): 419–43.

Secretaria de Desarrollo Social (Sedesol) (2007) 'Programa de Guarderías y Estancias Infantiles para Apoyar a Madres Trabajadoras: Cuarto Informe Trimestral' ['Federal Day-Care Programme for Working Mothers: Fourth Quarterly Report']. Mexico City: Sedesol.

Secretaria de Desarrollo Social (Sedesol) (2008) 'Programa de Guarderías y Estancias Infantiles para Apoyar a Madres Trabajadoras: Cuarto Informe Trimestral' ['Federal Day-Care Programme for Working Mothers: Fourth Quarterly Report']. Mexico City: Sedesol.

Serrano, C. (2005) 'La familia como unidad de intervención de políticas sociales. Notas sobre el programa Puente-Chile Solidario' ['The Family as a Unity of Intervention for Social Policy. Notes on the Puente-Chile Solidario Programme'], in I. Arriagada (ed.) *Políticas hacia las familias, protección e inclusión sociales* [*Family Policies, Social Protection and Inclusion*], pp. 231–44. Santiago de Chile: CEPAL.

Staab, Silke (2010) 'Social Investment in Chile and Latin America: Towards Equal Opportunities for Women and Children?', *Journal of Social Policy* 39(4): 607–26.

Staab, S. and R. Gerhard (2010) 'Early Childhood Education and Care Policies in Latin America: For Women or Children or Both?'. Gender and Development Programme Paper No. 10. Geneva: UNRISD.

Tabbush, C. (2009) 'Gender, Citizenship and New Approaches to Poverty Relief: Conditional Cash Transfer Programmes in Argentina', in S. Razavi (ed.) *The Gendered Impact of Liberalization: Towards 'Embedded Liberalism'?*, pp. 290–326. New York: Routledge in assoc with UNRISD.

Teichman, J. (2001) *The Politics of Freeing Markets in Latin America: Chile, Argentina and Mexico*. Chapel Hill, NC: The University of North Carolina Press.

Valenzuela, M.E. (2000) 'La Calidad del Empleo de Las Mujeres en los Países del Cono Sur' ['The Quality of Women's Employment in the Southern Cone Countries'], in M.E. Valenzuela and G. Reinecke (eds) *¿Más y Mejores Empleos para las Mujeres? La Experiencia de los Países del Mercosur y Chile* [*More and Better Jobs for Women? The Experience of Mercosur Countries and Chile*], pp. 59–102. Santiago de Chile: OIT.

Zaragoza, L. (2007) 'Poca Calidad en Guarderías Impulsadas por Calderón' ['Little Quality in Childcare Centres Promoted by Calderón'], *La Jornada* 8 August.

10

Going Global: The Transnationalization of Care

Nicola Yeates

INTRODUCTION

Ongoing processes of global restructuring have inspired the development of research agendas attentive to the diverse and complex ways in which socio-institutional formations and practices across distant and proximate territories are materially connected. These agendas are generating new theoretical understandings of social structures, relations, identities and practices as stretching across national terrains (rather than confined within them) and of a world made up of dense networks of border-spanning connections, interactions and effects.

Care occupies a key place in this research agenda because of what it reveals about the nature of these border-crossing webs of socio-economic relationships. At one level, it illuminates a facet of economic restructuring that tends to be neglected by orthodox literatures on the subject (e.g. OECD, 2006). Care services are essentially oriented to the (re)production of beings and do not necessarily 'add value', at least in the market exchange sense of the term. They are provided on an unwaged/unpaid as well as on a waged/paid basis and the majority of such services are not produced by for-profit firms, but by governments, non-profit organizations and households operating outside of the commercial sphere. They are guided as much by relations of social solidarity, obligation, altruism and reciprocity as by market exchange, preference, choice and economic gain. They constitute a major component of public and private economic activity and expenditure, make significant contributions to GDP and national wealth and are essential to social reproduction without which production systems could not operate. As such, a focus on care captures forms and dynamics of services restructuring obscured by a focus on commercialized operations and transactions revolving around the production of commodities ('things'). And it brings into view wider sets of considerations and calculations behind the provision and reform of services that a focus on marketized transactions and for-profit logics alone is not fully equipped to address.

At another level, a focus on care brings to light the ways in which the social organization, relations and practices of welfare are being 'stretched' over long distances and structured across national borders. Care provides a productive lens through which to examine how societies are structured,

The author wishes to thank Shahra Razavi and the two anonymous referees for their constructive feedback on an earlier version of this article.

Seen, Heard and Counted, First Edition. Edited by Shahra Razavi.
Chapters © 2012 The Institute of Social Studies. Book compilation © 2012 Blackwell Publishing Ltd.

how different social groups are positioned within them (including how these positions are mediated by economic and welfare institutions), and the consequences of these structures and modes of social organization for access to major resources (Pascall, 1997). Such questions have traditionally been addressed through the lens of methodological nationalism which privileges a single socio-spatial scale (the nation state) and attends only to domestic sources of power, political actors and modes of service provision (e.g. Daly, 2002a, 2002b; Williams, 2010). But as evidence of the significance of care to the formation of 'multi-stranded' social relations routinely linking societies of origin and settlement (Basch et al., 1994) mounts, so recognition of the implications of these relations for understanding the transnationalized nature of care formations is also growing.

This article critically examines the contours of 'care transnationalization' as an ongoing social process and as a field of enquiry. I argue that this body of scholarship usefully combines structural understandings of global power relations with an emphasis on social interactions between defined actors in ways that keep sight of human agency, impacts upon material welfare and wider social development. However, this scholarship has privileged particular forms, dynamics and sites of care transnationalization over others. In particular, the literature on migrant care workers, which is otherwise the most developed to date in respect of its engagement with transnationalizations, contains a number of important biases and omissions regarding different kinds of border-spanning care relations. Other modes and expressions of care transnationalization — such as those involving consumer-based care migration, corporate restructuring and policy formation — have not yet enjoyed similar levels of scholarly attention with that literature or have been developed outside a care transnationalization theoretical framework. I argue that addressing these biases and deficits is central to the future development of a transnational analysis of care. This involves deepening analyses of how different forms of care transnationalization are expressed across different country, social and policy contexts, as well as furthering understandings of the connections between seemingly disparate modes of care transnationalization. It will need to intensify the dialogue between methodological nationalists and transnationalists and deploy the methods of comparative policy analysis.

The discussion is organized around four main sections. The first section provides preliminary clarification of the concepts of 'care' and 'transnationalization', while the second section reviews varieties of care transnationalization and different kinds of transnational entity involved. Here, I argue that a transnationalization framework has the potential to reveal multiple forms and dynamics of care restructuring and the existence of diverse care structures linking populations and places around the world. The discussion in the third section critically reviews research literatures focused on producer-based care migration to elucidate the ways in which they reveal the transnationalization of economic flows, social formations, political action and ideational consciousness. The final section then takes overall stock of care transnationalization research as it has developed to date and considers the implications of this discussion for future research attentive to diverse expressions, sites, scales and dynamics of care transnationalization.

CARE TRANSNATIONALIZATION: DEFINITIONS AND APPROACHES

The concept of care refers to activities and orientations to promote the physical and social (re)production of 'beings' and the solidary-affective bonds between them. Care activities refer to the performance of tasks (and the supervision thereof) involved in 'catering for the material and other general well-being of the one receiving care'. These tasks range from the highly intimate (personal, social, health and sexual care) to the less intimate (cooking, cleaning, ironing and general maintenance work), and take place in diverse settings (household, community, institutional contexts) (Yeates, 2004, 2009a). The orientational aspects of care involve emotional labour, expressed variously as 'looking out for' the other, 'having affection and concern for the other and working on the relationship between the self and the other to ensure the development of the bond' (Lynch and McLaughlin, 1995: 256–7, cited in Yeates, 2004). In some formulations, these orientational aspects include those which are directed at oneself rather than only at others. It is also important to distinguish emotional care labour from spiritual (or religious) care labour. Spiritual care addresses the meta-physical dimensions of existence of the self and the well-being of the other; it is distinct from the emotional bonds developed from a personal, affective relationship between the self and the other. Like affective care, though, religious care entails a set of perspectives, which are often integrated and provided in conjunction with tasks, such as looking after the other. Thus, social, educational and healthcare services may involve one or all of emotional care, spiritual care and physical care (Yeates, 2009a).

This definition of care and of care services is able to accommodate incredibly diverse phenomena. By some accounts, it becomes operationally meaningless as most work contains elements of 'looking out for' the other. Because of this, often a more restricted interpretation of care is employed, referring to 'custodial or maintenance help or services, rendered for the well-being of individuals who *cannot* perform such activities themselves' (Waerness, 1985, in Hooyman and Gonyea, 1995: 3, emphasis added) — typically ill, disabled, elderly and children and young people (Daly, 2002a). However, this may miss important elements of care work, such as that provided for people who are able to perform such activities for themselves but are not inclined to do so (as in domestic work and 'breadwinning') (Folbre, 2002). These definitional problems of what care work is and what it is not alert us to the complexities of the subject. Such complexities have been the subject of extended (and inconclusive) debate across the social sciences for much of recent history. But, ultimately, what is important is to understand that care as an orientation and a practice is routinely 'stretched' over vast distances in ways that have material importance for questions of who provides and consumes care, under what conditions, and with what effects for access to services, the quality of rights and the distribution of resources within and between countries.

A second axis of debate concerns the relative merits of psychological, labourist and philosophical approaches to care. Psychological approaches to care giving emphasize individual motivations, emotional attachments and identities of care givers; labourist approaches conceptualize care giving as labour, be this physical, emotional or spiritual labour (as above); philosophical approaches emphasize the moral and ethical dimensions of care giving. Of the three, labourist approaches have been most developed in contemporary care transnationalization literatures and have most affinity with contemporary policy reform agendas. But each perspective has the potential to bring useful and complementary insights to the question of how transnationalizing forces mediate care as an orientation and as practice, how these forces are restructuring modes of social organization and social relations, and how these are giving rise to 'new' forms of consciousness and awareness that are finding their ways into political discourses, collective action and policy initiatives.

Finally, we need to recognize the distinctiveness of a transnationalization perspective and how it differs from internationalization and globalization perspectives. Internationalization refers simply to the geographical dispersion of ideas, activities and practices across political borders, from one country to the next; it implies no simultaneous 'backward' or 'forward' linkages, whereas transnationalization does. Indeed these multiple linkages are an essential definitional element of transnationalization. The distinction between the two is illustrated in relation to migration processes. An international perspective sees directed movement from one point of departure (country A) to a point of arrival (country B) and focuses on settlement and integration of migrants into country B. A transnational perspective emphasizes the blurring of social space and geographic space, as migration implies less a rupture of relations with country A after having arrived in country B than ongoing and simultaneous relations with countries A and B. The distinction is captured in the term trans-migrants in opposition to international migrants, echoing similar terminological distinctions in the characterization of corporations — transnational corporations (TNCs) vs multinational corporations (MNCs).

While transnationalists and globalists share a common interest in actors, entities and processes that transcend nation states, transnationalists are sceptical of 'meta-individual imaginations of "deep structures"' (Dicken et al., 2001) that read care migrations off macro-structuralist 'logics of capitalism' scripts of the global system. Instead, they place greater emphasis on the actual interactions and transactions involved and assign a greater role to agency power in shaping outcomes (Khagram and Levitt, 2004). This does not negate structural forces or lapse into banal methodological individualism: the relational approach emphasizes the (re)production of a border-spanning web of relationships while avoiding "'atomistic description(s)" of activities of individual actors' (Dicken et al., 2001: 91). The focus on social interactions between defined actors and their empirical outcomes enables structural understandings of global power relations and social structures propelling and sustaining trans-bordering processes (of people, ideas, capital) together with an emphasis on human agency to be kept in view (cf. Dicken et al., 2001; Holton, 2008; Yeates, forthcoming 2012b).

VARIETIES AND EXPRESSIONS OF CARE TRANSNATIONALIZATION

Care transnationalization refers to the processes of heightened connectivity revolving around consciousness, identities, ideas, relations and practices of care which link people, institutions and places across state borders. Following Vertovec (1999), we may distinguish between the different *conceptual premises* underpinning articulations of care transnationalization. These include border-spanning social morphologies (e.g. migrant networks, ethnic diasporas, transnational families); a type of consciousness (e.g. awareness and concern for the well-being of one or more 'distant' others; dual/multiple identities of belonging); a conduit for capital flows (e.g. remittances of goods and money, transnational care corporations); a site of political engagement (e.g. global public fora and cross-border spheres of governance through which claims making is directed and care policies are constructed), and the reconstruction of place or locality (e.g. care identities, orientations and practices that connect and position actors in more than one country). Care transnationalization is an ongoing process involving diverse phenomena, but it is not an amorphous or 'disembodied' one. We may identify a range of expressions of care transnationalization and actors involved. Table 1 accordingly identifies a range of *transnational entities* and provides examples to illustrate their involvement in the promulgation of ideas and practices around care.

Table 1 reveals the diverse range of transnational entities (epistemic communities, governmental networks, professions and social movement organizations), the motivating forces (contrast, for example, the logics of for-profit entities with the moral logics of advocacy coalitions and social movement entities) and the varied nature of transnational care networks (from transnational families to consumer organizations to labour recruitment networks to advocacy coalitions). These networks act as conduits through which economic, ideational and informational resources circulate and position dispersed people, places and institutions in relation to one another. Ideational circuits, for example, may involve, be directed at, or expressed through,

*Table 1. Transnational Entities and Examples of Care Ideas
and Practices Promulgated*

Type	Definition	Ideas and practices
Epistemic communities	Experts linked around the production and dissemination of scientific ideas, knowledge and policy advice	Research institutes, think tanks, consultants undertaking research and providing advice on policy relating to care migration, service provision and regulation
Transnational advocacy networks Transnational social movements	Individuals linked around common moral and political concerns and discourses	Articulation of ethical and moral concerns about care migration; defence of migrants' rights; claims making to enhance the quality of social protection
Transnational migrant networks; ethnic diasporas and networks Transnational family networks Transnational consumer networks	Individuals linked around a common experience; exchanges of information, goods and services; shared values or aspirations; familial and/or ethnic ties and bonds	Exchanges of care employment, recruitment and employer information Provision of emotional and practical support from a distance e.g. listening, homework tuition, financial support through remittances Exchange of information about health and social care providers, products and services
Transnational corporations Transnational criminal networks	Corporate and other economic entities in pursuit of economic gain and profit	Staffing/care labour recruitment Health and social care service provision (hospitals, nursing homes, home healthcare, childcare, nurseries). Trafficking and smuggling of humans e.g. for sex and domestic work
Transnational professions	Care professionals linked around knowledge and technical expertise	International Guild of Catholic Nurses; International Council of Nurses
Transnational governmental networks Cross-border spheres of governance	Governmental actors linked around a common issue or concern	IGOs (e.g. World Bank, OECD, European Union, ILO) promulgating care discourses and policies on health migration, medical travel, health and social care provision, work–family reconciliation

Source: author, adapted from Khagram and Levitt (2004).

border-spanning public fora and spheres of cross-border governance; but they also circulate through 'national' spheres of governance. Much of the focus on ideational modes of care transnationalization has been on highly visible sites of global governance (IGOs), but the circulation of ideas within and across countries (some of which emanate from global fora) is also of importance to understanding how 'national' formations, the definition of policy problems and the formulation of domestic responses to them are co-constructed by processes of transnationalization.

Conceptually, ideational networks are often distinguished from networks of care labour and economic resources. The latter networks are the subject of a more detailed review in the following section, so suffice it for now to simply note that examples include labour networks of migrant domestic workers or other kinds of care labour (e.g. health workers), and that they are at once constituted by, and formative of, personal, familial and institutional relations over long distances. We may also distinguish between different kinds of producer-based care networks: those based on the migration of care labour and those revolving around corporate entities. Transnational care corporations include recruitment agencies mobilizing and supplying care labour as well as entities directly providing care services. These may operate on a 'for-profit' basis (as in corporations providing medical care, childcare and long-term care) or on a not-for-profit basis (as in international voluntary sector organizations providing diverse kinds of care services within emergency and development aid contexts).

Producer-based care networks differ in nature from consumption-based networks based on movements of people to the point of care service provision. Examples of the latter include medical travel and retirement migration. Space constraints only permit the briefest of commentary, but both medical travel and retirement migration are motivated by the search for more affordable, accessible, timely and/or specialized medical and social care anticipated to deliver a better quality of life than is possible in the home country. These migratory dynamics reflect uneven development, emanating from wealthier groups (i.e. those with greater consumer power) in developing and industrialized countries. Whereas producer-based care migration tends to involve movements from poorer to richer countries, medical travel and retirement migration tend to involve movement from richer to poorer countries. (One exception to this is medical travel in contexts where access to certain kinds of healthcare services of member state citizens is facilitated by multilateral agreements on portability of entitlements, such as in the EU.)

In the expansion of medical migration we see the development of transnational corporate care markets. Such markets are sponsored by developing country governments seeking foreign revenue and the socio-economic development they believe it will deliver. These markets are also sponsored by governments in neighbouring countries in the region as well as by those further afield seeking to move particular forms of healthcare provision offshore at lower cost. As Whittaker makes clear in the Indian context, where private healthcare has significantly expanded over the last two decades:

> The Indian Apollo Hospital Enterprises, the largest medical corporation providing services to foreigners and which treated an estimated 60,000 patients between 2001–2004, exemplifies global corporatised health with either ownership or partnerships with hospitals in Sri Lanka, Muscat, Dubai, India, Nepal, Tanzania, and Bangladesh. It also provides 'outsourced' medical services to treat patients from Tanzania and Mauritius sponsored by their governments and has negotiated to provide tests and do operations for the British National Health Service (CBC news online 2004). (Whittaker, 2009: 4)

Medical markets tend to be dominated by hospitals owned or managed by large multinational medi-corporations providing advanced facilities oriented towards more profitable procedures and catering for wealthy patient-customers drawn from local elites and from abroad (often including from ethnic diasporas). They form a key part of wider healthcare complexes involving transnational circuits of medical technologies and techniques circulating between hospitals. These circuits are flanked by parallel circuits of health professionals drawn from skilled medical staff in the domestic public health system as well as those practising overseas (Leng and Whittaker, 2010; UNESCAP, 2008; Wibulpolprasert et al., 2004).

In retirement migration, too, we see poorer countries competing for a larger share of expanding international markets for rich retirees. Like medical migration, retirement migration also involves the relatively wealthy and well educated moving from richer to poorer countries to capitalize on their superior purchasing power whilst maintaining ongoing ties with the home nation. Often these markets develop on a regional basis. In Europe, retirees from the Nordic countries move to the Mediterranean region countries such as Portugal, Italy, Greece, Turkey, Hungary and Spain (King et al., 1998). In Oceania, Australia and New Zealand are popular among retirees from northern Europe and East Asia (Shinozaky, 2006, cited in Morales, 2010). In the Americas, Costa Rica, Guatemala, Colombia, Brazil, Argentina and Mexico attract retirees from the United States and Canada (MPI, 2006; Morales, 2010). South-East Asian countries, such as Malaysia, Thailand and the Philippines are popular destinations for Japanese, Chinese, Taiwanese and Korean retirees (Shimizu, 2009). With the development of these markets comes the redirection of purchasing power and other forms of economic activity, as well as substantial relocations of social and healthcare costs to the destination country (Gustafsen, 2001; Williams et al., 1997).

Of note is that retirement migration may involve a sexual element, in that access to sexual care is often closely bound up with access to social and health care. As Shimuzu (2009) notes, for many of the Japanese men moving to the Philippines starting a new life with a new young (Filipina) partner, sexual care is integral to the care package they anticipated accessing. Morales' (2010) study of US retirement migration to Mexico similarly draws attention to the significance of marriage; it notes the preponderance of retired citizens (mostly US men) marrying local people (Mexican women). Here, the strategic economic calculation behind such marriages is evident in that 'it allows [US men] to buy property without the expense of the trust that must be paid by foreigners to own property in Mexico' (Morales, 2010: 80).

The distinction between ideational and service-based care transnationalization is useful conceptually but such distinctions are not necessarily evident in practice. For example, migrant networks based on care work have evolved in conjunction with advocacy-based and professional networks. Commercial care corporations' networks have developed alongside transnational political coalitions representing their economic interests in spheres of policy formation. And the rise of consumer-based care migration has been accompanied by transnational consumer networks cohering around information exchange and advocacy campaigns.

CARE TRANSNATIONALIZATION: THE EXAMPLE OF PRODUCER-BASED CARE MIGRATION

The most studied forms of care transnationalization to date concern those involving cross-border migration processes. This emphasis on migration is unsurprising given the importance transnational studies attaches to the movement of people as a pre-eminent mode/expression of transnational activity and consciousness and as a conduit for further transnationalisms, be they economic (e.g. remittances), social (ethnic diasporas, migrant networks), or political (e.g. migrant advocacy and coalition campaigns) in nature. Of all the forms of care migration as a mode of transnationalism and as a conduit for transnationalization, most attention has been paid to the migration of care workers. Essentially concerned with 'natural persons' (i.e. as opposed to corporate or governmental entities) involved in the cross-border provision of care services, this literature emphasizes the formative role of migration in sustaining social relations between disparately-located individuals, families, welfare institutions and economic systems.

This section examines the main contours of such care migration in some detail, to illustrate some of the key ways in which it can be said to be transnationalized (or transnationalizing). This discussion emphasizes the following aspects of care labour networks: as conduits for transnational economic flows (remittances of goods and capital) and transnational ideational flows (ideas and ideologies of care); as constituted by and formative of border-spanning social formations (global care networks, transnational families); and as an object of transnational collective action (e.g. advocacy and coalition campaigns, policy formation/responses in and through domestic and/or global fora).

Over the last two decades feminist care research has emphasized the extent to which women from 'peripheral' countries migrate to 'core' countries to undertake care labour. Much of this work has focused on transfers of 'motherly' care (particularly domestic work and childcare) in individualized household contexts, and the forging of a web of personal relations spanning the globe based on the provision of paid and/or unpaid care work. Hochschild (2000) and Parreñas (2001, 2005) portrayed a world criss-crossed by 'chains' of migration and love where mothers in mainly peripheral countries leave their children to the care of others while travelling to mainly metropolitan areas in core countries to care for the children of other women, either to release these women to undertake paid work in the formal economy or for status reasons. Migrants are a crucial source of labour easing the care burden of a growing number of households (read: women) in richer countries as they struggle to balance the demands of paid employment with their continuing responsibility for domestic work and other (unpaid) forms of care (Yeates, 2009a).

These flows need to be placed in the context of greater population movements generally and the feminized nature of contemporary international migration in particular, both of which are a response to the problem of uneven development. State policy, including social policy, shapes the scale and directions of these flows. Recruiting households are embedded in socio-institutional formations that foster — to varying degrees — reliance upon forms of work characterized by socio-economic insecurity. The development of tax and welfare benefits and labour regulations in rich countries construct care work as poor work and facilitate migrants' entry into it, where they compensate for the inflexibility and inadequacy of public social and healthcare services (Bettio et al., 2006; Escrivá, 2004; Piper, 2007a; Ungerson, 2002; Williams, 2010). Bretton Woods policies require governments to spend more on debt repayments than on social and healthcare services provision and are supportive of pro-'free' market policy reforms in developing countries that erode livelihoods, suppress wages, devalue currencies and promote export-oriented economic development. This, together with the fact that those countries may have little else to sell on the world market but labour power, renders the export of female labour central to the international politics of debt. Indeed, migration to richer countries represents a major means by which individual families generate income necessary for economic survival and welfare provisioning, while remittances are one of the few means by which some poorer countries can generate foreign currency and securitize loans (World Bank, 2011). Not surprisingly, then, international export of female labour is explicitly sponsored or tacitly condoned by governments, with care labour export an increasingly significant element of industrialization and economic development strategies (Yeates, 2009a). With these export-led strategies also come attempts to foster migrants' continuing relations with their 'home' country, including the development of taxation policy to foster favourable returns on inward investment (cf. 'Non-Resident Indian' in Indian tax codes) and/or to harvest a share of migrant remittances for general purposes (e.g. Philippines, Ghana).

Care worker migration is formative of border-spanning family care networks. Through migration, transnational networks of families are established, comprised of links amongst the same families (through the formation of transnational families) as well as links between different families (through the employment nexus) (Yeates, 2004). The literature on this subject clearly demonstrates the extent to which the provision of care labour is integral to the active, regular connections between and among transnational families. Whether the subjects of care are young (e.g. Parreñas, 2005) or elderly (e.g. Baldock, 2000), emigration transforms rather than closes down migrants' roles and identities as carers. Migrants themselves conceptualize their labour overseas and their sending of remittances as an act of care itself and, as 'distant carers', they also continue to provide tangible amounts of emotional and practical care work — often on a daily basis — from afar. This care work ranges from emotional support around issues of health, education and personal relationships, to practical support in the form of homework tuition, organization of family finances and the sending of remittances. Migrants remain involved in key forms of daily care activities and major decisions about educational, health and social care of their child(ren) and/or parents, and they are incorporated into networks of care provision involving family, neighbours, friends living in the vicinity of the elderly parent or child (Baldock, 2000). Even if caring from a distance amounts, by some accounts, to no more than semblant intimacy (Parreñas, 2001), migration reconfigures care roles, identities, power and status hierarchies within families and social networks (Asis et al., 2004).

These analyses have been crucially important for revealing 'new' global dynamics of care provision and restructuring, including the formation of global relations of social inequality between geographically dispersed men, women and children. But migration is formative of global care networks beyond 'private' familial networks. The 'care migration-industrial complex' concept conveys the degree of coordinated action among public and private actors to produce, recruit, relocate and settle care labour abroad, and to facilitate them in actively maintaining their ties 'back home' (Yeates, 2009a). Networks are based on (but not limited to) economic exchange; they link health and social care institutions (including those involved in the formation of 'human care capital' such as education and training organizations), and generate significant (often negative) externalities for public health and welfare institutions and populations in poorest countries. The characteristics of global care networks are an expression of the global status of countries:

> Countries at the top of the chain are 'fed' by those lower down the ranks: for example, the United States draws nurses from Canada; Canada draws nurses from England to make up for its losses to United States; England draws from South Africa to fill its vacancies; South Africa draws on Swaziland. Countries at the bottom end of the nursing chain may supply international markets but not replenish their stocks by importing health workers

from other countries: the Philippines is a major example of this. The problem for such countries is that they have no further countries from which they may recruit to make up for the losses of their own nurses... and consequently experience nursing shortages. (Yeates, 2009a: 80)

Broadening the scope of attention from 'unskilled' care workers in individualized household contexts to also include more skilled migrant carers working in highly institutionalized, professionalized and regulated contexts draws attention to the 'public' face of transnationalizing care including the existence of looped circuits of connection from richer countries to poorer ones. It highlights how those countries which have no other (i.e. poorer) countries from which to recruit may become reliant on charity. This is evidenced in the case of health worker migration, where nursing (and medical) labour is often provided by the very same countries that have recruited nurses from poorer ones. This is illustrated in the case of Malawi, whose long history of nurse emigration (mostly to the UK) is paralleled by a more recent history of importing nurses from overseas under the auspices of donor aid programmes. In that context, nurses comprised a sizeable proportion (about one in five) of volunteers mobilized by UN Volunteers and the UK's Voluntary Services International as part of the Emergency Human Resource Programme, a donor aid package to Malawi operational since 2005 (MSH, 2010; Muula, 2006). This 'counter-migratory' dynamic is an integral part of the same global political economy of care propelling and sustaining migration from middle- and low-income countries to high-income countries (Yeates, 2009a, 2011a).

The complexities of global care networks are revealed in a markedly different form of care transmigration — that involving the religious. My research into the organized production and export of care labour by Ireland throughout the nineteenth and twentieth centuries testifies to the pivotal importance of the Catholic religious to the formation of sustained social relations linking Ireland to the many countries worldwide to which the Irish migrated (Yeates, 2009b). The female religious were central to the establishment of various care (and more general welfare) services — ranging from nursing care to shelter to food to job training and job placement — for Irish female emigrants overseas and other local Catholic populations. Such was the demand for the services offered that the nuns regularly returned to Ireland to recruit others to staff the further expansion of their emigrant services. These care services were significant conduits for the spread of Irish Catholic social teaching worldwide, but they also enabled contact to be maintained between emigrants and their families in Ireland (orders of nuns were involved in letter writing and delivery which ensured, amongst other things, that remittances actually reached families; see Fitzgerald, 2006) (Yeates, 2009a; forthcoming 2012a).

Sodalities (communities of lay and professional female religious) played a critical role in the formation of these care networks. They prepared girls and women for emigration, provided continued spiritual and pastoral support for them after emigration, and were a principal means by which they maintained regular contact with Ireland. These communities constituted a circuit by which emigrants kept in contact not only with nuns 'back home' but also with their families (Magray, 1998). Sodalities also played a significant role in the formation of transnational networks of care professionals. For example, the formation of a sodality of Catholic nursing labour force (the Irish Guild of Catholic Nurses (IGCN)) was pivotal in articulating and promoting Catholic nursing ethics and practices to Irish (and non-Irish) Catholic nursing diasporas. The IGCN was a major actor in the formation of a transnational care network of Catholic nurses through which nursing goods, values and ideas were circulated. Its professional nursing journal spread Catholic ideas and ideals of nursing and organized the financing and sending of care goods in the form of supplies of medicinal, surgical and general hospital equipment to the missionaries (Yeates, 2009b; forthcoming 2012a).

Alongside the effects of distance on the nature of care provision, the remaking of social inequality and exploitation on a global scale has been a particular focus of attention. Care migration entails the extraction of resources from poorer countries and their transfer to richer ones. Deprived of human care labour these extractive processes export to poorer countries social problems created by rich countries' under-investment in public care services. Sustained and intensive migration processes distort and erode social solidarities and the 'emotional commons' that female emigrants would have otherwise sustained in their home countries (Isaksen et al., 2008), while the overseas recruitment strategies of rich countries exacerbate shortages of nursing and medical staff that compromise local populations' access to healthcare services in poorer sending countries. The resultant increase in rates of death, disability and morbidity contribute to a widening population health gap, reduced productivity, and loss of public investment (Awases et al., 2004; Khaliq et al., 2009; OECD/WHO, 2010). It is possible to appreciate how these processes of care labour extraction and redistribution link the deteriorating health status of those in source countries with the improving status of those in destination countries (Yeates, 2011a).

Social relations of exploitation take on a personal dimension as many emphasize how care transnationalization involves not just service provision, but servitude itself. The rise in demand for domestic care labour is embroiled with that of 'post-industrial household structure[s] with pre-industrial values' (Parreñas, 2001), where relations between migrant domestic workers and their employers more closely resemble a state of subjection (and often in ways that approximate slavery) than one of exchange, freedom and reciprocity (Anderson, 1997; Chin, 1998; Ong, 2006). Indeed, the working conditions of migrant care workers have emerged as a major concern for agencies combating transnational crime in recent years. In many cases women are recruited with promises of legitimate jobs with good pay and conditions; when they arrive in the host country, the promises are revealed to be false (Redfoot and Houser, 2005). An ILO-sponsored study concluded from its review of international evidence that it is in the private sector where unionization rates are low that some of the worst abuses of migrant health-care workers occur (Bach, 2003: 19), while in some cases the position of nurses closely resembles that of bonded labour more commonly associated with domestic or sex workers (Browne, 2001; Jha, 2007).

The operation of work permit systems in destination countries is a major factor in this exploitation where the employer rather than the migrant owns the permit; but even where this is not the case there is a reluctance to report employer abuse for fear of work permits being withdrawn. A further problem is that migrants overseas can be pressurized into signing a supplemental contract that requires the payment of additional fees. When such problems occur abroad, they are outside the jurisdiction of the source country government (Martin, 2005). This effectively leaves migrant nurses who have legitimate grievances about the terms and conditions of their work in a difficult situation, since their only option is to pursue their complaints with the recruitment agency based in the country of origin. The disjuncture between the territorial reach of the state, recruit-ment agencies and labour compromises the quality of labour protection (Yeates, 2011b).

Transnational advocacy and policy campaigns have emerged to protect against such abuses, promote migrants' rights and influence policy discourse and formation. Through these organizations, migrant workers, who are often constituted as second-class citizens in the 'host' country, are asserting their rights to be treated as first-class citizens, and constitute themselves as such, through their claims, demands and practices. Amongst the key demands they are placing on reform agendas are labour and residency rights, including rights of family reunification. Supported by labour and social movement organizations within and across countries, such advocacy campaigns are directed at spheres of national governance where discriminatory policy and law are opposed and the practices of recruitment agencies and employers (through individual lawsuits and class action) are contested. This national focus of campaign is in part a function of present institutional arrangements whereby the receiving state, being the body that has ratified international conventions, is the only actor that can take action against the offending party (e.g. employer or recruitment agency).

These campaigns have been instrumental in policy formation processes. The Global Campaign for the Ratification of the UN Migrant Workers Con-vention was developed in global spheres of governance, but its implemen-tation was directed at national spheres of governance (to increasing ratifica-tions of the Convention). In 2003 the Philippines successfully led a coalition of six countries (also including Indonesia, Thailand, Vietnam, Myanmar and Sri Lanka) to pressure Hong Kong to withdraw its wage cuts for foreign workers (Oishi, 2005) and transnational advocacy networks filed a com-plaint to the ILO (Piper, 2007b). Other examples of campaigns initiated by transnational advocacy networks include placing issues of the trafficking of women and children on the global policy agenda, the development of new multilateral rights instruments (ILO Convention on domestic workers 2011, and the WHO 2010 code of practice on international recruitment of health personnel), and defence campaigns for domestic workers accused of crimes in countries such as Singapore and the Gulf states.

These 'bottom up' transnational practices demonstrate that transnational rights campaigns are not always or entirely directed at global institutions and agencies. Indeed, they may harness ideational, discursive and legal tools in support of coalition building and activism involving partnerships of states, NGOs and social movements and directed at spheres of national governance as well as at spheres of global governance. Care values and discourses circulate through these networks. Contemporarily this is evidenced through transnational advocacy networks centred on the defence and promotion of migrant workers' human rights in specific country contexts in ways that echo flows of socio-religious ideas and ideologies of care through border-spanning religious networks (Yeates, 2009b).

Although ideational transnationalization takes place outside the bureaux and boardrooms of elite global organizations, cross-border spheres of governance are a major arena through which such processes are manifested and struggles over ideas and ideologies played out. Of note here is research literature focusing on IGOs' policy discourses and prescriptions regarding childcare policy (Mahon, 2005), healthcare policy (Koivusalo and Mackintosh, 2005; Koivusalo and Ollila, 1997), and gender equality in care giving (Bedford, 2010). While these institutions may not have the necessary political, financial or legal leverage over sovereign governments to effect their direct and immediate implementation, they are nonetheless instrumental in framing normative ideals and ideas about care provision that are translated into 'national' policy debates, options and courses of action. Research has not yet traced the impacts of global care discourse and policy on policy implementation within and/or across country settings, but evidence from other policy areas (Deacon, 2007; Orenstein, 2008; Yeates, 2008) has demonstrated the extent to which global agencies have been involved in the co-construction of 'national' policy and the formation of 'national' regimes in both contemporary and historical contexts.

Overall, this literature effectively highlights the multitude of ways in which social relations, orientations and practices of care are routinely 'stretched' across political (state) borders. This has brought a clear understanding of the regularity of such interactions and the enduring nature of such relations. With this has come an appreciation of the textured and differentiated nature of transnationalization processes and their impacts. Despite the largely 'presentist' focus of much of the care migration literature, neither care labour migration nor the social formations to which it gives rise are historically unprecedented. Contemporary transnational families and transnationalizing (child) care practices have strong historical continuities in practices of children being raised by paid and unpaid care givers across a range of slave, colonial and settler societies (Hondagneu-Sotelo and Avila, 1997; Plaza, 2000; Vuorela, 2003). Indeed, such social formations are best understood as current expressions of an age-old means of fulfilling care responsibilities for a variety of family members — from small children to the ailing aged — when for a range of reasons and circumstances parents (or children) were not able to be physically proximate. Similar precedents to the systemic linkages and relations between recruiting and sending countries' care services can be found in histories of welfare colonialism that highlight the spread of Western ideologies and practices of education, medicine and nursing through migration from colonizing countries to colonized ones. The work of Rafferty (2005) and Yeates (2009a) on the influence of the UK's CAN/ONA on the development of nursing in UK colonies, and the work of Choy (2003) and Brush (1997) on the enduring influence of US intervention on nursing in the Philippines all show how earlier processes of transnationalization laid the foundations for mass recruitment from developing to developed countries that is a feature of contemporary care economies.

Contemporarily, just as in the past, transnationalization processes are neither homogenizing nor homogenized. There are marked differences in their pace, scale and significance within different countries and between different branches of the care sector. For example, there are major differences in the extent to which different recruiting countries are reliant on migrant health workers to staff their workforces and the countries from which they recruit in ways that bear on the expression of transnationalization processes in healthcare policy and provision (Yeates, 2011b). There are also marked differences between migration to provide for the survival of the immediate or extended family in a context where relatives depend on remittances for their economic survival and where state social provision is minimal, and emigration from a country where family members are not dependent on remittances for survival and where state provision is, in global terms, extensive and generous (Yeates, 2009a). Such differences emanate from historical and contemporary global political economies of development including the varied effects of differential health, welfare, trade, aid, development, and immigration regimes governing the scale and pace of transmigration. Place and locality continue to mediate social divisions of gender, class, age/generation, 'race' and ethnicity (Maher, 2003; Manalansan, 2004; Walton-Roberts, forthcoming 2012; Yeates, 2009a; forthcoming 2012b) and these, in turn, shape processes, practices and experiences of transnationalism and the distribution of risks and costs, benefits.

DEVELOPING RESEARCH AGENDAS

This article has reviewed key contours of care transnationalization as a field of research enquiry and as an ongoing social process. It has argued that care is a major transnational social field through which individuals, families, communities, socio-institutional formations, economies and policy actors are routinely connected and positioned across more than one country. Characterized by its attention to transactions among and relations between defined actors operating within contexts of global power relations, care transnationalization research has substantially engaged with and contributed to major policy debates and substantially contributed to broader intellectual endeavours challenging the relevance and coherence of 'container state' notions of social formations (past and present) and welfare systems.

Much of the literature on care transnationalization has been directed at the intersection of producer-based care migration and care restructuring, through which diverse transnationalizing social formations, relations and practices have been documented. This literature has expanded from an initial focus on familial contexts (household-based social care) to more public, institutionalized contexts of health and social care. With this has developed a rich analytical terrain cognizant of the border-spanning, multi-stranded webs of socio-economic relationships and the diverse ways in which they materially and synchronously affect individual and collective welfare at home and abroad. This includes attention to multi-stranded social relations and formations revolving around care provision and consumption, and the significance of care networks as conduits through which economic resources, ideas and practices are circulated. Far from offering banal accounts of uninterrupted flows, seamless circuits, and undifferentiated impacts, due emphasis is given to the incomplete and contested nature of transnationalizing processes and to the contexts in which border-spanning orientations, ideas and practices arise, take shape and 'touch down', including the ways in which the care transnationalization is mediated by social divisions of gender, 'race'/ethnicity, class, age, religion and locality.

This literature is not without its omissions and biases. Most of the research has attended to producer-based forms of transmigration of care workers while giving far less consideration to other expressions of care transnationalization. Foremost among these are consumption-based dynamics as a mode of care transnationalization and their implications for social development. One example is the extent to which corporate healthcare markets in medical travel contribute to the care drain through the intermeshing of internal and international healthcare migration and their consequences for access to healthcare. A second example concerns the extent to which the costs of social and health care are being borne by developing countries in their quest to attract consumer capital through retirement (and medical) migration and what this means for local populations' access to quality services. Research into these forms of care transnationalization would provide useful further insights into the territorial and social distribution of risks, benefits and costs of care transnationalization. Just as too little is known about how these processes are impacting upon the development prospects of poorer countries, so too little is known about ideational forms of care transnationalization.

Literatures on care worker migration have tended to neglect how transnational networks act as conduits through which orientations, ideas and ideologies of care are circulated and mediated within and across 'national' terrains. Some work has begun on ideational forms of care transnationalization in relation to IGOs and global agencies, but it is comparatively recent in origin and has not yet concretely attended to how global care policy is translated across different historical, regional, country and policy contexts. There is also a dearth of enquiry as to how ideas about care provision are constructed and flow through transnational networks not involving IGOs, how transnational ideas about care are variously taken up across different country, sectoral and historical contexts, and how ideas about care — wherever they are manifested — are themselves transnational constructs.

None of this negates the need to further examine care worker migration as a mode of care transnationalization. The literature has been biased towards the recruiting experiences of rich Anglophone zones such as North America, Western Europe and Australia, while middle- and low-income countries tend to be constructed as source countries. This overlooks the considerable extent of care migration that is occurring on a 'South–South' basis (Bakewell, 2009; Piper and Roces, 2003; Yamanaka and Piper, 2005), on a North–South basis (Yeates, 2009a) and on a North–North basis (Yeates, 2011a), especially among non-Anglophone countries. Incorporating the experiences of a wider range of countries, branches of the care economy and occupations would generate a better understanding of different textures of care migration and responses to it in both national and cross-border spheres of governance. At the same time, there is much more scope for research into the ways that producer-based care transmigration (and indeed, other forms of transmigration and transnationalization) is mediated by and played out in and through different socio-institutional formations. Here, the tools of comparative policy analysis need to be deployed to a far greater extent than they have been to date.

This latter signals an essential basis for a continuing and productive dialogue between methodologically transnationalist approaches, which bring a focus on the diverse ways in which transnationalizing phenomena and processes are embedded in social organization, identities, practices and relations of care, and methodologically nationalist approaches, with their attention to socio-institutional expressions of care provision in a wide array of country contexts. While not underestimating the challenges of such collaboration between two such notably divergent methodological and theoretical approaches, this dialogue must be a key priority for ongoing research into the development impacts of care restructuring worldwide.

REFERENCES

Anderson, B. (1997) 'Servants and Slaves: Europe's Domestic Workers', *Race & Class* 39(1): 37–49.

Asis, M.M.B., S. Huang and B. Yeoh (2004) 'When the Light of the Home is Abroad: Unskilled Female Migration and the Filipino Family', *Singapore Journal of Tropical Geography* 25(2): 198–215.

Awases, M., A. Gbary, J. Nyoni and R. Chatora (2004) *Migration of Health Professionals in Six Countries: A Synthesis Report.* Brazzaville: World Health Organization, Regional Office for Africa. Available at: http://www.afro.who.int/dsd/migration6countriesfinal.pdf (accessed 19 November 2006).

Bach, S. (2003) 'International Migration of Health Workers: Labour and Social Issues'. Sectoral Activities Programme Working Paper No. 209. Geneva: ILO.

Bakewell, O. (2009) 'South–South Migration and Human Development: Reflections on African Experiences'. Human Development Research Paper 2009/07. New York: UNDP.

Baldock, C.V. (2000) 'Migrants and their Parents: Caregiving from a Distance', *Journal of Family Issues* 21(2): 205–24.

Basch, L.N., G. Schiller and C.S. Blanc (1994) *Nations Unbound: Transnational Projects, Post-colonial Predicaments and Deterritorialized Nation-States.* Langhorne: Gordon & Breach.

Bedford, K. (2010) 'Harmonizing Global Care Policy? Care and the Commission on the Status of Women'. Gender and Development Programme Paper No. 7. Geneva: UNRISD.

Bettio, F., A. Simonazi and P. Villa (2006) 'Change in Care Regimes and Female Migration: The "Care Drain" in the Mediterranean', *Journal of European Social Policy* 16(3): 271–85.

Browne, A. (2001) 'Abused, Threatened and Trapped — Britain's Foreign "Slave Nurses"'. *The Guardian* 29 May. http://society.guardian.co.uk/NHSstaff/story/0,7991,497983,00.html (accessed 14 November 2005).

Brush, B.L. (1997) 'The Rockefeller Agenda for American/Philippines Nursing Relations', in A.M. Rafferty, J. Robinson and R. Elkan (eds) *Nursing History and the Politics of Welfare*, pp. 45–63. London: Routledge.

Chin, C.B.N. (1998) *In Service and Servitude: Foreign Female Domestic Workers and the Malaysian 'Modernity' Project.* New York: Columbia University Press.

Choy, C.C. (2003) *Empire of Care: Nursing and Migration in Filipino American History.* Durham, NC: Duke University Press.

Daly, M. (2002a) 'Care as a Good for Social Policy', *Journal of Social Policy* 31(2): 251–70.

Daly, M. (ed.) (2002b) *Care Work: The Quest for Security.* Geneva: International Labour Office.

Deacon, B. (2008) *Global Social Governance and Policy.* London: Sage.

Dicken, P., P.F. Kelly, K. Olds and H. Wai-chung Yeung (2001) 'Chains and Networks, Territories and Scales: Towards a Relational Framework for Analyzing the Global Economy', *Global Networks* 1(2): 89–112.

Escrivá, A. (2004) 'Securing Care and Welfare of Dependants Transnationally: Peruvians and Spaniards in Spain'. Working Paper No. 404. Oxford: Oxford Institute of Ageing.

Fitzgerald, M. (2006) *Habits of Compassion: Irish Catholic Nuns and the Origins of New York's Welfare System, 1830–1920.* Urbana, IL: University of Illinois Press.

Folbre, N. (2002) 'Accounting for Care in the United States', in Mary Daly (ed.) *Care Work: The Quest for Security*, pp. 175–91. Geneva: International Labour Office.

Gustafson, P. (2001) 'Retirement Migration and Transnational Lifestyles', *Ageing and Society* 21: 371–94.

Hochschild, A.R. (2000) 'Global Care Chains and Emotional Surplus Value', in W. Hutton and A. Giddens (eds) *On The Edge: Living with Global Capitalism*, pp. 130–46. London: Jonathan Cape.

Holton, R.J. (2008) *Global Networks.* London: Palgrave.

Hondagneu-Sotelo, P. and E. Avila (1997) 'I'm Here, but I'm There: The Meanings of Latin Transnational Motherhood', *Gender and Society* 11(5): 548–70.

Hooyman, N. and J. Gonyea (1995) *Feminist Perspectives on Family Care: Policies for Gender Justice.* Thousand Oaks, CA: Sage.

Isaksen, L., U. Devi and A. Hochschild (2008) 'Global Care Crisis: A Problem of Capital, Care Chain, or Commons?', *American Behavioural Scientist* 52(3): 405–25.

Jha, N.B. (2007) 'Indian Nurses Forced to Continue Working in Saudi', *Times of India* 17 January. http://timesofindia.indiatimes.com/articleshow/msid-1256307,prtpage-1.cms (accessed 17 July 2007).

Khagram, S. and P. Levitt (2004) 'Towards a Field of Transnational Studies and a Sociological Transnationalism Research Program'. Working Paper No. 24. Cambridge, MA: Hauser Center for Non-Profit Organizations at Harvard University. http://ssrn.com/abstract=556993 (accessed 12 January 2008).

Khaliq, A.A., R.W. Broyles and A.K. Mwachofi (2009) 'Global Nurse Migration: Its Impact on Developing Countries and Prospects for the Future', *World Heath & Population* 10(3): 5–23.

King, R., A.M. Warnes and A.M. Williams (1998) 'International Retirement Migration in Europe', *International Journal of Population Geography* 4: 91–111.

Koivusalo, M. and M. Mackintosh (eds) (2005) *Commercialization of Health Care: Global and Local Dynamics and Policy Responses*. Basingstoke: Macmillan.

Koivusalo, M. and E. Ollila (1997) *Making a Healthy World: Agencies, Actors and Policies in International Health*. London: Zed Books.

Leng, C.H. and A. Whittaker (eds) (2010) 'Medical Travel', Special Issue of *Global Social Policy* 10(3): 287–415.

Lynch, K. and E. McLaughlin (1995) 'Caring Labour and Love Labour', in P. Clancy, S. Drudy, K. Lynch and L. O'Dowd (eds) *Irish Society: Sociological Perspectives*, pp. 250–92. Dublin: Institute of Public Administration.

Magray, M. (1998) *The Transforming Power of the Nuns: Women, Religious and Cultural Change in Ireland 1730–1900*. Oxford: Oxford University Press.

Maher, K. (2003) 'Identity Projects at Home and Labour from Abroad: The Market for Foreign Domestic Workers in Southern California and Santiago, Chile'. Working Paper No. 75. San Diego, CA: Center for Comparative Immigration Studies, University of California-San Diego.

Mahon, R. (2005) 'The OECD and the Reconciliation Agenda: Competing Blueprints'. Ottawa: Institute of Political Economy, Carleton University.

Management Sciences for Health (MSH) (2010) 'Evaluation of Malawi's Emergency Human Resources Programme'. EHRP Final Report, July. London: Department for International Development.

Manalansan, M.F. (2004) 'Queer Intersections: Sexuality and Gender in Migration Studies', *International Migration Review* 40(1): 224–49.

Martin, P. (2005) 'Merchants of Labour: Agents of the Evolving Migration Infrastructure'. Discussion Paper DP/158/2005. Geneva: International Institute for Labour Studies.

Migration Policy Institute (MPI) (2006) 'America's Emigrants. US Retirement Migration to Mexico and Panama'. Washington, DC: Migration Policy Institute. www.migrationpolicy. org/pubs/americas_emigrants.pdf (accessed 8 June 2011).

Morales, O.L. (2010) 'US Citizens Retirement Migration to Los Cabos, Mexico. Profile and Social Effects', *Recreation and Society in Africa, Asia and Latin America* 1(1): 75–92. http://www.spreadcorp.org/rasaala/1VOL1/Morale_75–92.pdf

Muula, A.S. (2006) 'Nationality and Country of Training of Medical Doctors in Malawi', *African Health Sciences* 6: 118–19.

OECD (2006) 'How are Services being Internationalised?'. 7th OECD International Trade Statistics Expert Meeting ITS and OECD-Eurostat meeting of experts in trade-in-services-statistics (TIS), STD/NAES/TASS/SERV(2006)14. Paris: OECD.

OECD and WHO (2010) 'International Migration of Health Workers: Improving International Co-operation to Address the Global Health Workforce Crisis'. Policy Brief, February. Paris: OECD.

Oishi, N. (2005) *Women in Motion: Globalization, State Policies and Labor Migration in Asia*. Stanford, CA: Stanford University Press.

Ong, A. (2006) *Neoliberalism as Exception: Mutations in Citizenship and Sovereignty*. Durham, NC: Duke University Press.

Orenstein, M. (2008) *Privatizing Pensions: The Transnational Campaign for Social Security Reform*. Princeton, NJ: Princeton University Press.

Parreñas, R. (2001) *Servants of Globalization*. Stanford, CA: Stanford University Press.

Parreñas, R. (2005) *Children of Global Migration: Transnational Families and Gendered Woes*. Stanford, CA: Stanford University Press.

Pascall, G. (1997) *Social Policy: A New Feminist Analysis*. London: Routledge.

Piper, N. (ed.) (2007a) *New Perspectives on Gender and Migration: Rights, Entitlements and Livelihoods*. London: Routledge.

Piper, N. (2007b) 'Governance of Migration and Transnationalisation of Migrants' Rights — An Organisational Perspective'. COMCAD Working Paper 22. Bielefeld: Center on Migration, Citizenship and Development, Bielefeld University.

Piper, N. and M. Roces (2003) *Wife or Worker? Asian Women and Migration*. Lanham, MD: Rowman and Littlefield.

Plaza, D. (2000) 'Transnational Grannies: The Changing Family Responsibilities of Elderly African Caribbean-born Women Resident in Britain', *Social Indicators Research* 51: 75–105.

Rafferty, A.M. (2005) 'The Seductions of History and the Nursing Diaspora', *Health and History* 7(2): 2–16. www.historycooperative.org/journals/hah/7.2/refferty.html (accessed 17 July 2007).

Redfoot, D.L. and A.N. Houser (2005) '"We Shall Travel On": Quality of Care, Economic Development, and the International Migration of Long-Term Care Workers'. Washington, DC: AARP. www.mecf.org/articles/AARP_immigrant.pdf (accessed 9 November 2005).

Shimizu, H. (2009) 'Paradise in Dream or in Reality? Japanese Retirees Long-Stay in the Philippines'. Paper delivered at conference Transnational Mobilities for Care: State, Market, and Family Dynamics in Asia, Asia Research Institute, National University of Singapore (10–11 September).

UNESCAP (2008) 'Medical Travel in Asia and the Pacific: Challenges and Opportunities'. Bangkok: UNESCAP.

Ungerson, C. (2002) 'Commodified Care Work in European Labour Markets', *European Societies* 5(4): 377–96.

Vertovec, S. (1999) 'Conceiving and Researching Transnationalism', Ethnic and Racial Studies 22(2): 447–62.

Vuorela, U. (2003) 'Transnational Families: Imagined and Real Communities', in D. Bryceson and U. Vuorela (eds) *The Transnational Family: New European Frontiers and Global Network*, pp. 63–82. Oxford: Berg.

Walton-Roberts, M. (forthcoming 2012) 'Contextualizing the Global Nurse Care Chain: International Migration and the Status of Nursing in South India', *Global Networks*.

Whittaker, A. (2009) 'Medical Travel: Challenges to Equity, Access and Ethics in Asian Health Systems'. Paper delivered at conference Transnational Mobilities for Care: State, Market and Family Dynamics in Asia, Asia Research Institute, National University of Singapore (10–11 September).

Wibulpolprasert, S., C. Pachanee, S. Pitayarangsarit and P. Hempisut (2004) 'International Service Trade and its Implications for Human Resources for Health: A Case Study of Thailand', *Human Resources for Health* 2(10). http://www.human-resources-health.com/content/2/1/10

Williams, A.M., R. King and T. Warnes (1997) 'A Place in the Sun: International Retirement Migration from Northern to Southern Europe', *European Urban and Regional Studies* 4: 115–34.

Williams, F. (2010) 'Migration and Care: Themes, Concepts and Challenges', *Social Policy and Society* 9(3): 385–96.

World Bank (2011) *Migration and Remittances Fact Book 2011* (2nd edn). Washington, DC: World Bank.

World Health Organization (2010) 'International Recruitment of Health Personnel: Draft Global Code of Practice'. A63/8, 15 April. Geneva: WHO.

Yamanaka, K. and N. Piper (2005) 'Feminized Migration in East and Southeast Asia: Policies, Actions and Empowerment'. Geneva: United Nations Research Institute for Social Development.

Yeates, N. (2004) 'Global Care Chains: Critical Reflections and Lines of Enquiry', *International Feminist Journal of Politics* 6(3): 369–91.

Yeates, N. (ed.) (2008) *Understanding Global Social Policy*. Bristol: The Policy Press.

Yeates, N. (2009a) *Globalising Care Economies and Migrant Workers: Explorations in Global Care Chains*. Basingstoke: Palgrave.

Yeates, N. (2009b) 'Migration and Nursing in Ireland', *Translocations: Migration and Social Change* 5(1): 1–20. http://www.imrstr.dcu.ie/volume_5_issue_1/Vol_5_Issue_1_d.pdf

Yeates, N. (2011a) 'The Globalisation of Paid Care Labour migration: Policy Issues and Responses', *International Labour Review* 149(4): 423–40.

Yeates, N. (2011b) 'Ireland's Contributions to the Global Nursing Crisis', in R. Munck and B. Fanning (eds) *Immigration and the Irish Experience of European and Global Transformation*, pp. 35–50. Farnham: Ashgate.

Yeates, N. (forthcoming 2012a) 'The Irish Catholic Female Religious in the Transnationalisation of Care: An Historical Perspective', *Irish Journal of Sociology*.

Yeates, N. (forthcoming 2012b) 'Global Care Chains (GCCs): A State-of-the-Art Review and Future Directions in Care Transnationalisation Research', *Global Networks*.

Index

Note: Page numbers in *italics* refer to Figures; those in **bold** to Tables.

advocacy campaigns, 241, 246–7
affective care, 235
Africa, 2, 51, 57–8
ageing population, 80, 83–4, 87, 149,
   153, 160, 171
agricultural labour, 77, 85, 131, 184–5,
   190
AIDS,
   related deaths, 55, 66
   sick, 58–9
allowances-plus-wages, 16
anganwadi,
   centres, 185–6, 194–5
   workers, 195
anti-poverty, 180, 182, 188
anti-retroviral therapy (ART), 59
apartheid, 5, 52, 60, 61, 65, 67, 68
Ardington, C., 61, 66, 67
Argentina, 5, 17, 20, 23, 94, 95, 96,
   98–9, 104, 105, 109, 111, 113,
   115, 117, 223–4
Asia, 2, 51
   economic crisis of 1997, 36
assets, 157

Bachelot, M., 23, 222
Bakilana, A., 58
Barrientos, A., 35, 51, 96, 117
Beijing Migrant Family Survey, 82
benefits, 188, 220, 224, 248
Beneria, L., 1, 2, 123
Beveridge Plan (India), 183
birth rates, 205
bonded labour, 246
Botswana, 12, 57
Bradshaw, S., 141
Brazil, 4, 206
breadwinners, 171; *see also,* male
breadwinners
Bretton Woods, 242
budgets, 102, 188
Budlender, D., 2, 3, 5, 12, 13, 17, 51–69
Buenos Aires, 97, **105**, 108, 109–10

Calderón, F., 222
care, 5, 170
   centres among children under 5, **136**
   deficits, 81, 85, 192, 193, 197, 198,
    199
   definition, 12
   issue, 93
   work, 235–6
'care diamond', 94, 95, 117, 176, 191,
   197
care givers, 75–6, 78, 221, 248
   children aged 0–5, **103**
   role of, 52, 84–5
care provisioning, 176
care regime, 94, 95, 117, 122
care transnationalization, 234–6, 237,
   239, 241, 244, 245, 248–9, 250
cash transfer programmes, 4, 16, 17–18,
   65, 99, 112, 113, 114, 124, 133,
   139, 140, 141, 143, 153, 171, 187,
   205, 207, 213, 226, 228
Catholic Church, 102, 129, 132
Catholic doctrine, 225
Catholic dogma, 144
Central America, 126
Centres for the Assistance of Families
   and Infants, CAIF (Uruguay),
   165
Cerrutti, M., 11, 97
Chant, S., 3, 11, 57, 98, 115, 206
Chávez Metoyer, C., 123, 132
Child Care Act, South Korea, (1991), 38
Child Development Centres (CEDIS)
   (Argentina), 102, 107, 110, 111,
   116, 136
child education, 23–4, 86, 100–104,
   107–8, 167, 185
   attendance rates (Argentina), 107,
    108, 109–10, *110*
child health, 138
child inequality, 111
child rearing, 205, 227
childbearing, 155

Seen, Heard and Counted, First Edition. Edited by Shahra Razavi.
Chapters © 2012 The Institute of Social Studies. Book compilation © 2012 Blackwell Publishing Ltd.

childcare, 4, 8, 13, 16, 21, 26, 31, 33, 44,
    46, 65, 74, 78, 82, 86, 87, 102,
    107, 124, 175, 190–191, 208
    allowances, 38–9
    cutbacks, 78–9
    early, 25, 62, 86
    poor, 102, 103, 107
    private, 23, 44
    reforms, 32, 37, 41–3
childcare under five, 112
children, 2–3, 10, 13–14, 17, 18,
    42, 87
    low-income families, 23, 38
    rural (China), 80
    South Africa, 52, 53, 56–7, 59, 63,
    64–5
Chile, 5, 22–3, 134, 205, 206, 207, 208,
    214, 216, **218**, 219–20, 221, 223,
    226, 227
Chile Crece Contigo, 219, 220
China, 2, 5, 8–9, 14, 15, 18–19, 25, 73,
    75, 76, 77–8, 80–1, 83–4, 87
    care givers, 75–6, 80, 81
    childcare, 78–9, 82, 86
    elderly care, 12, 75, 78, 79
    one-child policy, 80
    women, 76, 77–8, 80–2
China Health and Nutrition Survey
    (CHNS), 81, 84, 85, 86
Chinchilla, N. S., 124, 129
Choi, E., 28, 39, 40
citizens, 189, 190, 246
class inequalities, 116
cluster analysis, 157
co-responsibility, 112, 220
Code of Children's Rights and
    Obligations (Nicaragua), 130
cohabitation, 151–2, 153, 154
collective action, 236
collective bargaining, 105
    women, 168
Collier, R. B., 100, 105
Committee on the Status of Women in
    India (CSWI), 190
commodification, 31, 46, 93, 112, 124,
    141, 179, 206
community/voluntary work, 25, 123,
    130, 143
community teachers, 165
compensatory measures, 94–5

conditional cash transfers (CCTs),
    205–6, 224; *see also,* cash transfer
    programmes
Confucian cultural heritage, 80, 87
contract staff, 187
Cook, S., 2, 12, 14, 18, 73–88
corporatism, 101, 156, 157–8, 160, 171,
    225
Cortés, R., 96, 113
costs, 138, 220, 226, 248
    day-care centres, 213
    social/health care, 249
crèches, 23, 26, 94, 98, 101–3, 105,
    107–11, 116, 183, 185, 187, 190,
    191, 194, 195, 196, 214–16, 217,
    219, 224

Daly, M., 1, 6, 7, 14, 15, 16, 93, 234–5
day-care centres, 105, 182, 187, 210,
    212, 219, 222, 224, 225, 226
    private, 196,
    quality, 195, 210
de-familialization, 10, 206, 213, 222
debt, 96, 126, 242
decentralization, 135, 142
decision-making, women, 170
democracy, 129, 207
demographic changes, 35, 153, 205
developed countries, 3, 6, 7, 34
developing countries, 6, 7, 11, 16, 20,
    24, 25, 239
Dicken, P., 237, 242
disabled people, 65
disadvantaged households, 217
discrimination, against women, 40–1,
    42, 74, 132, 228, 246
division of labour, 163, 171, 225
domestic service, 14–5
domestic violence, 168–9
domestic work, 3, 60, 64, 80, 123, 179,
    191, 193, 242, 245
domestic workers, 196–7, 247
Dong, X.-Y., 2, 12, 14, 18, 73–88
dual earner model, 39, 103, 160
dualist regimes, 19

early childhood education and care
    (ECEC), 22, 37–8, 38–9, 40, 42,
    195, 196, 199, 205, 207, 209, 215,
    216, 219–20, 221, 223, 226, 228

Early Childhood Education Promotion
Act, (South Korea, 1982), 38
early education, 107, 186
earnings,
female, 208–9
Eastern Europe, 5
economic crises, 10, 11
economic development, 60
economic growth, 80, 87, 99, 131, 209
economic participation rates by sex,
151
economic reform, and women's work,
74
economy, 44, 73, 77, 80
education, 21, 22, 53, 62, 63, 98, 123,
124, 129, 156, 182–3, 199
spending on, *127*
education (Uruguay), **162**, 171
education system (Nicaragua), 124
ecudation system, reform of (Argentina),
96, 110–111
Educational Funding Act (Law 26.075)
(Argentina), 101
elderly care, 8, 12, 13–14, 17, 35, 53, 65,
79, 81, 83–4, 85, 87, 168, 171, 199
South Korea, 31, **33**, 37, 37–8, 46
elderly people, 63, 65, 74, 80, 85,
149–50, 156, 163
elderly women, 86
Elderly Rights and Security Law, 1996
(China), 79–80
elementary education, 184
elite (India), 197, 198
Ellingsaeter, A, L., 105
emancipation, 152, 154, 156, 160, 170
from household of origin, *159*
Emergency Human Resource
Programme (Malawi), 244
emigration, 245
emotional care, 235
employees, public, 186–7
Chile, 216–17
employment, 16, 18, 25, 32, 36, 40, 44,
61, 166, 176–7
deregulation, 36
formal, 87, 149, 151, 167, 177, *179*,
187, 193, 209
informal, 18, 87, 106, 177, *179*, 208
opportunities, 23, 24, 221, 228
paid, 242

rate among married women, 35
service sector, 177
structures, 208
Employment Equity Act (South Africa),
60
Employment Insurance reform, South
Korea (1998), 34–5
employment-based care benefits, 116
employment-related childcare, 94, 95,
104, 106, 107
equal opportunities, 116, 222
Esping-Andersen, G., 9, 10, 25, 31, 51,
93, 122
Esquivel, V., 104
Etchemendy, S., 100, 105
Europe, 7, 15–16, 22, 25, 105, 117, 183,
240
exclusionary social policy, 9, 12, 18,
121, 124
exploitation, 245, 246
extended families, 122

fair price, 182
familialism, 5, 14, 24, 31, 34, 101, 122,
132, 138, 142, 166, 177, 189, 191,
249
carers, 197–9
gendered, 193–4, 197
stratified, 175, 180, 197–9
Families for Social Inclusion Programme
(Argentina), 112, 114–15
family, 6, 9, 11, 12, 13–14, 15–16, 17,
33, 40, 45, 131, 154–5, 160, 163,
175, 191
failures, 189
government expenditure on, 32–3
low-income, 219
multigenerational, 10, 33
old-age support, **33**
role of, 117, 121, 124–5, 131, 132–3,
140, 142,
family allowances, 104, 151, 166–7,
169, 171
family life, disruption 51, 52, 53, 55–6,
68
family planning programmes, 183
family wages, 152
family–work harmonization
South Korea, 31–2, 37, 40, 42,
45–6

fathers, 211, 227
    contribution to care activities, 3, 12,
        52, 53, 55–6, 57, 103
Faur, E., 5, 17, 23, 108, 109, 224
Federal Day-Care Programme for
        Working Mothers (Mexico), 207,
        211
Feeney, M., 132
female-headed households, 57, 60, 113,
        122, 132, 141, 149, 153, 161
female migration, 61, 77, 80, 82–3
feminism, 10, 22, 168, 169, 170, 190,
        199, 205–6, 225, 241–2
feminization, 136, 142
fertility, 3, 5, 56, 153–4, **154**, 156, 160,
        161, 166, 170
    decline in, 35, 42, 44
Filgueira, F., 18, 96, 117, 124, 155
fiscal powers, 181
foreign direct assistance, 127
funding, 135, 139
    from external sources, 140

GDP, 233
    Chile, 206
    India, 175, 176, 177, 181, 184,
        190
    Mexico, 206
    Uruguay, 149, 167
gender
    equality, 7–8, 16, 32, 35, 75, 93,
        130–131, 132, 141, 166, 171, 205,
        224–5, 225–6, 247
    inequalities, 95, 189, 206, 207, 228
    relations, 141
    roles, 122, 141, 206, 227
    wage gaps, 75, 76–7, 133, 161, 191,
        192, 208
gendered familialism, 191
gendered qualifier, 189
Gerhard, R., 23, 205–32
Gerssshberg, A., 125, 133
Gherardi, N., 104
girls, safety, 185
global care networks, 244
global governance (IGOs), 239,
        247
global restructuring, 233
globalization, 170, 236
Gough, I., 180, 183

governance, 3–4, 131, 175
    cross-border, 239, 247
    national, 246
government schools, 184
governments, 37, 38–41, 53, 59, 62, 64,
        68, 78, 99, 100, 101, 108,
        110–111, 115, 135
grants, 63, 65
Groisman, F., 113

health, 16–17, 19, 33, 182, 183, 224
    reform, 166
    South Africa, 53, 62, 63
health benefits, **158**
health spending, *127*
healthcare, 75, 96, 104, 123, 124, 139,
        140, 150, 156, 165–6, 171, 239–40
Heintz, J., 25
higher education, 184
HIV/AIDS pandemic, 2, 8, 11, 24, 26, 56
    South Africa, 5, 8, 52, 53, 56, 57–8,
        58, 59, 60, 62, 63, 68
homelands, 61
Honduras, 122
Hoszowski, A., 113
household heads, 57, 113
households, 10, 11, 13, 31, 73, 97–8,
        112, 116, 193
    composition with older people (65+),
        33
    fractured, 60
    high-income, 13, 117
    low-income, 3, 23, 104, 220–221, 228
    maintenance, 192
    structures, 208
    upper middle-class, 103
    women with children, *159*
housing expenditure, 127
Huber, E., 96
Hughes, J., 76, 77
human agency, 234, 236–7
human capital, 22, 39, 42, 87, 205
human resources, 199
human rights, 170

ideational circuits/networks, 234–8, 239,
        241, 249–50
ideology, 101, 102, 175, 176, 180, 193,
        247
IMF, 36

import-substitution industrialization
(ISI), 156, 170–1
income
decommodification, 158
elderly care, 33
inequality, 36, 37, 168
low, 18, 153–4, 155, 226–7
middle, 155, 220
policy development, 24
redistribution, 34
security, 59
India, 5, 10, 15, 18, 21, 24, 175, 176,
184, 189, 199, 240
industrialized countries, 52
inequalities, 26–7, 156, 170
information exchange, 241
infrastructure, 20–1, 25
Integra (Chile), 216, 217
Integrated Child Development Scheme
(ICDS) (India), 181, 185–6, 187,
191, 195, 199
international migrants, 236
International Monetary Fund (IMF), 129
internationalization, 236
Ireland, 244–5
Irish Guild of Catholic Nurses (IGCN),
245

Jenson, J., 4, 22, 130, 176, 219
job creation, 44–5, 131
Mexico, 213–14
job training, 206
jobs, for women, 36–7, 44, 112, 228
jurisdiction, 181

Kelly, P. F., 237, 242
Kim Dae-Jung, 42
kin ties, 189, 199
kindergartens, 38, 78, 79, 82, 94–5, 98,
101, 102, 103, 107, 109–10, 215,
219
Korea *see,* South Korea
Korean Women's Development Institute
(KWDI), 35, 37, 43

labour force
feminization, 60
women, 151
labour markets, 32, 34, 35–7, 59–62, 88,
106, 151, 152, 155, 169, 171, 227

deregulation, 37, 41, 46, 96
dualism, 40–1
flexibility, 25, 37, 45, 122
formal, 150
informal, 18–19
insecurity, 40
participation of women, **155**
programmes, 36–7
reforms, 20, 41
strategy, 45
women in, 22, 37, 39–40, 62, 74, 152
labour care networks, 239, 241, 242, 245
labour migration, 85–6, 87
labour regulations, 104, 105
labour system,
migrant, 52
labourist care, 236
Latin America, 2, 4, 10–11, 15, 16,
23–4, 51, 57, 93, 96, 112, 121,
122, 124, 129, 134, 136, 139, 143,
152, 165, 167, 205, 207, 208, 224
laws, 101, 102, 187
Left (Uruguay), 169–70
legislation, 55–6, 101, 105–6, 189–90,
191
legislative reforms,
South Korea, 39
legitimacy, 226
Lewis, J., 6, 7, 9, 12, 16, 31, 93, 104
liberalization, 4, 170, 190, 207
lifetime employment, 36, 74, 75
literacy, 184
living arrangements, 53–7, 132
of children aged *0–17* (South Africa),
55
for women (Uruguay), **154**
lower middle class, 182
Lund, F., 12, 13, 17, 25, 51–69

Mahon, R., 4, 22, 247
Malawi, 244
male breadwinners, 31, 32, 37, 40, 46,
97, 149, 151–2, 153, 177, 189, 208
male migration, 61
male providers, 122
Maoism, 74, 75, 78
marital patterns, 56, 59
market allocation, 73–4
market economy, 75
market participation, of women, **154**

market-led development, 9
markets, 160
marriage, 35, 52, 54, 56, 121–2, 153,
    160, 194, 240–241
Marshall, A., 96
Martinez-Franzoni, J., 5, 10, 18, 21, 24,
    51
Marxist doctrine, 74
maternalism, 14, 16, 111, 116, 117, 222,
    223
maternity, 190, 194
maternity/parental leave, 18, 19, 20, 39,
    46, 104–5, **105**, 106
Maurer-Fazio, M., 76, 77
means-tested programmes, 94–5, 112,
    168, 219–20
medical markets, 240
medical travel, 239, 249
men, 121–2
    care work, 192
    childcare, 54–56
    employment, 166–7
    paid work, 13, 161
    unpaid work, 133, 161
Mesa-Largo, C., 124, 125
Mexican Institute for Social Security
    (IMSS), 209–10, 211, 212–13,
    219, 220, 223, 224, 227
Mexico, 4, 5, 19, 23, 205, 206, 207, 208,
    209, 211–12, 216, 217, **218**,
    219–20, 221, 222–3, 225, 227,
    228, 240–241
middle class (India), 197, 198
middle-class lifestyle, 37
migration, 2, 6, 11, 80, 82, 122, 184–5,
    197, 236, 239, 242, 248, 249
    care workers, 241, 234, 242, 243–4,
    245–6, 250
    human rights, 247
    rural-urban (China), 77, 80, 85
    women, 80, 179, 241–2
Mineduc (Chile), 214–15, 217,
mining, 60
minimum wages, 15, 187, 211
Ministry of Education (Chile), 214
Molyneux, M., 4, 16, 67, 95, 112, 121,
    124–5, 129, 131, 206–7
Montaño, S., 136
Montgomery, R. J. V., 75

mortality rates, 183, 199
    decline in child, 186
mothers, 4, 14, 16, 17, 23, 40, 43, 57, 83,
    85, 86, 87, 93, 94, 103, 104, 105,
    113, 114, 115, 121, 140, 141, 143,
    144, 186, 191, 193, 194, 197, 198,
    199, 209, 211, 219, 220, 222–3,
    226, 227

Nari, M., 104
National Education Act (Law 26.206)
    (Argentina), 101
National Rural Employment Guarantee
    Act (India; NREGA), 188, 194
nationalism, 5–6, 234
neoliberal policies, 97, 99, 111, 116,
    121, 122, 124–5, 126, 130, 132,
    142, 176, 181
Neetha, N., 21
New Poverty Agenda (Mexico), 220
NGOs, 195–6, 247
Nicaragua, 5, 10, 17, 18, 21, 24, 121,
    122, 123–4, 125, *126*, 128, 130,
    131, 132, 133, 134, 135, 136, 138,
    139, 140, 142–3, 144
non-standard employment, 20
nuclear family/norms, 52, 53–4, 122,
    132, 163, 193
nursery schools, 107, 109, 111
nurses, 183, 244, 245, 246

old age pension, 17
old people *see,* elderly care
Olds, K., 237, 242
Oosthuizen, M., 60
Orloff, A. S., 93
Ostner, I., 91
outsourcing, 210

Palriwala, R., 21
parents
    working, 219
Pascall, G., 153
path-dependency, 22, 117
patrilineal norms (China), 79, 84, 85
patronage politics, 181–2
Pautassi, L., 104
pay-as-you-go pensions, 127, 168, 171
Peng, I., 5, 20, 26, 31–47, 51, 64, 224

pensions, 18, 61, 62, 63, 65–6, 75, 88, 100, 124, 150, 156, 167, 171, 187–8, 224
person care, 192
Philippines, 2, 246, 248
placement agencies, 197
Polanyi, K., 1
policies, 15–16
  care-related, 24
  development, 3
  initiatives, 236
  reforms, 81
poltical democratization, 36
political economy, 31
political instrumentalism, 41
political will, 220
politics, 24–7, 224, 225, 226, 236, 241
poor, 125, 182, 183
  children, 110, 111, 137–8, 156, 185
  women, 109, 112, 114–15, 116, 188, 206
population
  control, 183
  health gap, 245
  movements, 242
post-Washington Consensus, 3, 228
poverty, 16, 18, 21, 24, 36, 42, 65, 94, 95, 97, 100, 121, 140, 143, 157, 168, 170, 175, 176–7, 182, 187, 199, 205, 206–7
  feminization, 57, 62, 98, 136
  infantilization, 169
  reduction, 116, 209, 211
Poverty Reduction Strategies (Argentina), 95, 117
Prates, S., 152
pre-school education, 5, 19, 23–4, 33, 37–8, 39, 41, 64, 94, 95, 98, 101, 107, 109, 111, 114, 116, 125, 133, 135–6, **136, 137,** 139, 140, 161, 165, 169, 194, 209, 210, 214, 219, 227
pregnancy, 104, 112
primary education, 125, 133, 134, 143, 157, 182, 183–5, 214
primary carers, 221, 222–3
private education, 158
  fees, 185
private healthcare, 21

private savings, 66
private schools, 184
private Uruguay, 156, 157, 158, 170
privatization, 117, 181, 182–3
professionalization, 221, 226, 227
psychological care, 236
Puar, J. K., 135, 136
public distribution system (PDS) (India), 182
public expenditure, 34, 36
  social, *126*
  unemployment benefits, 36–7
public facilities, 183
public goods, 93
public health, 21, 158, 182–3
public institutions, 94
public policy, 2, 106
  care, 15–20, 175
public schools, 216
public social programmes, *127*–8
public welfare, 21
public-private-community mix, 22, 24
purchasing power, 158, 240

Quirós Viquez, A., 141

Razavi, S,. 1–27
real wages, 37, 152
regression, 83, 84, 85
religious care, 235, 247
'(re)production', 233
reproductive behaviour (Uruguay), 152, 159–60, 169
reproductive rights (Argentina), 100
retirement, 100, 167–8, 239, 240
risks, 156, 248
rural migration, 82
rural women, 19, 65, 87, 192–3
rural-urban inequality, 177

Sainsbury, D., 93, 94, 95, 105
Sandinista government (Nicaragua), 122, 123, 124, 126, 128–9, 130, 131–2, 135, 139, 142, 143
Scandinavian welfare model, 43
school autonomy, 135
school fund programmes, 139
secondary education, 134, 165, 184, 214
self-employment, 177

sexual rights (Argentina), 100
sick, 74
single mothers, 208
single-parent households, 209
single-person households, 35, 97, 98
social assistance, 17, 124, 205–6
social class, 117
social inequalities, 207, 243, 245
social insurances, 34–5, 166
social investment, 4, 21–2, 130, 131
    South Korea, 41, 42, 45
Social Investment Fund (FISE)
    (Nicaragua), 139
social justice, 180
social policies, 4–5, 6, 7, 8, 51, 68–9,
    226, 228
    India, 180, 181, 191, 199
    Nicaragua, 123, 125–6, 130, 143
    South Korea, 35, 41, 46
    welfare regime, 6
social protection, 96, 116, 124, 131, 149,
    150, 152, 187, 224, 227
Social Protection Network (RPS;
    Nicaragua), 140–141
social reproduction, 1, 73–4, 75, 76, 77,
    87, 88, 122, 132
social risks, 34, 122, 149
social sector expenditure, *181*
social security, 4, 17–18, 19, 34, 75, 78,
    96, 104, 140, 153, 169, 177, 181,
    208, 211, 220, 227
social services, lack of, 163
social spending, 34, 124, 125, *127*–8
    as percentage of GDP (Nicaragua),
    126
    public, *127*, 131
social welfare, 37, 40
socialist ideology, 76
societies, 233–4, 248
socio-economic relationships, **157**, 233,
    242
sodalities, 244–5
solidarity, 143
South Africa, 2–3, 5, 10, 11–12, 15, 17,
    19, 20, 51–2, 53, 59–60, 61, 61–2,
    63, 68
    abortions, 63
    child support grant (CSG), 66–7
    childcare, 52, 53, 54, 59

early development (ECD), 63, 64–5,
    68
    elderly care, 53
    family life, disruption, 52, 53, 68
    HIV/AIDS pandemic, 5, 52, 53,
        55–56, 57–8, **58**, 59, 60, 62, 63,
        68
    living arrangements, 53–7
    public works programmes, 53, 61, 62,
        64–5, 68
    women, 52–3, 59–60, 61–2
South African Household Composition,
    2005, **54**
South African Maintenance Act, 56
South Korea, 5, 10, 19, 23–4, 31, 32, 37,
    39, 40, 45, 46, 47, 60,
    gender equality, 31, 32, 35, 41, 45–6
    Ministry of Labour, 42–3, 44
    social care expansion, 31–47
Southern Africa, 2, 12
spiritual care, 235
Staab, S., 22, 23, 143, 205–32
standards of living, 176–7
state expenditures, 181
state institutions, 125, 130
state employees, 74
Stephens, J., 96
subsidies, 211–12, 215, 216, 217, **218**,
    221, 224
Sumayya, G., 60
Swaminathan, M., 186
Sweden, 25

Tabbush, C., 112, 206
Tanzania, 8, 58
tax benefits, 39
taxation, 219
teachers, 38, 44, 101, 106, 110, 111, 124,
    134, 135, 165, 184, 213, 217, 223
Three Worlds of Welfare Capitalism
    (Esping-Andersen), 9, 25
time use, 15, 86, 133, 153, 170, 175,
    192–3
Time Use Survey (TUS), 8, 12–13, 52,
    54, 55, 192
Township and Village Enterprises
    (TVEs) (China), 77, 79
trade unions, 101, 135, 156, 169, 221
trafficking, 247

trans-migrants, 236, 248, 250
transnational corporate care markets, 239
transnational entities, 237, **238**
transnational families, 2
transnational rights, 247
Tronto, J., 15, 26
two-tier systems, 81

UK, 244, 248
Unemployed Heads of Household Plan (PJJHD) (Argentina), 112, 113–14
unemployment, 18, 41, 36–37, 53, 61–2, 63, 68, 76, 97, 99
unequal care, 9
United States, 126
unpaid care, 9
 inequalties, 12–13
unemployment, 5, 155
universal provisioning, 219
universality, 96, 182
UNRISD project, 8
upper middle classes, 156
upper classes, 156
Uruguay, 2–3, 10, 11, 149, 150, 152, 153, 156, 157–8, 160, *161, 163,* 165, 167, 168, 169, 170, 171, 206
USA, 183

Van der Westhuizen, C., 60
Venezuela, 122
voluntarism, 24, 25, 195
volunteers, 124, 143

wages, 221
Wang, H., 83
Washington Consensus, 170
wealth, 175
 redistribution of, 65
welfare, 10, 37, 53, 62, 152, 155, 157, 180, 181–2
welfare benefits, 205–6
welfare colonialism, 248
welfare imbalance, 169
welfare pillars, 93, 115,
welfare regimes, 31, 34, 51, 52, 93, 122, 125, 149, 175, 176, 182, 183

welfare states, 7, 9–10, 21, 31, 36, 149, 153, 156, 171
 residual, 180
Whittaker, A., 240
women, 2–3, 10, 11, 14, 26, 35, 73, 87, 97, 113, 121–2, 129, 132, 138, 141, 168, 225
 as carers, 23., 55, 68, 74–5, 77–8, 81, 84, 87–8, 111–12, 151, 166, 170, 175, 187–8, 191, 194
 different strata, 156
 domestic service, 15
 employment, 39–40, 44, 76, 85, 113–14, 116, 122, 177–8, 190
 income earners, 81, 83
 informal work, 19, 189, 191, 193
 job creation, 44
 labour force, 76, 81, 104, 149
 labour markets, 22, 25, 39–40, 46
 movements, 4, 25, 100, 199, 225
 paid work, 2–3, 11, 13, 18, 40, 61–2, 81, 83, 86–7, 142, 160, 189, 191, 197, 205, 215
 roles, 170–171
 stereotypes, 100
 unpaid work, 16–17, 24, 31, 77, 86–7, 121, 122–3, 133, 143, 155, 160, *161*, 193, 205
 with young children, 3, 16, 81, 83, 155
women's rights, 224–5
women's work, 40–1, 46–7, 177, 227
women-specific programmes, 190
Woo, M. J., 36
work, *163*, 175, 177
 family life, 166
 permits, 246
 unpaid, 170
workers (India), 177, **178,** *179*
 informal, 187–8
World Bank, 22, 121, 140, 242

Yeates, N., 235, 237, 243, 244
Yeung, H. W., 237, 242

Zhan, H., 75
Zhang, D., 76, 77
Zimbabwe, 58